THE SECTION 199A (AND 1202) HANDBOOK

THE ADVISOR'S GUIDE TO SAVING TAXES ON BUSINESS AND INVESTMENT INCOME, STRUCTURING ENTITIES, AND ESTATE PLANNING UNDER THE 2017 TAX CUTS AND JOBS ACT

Alan Gassman, Brandon Ketron, Martin Shenkman, Jonathan Blattmachr and Robert Schenck

Disclaimer of Warranty and Limit of Liability

The authors and publisher make no representations or warranties with respect to the accuracy of the contents of this work and do hereby specifically and expressly disclaim all warranties, including without limitation, warranties of title, merchantability, fitness for a particular purpose and non-infringement. No warranty may be created or extended by sales or promotional material associated with this work.

Any advice, strategies, and ideas contained herein may not be suitable for particular situations. This work is sold with the understanding that the publisher is not engaging in or rendering medical or legal advice or other professional services. If professional assistance is required, the services of a competent professional person should be sought.

Although the authors and publisher have made every effort to ensure that the information in this book was correct at press time, the authors and publisher do not assume and hereby disclaim any responsibility or liability whatsoever to the fullest extent allowed by law to any party for any and all direct, indirect, incidental, special, or consequential damages, or lost profits that result, either directly, or indirectly, from the use and application of any of the contents of this book. The purchaser or reader of this book alone assumes the risk for anything learned from this book.

This book is not intended as a substitute for legal advice and should not be used in such manner. Furthermore, the use of this book does not establish an attorney-client relationship.

The information provided in this book is designed for educational and informational purposes only and is not intended to serve as legal or medical advice.

References are provided for informational purposes only and do not constitute or imply endorsement, sponsorship, or recommendation of any websites or other sources. Readers should be aware that the websites listed in this book may change.

The views expressed herein are solely those of the authors and do not reflect the opinions of any other person or entity.

ACKNOWLEDGEMENTS

The authors would like to thank:

Steve Leimberg, James Magner, Howard Le and the entire Leimberg Information Services (LISI) team and its subscribers for their support and guidance while writing this book.

Steven B. Gorin of Thompson Coburn LLP for his September 13, 2018 presentation for the Real Property Trust and Estate Law Section of the ABA, and his 425 pages of Section 199A outline entitled "IRS Guidance on Section 199A Deduction," which was excerpted from what is now over 1,700 pages in a fully searchable PDF "Structuring Ownership of Privately-Owned Businesses: Tax and Estate Implications," the latter of which can be obtained by contacting sgorin@thompsoncoburn.com, and for his helpful comments and his leadership of the April 4, 2019 ABA presentation entitled *Recent 199A Guidance: Hear From Practicing Experts and Government Officials*, which is mentioned in this book.

David Kirk who was a longtime, leading IRS regulation drafter and now a leading practitioner in this area of Ernst & Young LLP, for his input.

Michael E. Lloyd of Williams Coulson Attorneys at Law for his observations and input on the use of pension plans used in this book.

Leimberg commentators **Steve Oshins and Robert S. Keebler** for the countless hours and the wonderful materials that they have provided for LISI subscribers and others on Section 199A and related topics.

Michael Kitces for his contribution to the Section 199A literature, and for allowing us to use an improved version of his chart that summarizes the structural components of Section 199A that can be found in Chapter 2 of this book.

Christopher J. Denicolo, **John N. Beck**, **Kenneth J. Crotty**, **Debbie Grey**, **Shelley Weber** and many others of the law firm of **Gassman, Crotty & Denicolo, P.A.** for their countless hours of work and patience with changes with respect to the manuscript and charts in this book.

-Table of Contents

INDEX OF CHARTS AND TABLES

CASES

Revenue Rulings

Revenue Proceedings

ABOUT THE AUTHORS

Alan Gassman, JD, LL.M. is the founding partner of the law firm of Gassman, Crotty & Denicolo, P.A., in Clearwater, Florida. He is a frequent contributor to Leimberg Information Services, Inc. (LISI), has authored several books and many articles on estate and estate tax planning, trust planning, creditor protection planning, and associated topics, and is listed in Best Lawyers of America.

Brandon Ketron, CPA, JD, LL.M. is an associate at the law firm of Gassman, Crotty & Denicolo, P.A., in Clearwater, Florida and practices in the areas of estate planning, tax, and corporate and business law. Brandon is a frequent contributor to LISI and presents webinars on various topics for both clients and practitioners. Brandon attended Stetson University College of Law where he graduated cum laude and received his LL.M. in Taxation from the University of Florida. He received his undergraduate degree at Roanoke College where he graduated cum laude with a degree in Business Administration and a concentration in both Accounting and Finance. Brandon is also a licensed CPA in the states of Florida and Virginia.

Martin M. Shenkman, CPA, MBA, PFS, AEP, JD is an attorney in private practice in Fort Lee, New Jersey and New York City who concentrates on estate and closely held business planning, tax planning, and estate administration. He is the author of 42 books and more than 1,200 articles. His firm's website is www.shenkmanlaw.com where you can subscribe to his free quarterly newsletter Practical Planner and find an archive of webinar recordings and other planning materials.

Jonathan G. Blattmachr is the Director of Estate Planning for Peak Trust Company (formerly the Alaska Trust Company) which has offices in Alaska and Nevada, a principal of Pioneer Wealth Partners, LLC, and co-developer, with Michael L. Graham, Esq., of Dallas, Texas, of Wealth Transfer Planning, a computer system produced by Interactive Legal that provides artificial intelligence advice and automated document assembly systems for practitioners.

Robert Schenck is a law student at Duke University School of Law who acted as the managing editor of this book while working at the offices of Gassman, Crotty & Denicolo, P.A., in Clearwater, Florida. He has helped in the drafting of numerous articles and presentations on Section 199A.

DISCLAIMER OF WARRANTY AND LIMIT OF LIABILITY

This book is not intended as a substitute for legal advice and should not be used in such a manner. Furthermore, the use of this book does not establish an attorney-client relationship. The purchaser and/or reader of this book understands that they are responsible for risk from anything learned in this book.

CHAPTER 1.
INTRODUCTION

The 2017 Tax Cuts and Jobs Act (the "Act")[1] provides significant tax relief for business, professional practice, and investment income for many taxpayers, but the complexity of the rules and structural changes needed for many business and investment arrangements presents a challenge for taxpayers and their advisors.

This book has been written to allow both non-tax professionals and their tax advisors to have the necessary foundation and associated knowledge and techniques in order to allow taxpayers to best position their professional, business, and investment activities under the new law, while discussing a number of uncertainties and non- tax law considerations that should be evaluated in making restructuring decisions. In some instances, opting not to restructure entities or create new trusts might be the best answer, and that scenario will be explored as well so that a balanced view of what is feasible or optimal under 199A will be clear.

This book is being issued shortly after the issuance of Final Regulations on January 18, 2019, and in slightly revised form on February 4, 2019, which made substantial changes to the previous Proposed Regulations that were issued on August 8, 2018.

Tax law experts should find that the details and examples in this book are a good refresher and include some points and strategies that have not been considered or well understood by many.

This book uses progressive examples that show the mechanics and numbers of the law. Non-tax novices may find these examples especially helpful to gain the best possible understanding of how the law works, and how it can be applied to save taxes and reduce creditor exposure to individuals, businesses, and investment entities.[2]

The authors hope that readers find that the law is not as complicated or mysterious as one would think, if they have time to digest the contents with reasonable speed and diligence.

This book is accompanied by a number of aides and appendixes that will be useful to the reader, including:

- An Executive Summary in Chapter 3 that can help experienced tax practitioners to readily understand the structure of Section 199A.

- The actual text of the statute, redlined for the changes made by technical corrections on March 23, 2018, is in **Error! Reference source not found.**.

- The Final Regulations released to the public on February 4, 2019, are in **Error! Reference source not found.**.

---

[1] The Act's official title is "An Act to Provide for Reconciliation Pursuant to Titles II and V of the Concurrent Resolution on the Budget for Fiscal Year 2018.

[2] Thanks to Professor Jerome Hesch for pointing out that repetition and examples, preferably without citing very many Code Sections, are often the primary stepping stones to understanding the tax law.

- **Error! Reference source not found.** contains the Preamble to the Proposed Regulations.

- Contains Revenue Procedure 2019 11, which provides guidance on the definitions of wages for purposes of calculating the Section 199A deduction.

- **Error! Reference source not found.** contains Notice 2019-7 which provides a safe harbor for rental property to qualify as a trade or business.

- **Error! Reference source not found.**contains proposed Treasury Regulations that provide guidance on how the Section 199A deduction applies to Charitable Remainder Trusts.

- The Reports regarding Section 199A, including the conference agreement, Senate Amendments, House bill, and summary of previous law, are provided in **Error! Reference source not found.**.

- **Error! Reference source not found.** is an excerpt from the Conference Report on the Tax Cuts and Jobs Act of 2017, containing what the House of Representatives had proposed for Section 199A. The bill originated in the House and was introduced on November 2, 2017.

- **Error! Reference source not found.** is an excerpt from the Conference Report on the Tax Cuts and Jobs Act of 2017:

- **Error! Reference source not found.** includes the text of Section 1202.

- Charts which reflect the new income tax brackets and tax savings resulting from lower rates under the new tax brackets appear in **Error! Reference source not found.**, and which individual deductions are now permitted or included in the itemized deduction category in Chart 4 under the same Appendix.

- **Error! Reference source not found.**includes a discussion of the case called *Bross Trucking, Inc. v. Commissioner*, which deals with the transfer and ownership of goodwill in a company. This is important to planning under Section 199A because a transfer of a business or professional practice from one entity to another may be considered a taxable transfer of goodwill based upon the value of goodwill transferred.

- APPENDIX 13 includes Private Letter Rulings that expound upon what is considered a "qualified trade or business" under the subsections of Section 1202 that are cited in the definition of Specified Service Trade or Business in Section 199A.

CHAPTER 2.
SECTION 199A - STRUCTURAL CHART

The authors thank Michael Kitces for allowing us to use the following chart that provides an overview of Section 199A, and for his excellent website and writings which can be found at https://www.kitces.com:

Section 199A -- Structural Chart

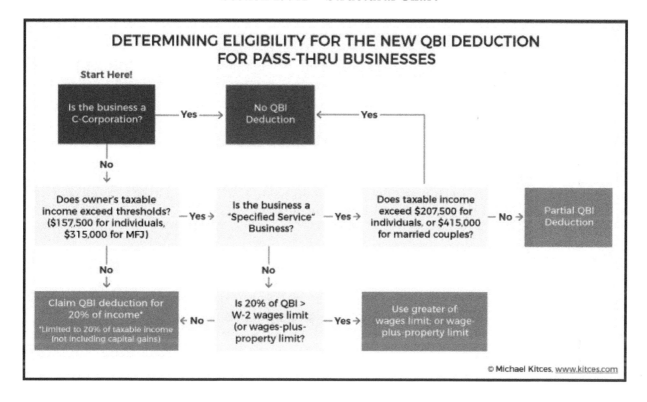

DETERMINING ELIGIBILITY FOR THE NEW QBI DEDUCTION FOR PASS-THRU BUSINESSES

© Michael Kitces, www.kitces.com

CHAPTER 3.
EXECUTIVE SUMMARY OF SECTION 199A

The following is a summary of important aspects of Section 199A, and presents Section 199A and its components, each of which is explained later in this book.

A.   OVERVIEW OF SECTION 199A

With the reduction of the federal corporate income tax rate to a flat 21%, the combined federal income tax on C corporations (36.8%) was actually lower than the highest individual rate for a flow-through entity, which would be 37%.[3] Congress wanted flow-through entities to continue to enjoy a preferential tax rate, and Section 199A was enacted to accomplish this. In addition to reducing the effective tax rate below that of a C corporation, Congress wanted to incentivize businesses to employ workers, make capital investments, and apparently punish specific industries resulting in two limitations on a taxpayer's ability to take the full 20% deduction, which are discussed in more detail throughout this book.

Section 199A provides a 20% tax deduction for trade or business income that meets certain requirements. The statute has many definitions and limitations, which need to be carefully applied, and for many of which considerable uncertainty remains.

1. TYPES OF INCOME THAT QUALIFY.

The deduction is taken on the individual tax return of the individual or married couple, Form 1040, or on the tax return of a separately taxed trust or estate, Form 1041, that may receive flow-through income. A separately taxed trust means a non-grantor trust that pays income taxes on undistributed income and is also known as a "complex trust" under Internal Revenue Code Section 661. The "Internal Revenue Code" is referred to throughout the remainder of this book as the "Code" and shall mean the Internal Revenue Code or the specific referenced Sections of the Internal Revenue Code.

2. QBI DEFINED.

QBI is discussed extensively in Chapter 9, Part One.

The deduction is for up to 20% of "Qualified Business Income" ("QBI"), which is the "flow-through" trade or business income, as defined in Section 162, as well as income from certain investment activities. Flow-through entities include S corporations, entities taxed as partnerships, and Schedule C and E businesses and rental activities, and Schedule F farming activities. The trade or business requirement is discussed in more detail in Chapter 12.

3. TYPES OF SSTBs DEFINED.

The statute created a new term and tax concept called "Specified Service Trades or Business" ("SSTB"), and these are subject to special limitations on claiming the 20% deduction. These are

---

[3] 21% Corporate tax ($100-$21=$79) and a 20% tax on dividends ($79-($79*.20)=$63.2). 100-63.2=36.8% effective tax rate on C corps.

trades or business that are engaged in the fields of: (1) health, (2) law, (3) accounting, (4) actuarial science, (5) performing arts, (6) consulting, (7) athletics, (8) financial services, (9) brokerage services, (10) investing, trading, or dealing in securities, partnership interest, or commodities, and (11) any business where the principal asset is the reputation or skill of one or more of its employees. While many practitioners feared that the last category would serve as a broad catchall that would subsume a wide array of businesses, the Final Regulations under Section 199A provided some leniency in narrowing the definition.

4. WHAT ARE WAGES?

Wages are discussed extensively in Chapter 4, with great charts.

Wages, to qualify for the purposes of the Section 199A Wage/Property Limitation, do not include:

A.   compensation paid by a partnership to a partner (which are known under the Code as "guaranteed payments" instead of wages),

B.   compensation paid to independent contractors or "statutory employees," or

C.   wages that are not properly and promptly reported to the Social Security Administration within sixty (60) days of the due date of the form reporting such wages. Wages paid by an individually-owned trade or business, or an LLC that is disregarded and owed directly by the individual taxpayer for income tax purposes, will not count for purposes of Section 199A if those wages are paid to the individual owner.[4] However, wages will be considered as wages if paid to the owner's spouse who does not have an ownership interest in the trade or business. This will be true even if the married couple files a joint return. Business income derived from an individual's personally owned trade or business or an LLC that is disregarded for income tax purposes and owned by the individual will not count as wages.

D.   Wages paid by an S corporation to its owner(s) will count as wages for the purposes of Section 199A.

5. QUALIFIED PROPERTY.

Qualified Property, for purposes of the 2.5% tangible property calculation that is part of the Section 199A deduction phase-out, does not include any asset that has been fully depreciated, except that a fully depreciated asset can still be counted until it has been in service for ten (10) years. The Statute refers to this property as the "Unadjusted Basis Immediately After Acquisition" of Qualified Property, which was given the acronym "UBIA" by the drafters of the Regulations.

Qualified Property and UBIA are discussed extensively in Chapter 4.

---

[4] The same would apply for a trade or business owned under a grantor trust where the grantor is treated as the owner of the trust for income tax purposes, or a "Section 678 Trust," which has its income considered as having been received by a beneficiary who has had a certain withdrawal power as further discussed in Chapter 12.

6. LOW INCOME TAXPAYERS.

Any trade, business, or permitted rental income from a flow-through entity can qualify for the deduction if the taxpayer is single or married filing separately or as a trust or an estate with $157,500 or less of income, or if a married couple has less than $315,000 of taxable income. Taxpayers with taxable income below the $157,500/$315,000 thresholds will normally qualify for the full 20% deduction without reference to wages, Qualified Property, or the type of trade or business involved. These "Threshold Amounts" are inflation adjusted[5] and have been increased to $160,700 for single filers and trusts, and $321,400 for taxpayers married, filing jointly, for the 2019 tax year. In this book, we usually refer to the original $157,500 and $315,000 thresholds.

The following example from the Final Regulations illustrates how the calculation applies for a low-income taxpayer:

Example 1 - A, an unmarried individual, owns and operates a computer repair shop as a sole proprietorship. The business generates $100,000 in net taxable income from operations in 2018. A has no capital gains or losses. After allowable deductions not relating to the business, A's total taxable income for 2018 is $81,000. The business's QBI is $100,000, the net amount of its qualified items of income, gain, deduction, and loss. A's Section 199A deduction for 2018 is equal to $16,200, the lesser of 20% of A's QBI from the business ($100,000 x 20% = $20,000) and 20% of A's total taxable income for the taxable year ($81,000 x 20% = $16,200).[6]

7. $157,500 / $315,000 THRESHOLD AMOUNT.

When the taxable income of an individual or separately taxed trust exceeds the $157,500 /$315,000 2018 lower thresholds, the following two limitations will apply:

A.   A wage/property limitation, whereby there must be sufficient wages paid by the entity and/or tangible depreciable assets meeting certain requirements, as described below, to qualify for the deduction.

B.   An SSTB Limitation, as further described below, applies if the trade or business is engaged in furnishing any of the "tainted" services identified above. The taxpayer's Section 199A deduction is subject to a phase-out on taxable income above the Threshold Amount as described above.

Wage/Property Limitation. The activity will be subject to the "Wage/Property Limitation," based on the W-2 wages paid and/or Qualified Property held by the business at the entity level. This limitation applies to all activities, regardless of whether they are SSTBs or not, but unlike the SSTB Limitation in the next section, the deduction will not necessarily be eliminated when the

---

[5] Treas. Reg. § 1.199A-1(b)(12) Threshold amount. In the case of any taxable year beginning after 2018, the dollar amount in the preceding sentence shall be increased by an amount equal to—(i) such dollar amount, multiplied by (ii) the cost-of-living adjustment determined under Section 1(f)(3) for the calendar year in which the taxable year begins, determined by substituting "calendar year 2017" for "calendar year 2016" in Section 1(f)(3)(A)(ii). The amount of increase is rounded pursuant to Section 1(f)(3) for the calendar year in which the taxable year begins, determined by substituting "calendar year 2017" for "calendar year 2016" in Section 1(f)(3)(A)(ii). The amount of increase is rounded pursuant to Section 1(f)(7).

[6] Treas. Reg. § 1.199A-1(c)(3), Example 1.

taxpayer's taxable income reaches the $207,500/$415,000 thresholds. The stated objective of this part of the law is to encourage businesses to own more property and pay more wages. There are two tests that make up this limitation: (1) the 50% Wage Test (referred to as the "Wage Test"); or (2) a 25% Wage Test and 2.5% tangible property test (referred to as the "Property Test"), and the limitation is equal to the greater of the following two amounts:

(1) **50% Wage Test.** This is the taxpayer's allocable share of 50% of W-2 wages paid by the entity, which is pro rata to ownership with an S corporation and usually pro rata to ownership for a partnership.

(2) **25% Wage and 2.5% Property Test.** This is the taxpayer's allocable share of 2.5% of the entity's unadjusted cost basis in qualified depreciable property, plus 25% of W-2 wages paid by the entity.

In applying the above tests, if the high-income taxpayer directly owns the entire enterprise, e.g., a sole proprietorship or a disregarded LLC, the full amount of wages and property would be subject to the test. The IRS has provided rules for determining the W-2 wages which generally follow the rules that applied to the former Section 199 domestic production activities deduction.[7] If a taxpayer owns an interest in a pass-through entity, like a partnership, LLC taxed as a partnership, or a partial interest in an S corporation, then the taxpayer's allocable share of these items of that entity would be used in that specific taxpayer's calculation.

If the greater value of the two tests is less than the taxpayer's tentative deduction (20% of flow-through income, QBI, from the entity), then the deduction will be limited. Otherwise, the taxpayer can claim the full 20% deduction.

For taxpayers with taxable income between the $157,000-$207,500 (for single filers) or $315,000-$415,000 (for joint filers) thresholds, the deduction limitation is phased-in and the Wage/Property Limitation gradually applies as the taxpayer exceeds the lower ($157,500/$315,000) thresholds. These calculations are described in detail in Chapter 10.

If the taxpayer's taxable income exceeds the $207,500/$415,000 thresholds, and the Wage/Property Test is less than the taxpayer's tentative deduction (20% of flow-through income,) then the value from the Wage/Property Test will establish the taxpayer's Section 199A deduction in that particular year. The fact that these tests will fluctuate from year to year suggests that planning opportunities exist, but also that complexity exists. Those preparing forecasts for future year's tax planning, and returns, must be careful to corroborate the underlying data and not merely rely on a prior year's results. It might be cost effective to create an Excel model for a particular client and update that each year.

A comprehensive phase-out summary chart is available in Chapter 4.

Comprehensive Example from Regulations:

> For example, assume that an S corporation has $200,000 of K-1 income
> so that the tentative Section 199A deduction would be $40,000

---

[7] *Rev. Proc. 2019-11.*

> ($200,000 QBI x 20% rate). Assume further that the S corporation pays $70,000 in wages and is owned by an individual who is a single filer with Taxable Income in excess of $207,500. The deduction will be limited to 50% of W-2 Wages, or $35,000 (50% x $70,000 = $35,000) which is less than 20% of the $200,000 of the taxpayer's flow-through income ($200,000 x 20% = $40,000).

The loss of the Section 199A deduction in the above example can be salvaged by having the entity pay $80,000 in wages ($80,000 x 50% = $40,000). This might be achieved by paying W-2 wages to individuals who were formerly independent contractors but converted to employee status. Obviously while these types of planning options exist, merely restructuring relationships for the purpose of passing the Wage/Property Limitation may not be simple or worthwhile. The change in status might affect insurance coverage, contracts between the parties, and other factors. Also, if the change in status is merely that, and not substantive, the IRS might challenge the purported change.

This same idea applies if a flow-through entity plans to use "UBIA."

Example:

> If an S corporation owned by an unmarried individual actively leases property that is nine years old and cost $100,000 for the land and $800,000 for the building, the owner would use $20,000 for the Wage/Property Test calculation (2.5% x $800,000 building undepreciated cost = $20,000). The land is not included in the calculation since it is not depreciable. Assume that the S corporation has $200,000 QBI and the owner has $250,000 of taxable income. The owner's tentative Section 199A deduction would be $40,000 ($200,000 QBI x 20%); however, the deduction would be limited to only $20,000 because of the Wage/Property Limitation.

8. SPECIFIED SERVICE TRADE OR BUSINESS ("SSTB") INCOME LIMITATION RULES.

SSTBs are discussed extensively in Chapter 9, Part One.

The income from an SSTB will not qualify for the deduction under any circumstances if the taxable income of the individual or trust receiving such income is over the $207,500/$415,000 threshold.

There is also a phase-out of the deduction that can occur between taxable income ranges from $157,500 and $207,500 for single filers and separately taxed trusts, and between $315,000 and $415,000 for married couples, and the phase-out result will be more severe if the SSTB income does not meet the wages or qualified property test. It is also noteworthy that SSTBs are not eligible to be aggregated with other commonly controlled trades or businesses, and therefore must independently satisfy the Wage/Property Test for high income taxpayers.

As the taxable income of the individual or trust increases above the $157,500/$315,000 lower thresholds toward the $207,500/$415,000 higher thresholds, the deduction will be phased-out proportionally. So, if married taxpayers have taxable income of $365,000 in 2018, from an SSTB, then they would qualify at this mid-point for only one-half of the deduction if there are sufficient wages or qualified property. This is further discussed in Chapter 10.

Additionally, it appears that Publicly Traded Partnership income, while not subject to the Wage/Property Test, is subject to the SSTB Limitation.[8]

9. UNITED STATES OR PUERTO RICO.

Only income that is derived from business operations in the United States or Puerto Rico will qualify for the deduction, and only Qualified Property located in the United States will be counted for purposes of applying the Wage/Property Limitation.

10. FILING JOINTLY OR SEPARATELY.

A married couple may choose to file separate individual returns, so that the $157,500 threshold applies to each of them in lieu of a cumulative threshold of $315,000, so that a spouse who has $157,500 or less of Section 199A income can take the deduction even if the other spouse has significantly more than $207,500 of income. However, this and many other Section 199A calculations, will be intertwined with other planning for the client. If clients who previously filed married filing jointly begin filing as married filing separately, what other tax benefits might be affected?

Will there be possible matrimonial ramifications? Depending on the terms of a prenuptial or post-nuptial agreement there might be significant consequences. Even in the absence of such an agreement the manner in which income is divided and reported between each spouse may have ramifications on a future divorce. Practitioners should exercise care and caution clients of potentially adverse ramifications, and whether addressing those potential consequences raises conflict of interest issues. A chart summarizing these considerations can be found in Chapter 11 (Chart 18).

11. LOSSES.

Losses and coordination with the Section 199A rules are discussed extensively in Chapter 9, Part Two.

The deduction cannot exceed 20% of the taxpayer's total taxable income, so losses that reduce taxable income to below the taxpayer's Section 199A deduction can cause a reduction of the Section 199A deduction. Taxable income can obviously be affected by a myriad of planning steps. Bunching charitable contributions into a particular year may maximize charitable deductions but also lower taxable income for the Section 199A tests for that year, and years from which deductions were shifted might have higher taxable income. There are a host of other examples,

---

[8] Publicly Traded Partnership income includes the taxpayer's "qualified item[s] of income, gain, deduction, and loss," which are one of the three items reduced by the Specified Service phase-out.

but the point is that practitioners might need to prepare tax forecasts for several years in order to identify an appropriate strategy.

12. TRUST PLANNING.

Trusts for the benefit of children, spouses and others will commonly be used in Section 199A planning, so that income thresholds can be met, although the Final Regulations limit some applications of this, as explained in Chapter 13 and Chapter 14.

Example:

> Mother is a high-income taxpayer and sells stock in her S corporation, which owns a profitable trade or business and does not pay wages or have any qualified property, to non-grantor trusts that were formed and funded in 2016 for each of her two children. If the trusts were formed and funded before 2017 and pass muster under the multiple trust rules that may apply under the Section 643(f) Final Regulations, then each trust may recognize part of the S corporation's income and have its own $157,500 threshold for phase-out purposes. Income from each trust would be taxed to the trust if retained by the trust, or taxed at the beneficiaries' brackets if distributed to the beneficiaries depending on the distribution of Distributable Net Income ("DNI") to each beneficiary, which could be much lower than the original Mother's bracket to facilitate eligibility for the Section 199A deduction. If the trust was formed or funded after enactment of Section 199A in December of 2017, then the anti-abuse rules described in Chapter 13 may apply.

13. PENSION PLANNING.

Pension planning is discussed extensively in Chapter 4.

Certain pension plans, such as defined-benefit or cash balance plans, may lower the taxable income of the taxpayer, while facilitating better planning for retirement, deferral of income taxes, and a greater Section 199A deduction. Further, pension plan expenses are often accrued in the tax year before the actual contribution is made, so that some degree of "after the tax year is over" planning may occur.

14. AGGREGATION FOR WAGE AND QUALIFIED PROPERTY PURPOSES.

It is not always clear whether and to what extent, entities that have multiple activities and properties can be aggregated for purposes of the wages and Qualified Property tests, as further discussed in Chapter 9.

15. **SSTB AND NON-SSTB INCOME SEPARATION AND VERIFICATION.**

The Final Regulations provide new tests for determining if and when a non-Specified Trade or Business activity that occurs in the same entity as a Specified Trade or Business activity will qualify for the Section 199A deduction, as further discussed in Chapter 9, Part Two.

16. **EMPLOYMENT AND MEDICARE TAX INTERACTION.**

The Section 199A deduction does not reduce employment taxes that are payable on partnership and personal income and does not reduce income subject to the 3.8% Net Investment Income Tax ("NIIT"). Most states have issued conforming changes to their applicable state income tax so that the Section 199A deduction will presumably apply for state income tax calculation purposes. Thus, in evaluating the benefits of the possible Section 199A deduction, practitioners should consider all these limitations. The fact that a taxpayer may still incur NIIT and state income taxes on the QBI may still result in the taxpayer facing a larger than anticipated net tax cost.

B. **REDUCING TAXABLE INCOME TO INCREASE THE SECTION 199A DEDUCTIONS**

The following is a quick list of ways that a taxpayer may reduce taxable income when necessary to qualify for Section 199A deductions for high-income taxpayers.

1. Buy a business car and use Section 179 expensing or Section 168(k) bonus depreciation to write off the cost.
2. Buy equipment, computer software, and other business assets that can be completely expensed in the year acquired and placed in service under the Section 179 expensing or 168(k) bonus depreciation rules.
3. 1031 Exchanges.
4. Pay children's management companies.
5. Establish a new or additional pension or profit-sharing plan to create business deductions and reduce wages or flow-through income. There will be costs to maintain and administer a plan and non- family members may have to receive specified benefits for the plan to succeed.
6. Consider putting other family members to work and on the payroll to reduce the owner's taxable income in addition to increasing W-2 wages paid by an entity.
7. Defer the sale of a capital gain asset to the next year if the sale will increase income above the threshold levels.
8. Use a Charitable Remainder Trust to defer large gains over multiple tax years.
9. Establish separate profit centers with separate books and records as required to maximize the deductibility of non-Specified Trade or Business income that occurs under an entity that also conducts one or more specified trades or businesses.

   If planning is feasible, then it may be worthwhile to proceed by establishing a management or factoring company and/or rental activity with arm's-length arrangements which may be owned in part or in whole by related taxpayers. See Chapter 9, Part Two and Chapter 11.
10. Create a qualified conservation easement by agreeing to allow real estate to be subject to ecologically friendly prohibitions (called "Perpetual Conservation Restrictions") for the

preservation of the land in favor of a qualified charity or governmental organization under Section 170.[9] Before proceeding down this path the conservation easement should be feasible and worthwhile in its own right, and then it might be planned and implemented in a manner that also provides benefits under Section 199A.

11. Buy personally owned oil and gas well interests to deduct 100% of the intangible drilling costs.

Chapter 11 contains a much more comprehensive list of planning techniques, with more detail as to each technique discussed above.

C.   WHERE DID THE LANGUAGE OF SECTION 199A COME FROM?

Section 199A replaced what is now referred to as "former" Section 199,[10] which provided a deduction for certain forms of manufacturing income, which were defined as "Qualified Production Activities Income." The following will be helpful for those tax advisors who would like to be familiar with the formerly effective Section 199 Regulations for situations where uncertainty exists under Section 199A and the Final Regulations thereunder.

Former Section 199 afforded a 3.564% deduction for taxpayers in the highest income bracket (39.6% x 9% = 3.564%). In total, manufacturers received roughly 65% of the tax benefits of the deduction in each year from 2005-2009.[11]

Qualified production activities income was defined as a taxpayer's domestic production gross receipts, less (i) the costs of goods sold that were allocable to domestic production, (ii) other deductions directly allocable to domestic production, and (iii) a ratable portion of deductions not directly allocable to domestic production or other classes of income.

The deduction was only applicable to gross receipts derived from:

1. qualifying production property which was manufactured, produced, grown, or extracted by the taxpayer;

2. any qualified film produced by the taxpayer;

3. electricity, natural gas, or potable water produced by the taxpayer;

4. construction performed; or

5. engineering or architectural services performed for construction projects in the United States

---

[9] *See* Treas, Reg § 1.170A-14, regarding qualified conservation contributions. *See also* Barbara Kirschten and Carla Freitag, 521-4th T.M. at II.F.1.b.(5) (BNA), *Charitable Contributions: Income Tax Aspects.*

[10] The authors prefer not to call something created in 2004 "old." Congress created the Code Section with the American Jobs Creation Act of 2004, which became Public Law No: 108-357.

[11] *See* Robert J. Shapiro, *Anatomy of a Special Tax Break and the Case for Broad Corporate Tax Reform*, Progressive Policy Institute (March 2013), citing I.R.S. Statistics of Income Tax Statistics. (2012). http://www.irs.gov/uac/SOI-Tax-Stats-Returns-of-Active-Corporations-Table-6.

The term "qualifying production property" was defined in the statute as any tangible personal property, any computer software, and any property described in Section 168(f)(4).[12] Additionally, Section 199 applied to C corporations and flow-through entities. Similar to Section 199A, the deduction was limited to 50% of W-2 wages paid by the employer for the taxable year, and the deduction could not exceed a taxpayer's taxable income.

---

[12]IRC § 168(f)(4) applies to works that result from the fixation of sound onto a material "in which such sounds are embodied," such as discs, tapes, or other phono-recordings.

CHAPTER 4.
SECTION 199A DEFINITIONS AND TERMINOLOGY

We start with a few definitions and some basic terminology that will be built upon later in this book.

A.   SECTION 199A

A new Code Section provision that allows for a 20% income tax deduction from the net taxable income derived from certain trades and businesses, which are reported on an individual or trust or estate income tax return as coming from S corporations, entities taxed as partnerships and individual Schedule C, F or E activities or proprietorships (often referred to as "flow-through entities"). LLCs taxed as S corporations, partnerships, or as disregarded and owned by individuals or trusts can all have income that qualifies for the Section 199A deduction.

Section 199A also permits the deduction to apply where a landlord is considered to be in the "trade or business" of leasing based upon the Internal Revenue Code Section 162 definition of "trade or business," and the Final Regulations provide that the property rented or leased to a trade or business that is 50% or more commonly owned by the same taxpayers will be considered to be an active trade or business, even if there is a triple net lease in place.

On the other hand, the Final Regulations generally provide that a triple net lease will not be considered to be a "trade or business" unless there is a significant amount of landlord activity involved and provide a safe harbor for non-triple net leased property as described in Chapter 12, Part Two.

Taxpayers engaged in agricultural and horticultural cooperatives have their own deduction under this statute, which is equal to 20% of the excess of gross income of the cooperative over any qualified cooperative dividends, as defined in Section 199A(g)(4) reads as follows:

(4)   Specified agricultural or horticultural cooperative. For purposes of this section

(A)   In general, the term "specified agricultural or horticultural cooperative" means an organization to which part I of subchapter T applies which is engaged—

(i)   in the manufacturing, production, growth, or extraction in whole or significant part of any agricultural or horticultural product, or

(ii)   in the marketing of agricultural or horticultural products.

(B)   Application to marketing cooperatives.

A specified agricultural or horticultural cooperative described in subparagraph (A)(ii) shall be treated as having manufactured, produced, grown, or extracted in whole or significant part any agricultural or horticultural product marketed by the specified agricultural or horticultural cooperative which its patrons have so manufactured, produced, grown, or extracted.

The Section 199A deduction is limited to the excess of 20% of a taxpayer's taxable income over the sum of net capital gains and qualified cooperative dividends.

The following example from the Final Regulations illustrates the above:

A, an unmarried individual, owns and operates a computer repair shop as a sole proprietorship. The business generates $100,000 in net taxable income from operations in 2018. An also has $7,000 in net capital gain for 2018 and that, after allowable deductions not relating to the business, A's taxable income for 2018 is $74,000. A's taxable income minus net capital gain is $67,000 ($74,000 - $7,000). A's section 199A deduction is equal to $13,400, the lesser of 20% of A's QBI from the business ($100,000 x 20% = $20,000) and 20% of A's total taxable income minus net capital gain for the taxable year ($67,000 x 20% = $13,400).[13]

1.   WAGE AND QUALIFIED PROPERTY LIMITATION.

A Section 199A deduction will not be available to high-income taxpayers unless a Wage and Qualified Property test is met, which is referred to in this book as a "Wage/Property Limitation." Simply put, at certain income levels, a taxpayer's deduction will be limited if it is less than the greater of the following: (1) 50% of wages that a business pays ("50% Wage Test") or (2) the sum of 2.5% of certain depreciable property plus 25% of wages ("Property Test"). Therefore, not paying sufficient wages or keeping sufficient property could result in the limitation or loss of a Section 199A deduction.

This is also illustrated in the following example from the Final Regulations:

Example:

> E, an unmarried individual, is a 30% owner of LLC, which is classified as a partnership for Federal income tax purposes. In 2018, the LLC has a single trade or business and reports QBI of $3,000,000. The LLC pays total W-2 wages of $1,000,000, and its total UBIA of qualified property is $100,000. E is allocated 30% of all items of the partnership. For the 2018 taxable year, E reports $900,000 of QBI from the LLC. After allowable deductions unrelated to LLC, E's taxable income is $880,000. Because E's taxable income is above the threshold amount, the QBI component of E's section 199A deduction will be limited to the lesser of 20% of E's share of LLC's QBI or the greater of the W-2 wage or UBIA of qualified property limitations. Twenty percent of E's share of QBI of $900,000 is $180,000. The W-2 wage limitation equals 50% of E's share of the LLC's wages ($300,000) or $150,000.
>
> The UBIA of qualified property limitation equals $75,750, the sum of 25% of E's share of LLC's wages ($300,000) or $75,000 plus 2.5% of E's share of UBIA of qualified property ($30,000) or $750. The greater of the limitation amounts ($150,000 and $75,750) is $150,000. The QBI

---

[13] Treas. Reg. § 1.199A-1(c)(3), Example 2.

component of E's section 199A deduction is thus limited to $150,000, the lesser of 20% of QBI ($180,000) and the greater of the limitations amounts ($150,000). E's section 199A deduction is equal to the lesser of 20% of the QBI from the business as limited ($150,000) or 20% of E's taxable income ($880,000 x 20% = $176,000). Therefore, E's section 199A deduction is $150,000 for 2018.[14]

Notably, the statute applies the Wage/Property Limitation before the taxpayer's deduction is increased by REIT dividends and Publicly Traded Partnership income, meaning that both of these amounts are not subject to limitations based on wages paid or Qualified Property held, as illustrated by the following example contained in the Final Regulations:

B and C are married and file a joint individual income tax return. B earns $50,000 in wages as an employee of an unrelated company in 2018. C owns 100% of the shares of X, an S corporation that provides landscaping services. X generates $100,000 in net income from operations in 2018. X pays C $150,000 in wages in 2018. B and C have no capital gains or losses. After allowable deductions not related to X, B and C's total taxable income for 2018 is $270,000. B's and C's wages are not considered to be income from a trade or business for purposes of the section 199A deduction. Because X is an S corporation, its QBI is determined at the S corporation level. X's QBI is $100,000, the net amount of its qualified items of income, gain, deduction, and loss. The wages paid by X to C are considered to be a qualified item of deduction for purposes of determining X's QBI. The section 199A deduction with respect to X's QBI is then determined by C, X's sole shareholder, and is claimed on the joint return filed by B and C. B also earns $1,000 in qualified REIT dividends and $500 in qualified PTP income in 2018, increasing taxable income to $271,500. B and C's section 199A deduction is equal to $20,300, the lesser of (i) 20% of C's QBI from the business ($100,000 x 20% = $20,000) plus 20% of B's combined qualified REIT dividends and qualified PTP income ($1500 x 20% = $300) and (ii) 20% of B and C's total taxable for the taxable year ($271,500 x 20% = $54,300).15

A second example related to Publicly Traded Partnerships illustrates that losses attributable to Publicly Traded Partnerships and REIT dividends do not offset QBI, but instead are carried over to be netted against Publicly Traded Partnership or REIT dividends in future tax years. The example reads as follows:

F, an unmarried individual, owns a 50% interest in Z, an S corporation for Federal income tax purposes that conducts a single trade or business.

---

[14] Treas. Reg. § 1.199A-1(d)(4), Example 3.
[15] Treas. Reg. § 1.199A-1(c)(3), Example 4.

In 2018, Z reports QBI of $6,000,000. Z pays total W-2 wages of $2,000,000, and its total UBIA of qualified property is $200,000. For the 2018 taxable year, F reports $3,000,000 of QBI from Z. F is not an employee of Z and receives no wages or reasonable compensation from Z. After allowable deductions unrelated to Z and a deductible qualified net loss from a PTP of ($10,000), F's taxable income is $1,880,000. Because F's taxable income is above the threshold amount, the QBI component of F's section 199A deduction will be limited to the lesser of 20% of F's share of Z's QBI or (ii) the greater of the W-2 wage and UBIA of qualified property limitations. Twenty percent of F's share of Z's QBI ($3,000,000) is $600,000. The W-2 wage limitation equals 50% of F's share of Z's W-2 wages ($1,000,000) or $500,000. The UBIA of qualified property limitation equals $252,500, the sum of 25% of F's share of Z's W-2 wages ($1,000,000) or $250,000 plus 2.5% of E's share of UBIA of qualified property ($100,000) or $2,500. The greater of the limitation amounts ($500,000 and $252,500) is $500,000. The QBI component of F's section 199A deduction is thus limited to $500,000, the lesser of 20% of QBI ($600,000) and the greater of the limitations amounts ($500,000). F reports a qualified loss from a PTP and has no qualified REIT dividend. F does not net the ($10,000) loss from the PTP against QBI. Instead, the portion of F's section 199A deduction related to qualified REIT dividends and qualified PTP income is zero for 2018. F's section is 199A deduction is equal to the lesser of 20% of the QBI from the business as limited ($500,000) or 20% of F's taxable income over net capital gain ($1,880,000 x 20% = $376,000). Therefore, F's section 199A deduction is $376,000 for 2018. F must also carry forward the ($10,000) qualified loss from a PTP to be netted against F's qualified REIT dividends and qualified PTP income in the succeeding taxable year.[16]

2. FLOW-THROUGH INCOME.

This is trade or business income that is received by an individual (which would include grantor trust income), trust, or estate that is the owner of a flow-through entity. This does not include employment wages as mentioned in the definition of S corporation and Wages described below in this Chapter.

The statute refers to this amount as Qualified Business Income "QBI." Some refer to this as "pass-thru" or "pass-through" income."

The trade or business requirement is discussed in more detail in Chapter 12.

The following example from the Final Regulations illustrates the above:

---

[16] Treas. Reg. § 1.199A-1(d)(4), Example 4.

Example:

> B and C are married and file a joint individual income tax return. B earns $50,000 in wages as an employee of an unrelated company in 2018. C owns 100% of the shares of X, an S corporation that provides landscaping services. X generates $100,000 in net income from operations in 2018. X pays C $150,000 in wages in 2018. B and C have no capital gains or losses. After allowable deductions not related to X, B and C's total taxable income for 2018 is $270,000. B's and C's wages are not considered to be income from a trade or business for purposes of the section 199A deduction. Because X is an S corporation, its QBI is determined at the S corporation level. X's QBI is $100,000, the net amount of its qualified items of income, gain, deduction, and loss. The wages paid by X to C are considered to be a qualified item of deduction for purposes of determining X's QBI. The section 199A deduction with respect to X's QBI is then determined by C, X's sole shareholder, and is claimed on the joint return filed by B and C. B and C's section 199A deduction is equal to $20,000, the lesser of 20% of C's QBI from the business ($100,000 x 20% = $20,000) and 20% of B and C's total taxable income for the taxable year ($270,000 x 20% = $54,000).[17]

3. SECTION 199A REQUIREMENTS FOR HIGH-INCOME TAXPAYERS.

Taxpayers who are married joint filers with more than $415,000 of taxable income, and single filers, trusts, and estates that have more than $207,500 of taxable income are not eligible for the 20% Section 199A deduction on either of (1) income from one of the 11 enumerated categories of "Specified Service Trade or Businesses," [18] or (2) income from a trade or business that does not satisfy the Wage/Property Test. These limitations are phased-in for taxpayers who are joint filers with more than $315,000 of net income and single filers and trusts with over $157,500 of income and is summarized by the following chart:

---

[17] Treas. Reg. § 1.199A-1(c)(3), Example 3.
[18] Treas. Reg. § 1.199A-3(b)(1). Defined as "the net amount of qualified items of income, gain, deduction, and loss with respect to any qualified trade or business of the taxpayers."

Chart 1 – 2018 Phase-Out Summary Chart

$0-$157,500 (single filers, trusts, and estates)	$157,500-$207,500 (single filers)	$207,500+ (single filers)
$0-$315,000 (married joint filers)	$315,000,$415,000 (joint filers)	$415,000+ (joint filers)
Full Deduction: No limits from Wage/Property Limitation; no limitation from being a Specified Service (i.e., **s and phase-outs have not started in this income bracket)**	**Phase-In/Phase-Out Zone: Wage/Property Limitation is phased-in, *and* deduction for Specified Service income starts being phased-out, as income exceeds lower income thresholds**	**Fully Phased-In/Phased-Out: No deduction under any circumstances for Specified Service income, Wage/Property Limitation is fully phased-in for other businesses**

Chart 1A – 2019 Phase-Out Summary Chart

$0-$160,700 (single filers, trusts, and estates)	$160,700-$210,700 (single filers)	$210,700+ (single filers)
$0-$321,400 (married joint filers)	$321,400-$421,400 (joint filers)	$421,400+ (joint filers)
Full Deduction: No limits from Wage/Property Limitation; no limitation from being a Specified Service (i.e., phase-ins and phase-outs have not started in this income bracket)	**Phase-In/Phase-Out Zone: Wage/Property Limitation is phased-in, *and* deduction for Specified Service income starts being phased-out, as income exceeds lower income thresholds**	**Fully Phased-In/Phased-Out: No deduction under any circumstances for Specified Service income, Wage/Property Limitation is fully phased-in for other businesses**

4. S CORPORATIONS.

A company, professional practice entity or LLC that elects to be treated as an S corporation by filing a Form 2553 with the IRS and meets certain strict organizational and ownership requirements. S corporation income is not taxed to the company, but instead is considered to be received by its owners pro rata to their ownership thereof, except if the company is a C corporation that elected S corporation status, in which event taxes imposed by Sections 1374 and 1375 may apply. See Chapter 7. The flow-through income of the S corporation is reported on "K-1" forms, as discussed in Chapter 3 that are attached to the S corporation's Form 1120S income tax return and then reported on the individual owners' Form 1040 or on a trust's or estate's Form 1041 income tax returns. This happens whether the owners have received distributions or not. It is noteworthy that S corporation K-1 income is not subject to employment taxes, but reasonable compensation for services rendered must be paid to S corporation owners and is subject to employment taxes.

Under the "second class of stock" rules, S corporation distributions and liquidation proceeds must be strictly pro rata to ownership and cannot take capital contributions or preferential rights into account, other than legitimate shareholder loans and compensation amounts.[19] This can make S corporations inflexible when shareholders wish to distribute income in a manner other than pro rata to ownership.

It is not safe for an S corporation shareholder to share income pro rata to productivity under an S corporation by adjusting wages so that the remaining profits come out pro rata to ownership because the second class of stock rules might be violated, so the S Election might be lost because of an implied agreement to allocate income other than strictly pro rata to ownership. The IRS may recharacterize wages paid as disguised distributions that would constitute a separate class of stock, which can cause the company to be treated as a C corporation and can lead to double taxation, as described below.

It is essential that S corporation shareholder or operating agreements be carefully reviewed to be sure that the contractual provisions do not violate the S corporation rules, which may cause C corporation status to be imposed, loss of the Section 199A deduction, and consequent double taxation on what would have been flow-through income.

5. PARTNERSHIPS.

Two or more persons or entities engaged in business or investment activities, an LLC, or other entity that is properly treated as a partnership for income tax purposes. Like an S corporation, the partnership's income is not taxed to the entity, but is instead considered to be received by its "partners" pro rata to their percentage of ownership, or as otherwise properly allocated if special rules are followed then their partners, whether it is actually paid out or not[20]. Partnerships file Form 1065 tax return and also issue K-1 forms to their partners. Unlike an S corporation, most active partners must pay employment taxes on their share of all partnership income.

6. REAL ESTATE INVESTMENT TRUSTS (REITs).

Real estate investment trusts are corporations, trusts or associations that have at least one hundred (100) beneficial owners and meet the requirements of Sections 856 through 589, which include

---

[19] S Corporations are required to pay reasonable compensation to owners, but compensation may be deferred in a reasonable manner.

[20] Under Code Section 704(b), the allocation of income and deductions under a partnership must satisfy some very complicated and strict rules that are called the "Substantial Economic Effect Rules." These rules require that capital account balance and the economics of any partnership arrangement should justify anything other than distributions and tax reporting that is pro-rat to ownership. Partners are taxed on partnership K-1 income regardless of whether distributions are made.

ownership,[21] distribution, and special tax treatment rules.[22] REITs are taxed on income not distributed to owners.

It is noteworthy that REIT income will qualify for the Section 199A deduction regardless of whether the REIT is actively engaged in a trade or business, has Qualified Property, or pays wages. Unfortunately, Publicly Traded Partnerships do not have the same immunities.

REIT dividends are eligible for the Section 199A deduction, based upon the lesser of (1) 20% of the excess of the taxable income over the net capital gains, or (2) the sum of 20% of flow-through income plus 20% of the sum of the aggregate amount of REIT dividends and publicly traded partnership income. Additionally, REIT dividends are only included to the extent they are not capital gain dividends or dividend income from C corporations.[23]

While the Section 199A definition of QBI specifically excludes REIT dividends, these amounts are still included in the general deduction because technically the deduction is for the "combined QBI amount," which is defined as the sum of 20% of flow-through income plus 20% of the aggregate amount of REIT dividends and qualified publicly traded partnership income. As a result of the above, REITS can qualify for the full 20% deduction without regard to how much they pay in wages or how much Qualified Property they have.[24]

7. PUBLICLY TRADED PARTNERSHIPS.

Publicly traded partnerships are entities that are taxed as partnerships and traded on a recognized stock exchange.[25]

Income from PTPs will qualify for the Section 199A deduction, regardless of the recipient taxpayer's income level or Wage or Qualified Property amounts, provided that any Specified Service Trade or Business income will be subject to the normal SSTB Section 199A deduction limitations that apply to high-earner taxpayers.

Unfortunately, mutual funds that own REITs will not qualify for the Section 199A deduction due to what appears to be an oversight in the statute which applies even if the mutual fund owns only REITs. The largest REIT mutual fund is sponsored by Vanguard and has over $58.17 billion in

---

[21]IRC § 856. REIT ownership must meet the following 7 requirements: (1) the REIT must be managed by at least one trustee or director, (2) beneficial ownership must be evidenced by transferable shares or certificates of beneficial interest, (3) which would otherwise be taxable as a domestic corporation, (4) is not a financial institution or insurance company, (5) the beneficial ownership must be held by at least 100 persons, (6) subject to provisions in § 856(k), and (7) meet the requirements of § 856(c). As part of subsection (c), REITs are required to have 95% of their gross income derived from factors listed at § 856(c)(2) and 75% of their gross income derived from factors listed at § 856(c)(3).

[22]IRC §§ 857–59.

[23] Treas. Reg. § 1.199A-3(c)(2).

[24] The Wage/Property Limitation is applied before REIT dividends and Publicly Traded Partnership income are added to the taxpayer's deduction. This means that REIT and Publicly Traded Partnership income avoids the phase-in of the Wage/Property Limitation. However, the phase-out will reduce Publicly Traded Partnership income, as discussed in the Executive Summary and Chapter 6 of this book.

[25] See IRC Section 7704.

market value and will therefore have many very disappointed investors who still wonder why they are not able to participate in this deduction.[26]

8. TAXPAYER.

An individual or married couple, who file jointly, will report the Qualified Business Income on their Form 1040, or a separately taxed non-grantor trust or an estate that would file a Form 1041.

(a)   **Under-Threshold Taxpayers.**

These are taxpayers with total taxable income (including flow-through income) less than the lower income thresholds of $157,500 as single filers, or $315,000 as joint filers for 2018, as adjusted for inflation in future tax years. The inflation adjusted thresholds for 2019 are $160,700 for single filers and $321,400 for joint filers with the phase-out described below being from $160,700 through $210,700 and $321,400 through $421,400 for 2019.

(b)   **Partially Phased-Out Taxpayers.**

These are taxpayers with total taxable income exceeding the lower thresholds but less than the higher thresholds. These are single filers with taxable income between $157,500 and $207,500, and joint filers with taxable income between $315,000 and $415,000 for 2018, and as adjusted for inflation in future tax years. They are referred to as "phased-out" because these taxpayers will be subject to the SSTB Limitations. Additionally, they may also be subject to a partial deduction under the phase-in rules of the Wage/Property Limitation, as discussed further Chapter 4 of this book.

(c)   **High-Income Taxpayers.**

These are taxpayers with a total taxable income exceeding $207,500 as single filers or $415,000 as joint filers for 2018, as adjusted for inflation in future tax years.

(d)   **Single Filers.**

These are individuals, a married person filing separately, a trust, or an estate. If a married couple files separately, each person will have a single filer threshold ($157,500/$207,500) to use Section 199A, which may be useful in some scenarios.

9. WAGE/QUALIFIED PROPERTY LIMITATION FOR HIGH-INCOME TAXPAYERS.

High-Income taxpayers cannot take the Section 199A deduction if the flow- through entity that is owned by the taxpayer does not pay certain levels of W-2 wages or own certain amounts of "Qualified Property," as described below. In many circumstances, flow-through business or activity income will not qualify for the Section 199A deduction unless the business or activity pays sufficient wages to employees thereof. Wages normally include compensation paid to S corporation employees, including shareholders, compensation that non-owner employees

---

[26]VGSIX Real Estate Index Fund by Vanguard has the largest asset pool, with the next largest REIT mutual fund, DFA Real Estate Securities Portfolio, having only $8.76 billion in assets.

receive from entities taxed as partnerships, and compensation paid by proprietorships to individuals other than owner of the proprietorship, which can include the owner's spouse who files a joint tax return with the owner.[27]

For Section 199A, wages must meet three qualifications: Timeliness of Filing, Attribution, and Type of Compensation.

(a) **Timeliness of Filing.**

Wages must be properly reported on a return filed with the Social Security Administration within 60 days of when the return is due in order to qualify for the Section 199A Wage/Property Test. For the repealed Section 199 deduction, the return filed was the W-2 or W-3 forms or W-2c or W-3c forms for corrections, [28] and the Final Regulations and Notice 2018-64 confirm that these forms will also be used for Section 199A. For 2018, Forms W-2 and Forms W-3 are due by January 31, 2019, and the 60-day deadline for Section 199A includes all extensions, making the latest date Forms W-2 and W-3 may be filed April 1, 2019 for wages paid in 2018.

Additionally, Section 199A specifies that wages must be paid during the calendar year, so bonuses cannot be accrued after the year's end to meet the Wage/Property Limitations, although pension obligations may count as wages and may be deductible in the year accrued, as opposed to having to be funded in cash.

(b) **Attribution.**

Wages or Qualified Property must be allocable to the Qualified Business Income they are applied to, unless aggregation rules apply.[29]

(c) **Types of Compensation.**

Section 199A defines wages as "the amounts described in paragraphs (3) and (8) of Section 6051(a) paid by [the taxpayer] with respect to employment of employees during the calendar year." [30] This does not include compensation or benefits paid to independent contractors, including independent contractors who are characterized as "statutory employees" as described in Chapter 11, but does include two categories of payments to employees, which go well beyond traditional wages and will therefore help a great many high-income taxpayers qualify for the Section 199A deduction:

(d) **§ 6051(a)(3)**

Wages and certain benefits actually paid, defined under Section 3401(a) as being compensation given for services rendered by an employee for their employer, whether in cash or in kind.[31]

---

[27]The authors believe this is possible as long as the employee spouse being paid wages does not have an ownership interest in the company.

[28]Treas. Reg. § 1.199-2(a)(3).

[29]Treas. Reg. § 1.199A-2(b)(4).

[30]Treas. Reg. § 1.199A-2(b)(2)(i).

[31] IRC § 6051(a)(3) uses § 3401(a) as the definition of wages, which includes 22 exceptions for remuneration not to

This includes salaries, bonuses, commissions, health and accident plan premiums for employees, certain taxable fringe benefits, and vacation and sick pay.[32] For a list of incorporated benefits, see the Treasury Regulations at **Error! Reference source not found.**, under "Certain Specific Items." There are some forms of compensation specifically excluded from being considered wages under Section 3401(a), including premiums paid on group term life insurance and benefits received under a self- insured medical reimbursement plan, among other exceptions (items that are not considered as wages) which are enumerated in the footnote below.[33]

---

be classified as wages.

[32]A more extensive list of items considered to be wages under § 3401(a) can be found at Treas. Reg. § 31.3401(a)-1.

[33] IRC §§ 3401(a)(1)-(23) These exceptions are for (1) compensation for active service in a combat zone, (2) agricultural labor unless it qualifies as wages under § 3121(a), (3) domestic service in a private home, local college club, or local chapter of a college fraternity or sorority, (4) for service not in the course of the employer's trade or business performed by an employee, unless the compensation is $50 or more to a "regularly employed" individual, as defined in § 3401(a)(4), (5) work done by a U.S. citizen or resident for a foreign government or international organization, (6) for services by a nonresident alien individual as prescribed by the Secretary of the Treasury, (7) REPEALED (8) services rendered for an employer other than the U.S. government by a U.S. citizen where (A) the compensation is excluded from gross income under § 911, (B) the services are done in a foreign country or possession of the U.S. where the foreign country or possession withholds income tax upon such compensation, (C) the services are done in a U.S. territory (other than Puerto Rico) if it is reasonable to believe that 80% of compensation paid to the employee by an employer will be for such services, (D) the services are done in Puerto Rico if it is reasonable to believe that during the calendar year the employee will be a bona fide resident of Puerto Rico, and (E) the services are done in a territory of the U.S. where the U.S. withholds taxes on such compensation pursuant to an agreement with the territory, (9) services performed by a duly ordained, commissioned, or licensed minister of a church, or by a member of a religious order in the exercise of duties required by such order, (10) services relating to the delivery and distribution of newspapers or shopping news by individuals under the age of 18 or relating to the sale of newspapers or magazines under a fixed-price sale to the individual, (11) for services not in the course of the employer's trade or business, paid in a medium other than cash, (12) payments made on behalf of the employee or his beneficiary (A) to a trust described in § 401(a) unless it is paid to an employee of the trust as compensation for services rendered, (B) to an annuity plan described under § 403(a), (C) payments made to simplified employee pensions if it is reasonable to believe the employee will be entitled to an exclusion, (D) under a § 408(p) arrangement, (E) under a deferred compensation plan described in § 457(b), (13) services performed as a volunteer or volunteer as described in the Peace Corps Act (excluding 5(c) or 6(1) under that act), (14) compensation in the form of group-term life insurance, (15) compensation if it is reasonable to believe that such compensation will give a deduction under § 217 without regard to § 274(n), (16) tips in any medium other than cash and cash tips for less than $20 in a calendar month, (17) compensation for services performed on a boat engaged in catching fish or other aquatic life, (18) any compensation or benefit if it is reasonable to believe the employee will be able to exclude such compensation under § 127, § 129, § 134(b)(4), or § 134(b)(5), (19) any benefit where it is reasonable to believe that the employee can exclude it under § 74(c), §108(f)(4), §117, or § 132, (20) any medical care reimbursement made to or for the benefit of an employee under a self-insured medical reimbursement plan, (21) any payment where it is reasonable to believe it will be excludable by the employee under § 106(b), (22) any payment or benefit where it is reasonable to believe it will be excludable by the employee under § 106(d), and (23) any payment or benefit that is excludable from gross income of the employee under § 139B(b). (As noted above, number (7) in this list was repealed and dealt with services performed by nonresident alien individuals other than residents of contiguous countries who enter and leave the United States at frequent intervals, residents of Puerto Rico if such services are performed as an employee of the United States or any agency thereof, or individuals temporarily present in the United States as nonimmigrants under certain conditions.

(e) **§ 6051(a)(8)**

Elective deferrals under Section 402(g)(3), compensation deferred under Section 457, and Roth contributions as defined in Section 402A.[34]

Section 402(g)(3) provides that such elective deferrals, which are included in the definition of wages, are limited to $18,500 per employee, and include the following four (4) categories of contribution:

1. any employer contribution to a 401(k)(6) qualified cash or deferred compensation arrangement; [35]

2. any employer contribution to a Section 408(k) simplified employee pension where an employee elects to have the employer contribute to said plan;

3. any employer contribution to purchase a Section 403(b) annuity contract as part of a salary reduction agreement;" and

4. any employer contribution to a SIMPLE IRA as part of a salary reduction agreement that the employee elects.[36]

All of the above Section 402(g)(3) contributions are limited to $18,500 per employee in 2018, and elective deferrals paid in excess of this amount are included in the employee's taxable income. Under Section 401(a)(30), a plan must provide that contributions cannot exceed the 402(g) limitation, so it is unlikely that contributions will exceed this amount, and excess contributions for an employee, if any, will be paid back to said employee as taxable compensation.[37]

It is also important to note that matching contributions made by employers do not count as elective deferrals, and therefore do not count as wages for Section 199A. However, it appears that employer contributions to 401(k) plans can be counted as wages in some situations where the employee has the option to choose between a taxable benefit (or cash) and a contribution to their 401(k) plans.[38]

---

[34]IRC § 6051(a)(8). Elective deferrals are reported in Box 12 of the Form W-2 with code D for § 401(k) plans, code E for § 403(b) agreements, code F for § 408(k)(6) agreements, code G for § 457(b) deferred compensation, and codes AA for designated Roth contributions under § 401(k), BB for designated Roth contributions under a § 403(b) plan, and EE for designated Roth contributions under a § 457(b) plan.

[35]IRC § 402(g)(3)(A). "any employer contribution under a qualified cash or deferred arrangement (as defined in Section 401(k)) to the extent not includible in gross income for the taxable year."

[36]IRC § 402(g)(3)(D). The employee must elect these contributions according to IRC § 408(p)(2)(A)(i): "an employee eligible to participate in the arrangement may elect to have the employer make payments (I) as elective employer contributions to a simple retirement account on behalf of the employee, or (II) to the employee directly in cash."

[37]IRC § 401(a)(30).

[38]This is because the employee had to either continue rolling over their paid time off or contribute it to a pension plan, but they could not elect between payment and a deferral of payment required by the definition of "elective deferral" under Treas. Reg. § 1.401(k)-6.

In Revenue Ruling 2009-32, the IRS concluded that an elective deferral does not include workers converting unused vacation time (a non-taxable benefit)[39] to pension contributions when there is no option to elect payment in cash as compensation for unused paid time off.[40] It appears that this would have been an elective deferral if the employees were offered three options: (1) keep the vacation time, (2) take the cash value of the vacation time, or (3) have it contributed to a pension plan. Similar outcomes would occur if deferral of income was required as a condition of employment, and this would not be an elective deferral because the employee has no control over whether the deferral happens or not. If an employer gives workers the option of receiving a bonus or having the amount of such bonus contributed to their 401(k) plan, this would likely count as an elective deferral, includable in the employer's W-2 wages for Section 199A purposes. For the employee, these contributions would be subject to the 402(g)(3) limit, as discussed above, and includable in the employee's income during the year if it exceeds $18,500.

It is important to keep in mind that W-2 wages do not count as flow-through income that can qualify for the Section 199A deduction. While owners of sole-proprietorships, partnerships, and Schedule C, E and F, and S corporation entities cannot be paid wages for Section 199A qualification purposes, the law does not appear to preclude Schedule C, E, or F businesses from paying wages from the owner-spouse's proprietorship to the other spouse who does not have an ownership interest, although this is not absolutely clear.[41] Should this be permissible, if the wages are suddenly new (i.e., after the enactment of Section 199A) they may be more suspect. In all events the reasonableness of the wages should be corroborated. If the couple is above the phase-out range, it might not provide any net Section 199A benefit and would add to the net tax cost as a result of payroll taxes.

An employee's wages are subject to employment taxes that are paid by the employer based upon 7.65% of the first $128,400 of wages and 1.45% above that amount.[42] This is addition to the cost of worker's compensation, unemployment compensation, and other expenses. The employee also pays employment taxes based upon 7.65% of the first $128,400 of wages and 1.45% above $128,400. There is an additional 0.9% (9/10ths of 1 percent) Medicare tax imposed upon the employee on earnings exceeding $200,000 if a single filer, or $250,000 if filing jointly.[43]

Compensation paid to independent contractors will not be considered to be W-2 wages for Section 199A Wage Testing purposes, as described below, but may qualify for the Section 199A deduction on the tax return of the contractor.

---

[39]Vacation pay constitutes a wage under Treas. Reg. § 31.3401(b)(3), but vacation time without the ability to receive the dollar value of such vacation time is not a taxable benefit.

[40]*Rev. Rul. 2009-32* (2009).

[41]*See* I.R.S. Pub. No. 15, Cat. No. 10000W, (Jan. 15, 2018), https://www.irs.gov/pub/irs-pdf/p15.pdf (see "One spouse employed by another" under Chapter 3, noting that an employed spouse's compensation is still subject to wage taxes and withholding, but not to Federal Unemployment Tax).

[42]*See* IRC § 3111 for the employer's tax rates. IRC § 3121(a)(1) states that employers are responsible for Social Security Tax on wages below the "contribution and benefit base" (also known as the Social Security cap) that changes yearly based on the national average wage index, according to 42 U.S.C. 430.

[43]IRC § 3101(b)(2). *See also* Treas. Reg. § 31.3102-4.

Individuals working as independent contractors or having unincorporated trades or businesses must pay self-employment tax based on 15.3% of the first $128,400 of self- employment income, and the 2.9% Medicare employment tax on any income over that, plus the additional 0.9% Medicare tax on wages exceeding $200,000 for single filers or $250,000 for employees filing jointly.[44] Individuals who own LLCs that are disregarded for income tax purposes must treat the activities of the LLC as if they were personally owned. Wage taxes paid by an employer are income tax deductible by the employer, but wage taxes, Medicare taxes, and one-half (½) of self-employment taxes paid by an employee, contractor, or independent contractor are not tax deductible.

Additionally, businesses may be able to count wages paid to employees through common paymasters or leasing organizations. Under the old Section 199 regulations, taxpayers were allowed to consider "any wages paid by another entity and reported by the other entity on Forms W-2 with the other entity as the employer listed in Box c of the Forms W-2, provided that the wages were paid to employees of the taxpayer for employment by the taxpayer," as long as the taxpayer was the common law employer of the employees.

The Preamble to the Proposed Regulations specifically stated that the Regulations under former Section 199 addressed this, and the Final Regulations indicate that wages paid under common paymasters and similar arrangements will be considered as paid by the common law employer of the employees, and almost directly follow the previous regulations under Section 199.

It is noteworthy that on audit, the IRS may choose to reclassify K-1 income as being W- 2 wages, or vice versa. For example, lawyers using S corporations might have preferred to have more dividends and fewer wages to reduce employment taxes or prefer to have at least $275,000 in wages because the first $275,000 of income is counted in determining relative pension and profit-sharing plan contributions. Since wages above $275,000 would be irrelevant for such purposes, the IRS may claim that a portion of wages are actually dividends to reduce pension contribution amounts. Post-Section 199A it might be more advantageous to have lower wages which would not qualify for the Section 199A deduction and higher flow-through income which might.[45]

The above concepts are summarized by the following charts.

---

[44]IRC § 1411.

[45]Eric Yauch, *ABA Section of Taxation Meeting: Existing Tax Code Helpful for Addressing Section 199A Issues*, Tax Notes Today (May 28, 2018).

Chart 2 – W-2 Wages by Entity Chart

This chart simplifies who can be paid W-2 wages for the purposes of maximizing a Section 199A deduction from the standpoint of the flow-through entity:

Which employees below can be paid W-2 wages by the business structures listed on the right?	Sole Proprietorship	Partnership	S Corporation
Owners/employees with ownership interest	No	No	Yes
Non-owner employees	Yes	Yes	Yes
Spouses (with no ownership interest)	Yes	Yes	Yes
Independent contractors	No	No	No

Chart 3 – 2018 Employment Tax Summary Chart

This chart describes employment tax rules that will impact Section 199A planning:

Taxes	Employer	Employee	Self-Employed
Social Security Tax (12.4% on income up to $128,400).	Yes, the employer contributes 6.2% and withholds the employee's contribution of 6.2%.	Yes, the employee is expected to pay 6.2% Social Security Tax, which is withheld by the employer from payroll.	The self-employed individual pays 12.4% (combined employer and employee share).
Medicare Tax (2.9% on all income).	Yes, the employer contributes 1.45% and withholds the employee's contribution of 1.45%.	Yes, the employee is expected to pay 1.45%, which is withheld by the employer from payroll.	The self-employed individual pays 1.45% (the combined employer and employee share).
Additional Medicare Tax (0.9% on income exceeding $200,000 if single filer, $250,000 if joint filers).	No, but must withhold if employee makes over $200,000/$250,000.	Yes, the employee will pay .9% on wages/compensation exceeding $200,000 for single filers or $250,000 for joint filers.	Yes, if self-employment income is over $200,000 for single filers, or $250,000 for joint filers.

Chart 3A - 2019 Employment Tax Summary Chart

Taxes	Employer	Employee	Self-Employed
Social Security Tax (12.4% on income up to $132,900).	Yes, the employer contributes 6.2% and withholds the employee's contribution of 6.2%.	Yes, the employee is expected to pay 6.2% Social Security Tax, which is withheld by the employer from payroll.	The self-employed individual pays 12.4% (combined employer and employee share).
Medicare Tax (2.9% on all income).	Yes, the employer contributes 1.45% and withholds the employee's contribution of 1.45%.	Yes, the employee is expected to pay 1.45%, which is withheld by the employer from payroll.	The self-employed individual pays 1.45% (the combined employer and employee share).
Additional Medicare Tax (0.9% on income exceeding $200,000 if single filer, $250,000 if joint filers).	No, but must withhold if employee makes over $200,000/$250,000.	Yes, the employee will pay .9% on wages/compensation exceeding $200,000 for single filers or $250,000 for joint filers.	Yes, if self-employment income is over $200,000 for single filers, or $250,000 for joint filers.

Chart 4 – 2018 Employment Tax Rates Summary Chart

This chart gives the rates for the above employment taxes. For this chart, assume the employer is in the highest tax bracket, so that an employer in the 37% tax bracket will pay 63% of the employment tax rate (after taking into account that the payments are tax deductible), which will be $6,189 on the first $128,400 of income ($128,400 x 4.82% is $6,189). Also, if the employee is married the additional Medicare tax threshold will be $250,000, or $200,000 if the employee is single.

Income	Employer (Deductible)	Employee	Combined	Independent Contractor
				Self Employed*
$100,000	(63% x 7.65%) = 4.82% **Cumulative Cost: $4,820**	7.65% **Cumulative Cost: $7,650**	12.47% **Cumulative Total: $12,470**	12.47% **Cumulative Total: $12,470**
$128,400	(63% x 7.65%) = 4.82% **Cumulative Cost: $6,189**	7.65% **Cumulative Cost: $9,823**	12.47% **Cumulative Total: $16,012**	12.47% **Cumulative Total: $16,012**
$200,000	(63% x 1.45%) = 0.914% over $128,400 **Cumulative Cost: $8,016**	1.45% **Cumulative Cost: $11,650**	2.34% **Cumulative Total: $19,666**	2.34% **Cumulative Total: $19,666**
$250,000	(63% x 1.45%) = 0.914% over $128,400 **Cost: $8,474**	1.45% **Cumulative Cost: $12,108**	2.34% **Cumulative Total: $20,582**	2.34% **Cumulative Total: $20,582**

*Self-employed taxpayers act as employer and employee and can deduct one-half of their employment tax against their income tax.

Chart 4 A – 2019 Employment Tax Rates Summary Chart

Income	Employed			Independent Contractor
	Employer (Deductible)	Employee	Combined	Self Employed*
$100,000	(63% x 7.65%) = 4.82% **Cumulative Cost: $4,820**	7.65% **Cumulative Cost: $7,650**	12.47% **Cumulative Total: $12,470**	12.47% **Cumulative Total: $12,470**
$132,900	(63% x 7.65%) = 4.82% **Cumulative Cost: $6,406**	7.65% **Cumulative Cost: $10,167**	12.47% **Cumulative Total: $16,573**	12.47% **Cumulative Total: $16,573**
$200,000	(63% x 1.45%) = 0.914% over $132,900 **Cumulative Cost: $8,233**	1.45% **Cumulative Cost: $11,994**	2.34% **Cumulative Total: $20,227**	2.34% **Cumulative Total: $20,227**
$250,000	(63% x 1.45%) = 0.914% over $132,900 **Cost: $8,691**	1.45% **Cumulative Cost: $12,452**	2.34% **Cumulative Total: $21,143**	2.34% **Cumulative Total: $21,143**

*Self-employed taxpayers act as employer and employee and can deduct one-half of their employment tax against their income tax.

10. AGGREGATION VS. SEPARATION FOR WAGE/QUALIFIED PROPERTY TESTING AND FOR TAXPAYERS WITH MULTIPLE TRADES OR BUSINESSES.

An individual, married couple, trust or estate may own interests in two or more separate trades or businesses which may be aggregated for purposes of satisfying the Wage/Property Limitations that apply for high-earner taxpayers if certain requirements are met. The rules require that a trade or business with net losses that could be aggregated will cause reduction of the combined net income of the trades and businesses that are aggregated.

Further, certain related entities that perform services for, or sell products to, an SSTB that is under 50% or more common control will be treated as a separate SSTB. For example, lawyers or family members who have a law firm and a separate entity that owns a building leased to the law firm will have the building income considered to be a Specified Service Trade or Business to the extent that the gross revenue of the building entity is attributable to the law firm's payment of rent, and expenses and deductions properly allocable thereto. Alternatively, if control and related party revenue provisions can be skirted, this may be considered to be a law firm, a title company, and a landlord/tenant arrangement if separate accountings can be facilitated, and deductions for the title company and landlord activities would be permitted, that may not otherwise be allowed. For more detail, see Chapter 9, Part Two.

The Final Regulations provide that results based on "lines of business" may not be effective based on using separate entities, or a single entity with a reasonable grouping of income-generating activities.

Example:

> A law firm partnership offers legal, title insurance, and trustee services, and owns its own building. Would these be classified as a single legal service business, four businesses with no deduction, or four separate businesses, with three (the non-Specified Service Trades or Businesses) able to claim a deduction under Section 199A? How will wages paid by the law firm and the qualified property aspect of the building be treated as far as the Wage/Property Test is concerned? Under the Final Regulations, if the businesses are commonly controlled and provide services to the SSTB, then revenue that would otherwise not be considered to be from legal services, will nevertheless be treated as non-SSTB income.

The American Institute of Certified Public Accountants (AICPA) had strongly suggested that reasonable allocations of activities be allowed without requiring separation of entities, assets and activities. [46] Despite this and similar industry requests, the Final Regulations released on January 18, 2019 took a strict view concerning SSTB related operations qualifying for the new Section 199A deduction and seemed to require that separate books and records would be maintained. The Preamble to the Final Regulations misquoted an excerpt from the Final Regulations, and included examples that had taxpayers with separate books and records, but also other "indicia of separateness," qualifying for the segregation. The February 4, 2019 Regulations corrected the quotation from the Section 446 Regulations by using the word "separable," but the examples were not changed, causing concern that separate books and records would be required. This was further clarified by the ABA Webinar entitled *Recent 199A Guidance: Hear From Practicing Experts and Government Officials* on April 4, 2019, during which the Treasury lawyers who drafted the Regulations confirmed that the intention was to not actually require separate books and records so long as "separable" business records are maintained, so that separate financial statements can be prepared if needed. This would allow for "severability" after the fact, to the relief of many, and is discussed in more detail in Chapter 9, Part Two.

Not to be confused with "aggregation," which has a technical meaning under Section 199A, taxpayers owning multiple disregarded entities that are in the same trade or business should be able to combine the activities of each entity for purposes of determining whether a trade or business exists, or if the 250-hour safe harbor for real estate is met. This is discussed in more detail in Chapter 9, Part Two.

---

[46]Letter from Annette Nellen, Tax Executive Committee Chair, AICPA, to David J. Kautter, Assistant Secretary for Tax Policy, I.R.S., and William M. Paul, Deputy Chief Counsel, I.R.S. (Feb. 21, 2018) (on file with AICPA).

11. GUARANTEED PAYMENTS.

Guaranteed Payments are the name given in the Code to compensation paid to a partner by a partnership.[47][48] Therefore, compensation paid by a partnership to a partner can never be considered "Wages" for purposes of Section 199A, even if paid for legitimate purposes, and employment and other wage taxes are paid thereon. As a result of this, many partners may place their partnership interests into S corporations so that the "partner" for income tax purposes is the S corporation and wages can be paid to the individual S corporation owner who is no longer a partner. S corporations will be preferred over partnerships in many situations, especially for non-real estate and leasing trades and businesses.

The Final Regulations provide that payments received by a partner in a partnership as income that is based upon capital will not be considered to be deductible as QBI under Section 199A.

12. QUALIFIED PROPERTY.

For high-income taxpayers, as defined below, the Section 199A deduction will only apply for QBI from a business or entity that has sufficient wages and/or qualified property acquisition costs referred to as Unadjusted Basis Immediately After Acquisition or UBIA for short (which will be referred to as "Qualified Property" in this book) that meet certain thresholds. Only tangible assets, other than land, that have not yet exceeded the greater of (1) their depreciable life, regardless of whether the asset has been fully depreciated using bonus depreciation, or (2) 10 years since placed in service can qualify for this testing. This definition will be very important for high-income taxpayers who have income from rental activity.

Qualified Property must be used in the generation of flow-through income, and can include buildings (but not land), office furniture, printers, computers, and equipment owned by the flow-through entity or individual taxpayer. As defined by Section 199A, the "depreciable period" for Qualified Property is the later of (1) 10 years after the date the property is first placed into service or (2) the depreciable period that would apply under Section 168.[49] Accordingly, property with a depreciable life of shorter than 10 years can still be used for the Wage/Property Test under Section 199A until the 10-year period expires. Property fully expensed under the bonus depreciation rules will still be counted for the longer of (1) its normal depreciable life or (2) 10 years after acquisition. This will cause fewer taxpayers to use write off components of buildings as 5- or 7-year assets using "segregation studies" which became popular in the 1990s and still often used.

Chart 5 – Depreciable Periods Chart

This chart shows examples of some applicable depreciable periods:

---

[47]IRC § 707(c).

[48]Despite the connotation of the term "guaranteed," state contract law is not a factor in the determination of whether or not partnership payments will be characterized as a Guaranteed Payments.

[49]Treas. Reg. § 1.199A-2(c)(2)(i). This holds true even if the property was placed into service after 1981, the enactment year of Section 168.

Type of Property	Depreciable Period	Depreciable Period For 199A Purposes
Non-residential Real Property (post-1986)	39 Years	39 Years
Office Furniture (Desks, files, safes, etc.)	7 Years	10 Years
Automobiles and Taxis	5 Years	10 Years
Light General-Purpose Trucks	5 Years	10 Years
Information Systems (Computers, card readers, printers, etc.)	5 Years	10 Years

The Act authorizes the Treasury Department to issue regulations for the purpose of determining the depreciable period of assets acquired with a 1031 exchange or in an involuntary conversion.[50] Property received in a Section 1031 exchange or a Section 1033 involuntary conversion is treated under the Final Regulations as replacement MACRS property.[51] The Final Regulations provide detailed rules governing when property will be considered as having been placed in service, and state that deferred exchange assets will be considered to retain the UBIA of the relinquished property and are considered as having been placed in service on the same date that the relinquished property was placed into service, except that new consideration paid by the exchanger for the replacement property will be considered to be a new separate asset, and UBIA will be reduced to the extent that the exchanging taxpayer received cash or other taxable "boot" in the 1031 transaction.[52]

The calculation of the share of wages and Qualified Property that is allocated to a taxpayer will depend upon the circumstances of the partnership and partnership tax law. Section 199A(f)(1)(A) states that "199A applies at the partner or S corporation shareholder level, and that each partner or shareholder takes into account such person's allocable share of each qualified item" of the W-2 wages and the UBIA of qualified property by the partnership or S corporation for the taxable year."[53]

Section 199A goes on to say that a "partner's or shareholder's allocable share of the UBIA of qualified property shall be determined in the same manner as the partner's or shareholder's allocable share of depreciation." Generally, the allocation of items such as depreciation and wages are allocated pro rata to ownership unless otherwise stated in the partnership agreement and

---

[50]Treas. Reg. § 1.199A-2(c)(2)(iii).
[51]Replacement MACRS Property is defined in Treas. Reg. 1.168(i)-6(b)(1).
[52] Treas. Reg. § 1.199A-2(c)(2)(iii).
[53]IRC § 199A(f)(A)(iii).

permitted under applicable partnership tax law.[54] [I]n the case of an S corporation, an allocable share shall be the shareholder's pro rata share of an item."[55]

Example:

> John Doe and Ron Doe each own 50% of ABC, LLC, which acquired $100,000 of Qualified Property 5 years ago. John and Ron would each have $50,000 in Qualified Property that can be used for the Wage/Property Limitation of Section 199A. If they were to bring on a new shareholder and adjust their ownership so that each person owned 33% of the company, each shareholder would now have $33,333 to use for the Wage/Property Limitation.

Wages are allocated in a similar way.

Finally, it is important to remember that buildings are depreciable, but the land that they are placed on is generally not.[56] Whenever there is real estate, a certain portion is apportioned to the value of the land.[57] The IRS suggests in Publication 17, which is known as Tax Guide 2018 for Individuals, that the cost basis in real property should be allocated "according to the respective fair market values of the land and buildings at the time of purchase." [58]

For Section 199A purposes, it can be presumed that office and building condominium interests will need to be considered partly land and partly real estate based upon a reasonable allocation. The Tax Court has ruled that the acquisition of condominiums constitutes a purchase of depreciable and non-depreciable property in a lump sum, and the basis in land and the building must be allocated.[59] In Publication 17, the IRS notes that for those who are uncertain of the fair market values, the basis in land and buildings can be allocated according to their assessed value for real estate tax purposes.[60]

---

[54]IRC § 704(a). *See supra* fn. 15.

[55]IRC § 199A(f)(A)(iii).

[56]In some limited instances land may be depreciated, for example, if special grading or berms are created that may have a useful life related to the building, etc.

[57]*See United States v. Hill*, 506 U.S. 546 (1993) ("a taxpayer who bought an apartment building and the land it sits on for a single price must determine how much of that price went to pay for each and must treat each cost as a separate asset"). *See also Nielsen v. Commissioner*, T.C. Summary Opinion 2017-31 (2017) (citing to Treas. Reg. § 1.167(a)-5, as well as *United States v. Hill*) ("If depreciable property and nondepreciable property such as real property with improvements are bought for a lump sum, the cost must be apportioned between the land and the improvements").

[58]*See* I.R.S. Pub. No. 17, Cat. No. 10311G, at 100 (Dec. 12, 2017), https://www.irs.gov/pub/irs- pdf/p17.pdf. Taxpayers relying on guidance published in IRS Publications should use caution as this is not binding on the IRS. *See Bobrow v. Comm'r*.

[59]*Willits v. Commissioner*, 38 T.C.M. 1152 (1979) (holding that California state law gave petitioner an interest, owned as tenants in common, in the non-depreciable land of the condominium unit, and that petitioner needed to allocate some portion of their basis in the real estate to land). *See also Meiers v. Commissioner*, T.C. Memo 1982-51 (1982).

[60]*See* I.R.S. Pub. No. 17, Cat. No. 10311G, at 100 (Dec. 12, 2017), https://www.irs.gov/pub/irs- pdf/p17.pdf.

13. EFFECTIVELY CONNECTED ("U.S. OR PUERTO RICO BASED") INCOME.

Income that is derived from assets and activities in the U.S. or Puerto Rico that are a material factor in the realization of such income, as defined under Section 864(c), which controls when a non-resident person is considered to have income that will be taxed by the United States.

Section 864(c) states that "All income, gain, or loss from sources within the United States shall be treated as effectively connected with the conduct of a trade or business within the United States." There is an exception to this rule for certain types of income in the statute, and a two-factor test is applied to determine whether such income is effectively connected.[61] The test considers whether (1) the income is derived from assets used in or held for the conduct of such business and (2) the activities of the business were a material factor in the realization of the income, gain, or loss.

Non-Effectively Connected Income does not qualify for the Section 199A flow-through deduction and may be taxed differently under the foreign tax law provisions of the Code and under treaties that exist between the U.S. and the country or countries where a business or investments are used.

"Trade or business" in Section 199A applies to domestic American business and business in Puerto Rico. Activity, even for a flow-through entity, that happens or is located outside of the United States is barred from the definition of trade or business income under Section 199A. This definition excludes American territories other than Puerto Rico. If an entity has moved parts of their business overseas/offshore, such as billing, IT, and customer service, it might be best for the taxpayer to sequester these activities from their main business. Even though the Section 199A deduction is not available, offshore companies may be able to qualify for other tax deferral or reduction opportunities that are available.

The Preamble to the Proposed Regulations provides as follows:

> *"Thus, for example, a U.S. partner of a partnership that operates a trade or business in both the United States and in a foreign country would only include the items of income, gain, deductions, and loss that would be effectively connected with a United States trade or business. Similarly, a shareholder of an S corporation that is engaged in a trade or business in both the United States and in a foreign country would only consider the items of income, gain, deduction, and loss that would be effectively connected to the portion of the business conducted by the S corporation in the United States, determined by applying the principles of Section 864(c). In general, whether a nonresident alien is engaged in a trade or business within the United States, as opposed to a trade or business conducted solely outside the United States, is based upon the all the facts and circumstances, as developed through case law and other published guidance. Pursuant to Section 875(1), a nonresident alien is considered engaged in a trade or business within the United States if the partnership of which such individual is a member is so engaged."*

---

[61] IRC § 864(c)(2) states that income that is (A) received by nonresident alien individuals from sources other than capital gains, (B) debt portfolio interest received by nonresident alien individuals, (C) certain foreign corporation income under § 881(a), (D) debt portfolio interest received by a foreign corporation, and (E) from the sale or exchange of capital assets.

14. HOW TO CALCULATE TAXABLE INCOME.

This number reflects the "net income after deductions" of the individual taxpayer, S corporation, or partnership, and generally constitutes all income, minus deductions for permitted business expenses and certain above-the-line deductions allowed for individual taxpayers.[62] A taxpayer's Section 199A deduction is limited to 20% of the excess of the taxpayer's taxable income over the taxpayer's net capital gain, plus qualified cooperative dividends.

Chart 6 – Taxable Income Summary Chart

Taxable Income for	Calculation/Definition
Individual	Gross income minus above-the-line deductions, as well as other deductions (including standard/itemized deductions)
Trust or estate	Gross income minus trust expenses, trust/estate exemption amount ($100 for complex trust, $300 for simple trust, $600 for estates) [63], and distribution deductions[64]
S corporations	Calculated in the same manner as the individual's taxable income, except that Section 703(a)(2) (certain deductions not available to partnerships) deductions are not allowed, deductions for organizational expenditures are allowed, and certain restrictions exist on tax preference items [65]

While the majority of individual taxpayers will have taxable income based upon the excess of total earnings minus the $12,000 or $24,000 ($12,400 and $28,800 in 2019) standard allowance, many will have itemized deductions exceeding the $12,000/$24,000 level, net operating losses from previous years, which may reduce taxable income, "above-the-line" expenses for items such as health savings account contributions, student loan interest, and IRA contributions, which are deductible regardless of whether the taxpayer itemizes.[66]

Above-the-line deductions are expenses excludible from gross income (and therefore not itemized) and are reported on the IRS Income Tax Form 1040. Taxable income will consist of gross income, minus the above-the-line deductions, minus the greater of itemized deductions or the standard

---

[62]*See* IRS Form 1040, lines 23-35.
[63] While the personal exemption was suspended through 2025 for individuals, it remains unchanged for trusts and estates.
[64]The distribution deductions for simple trusts can be found at IRC § 651 and for complex trusts and estates, this deduction can be found at IRC § 661.
[65]IRC § 1362(b).
[66]Above-the-line deductions are found in IRC § 62(a).

allowance of $12,000 for an individual or $24,000 ($12,400 and $24,800 in 2019) for a married couple. Above-the-line deductions for 2018 consist of:

(1)   trade and business deductions under Code§§ 211-224,
(2)   certain trade and business deductions for employees under Code§§ 161-199A,
(3)   losses from sale or exchange of property under Code§§ 161-199A,
(4)   deductions attributable to property held for rent or royalties under Code§ 212,
(5)   § 611, and §§ 161-199A,
(6)   the deduction for depreciation allowed for life tenant of property, or an income beneficiary of property held in trust, or an heir, legatee, or devisee of an estate, under § 167 and § 611,
(7)   payments to pension, profit-sharing, and annuity plans by self-employed individuals,
(8)   payments to retirement savings accounts under § 219,
(9)   deductions under § 165 for losses incurred as penalties because of premature withdrawal of funds from deposits or time savings accounts,
(10)   reforestation expenses under § 194,
(11)   the deduction under § 165 for certain repayments of supplemental unemployment compensation,
(12)   jury duty pay remitted to an employer,
(13)   moving expenses allowed under § 217,
(14)   the deduction for Archer Medical Savings Accounts (MSAs) under § 220,
(15)   the deduction for interest on educational loans under § 221,
(16)   the deduction for higher education expenses under § 222,
(17)   the deduction for health savings accounts under § 223,
(18)   costs involving discrimination suits,
(19)   and attorneys' fees relating to awards for whistleblowers.

The Tax Cuts and Jobs Act made several significant changes to above-the-line deductions including:

(1)   The Act repealed the alimony deduction for payers, but excluded payments from the taxable income of alimony recipients, for divorce decrees or agreements entered into after December 31, 2018; and

(2)   The Act repealed the moving expense deduction for any individual who is not on active-duty in the armed forces or family thereof.

Itemized deductions include certain mortgage interest payments (on up to $1,000,000 of acquisition indebtedness incurred prior to December 15, 2017 and after 2025, or $750,000 of indebtedness taken after December 15, 2017 but before 2026), up to $10,000 of state and local taxes (including taxes on real estate), charitable donations, and medical expenses which are in excess of 7.5% of gross income for the taxable year.[67]

Before 2017, the Code provided a deduction for interest paid on home acquisition mortgages of up to $1,000,000, and home equity mortgages of up to $100,000. The value of the combined mortgages/loans, both acquisition and equity, is subject to the $750,000 cap that was intended to

---

[67]*See* IRS Form 1040, Schedule A. The medical deduction threshold reduction applies from the 2016 tax year to the 2018 tax year.

apply only to acquisition interest. Many practitioners assumed that this removed all deductions for interest paid on home equity loans, second mortgages, and home equity lines of credit. Fortunately, the IRS released guidance in February of 2019 stating that interest paid on these types of loans would be deductible if the money was used to buy, build or substantially improve the home that secures the loan.[68] For example, if a taxpayer takes out a $500,000 mortgage to purchase a first home, and another $500,000 mortgage in home equity to put an addition on the home, only the interest attributable to $750,000 of the debt would be deductible.

Example:

> A married couple may wish to "bunch" itemized deductions every two or three years to facilitate income tax savings. Assume that the couple pays $6,000 a year in property taxes, $7,000 a year in interest and donates $10,000 a year to charity, for a total of $23,000. The couple is better off with the $24,000 standard deduction. If the same couple instead donates $30,000 to charity every three years (instead of the $10,000 every year) then they will have the standard $24,000 deductions in years one and two, and a $43,000 deduction in year three, saving 40.8% (the combined 3.8% Net Investment Income Tax and 37% income tax) of $19,000 ($43,000 minus $24,000), totaling $7,752 every three years, instead of only taking the $24,000 standard deduction every year. While there has been much discussion of "bunching" in consumer articles, it is not clear that this will be useful to many clients. Given the elimination and severe restriction of many former itemized deductions the latitude for this planning to be effective is quite limited.

Section 199A and 1202 planning is further impacted by the lower tax rates that many taxpayers will be paying. While practitioners have been touting the reduction from a 37% rate to a 29.6% rate on flow-through income, this 7.4% difference only applies to those in the highest tax brackets. Those who are in lower tax brackets will have a smaller difference.

For example, Chart 5 in **Error! Reference source not found.**shows that a single individual with $200,000 in taxable income in 2018 was in the 32% tax bracket, and Section 199A deductible income at his or her bracket with a 20% deduction will be taxed at 25.6%, which is a difference of 6.4%. If that person was in the 24% ($82,501-$157,500) tax bracket, flow-through income would be taxed at 19.2%, which is a difference of only 4.8%. If there are no steps necessary to claim the deduction, even a small benefit might be advantageous. However, if costs will be incurred to restructure a business endeavor or its ownership in order to claim the deduction, it may not be worthwhile.

If this was a married couple with $150,000 of taxable income (24% tax bracket), then an additional $50,000 of 2018 flow-through income would be taxed at 19.2% with a full deduction.

---

[68]IR-2018-32 (Feb. 21, 2018).

The Chart below provides a list of the former itemized deductions, and has the itemized deductions that have been unchanged in white, the itemized deductions that have been changed in gray, and the itemized deductions that have been eliminated with a dashed underline and in red.

Itemized Deductions

	Deduction	Current Law Tax Year 2017	New Law Tax Year 2018	Notes	Effective/Expiration Date
1	State and Local Taxes	Unlimited	Capped at $10,000	Applies to state and local: (1) property taxes; plus (2) income or sales taxes.	Begins in tax year 2018 Expires after tax year 2025
2	Mortgage Interest	Limited to interest paid on debt of up to $1,000,000	Lowered to $750,000	Current homeowners (or homes acquired under contracts entered into before Dec. 15, 2017, which transactions close before April 1, 2018) will remain subject to the $1 million limitation	New limitation applies to homes acquired under contracts entered into before Dec 15, 2017, which close before April 1, 2018. Expired after tax year 2015.
3	Home Equity Debt Interest	Interest paid on home equity debt of up to $100,000	Repealed		
4	Unreimbursed Medical Expenses	Limited to 10% of AGI. Over 65, reduced to 7.5%	Reduced to 7.5% of AGI for all taxpayers		*Begins in tax year 2017. Expired after tax year 2018.
5	Personal Casualty and Theft Loss	Generally allowable for any such loss	Only available if such loss is attributable to a disaster, as declared by the President		
6	Miscellaneous Itemized Deductions	Total of miscellaneous deductions must be more than 2% of AGI	Repealed	Generally include expense for production or collection of income tax preparation, unreimbursed employee expenses.	Begins in tax year 2018. Expires after tax year 2015.
7	Charitable Deductions	Generally available for contributions to charitable organizations, certain limitations apply	Adjusted limit of cash contributions to 60%	Exception for contemporaneous written acknowledgment repealed. No deduction allowed for a donation in exchange for college sport seating rights.	Begins in tax year 2018. Expires after tax year 2025.
8	Limitation/Phase-Out of Itemized Deductions	Single filer with AGI over $266,700 or married jointly AGI over $320,000	Repealed		Begins in tax year 2018. Expires after tax year 2025.
9	Moving Expenses	Allowed for unreimbursed qualified moving expenses	Repealed	Deduction remains for members of the Armed Forces for their spouse or dependents on active duty who move due to military order.	Begins in tax year 2018. Expires after tax year 2025.

The pension census form on the next page can be used to provide an actuarial firm or other qualified advisory group with information on the ages, time with the company, date of birth, category of employee, and expected compensation.

Name of Employer:

Provide complete information for all employees employed during the year, even if they have terminated.

Employee Name	Date of Birth	Date of Hire	Date of Termination	Annualized W-2 Compensation	Hours Per Week	Ownership %

Businesses and practices will be well advised to consult periodically with pension plan advisors to determine if and when a defined benefit or cash balance plan might be added to a cross-tested 401(k) plan arrangement or other arrangements to reduce income. Section 412(i) plans may also be considered, and are very similar to defined benefit plans, but must invest only in life insurance, which can be a very expensive investment vehicle. Nevertheless, a 412(i) plan can be converted to an IRA and is much less expensive and time consuming to establish and operate.

The maximum contribution that can be made for a highly compensated employee under a normal 401(k) defined contribution plan, a cash balance plan, and a defined benefit plan are as follows:

Comparison of Maximum Contributions[69]

	Defined Contribution	Defined Benefit	Maximum Contribution for a Cash Balance Plan
Employee Age 60	$62,000	$254,000	$261,000
Employee Age 55	$62,000	$194,000	$203,000
Employee Age 50	$62,000	$148,000	$158,000
Employee Age 45	$56,000	$113,000	$123,000
Employee Age 40	$56,000	$ 87,000	$ 96,000

Permanency Requirement – A defined benefit or cash balance plan must be "permanent," which normally means that it will be in place at least five years, unless there are circumstances beyond the reasonable control of the Employer.

The following spreadsheet shows that a taxpayer earning $270,000 can contribute up to $206,469 into a cash balance and profit-sharing plan for himself or herself, while only having to contribute $12,669 for other employees. As discussed above, the use of cash balance plans or other arrangements can significantly reduce a taxpayer's income to allow the taxpayer to remain under the threshold limitations.

---

[69] The authors would like to thank Stephen Evers at Ascensus TPA Solutions for providing us with this chart.

JOHN SMITH
A Combination 401(k) / Profit Sharing / Cash Balance Plan
For the Plan Year 01/01/2017 – 12/31/2017

CONTRIBUTION REPORT – DETAIL

POH	Class	Last Name	First Name	AA	RA	Considered Earnings	Cash Balance Amount	%	Profit Sharing Amount	%	Total Contribution Amount	%	Employer Cost	%	% of Total
***	A	Smith	John	56	65	270,000	198,369	73.5	8,100	3.0	206,469	76.5	206,469	76.5	94.2
	B	Jones	Tom	27	65	22,724	909	4.0	1,932	8.5	2,840	12.5	2,840	12.5	1.3
	B	Doe	Jane	37	65	28.948	1,158	4.0	2,461	8.5	3,618	12.5	3,618	12.5	1.7
	B	White	Amy	47	65	24,394	976	4.0	2,073	8.5	3,049	12.5	3,049	12.5	1.4
	B	Adams	Martha	39	65	25,284	1,011	4.0	2,149	8.5	3,160	12.5	3,160	12.5	1.4

Legend: P – Principal; O – Owner; H – Highly Compensated Employee

CONTRIBUTION REPORT -- SUMMARY

	Considered Earnings	Cash Balance Amount	%	Profit Sharing Amount	%	Total Contribution Amount	%	Employer Cost	%	% of Total
Principals	270,000	198,369	73.5	8,100	3.0	206,469	76.5	206,469	76.5	94.2
Non-Principals	101,350	4,054	4.0	8,615	8.5	12,669	12.5	12,669	12.5	5.8
Grand Total	**371,350**	**202,423**	**54.5**	**16,715**	**4.5**	**219,138**	**59.0**	**219,138**	**59.0**	**100.0**

The employer's contribution to a pension plan for employees may be considered wages for purposes of the Wage and Qualified Property Test, and these payments will help the employer/owner avoid the limitations described in this book for higher-income taxpayers. It is important to note that only elective deferrals (also known as salary reduction agreements or elective employer contributions), as described in the definition of wages earlier in this chapter, count as wages. It does not appear that employer matching contributions will qualify as wages under Section 199A, which may have been an oversight of the legislation.

It is also noteworthy that pension planning can backfire. If the taxpayer is a low-income taxpayer, or operates a non-SSTB trade or business, the highest applicable income tax rates may now be only 29.6%. The taxpayer may face a much higher bracket upon retirement, so deductible IRA and pension contributions may not be the best strategy. The taxpayer might consider contributing to a Roth IRA or Roth 401(k) plan. Planners should keep in mind that contributions to pension plans and deductible IRAs can reduce employment and Medicare taxes, depending upon circumstances, and will not be subject to employment or Medicare taxes upon withdrawal under present law.

15. PHASE-IN.

For Section 199A, the Wage/Property Limitation is phased-in ratably as a taxpayer's income exceeds the lower income thresholds ($157,500 for single filers, $315,000 for joint filers). This applies to all trades and businesses, regardless of whether or not they are classified as Specified Service Trades or Businesses.

A more extensive discussion of the phase-in calculations is provided in Chapter 10.

16. PHASE-OUT (OF DEDUCTION FOR SPECIFIED SERVICE TRADES OR BUSINESS).

For Section 199A, the deduction for SSTB income is phased-out as the taxpayer exceeds the lower income threshold. This term only applies to SSTBs.

Once the taxpayer's taxable income exceeds the higher-income thresholds ($207,500/$415,000), their deduction for Specified Service flow-through income is completely phased-out. See Chapter 10.

Where the taxpayer's taxable income is less than the higher-income thresholds ($207,500/$415,000) but exceeds the lower-income thresholds ($157,500/$315,000), the taxpayer's deduction is proportionally reduced ("phased-out") as the taxpayer's taxable income exceeds the lower-income thresholds. By the simplest terms, the deduction will simply be pro-rated, going from 20% to 0%.

Example:

> A joint filing married couple with $365,000 of taxable income is 50% phased-out, and their deduction will be 50% of the deduction that would have otherwise applied.

17. TRADE OR BUSINESS.

The Final Regulations indicate that the definition of Trade or Business will be the same definition as applies under Section 162. This is further discussed in Chapter 14. There is significant case law under Section 162. It is noteworthy that many rental arrangements may not be active enough to qualify as a "Trade or Business" to facilitate qualification for the Section 199A deduction. The Preamble to the Final Regulations indicate that "key factual elements that may be relevant include, but are not limited to, the type of property (commercial real property versus a residential condominium versus personal property), the number of properties rented, the day-to-day involvement of the owner or its agent, and the type of rental (for example, a net lease versus a traditional lease, short-term versus long-term lease). It is apparently much easier to qualify as a "Trade or Business" when physical items other than real estate are being leased.

B.   PRIMARY RULES THAT APPLY

To build upon the above, the following is a list of primary rules that apply:

1. **FLOW-THROUGH INCOME.**

A flow-through entity is a trade or business which has reported income that passes through to the owners and is reported on their individual tax returns. This classification is only for the following three categories of entities: (1) entities treated as S corporations, which file annual Form 1120S tax returns, (2) entities treated as partnerships, which file annual Form 1065 tax returns, and (3) individuals who own or are individually considered to own trades and businesses that file Schedule C's attached to their personal Form 1040's for trades and businesses and Schedule E's for rental activities, and Schedule F for farming activities. When an individual owns 100% of an LLC, it can be disregarded, and its income and deductions can be considered as owned by the individual and reported on Schedule C or E. When an LLC is owned by a married couple in a community property state it can also be disregarded, and the tax law is not clear with respect to whether an LLC owned by a married couple outside of a community property state is treated as disregarded or as a partnership.[70]

2. **WHO IS THE TAXPAYER?**

For Section 199A purposes, the taxpayer is the person, married couple, trust, or estate that owns part or all of the ownership interest of the flow-through entity. For the purposes of this book, a "taxpayer" will always be an individual or married couple, a trust that is taxed as a separate entity, or an estate. C corporations and other taxable entities do not qualify for the Section 199A deduction.[71]

3. **SINGLE FILERS.**

Single filers and separately taxed trusts having less than $157,500 in taxable income qualify for the Section 199A deduction regardless of the Wages paid by or Qualified Property owned and used by the flow-through entity. Single filers and separately taxed trusts having more than $207,500 in taxable income will not qualify for the Section 199A deduction on any SSTB income whatsoever. Also, high-income taxpayers cannot take the Section 199A deduction on flow-through income of a non-SSTB unless the Wage/Property Limitation is met.[72]

4. **JOINT FILERS.**

Joint filers that have taxable income below $315,000 will qualify for the Section 199A deduction on the flow-through income from a Specified Service Trade or Business, and other flow-through

---

[70]For further discussion, *see* Gassman, Ketron *Yes, it is Usually Safe to Consider an LLC Owned as TBE as Disregarded for Income Tax Purposes*, The Thursday Report (December 11, 2014), available at https://gassmanlaw.com/thursday-reports/the-thursday-report-12-11-14/. *See also Rev. Proc. 84-35*, 1984-1 C.B. 509. There are no Section 6698 penalties (for failure to file a partnership return) imposed on a partnership with 10 or fewer partners, as long as the partners fully and timely report their share of partnership income on their individual income tax returns. Normally, an LLC with more than one member/partner is treated as a partnership, but because of the Revenue Procedures, LLCs with 10 or fewer members will meet the reasonable cause test and not be subject to 6698.

[71]*See* David Kautter and William Paul, *2017-2018 Priority Guidance Plan*, Dep't of the Treasury (February 7, 2018), https://www.irs.gov/pub/irs-utl/2017-2018_pgp_2nd_quarter_update.pdf.

[72]The I.R.S. in its Chief Counsel Regulation Handbook states that it takes comments through www.regulations.gov or direct comment to the drafting attorney. *See* I.R.S, "Chief Counsel Regulation Handbook," Section 7 (August 19, 2011), available at https://www.irs.gov/irm/part32/irm_32-001-007.

income regardless of whether the Wage/Property Test is met. Married couples with more than $415,000 of taxable income will not qualify for the Section 199A deduction on any Specified Service income whatsoever.[73]

5. PHASING OUT.

Where a single filer taxpayer or trust has more than $157,500, but less than $207,500 of taxable income, a portion of the Section 199A deduction will be available based upon a pro rata calculation and other factors as described above. The same applies when a married couple makes taxable income over $315,000, but below $415,000. Remember, these threshold amounts are all inflation adjusted.

6. 20% OF TAXABLE INCOME.

"The Personal Taxable Income Limitation Rule." The Section 199A deduction for an individual or trust will not exceed 20% of the taxpayer's taxable income for any given year, so that a taxpayer having losses that offset other applicable income may not receive the full deduction. For example, a married couple with $200,000 of flow-through income, otherwise deductible under Section 199A, and $100,000 of other income, who suffered a deductible theft loss of $200,000, will only have a $20,000 Section 199A deduction because of having only $100,000 of taxable income.

7. TREASURY'S AUTHORITY TO ISSUE REGULATIONS UNDER SECTION 199A.

The Treasury can issue two types of regulations: interpretative and legislative. The Treasury will often have to interpret ambiguous clauses of legislation passed by Congress. At other times, Congress intentionally defers its law-making power to the Treasury, so that they can create regulations in areas where they have the best knowledge of what is needed.

The Treasury issued Final Regulations and two Revenue Procedures on January 18th, 2019 and reissued revised Final Regulations on February 4th, 2019 which may in part exceed its authority.

This is because Section 199A only gives the IRS the ability to promulgate legislative regulations in the following five areas:

A. **Short Taxable Years:** Subsection 199A(b)(5) gives the Treasury the ability to create regulations regarding how QBI works for short taxable years, where a taxpayer acquires or disposes of a major portion of a trade or business, or where a taxpayer acquires or disposes of a major portion of a separate unit of a trade or business.

B. **Allocation of Items/Wages:** Subsection 199A(f)(4)(A) gives the Treasury the ability to create regulations to determine how the allocation of items and wages will apply. Additionally, it

---

[73]*Chevron U.S.A., Inc. v. National Resources Defense Council, Inc.*, 467 U.S. 837 (1984) ("If Congress has explicitly left a gap for the agency to fill, there is an express delegation of authority to the agency to elucidate a specific provision of the statute by regulation.")

gives the Secretary the authority to issue regulations determining the wage payment reporting requirements.[74]

C.   **Tiered Entity Structures:** Tiered entities are arrangements where one entity owns another entity, which may own another entity, in some combination. Subsection 199A(f)(4) gives the Treasury the ability to create regulations to restrict allocations of items under tiered entities. Section 199A(f)(4)(B) states: "The [Treasury] Secretary shall prescribe such regulations as are necessary to carry out the purposes of this section, including regulations – ... (B) for the application of this Section in the case of tiered entities."

For example, Final Regulation Section 199A-3 discourages the creation of tiered partnerships purely for the purpose of avoiding tax under Section 199A, but does not appear to prevent the payment of wages from a partnership to an individual who is the owner of another partnership that is a partner in the wage paying partnership for purposes of the 50% or 25% wage test.

D.   **Depreciable Periods and 1031 Exchanges:** Subsection 199A(h) gives the Treasury the ability to create anti-abuse rules. Subsection (1) of this Section gives the Treasury the right to use similar rules to Section 179(d)(2) to prevent manipulation of depreciable periods, and Subsection (2) gives the Treasury the right to create regulations to apply for determining the Unadjusted Basis in Qualified Property acquired in like-kind exchanges (Section 1031 exchanges) or involuntary conversions.

E.   **Agricultural and Horticultural Cooperatives:** In March of 2018, Section 199A was updated as a technical correction to remedy what was known as the "grain glitch," which was an oversight that would have allowed farmers selling to cooperatives to have unintended benefits.[75] The updates gave the Treasury the authority to make regulations to effectively implement a new subsection (g) for agricultural and horticultural cooperatives. These alterations can be seen in **Error! Reference source not found.**.

---

[74]Treas. Reg. § 1.199-2(a)(3)(i).

[75]See Christine Haughney, A Tax Law Boon to Farm Co-ops, Politico (January 10, 2018), https://www.politico.com/newsletters/morning-agriculture/2018/01/10/a-tax-law-boon-to-farm-co-ops-069726. This article does a good job of explaining how the grain glitch might have allowed co-op selling farmers to wipe out their tax burden completely.

CHAPTER 5.
LESSER KNOWN RULES

Now that the reader has a general understanding of how the Section 199A rules work, the following considerations should be kept in mind:

A.   NO REDUCTION FOR EMPLOYMENT OR SELF-EMPLOYMENT TAXES

The Section 199A deduction will not decrease employment or self-employment taxes, which may need to be paid on all flow-through business structures except for an S corporation's K-1 income.[76] A taxpayer reporting $100,000 a year from her sole proprietorship law firm will still owe self-employment taxes of $12,470 on the $100,000 of income, although with the Section 199A deduction she may only pay income taxes on $80,000 of income.

It is noteworthy that when calculating Qualified Business Income, a taxpayer must reduce QBI to take into account the deduction that would normally apply for the payment of one-half of self-employment taxes paid by the taxpayer.

For example, if a taxpayer has $10,000 of self-employment income, the taxpayer will only owe $1,530 in employment taxes and therefore must reduce his QBI by $765 (one-half of $1,530).

The taxpayer would then receive a Section 199A deduction based upon 20% of $9,235 ($10,000 - $765), rather than the $10,000 of self-employment income.

B.   THE RENTAL BUSINESS ARENA

Rental business has some quirks and rather unique stepping stones to being classified as a "trade or business." Landlords may have to provide tenant services, including but not limited to maintenance, landscape management, and other functions, in order qualify as a trade or business under Section 162.[77] Rental operations may qualify for the deduction even if they are passive double or triple net leases.[78] It is important to note that the Final Regulations for Section 199A have held that rental activities will be considered as trades or businesses if they meet the common ownership test of Final Regulations Section 1.199A-4(b)(1)(i), without necessarily passing the other aggregation requirements under the same subsection.

Businesses and their related real estate owner entities might check to see if rent can be increased to reduce the income of listed services or income that would be earned by a business that would not have sufficient wages or replacement property if its owners are above the $157,500/$315,000

---

[76] IRC § 199A(f)(3).

[77] The courts have essentially required trades or businesses, as defined under Section 162, to be engaged in an activity (1) for profit with (2) continuity and regularity.

[78] William E. Ebersole, *Triple Net Leases: An Investment Opportunity Fraught with Peril*, Pennsylvania Institute of Certified Public Accountants (March 1, 2017), https://www.picpa.org/articles/picpa- news/2017/03/01/pa-cpa-journal-triple-net-leases-an-investment-opportunity-fraught-with-peril. "A triple net lease requires a tenant to pay the landlord rent and to be directly responsible for property taxes, insurance, and maintenance."

levels, taking into consideration state or local sales taxes or other expenses that can occur when rent is adjusted.[79]

C.   <u>SUBSTANTIAL UNDERSTATEMENT PENALTY</u>

Income tax planners need to understand the substantial understatement penalty, which can be made much harsher when a taxpayer has qualified for a Section 199A deduction because of the reduction of the 10% threshold to 5%, as further explained below. Many people incorrectly believe that tax penalties are only exacted on those who show bad intent or negligence, but this is not the case. There are eight enumerated ways for the IRS to impose accuracy-related penalties, and while negligence is one of these reasons, the IRS only needs to demonstrate that the taxpayer "substantially underpaid" their taxes in order to impose a penalty equal to 20% of the underpayment under Section 6662. The understatement penalties are subject to daily compounding interest at a rate equal to the federal short-term rate plus three percentage points, which is presently a total rate of approximately 5% as of August 2018.[80]

A substantial understatement of tax normally occurs where the understatement exceeds the greater of (1) 10% of the tax required to be shown, or (2) $5,000.[81] For some reason, the 10% of tax threshold is lowered to 5% of the tax if any Section 199A deduction is taken, even if it is only $1! As a result of this, many taxpayers will take special steps to assure that they do not qualify for the Section 199A deduction where the tax savings is less than the risk value of possibly being subject to the substantial understatement penalty.

For example, a married taxpayer owning a Specified Service Trade or Business with income of $414,999 who claims a $4 Section 199A deduction on $400,000 of flow-through income, but fails to report $25,000 of income received from another entity, will owe an additional $8,741,[82] and will now be subject to the 20% penalty for a substantial understatement, because the threshold for determining whether a substantial understatement incurred was reduced to 5% of the tax required to be shown ($5,268). If no Section 199A deduction had been taken, then the taxpayer would have not been subject to the penalty for a substantial understatement, because his threshold for penalty purposes would have been 10% of the taxpayer's assessed tax liability ($10,537). As a result, the taxpayer now owes additional penalties of $1,748.

There is a reasonable cause exception where no penalty will apply if it can be shown that the taxpayer acted in good faith with reasonable cause for the understatement. This should be available for many taxpayers who claim a Section 199A deduction that is not allowed due to the complexity of the statute. There is no explanation as to why taking a Section 199A deduction would cause

---

[79] For example, Florida imposes a 6.8% sales tax on residential leases that are for more than 1 year and for commercial leases. The rental sales tax is deductible at the 37% income tax bracket, creating a savings of 4.284% (63% x 6.8% = 4.284%), and therefore, the 20% deduction gives a net savings of 3.116% on a rent increase (20% * 37% = 7.4% - 4.284% = 3.116%), assuming that Section 199A applies.

[80] IRC § 6601(e)(2) and IRC § 6621(a)(2). This rate is calculated quarterly, and was 4% from January 1, 2018, to March 31, 2018, and 5% from April 1, 2018, to June 30, 2018.

[81] IRC § 6662(d)(1). For C corporations, an understatement of tax is considered substantial if it exceeds the lesser of (1) 10% of the tax required to be shown on the return (or, if greater, $10,000), or (2) $10 million.

[82] This taxpayer is liable for $96,627 of income taxes for the $414,999 of income, which includes the reduction by the $4 Section 199A deduction. Additionally, the $25,000 of unreported income added onto the taxpayer's income would make them liable for $109,227 in total income taxes for the year, based on 2018 tax rates and brackets.

this unfair tripwire standard that will apply to many innocent taxpayers who may not even know that they are eligible for the deduction and may not even claim the deduction or reduce tax liability as the result of it.

CHAPTER 6.
WORKING EXAMPLE OF SECTION 199A

The previous principles can be summarized by the following example using 2018 brackets and thresholds, and the charts below will be helpful to have while reviewing this example.

Example:

> **Melissa** is a lawyer with her own practice, which has an income of $315,000 a year. Melissa is married to a spouse who has no income. She also owns the office condominium unit where the law practice is located, which has a net rental value of $40,000 a year. She also owns 30% of an S corporation, which has a factory that makes widgets and pays $100,000 in wages to the factory workers and makes $200,000 of taxable income each year, so that her K 1 income is $60,000. She does no work for the widget company, and therefore, does not have to pay herself a salary for her mere ownership. Therefore, her total taxable income is $415,000.
>
> Melissa is able to take the Section 199A deduction on the widget company, but not with respect to the real estate, because real estate owned by an SSTB owner and leased to an SSTB will be considered to be SSTB income.[83]
>
> Since the legal practice is not taxed as a partnership or S corporation, she pays self- employment taxes of $25,642 and Net Investment Income Tax of $1,520. Her law practice is a Specified Service Trade or Business and does not qualify for the Section 199A deduction. The shifting of income from the law firm to her Schedule E rental activity is subject to the 3.8% Net Investment Income Tax, and Melissa makes over $128,400 in income from the law firm, so she does not save on Social Security taxes.
>
> If Melissa placed the law practice in an LLC taxed as an S corporation, and took a salary of $100,000, then she and the company would pay a total of $15,300 of employment taxes and Medicare taxes, but the $215,000 of remaining K 1 income would not be subject to employment taxes, thus saving $10,370 in employment taxes. When her law firm was a proprietorship, all of its income was subject to employment tax.
>
> Melissa's total taxable income ($415,000) would still be over the $315,000 threshold. To reduce this, the law firm may establish a type of pension plan known as a cash-balance plan, which may receive a $100,000 tax-deductible contribution,[84] so her K 1 income from the law firm is now only $115,000, and

---

[83]Treas. Reg. § 1.199A-5(c)(2) provides that an SSTB includes any trade or business with 50% or more common ownership that provides its property or services to an SSTB.

[84]The amount a person can give to defined benefit pension plans depends on their age and the amount of their compensation. The $100,000 contribution assumes that the owner has been in business several years with historic income of greater than $100,000 and that this contribution meets the defined benefit pension plan rules.

her total taxable income is reduced to $315,000. Now her law firm and real estate K 1 income will qualify for the 20% deduction because she is no longer a high-income taxpayer. Melissa now has a Section 199A deduction of $43,000 ($215,000 x 20%) from all of her flow-through income, which saves her roughly $13,760 in income taxes (based upon the income being taxed at the 32% tax bracket).

John is also a married lawyer unrelated to Melissa who shares space with her and has been making $200,000 a year from his individually owned and operated law practice and has no other income. He has been paying $21,722 per year in employment taxes.

He forms an S corporation that becomes a partner with Melissa's S corporation so that they are a "partnership of professional corporations." They do this by forming an LLC that is taxed as a partnership and owned 61.2% by Melissa's professional S corporation and 38.8% by John's professional S corporation. They share the net income after expenses from the partnership pro rata to their respective generated receipts, which could not be done if they shared ownership of one S corporation professional corporation because of the "second class of stock rules."

The net income of the partnership is $515,000, which is distributed $200,000 to John's S corporation and $315,000 to Melissa's S corporation. Therefore, Melissa has the same income, can have the same cash balance pension plan, and can pay herself a $100,000 salary from her S corporation, leaving her tax result unchanged. John may have to participate in Melissa's pension plan unless he is considered a "highly compensated employee."[85]

Since John now has his practice under an S corporation, he also has to take a reasonable salary. If John takes a $100,000 salary from his S corporation, he will pay $15,300 in employment taxes and qualify for a $20,000 Section 199A deduction on the $100,000 of K 1 income from his legal practice. This saves

---

[85]The Section 414 rules require most employees of multiple businesses to be included in the pension plan of any one business in a comparable manner where the businesses work together, have common ownership, or are otherwise subject to aggregation to satisfy Congress' intention that affiliated companies will all be covered under one or more comparable pension plans.
 Nevertheless, a highly compensated employee, being an individual making more than $120,000 in 2018, or who has more than a 5% ownership interest in a company under Section 414(q) may waive participation in a pension plan but doing so may be a permanent waiver so that the individual may never be included in a plan sponsored by the same employer. Non-highly compensated individuals cannot waive their participation in a pension plan.
IRC § 410(b) requires these plans to benefit a certain percentage of employees who are not highly compensated under complex rules that are beyond the scope of this book. If John was not considered to be highly compensated, his waiver would cause the plan to fail. IRC § 410(b)(6)(F) allows an exception to this requirement for employers with only highly compensated employees. Other rules require a certain percentage of all employees, whether highly compensated or not, to be included in the plan, so consulting with a pension expert is a must in this area.

him $6,422 in employment taxes and $4,400 in income taxes (assuming that the income is taxed at the 22% tax bracket), adding up to $10,822 in total savings.

Alternatively, if John were a direct partner in the law firm partnership, all of his income from the partnership would be subject to employment and Medicare taxes.

Obviously both John and Melissa must carefully evaluate whether, independent of tax reasons, they are desirous of being associated in this manner. The liability, nature of practices, marketing considerations and other factors all need to be addressed.

The following are charts that will allow readers to better visualize the example above:

Chart 7A – Working Example Initial Structure Chart

The following chart demonstrates the initial facts for John and Melissa:

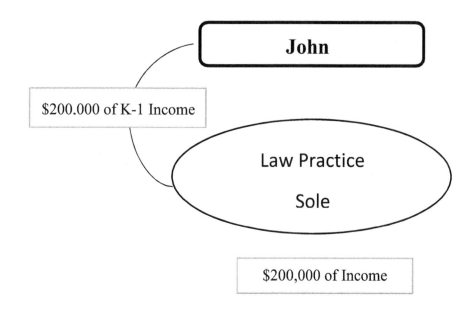

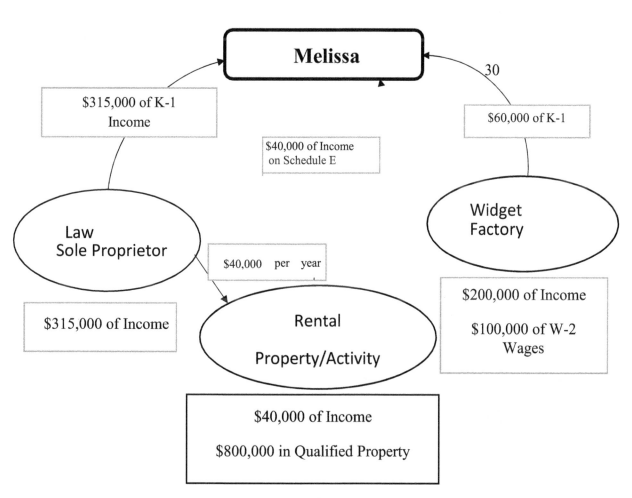

John's Initial Tax Liability	
100% of Law Practice	$200,000
Taxable Income for Section 199A Purposes	$200,000
Section 199A Deduction	$ (40,000)
Post-Section 199A Taxable Income	$160,000
Total Income Taxes	$27,079
Total Employment Taxes	$21,722
Net Investment Income Tax	$0
Total Taxes Paid by John	$48,801

Melissa's Initial Tax Liability	
100% of Law Practice	$315,000
100% of Rental Activity	$40,000
30% of Widget Factory	$60,000
Taxable Income for Section 199A Purposes	$415,000
Section 199A Deduction (Reduced to $12,000 if Rental Activity is an SSTB under the Final Regulations)	$ (20,000)
Post-Section 199A Taxable Income	$395,000
Total Income Taxes	$89,779
Total Employment Taxes	$25,642
Net Investment Income Tax	$1,520
Total Taxes Paid by Melissa	$116,9419

Since Melissa makes more than the higher-income threshold she does not receive a deduction for her law firm income. She can qualify for the Section 199A deduction on the widget business income ($60,000), but under the Final Regulations, the rental income is aggregated with the law practice income.	Self-employment taxes paid on the legal practice; Assume rental activity is considered passive.

Chart 7B – Working Example Final Structure Chart

This chart demonstrates the final posture of John and Melissa:

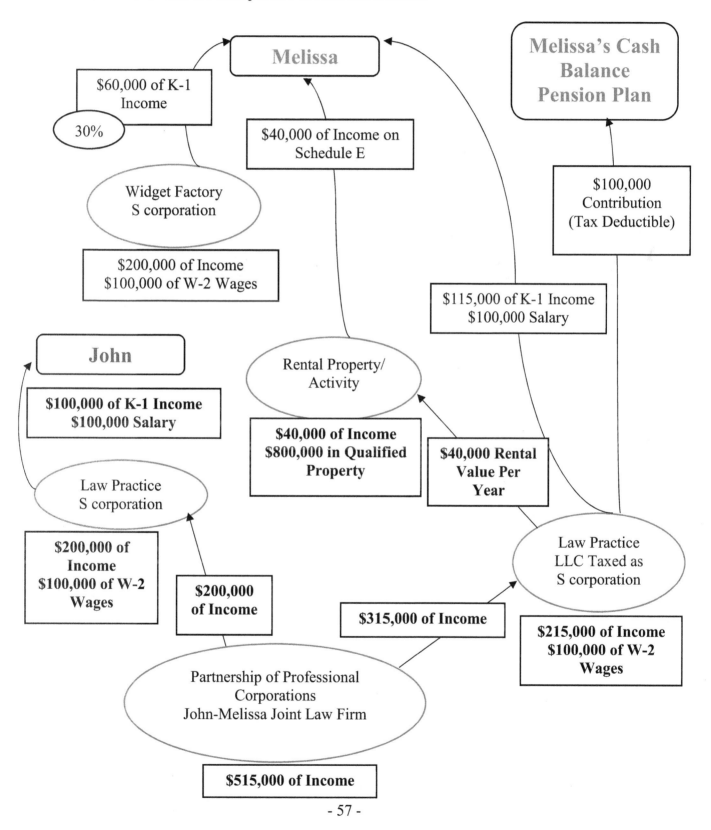

John's Final Tax Liability

100% of Law Practice	$100,000
Law Practice Salary	$100,000
Taxable Income for Section 199A Purposes	$200,000
Section 199A Deduction	$ (20,000)
Post-Section 199A Taxable Income	$180,000
Total Income Taxes	$31,779
Total Employment Taxes	$15,300
Total Taxes Paid by John	$47,079

Remember, because John took a $100,000 wage to qualify for the reasonable salary rule of S corporations, he can only deduct 20% of $100,000 of flow-through income from the law practice.

Melissa's Final Tax Liability

100% of Law Practice	$115,000
Law Practice Salary	$100,000
100% of Rental Activity	$40,000
30% of Widget Factory	$60,000
Taxable Income for Section 199A Purposes	$315,000
Section 199A Deduction	$ (43,000)
Post-Section 199A Taxable Income	$272,000
Total Income Taxes	$43,859
Total Employment Taxes	$15,300
Total Taxes Paid by Melissa	$69,159

Now that Melissa is at the $315,000 lower-income threshold, all of her law firm flow-through income can qualify for a 20% deduction.

Employment Taxes are paid on legal practice salary only ($100,000); assume Rental Activity is considered passive.

CHAPTER 7.
USING C CORPORATIONS AND CONVERTING FROM C TO S STATUS

A. 21% FLAT FEDERAL INCOME TAX RATE AND OTHER ADVANTAGES AND DISADVANTAGES

While the majority of closely held businesses and investment entities are treated as individually owned, S corporations, partnerships, regular business companies, professional corporations, LLCs, or other entities that elect on a Form 8832 to be treated as C corporation[86] are taxed as separate entities under Subchapter C of the Code. Some C corporations will qualify for Section 1202 treatment, which can enable shareholders to sell their stock without paying income tax. For more detail on Section 1202 see Chapter 8.

C corporations add revenues and other income, subtract deductible expenses (including wages), and then pay tax on the resulting taxable income as calculated on a Form 1120 tax return. C corporations do not issue K-1 forms to their shareholders, and C corporation dividends paid to their shareholders are subject to tax (thus known as "double tax") and do not qualify for the Section 199A 20% flow-through income tax deduction. Until the passage of the Tax Cuts and Jobs Act, professional service C corporations were taxed at a flat 35% of net income,[87] plus any state income taxes, and non-professional C corporations were taxed at the following brackets:

2017 C Corporation Tax Brackets

C Corporation Income	2017 Tax Rate
$0-$50,000	15% + $0
$50,000-$75,000	25% + $7,500
$75,000-$100,000	34% + $13,750
$100,000-$335,000	39% + $22,250
$335,000-$10,000,000	34% + $113,900
$10,000,000-$15,000,000	35% + $3,400,000
$15,000,000-$18,333,333	38% + $5,150,000
$18,333,333+	35% + $6,416,666.54

---

[86]Rev. Proc. 2009-41 2.04. Limited liability companies ("LLCs"), limited liability partnerships, and limited partnerships can elect to be treated as C corporations by filing a Form 8832 with the IRS within 75 days after when the election is considered to be effective, or later if there was an intent to make the election but the election is filed late and there is reasonable cause.
[87]IRC § 11(b)(2) (2016).

The 2017 Tax Act replaced the above graduated rates with a flat 21% rate, and as a result, C corporations that have less than $90,385 in net income received a federal tax increase and those with more than $90,385 had lower federal income tax to pay (ignoring the myriad of other tax law changes made by the 2017 Tax Act). It is noteworthy that dividends received from other domestic C corporations will be taxed at a maximum rate of 10.5% after taking into account the dividends received deduction discussed in more detail below.[88]

State taxes are relevant in many instances as well. For example, Florida imposes a 5.5% income tax on C corporation income but does not tax S corporations.[89] The state income tax paid by a C corporation is deductible for federal tax purposes so that the combined rate for a Florida C corporation will generally be 25.345% (21%, plus 79% of 5.5%).

As stated above, C corporation shareholders must treat all dividends, and also liquidation proceeds exceeding the shareholder's basis of the stock, as income, which is normally taxed at the 20% rate for individual taxpayers having more than $425,800 of taxable income (the 15% rate applies for individuals having more than $38,600 and up to $425,800 of taxable income) and trusts having more than $12,500 of retained taxable income.[90]

Chart 8 – 2018 Capital Gain Tax Rates Chart

This chart summarizes the tax brackets for capital gains and qualified dividends, and it can be found with more tax bracket charts in **Error! Reference source not found.**.

It appears more likely that capital gains will be audited when an entity that has active real estate development reports both ordinary income from development and capital gains from the sale of long-term investment property.

It may be best to separate out long-term gains property into a separate taxable entity to reduce the risk of audit and a higher level of scrutiny by the IRS.

Tax Rate	2018 Long Term Capital Gain/Qualified Dividend Income	
	Married Filing Jointly	Single
0%	$0 - $77,200	$0 - $38,600
15%	$77,201 - $479,000	$38,601 - $425,800
20%	$479,001 +	$425,801 +

---

[88]IRC § 24.
[89]Fla. Stat. § 220.11(2)(a).
[90]IRC § 1(h)(11)(ii).

Chart 8 A – 2019 Capital Gain Tax Rates Chart

Tax Rate	2019 Long Term Capital Gain/Qualified Dividend Income	
	Married Filing Jointly	Single
0%	$0 - $78,750	$0 - $39,375
15%	$78,751-488,850	$39,376-$434,550
20%	$488,851 +	$434,551 +

In addition, the 3.8% Section 1411 Net Investment Income ("Medicare") Tax will apply to the extent that single filer individuals have more than $200,000 of taxable income and married couples have more than $250,000 of taxable income.[91] This brings the highest bracket combined C corporation federal and Medicare tax rate to 43.11% in Florida or 38.765% in states that do not impose income tax on C corporations.

Under the 2018 income tax brackets, any dividends paid to single individuals with more than $425,800 of taxable income or to married couples having more than $479,000 of taxable income, will be subject to the highest capital gain tax rate.

Some C corporation shareholders are taxed very favorably under Section 1202, which allows there to be no capital gains tax on the sale of C corporation stock that has been held for at least 5 years if certain requirements are met. Section 1202 companies are further described in Chapter 8 of this book. **Error! Reference source not found.**provides the text of Section 1202.

It is noteworthy, however, that unlike S corporations and partnerships, C corporations can deduct non-discriminatory medical and disability insurance premiums,[92] medical expenses paid for owner employees, non-discriminatory group-term life insurance with a death benefit of up to $50,000 per employee, long-term care premiums, and certain fringe benefits, such as employer-provided vehicles and public transportation passes.[93] Therefore, individuals having high non-insured medical expenses, including in vitro procedures to facilitate pregnancy, and home care expenses incurred based upon the recommendation of a physician may want to operate under C corporations if these expenses can meet the non-discrimination rules required for deductibility.

Further, C corporations that accumulate more than is reasonably needed to operate the business may be subject to the accumulated earnings tax and the personal holding company taxes.[94]

---

[91] IRC §§ 1411(a)-(b).

[92] If disability insurance premiums are deducted then the disability income will be taxable, so this is usually not advised except in rare circumstances. Many tax advisors advocate having the individual pay the premiums and be reimbursed at the end of the year if they do not become disabled.

[93] *See generally* IRC § 162.

[94] *See* IRC § 541 (accumulated earnings tax is 20%). *See also,* IRC § 541 (personal holding company tax is 20%).

Accumulated earnings and personal holding company taxes presently apply at a rate of 20%, in addition to the flat 21% tax rate that applies to C corporation income. Some corporations will therefore pay dividends to avoid this tax. As a result, what would have been K-1 income for a flow-through entity will be subject to double taxation for a C corporation.

The transfer of goodwill from an S corporation or a C corporation to its shareholders will usually trigger capital gains tax, so it may not be safe to transfer a business or professional practice from one entity to another.[95] For more information on transfers of goodwill, see the article in **Error! Reference source not found.**that also discusses the important and relevant Tax Court decision under *Bross Trucking, Inc. v. Commissioner.*[96] The following article may be of interest with respect to the *Bross Trucking* case.

C corporations also receive a deduction on dividends received from other domestic C corporations. The deduction is based upon the percentage ownership of the corporation from which the dividend was received. The deduction is as follows: [97]

Percentage Ownership	Dividends Received Deduction	Effective Tax Rate
Less than 20%	50% Deduction	**10.5%**
20% to 80%	65% Deduction	**7.35%**
More than 80%	**100% Deduction**	**0%**

There are limitations on the C corporation's ability to take a dividends received deduction. The first is that the stock must be held for a period of 45 days, so a C corporation cannot simply purchase a stock the day it goes ex dividend and sell the stock immediately thereafter. In addition, the dividends received deduction only applies to common stock and does not apply to dividends received from a preferred stock interest.

Finally, there is a taxable income limitation, in that the dividends received deduction for corporations claiming the 50% deduction cannot exceed 50% of its taxable income, and for corporations claiming the 65% deduction, the deduction cannot exceed 50% of its taxable income. There is no limit on the deduction for corporations claiming the 100% deduction.

---

[95]*Bross Trucking, Inc., et al. v. Commissioner*, T.C.M. 2014-107 (June 5, 2014).

[96]Alan Gassman, *Bross Trucking: Set Up, Like a Bowlin' Pin. Knocked Down, it Gets to Wearin' Thin. They (the IRS) Just Won't Let You Be, Oh No.*, The Thursday Report (October 2, 2014) http://gassmanlaw.com/thursday-report-10-2-14-boss-fresca-edition/.

[97]Prior to the passage of the Tax Cuts and Jobs Act, the deduction was 70%, 80%, and 100% respectively.

B. CONVERTING FROM S CORPORATION TO C CORPORATION

Many S corporations will be converted to C corporations to take advantage of the lower corporate rates.

Steve Gorin recommends that a new S corporation should be formed to own an existing S corporation before it converts to being taxed as a C corporation for the following reasons, which can be found at part II.E.2.b of "Structuring Ownership of Privately-Owned Businesses: Tax and Estate Planning Implications":

1.   This can preserve the corporation's AAA account for if and when it converts back to being an S corporation.

2.   It appears that this will allow avoidance of having to wait five years before converting back to an S corporation.

3.   This may allow for qualification as a Section 1202 company that is newly incorporated and owned.

Hats off to Steve for this great planning idea. Steve's outline can be obtained by emailing him at sgorin@thompsoncoburn.com.

C. CONVERTING FROM C CORPORATION TO S CORPORATION

Some C corporations may be converted to S corporations in order to have income reported by the owners qualify for the Section 199A 20% deduction.

C corporations can elect to convert to an S corporation within 75 days after the date upon which the S election will be effective, but entity documents that comply with the S corporation rules must have existed on the first S corporation date.[98] For calendar year taxpayers, the election must be made by March 15 in order to be effective as of January 1. Elections made after March 15 will not be effective until the following calendar year. In the majority of cases, the S corporation taxable year will end on December 31 of the year the conversion is effective, and each year thereafter.

Because a professional service corporation ("PSC") is generally required to be on a calendar year end, an S election for a PSC will need to be effective on the first day of January. Section 1362(b) states that an S election will be effective for a taxable year as long as it takes place any time during the preceding taxable year or in the current taxable year if made on or before the 15th day of the third month of the taxable year. It is noteworthy that *Rev. Proc. 2013-30* allows the IRS Form 2553 for an S election to be filed up to 3 years and 75 days after the effective date of the election, as long as the election would have been otherwise valid for the taxable year. That Revenue Procedure requires a statement to be made that the S election was intended to have been made on the effective date and that the corporation has reasonable cause for the failure to file within 75 days from the effective date of the S election, which needs to be something more than just an

---

[98]IRC § 1362.

inadvertent oversight. *Rev. Proc. 2013-30* has several strict requirements for late elections, which is beyond the scope of this book.

Some advisors believe that the Form 2553 reasonable cause statement can be filed even if the taxpayer had not intended to make the S election until after the effective date requested, but this is not the case, and a fraud penalty, along with other penalties that apply to paid preparers of tax returns and forms, could be imposed where there is no documentation or evidence that an S election was intended as of the effective date requested on the late filed Form 2553.

Excellent materials on converting a C corporation to an S corporation can be found in Jerald August's thorough outline presented with his 2 ½ hour webinar with IRS counsel, Wendy L. Kribell, which was presented on April 16, 2019 and May 2, 2019 for The American Law Institute.

This can be ordered from the ABA or directly from Jerry at jaugust@foxrothschild.com.

D.   STING TAX CONSIDERATIONS FOR CONVERTED S CORPORATIONS WITH PASSIVE INCOME

Under Section 1375, an S corporation that was formally a C corporation with "earnings and profits" that were accumulated before making the S election may be subject to a corporate level tax on passive income, such as rental income. Even rental income that may be considered to be a "trade or business" for Section 199A purposes may trigger the Section 1375 Sting Tax, depending upon the level of activity. The tax will only apply to the extent that passive income exceeds 25% of the corporation's gross receipts. This "sting tax" can be avoided by making a tax-deductible compensation distribution and/or paying out dividends to eliminate all accumulated earnings and profits before the S election effective date, or by having active business revenues in the company after the election is made that exceed 25% of the corporation's gross receipts. Many taxpayers consider having the corporation buy a convenience store that sells gasoline because of the high revenue numbers and relatively safe economic results that a convenience store can generate.

E.   UNRECOGNIZED BUILT-IN GAINS RULES

The more challenging tax imposed as the result of a conversion is under Section 1374, which provides that assets owned by a C corporation that are worth more than their tax basis at the time that the S election is made must be tracked and the revenues from the liquidation or sale of those assets within 5 years of conversion will be taxed at the S corporation level as if it were a C corporation each year for purposes of measuring the income and paying the 21% corporate level tax.

Examples of unrecognized built-in gain items owned by a cash basis professional corporation would include accounts receivable, furniture and equipment (including furniture and equipment that is fully depreciated and subject to depreciation recapture), and any goodwill owned by the entity.

The most common and expedient way to avoid the unrecognized built-in gain rules is to accrue a large expense on the books of the company that equals or exceeds the unrecognized built- in gain that is otherwise applicable on the last day of the C corporation year before the S election is made (normally December 31st, with the S election to be effective the following January 1st).

For example, if a cash basis professional practice S corporation has $100,000 of accounts receivable, $200,000 of goodwill, and the fair market value of its furniture and equipment exceeds the tax basis by $100,000, then an amount that is equal to or exceeds the total of these three amounts ($400,000) may be declared to be owed as compensation for services previously rendered to the company by one or more of the employees of the corporation. The compensation may also then be declared as accrued as a bonus payable to them as of the last day of the last C corporation year, assuming that this will qualify as reasonable compensation.[99] This bonus must actually be paid within two and half months (75 days) of the effective date of the S election with respect to any individual who is a 5% or more shareholder in the company. [100] Taxpayers may also consider executing deferred compensation agreements and corroborating the reasons for the compensation being offered.

Further, this example assumes that the corporation is on the cash method of accounting, as opposed to the accrual method of accounting. The 2017 Tax Cuts and Jobs Act provides that corporations having less than $25 million per year in gross receipts for the previous 3 years may use the cash method of accounting in lieu of the accrual method. The former threshold was $5,000,000.[101] Additionally, the Act provides that inventory-based businesses can now use the cash method if they have less than $25 million in gross receipts.

Those who want to change their current method of accounting must file a Form 3115 to obtain the Commissioner's consent.[102] Please note that a change in accounting can only be requested five years after the previous request has been granted pursuant to Revenue Procedure. 2015-13. [103]

Another method of reducing unrecognized built-in gains would be to purchase assets that would yield a depreciation deduction for the corporation. In the example above, for instance, the practice corporation might purchase $80,000 worth of computer and copier equipment that can be immediately expensed via a Section 179 deduction or under the new bonus deprecation rules under Section 168, so that the bonus compensation would only need to be $320,000. The furniture and equipment would have to be actually purchased and "placed in service" on or before the last day of the C corporation tax year to qualify. Other assets and liabilities must also be considered but are beyond the scope of this simplified example.

Any accrued bonus should be paid within a reasonable time in addition to the normal compensation that shareholder employees would receive. For example, if a shareholder employee is normally paid $20,000 a month and a $60,000 bonus is declared, it would not be safe to stop paying the salary and to instead classify the $20,000 a month as a bonus, because the IRS may argue that the accrued bonus was not genuine. Many practices will therefore borrow money from a bank or shareholders, and actually pay the bonus, while then repaying the loan amounts over a period of months or years. The lender can receive a lien on the assets of the professional practice to stay in

---

[99]Rev. Rul. 74-44.

[100]Treas. Reg. § 1.1374-4(c).

[101]IRC § 448(c)(1).

[102]Treas. Reg. § 1.446-1(e)(3)(i).

[103]Rev. Proc. 2015-13 § 05.04(1) ("if during any of the five taxable years ending with the year of change a taxpayer changed, or applied for consent to change, its overall method of accounting … the taxpayer may not request the Commissioner's consent … under the automatic change procedures."). For more on changes in accounting, *see* Treas. Reg. § 1.381(c)(4)-1.

front of any potential future creditors of the practice. For this reason, many practices elect to keep the debt in place indefinitely, and to simply pay reasonable and tax-deductible interest on that loan.

While the bonus paid will be taxable to the employee shareholder, a deduction will be received on the S corporation tax return at the time of payment, so the bonus will "wash" for income tax purposes, but employment taxes will be payable thereon.

CHAPTER 8.
SECTION 1202 CORPORATIONS AND RELATED C CORPORATION PLANNING CONSIDERATIONS

Section 1202 of the Code permits the shareholder of a qualifying C corporation that meets certain requirements[104] to sell stock held for more than five years without paying capital gains tax on the sale. Also, a shareholder who has held Section 1202 qualifying stock for less than five years can reinvest the monies received from the sale of such stock to buy other Section 1202 qualifying stock on a tax-deferred basis. The holding period will be tacked to the holding period of the previously held Section 1202 stock, so that the sale of the subsequently acquired Section 1202 stock can be tax-free after a five-year combined holding period if the requirements discussed below are met.[105]

There are many requirements that must be satisfied to qualify for Section 1202 status. These include having the company engaged in an active trade or business that is not one of the "Specified Service Trades or Businesses" enumerated in the Statute and having at least 80% of the corporate assets being used or needed in the business or businesses of the company.

A Section 1202 company may perform management, marketing, billing, or associated services for a related entity, and may invest its profits in one or more other businesses. Another aspect of Section 1202 planning is that the liquidation of the company or distribution of assets to the shareholders after five years will still be subject to tax. The only way to avoid the tax is to sell the ownership of the company.

As above indicated, Section 1202 companies are not permitted to engage in any of the following enumerated trades or businesses, with the first eleven being the same as the list of Specified Service Trades or Businesses under Section 199A:

1.   Health,*

2.   Law,*

3.   Accounting,*

4.   Actuarial science,*

5.   Performing Arts,*

6.   Consulting,*

7.   Athletics,*

8.   Financial Services,*

---

[104]Named after IRC § 1202. *See* Gassman & Ketron: *1202 Things to Consider When Setting Up a Related Business Servicing Company* LISI Business Entities Newsletter #152, (July 13, 2016).
[105]*See generally* IRC § 1202.

9.	Brokerage Services,*

10.	Investing, Trading, or Dealing in Securities, Partnership Interest, or Commodities,*

11.	Any business where the principal asset is the reputation or skill of one or more of its employees.*

12.	Engineering;

13.	Architecture;

14.	Oil and Gas;

15.	Hotels and motels;

16.	Restaurants;

17.	Businesses similar to hotels, motels or restaurants.

---

*These 11 items are the same as the Specified Service Trades or Businesses defined below under Section 199A.

Section 1202 companies can be very tax effective when there is management or royalty income that might be earned and reinvested in the company to enable it to have sufficient working capital to operate a business or businesses, which are not listed above. An example would be to have management and advertising income used to purchase convenience stores or a horse-breeding business so that the company could accumulate income by paying the 21% federal income tax, with no additional tax to be paid when the company is sold.

What rules have to be followed in order to achieve this result or similar results that can apply any time that a client or family's business and investment arrangement can entail arm's-length payments for management services, or other similar arrangements? If a Specified Service Trade or Business ("SSTB"), such as a law practice, signs a long-term management, marketing and intellectual agreement at arm's-length with a related company and is later sold, the purchaser may pay significant monies for ownership of the management and advertising company, which would be received tax-free by the selling lawyer/lawyers.

Advisors should be careful to warn clients of risks associated with these arrangements, as discussed in the Downsides/Risks Section below, and as evidenced by the *Owen* case which is also discussed in the Active Business Requirement Section at footnote 1365.

Section 1202 company owners who sell their stock after holding it for more than six months, but not the five year holding requirement required by Section 1202, can use what is known as a Section 1045 exchange, to roll over and thus defer the gain by purchasing replacement Section 1202 stock within sixty days following the sale of qualified small business stock.[106] Gain

---

[106]IRC § 1045.

from these sales will be recognized only to the amount they exceed the cost of the new stock purchased by the taxpayer.

Additionally, it appears that a Section 1202 company that holds only intellectual property and receives significant royalty income would meet the requirements for Section 1202, but there is a risk that the company would be classified as a Personal Holding Company and thus subject to a 20% tax on undistributed income in addition to the 21% flat tax. There is an exception in Section 1202 and the Personal Holding Company rules under Section 543(d)(1) to treat royalty rights from copyrights and computer software as being used in the active conduct of a trade or business and thus eligible for Section 1202 treatment and exempt from the Personal Holding Company tax, but strict requirements must be met as discussed in more detail below.

A. GENERAL REQUIREMENTS TO QUALIFY FOR SECTION 1202 GAIN EXCLUSION

In order to be eligible to exclude gain under Section 1202, the taxpayer must meet the following requirements, each of which will be discussed in more detail below:

(1)   Must be stock of a C corporation acquired after 1993.[107]

(2)   Stock must have been acquired at original issue in exchange for money or other property, or as compensation for services performed for the corporation.[108]

(3)   The Corporation must be a "qualified small business" immediately before and immediately after the issuance of stock.[109]

(4)   During substantially all of the taxpayer's holding period, the Corporation meets the active trade or business requirements of Section 1202(e).[110]

(5)   The qualifying stock must be held for more than five years.[111]

1.   STOCK OF A C CORPORATION REQUIREMENT.

In order to qualify for the exclusion the stock must be stock of a C corporation.[112] Interests in S corporations, Partnerships, or LLCs will not qualify for this exclusion. Also, in order to qualify, the C corporation must be an eligible corporation defined in Section 1202(e)(4).

An eligible corporation is any domestic C corporation except for:

(1)   A DISC ("domestic international sales corporation" or former DISC;[113]

---

[107]IRC § 1202(c)(1).
[108]IRC § 1202(c)(1)(B).
[109]IRC § 1202(c)(1).
[110]IRC § 1202(c)(2)(A).
[111]IRC § 1202(b)(2).
[112]IRC § 1202(c)(1).
[113]IRC § 1202(e)(4)(A); *See* IRC § 992(a) for the definition of a DISC.

(2)   A corporation with respect to which an election under Section 936 is in effect or which has a direct or indirect subsidiary with respect to which an election is in effect;[114]

(3)   A regulated investment company (RIC), real estate investment trust (REIT), or a real estate mortgage investment conduit (REMIC);[115] and

(4)   A cooperative [116]

2. ORIGINAL ISSUANCE REQUIREMENT.

In order to be eligible for gain exclusion the stock of the C corporation must have been acquired at "original issue" (directly or through an underwriter) in exchange for money or other property, or as compensation for services performed for such corporation (other than services performed as an underwriter of such stock).[117] If the stock is acquired through the exercise of options or warrants, or through the conversion of convertible debt, it is also treated as acquired at original issue according to legislative history reports.[118] Additionally, the stock must have been acquired after 1993, which is the date of the enactment of this provision under the Revenue Reconciliation Act of 1993.[119] The exclusion is not limited to the C corporation's initial stock offering, but can also apply to any subsequent issuance of stock so long as the requirements of Section 1202 are met.

As discussed in Chapter 4, owners of an S corporation that will be converted to a C corporation might first establish a new S corporation to own the preexisting S corporation before it converts, so that the converted subsidiary may be considered to be an "original issue" ownership.

The C corporation also may not redeem its stock within specified time periods, which was enacted to prevent manipulation of the above rules.[120] Section 1202(c)(3) provides that stock acquired by the taxpayer is not treated as qualified small business stock ("QSB") if the issuer purchased stock from the taxpayer, or a person related to the taxpayer (within the meaning of Sections 267(b) or 707(b)), at any time during the four-year period beginning two years before the issuance of the stock. Additionally, stock issued by the C corporation will not be QSB stock if, during the two-year period beginning on the date one year before the issuance of such stock, such corporation made one or more purchases of its stock with an aggregate value exceeding 5% of the aggregate value of all of its stock as of the beginning of such two-year period. [121]

---

[114]IRC § 1202(e)(e)(B).

[115] IRC § 1202(e)(4)(C).

[116] IRC § 1202(e)(4)(D).

[117]IRC § 1202(c)(1).

[118]David B. Strong, *Section 1202: Qualified Small Business Stock* available at http://www.mofo.com/files/Uploads/Images/110811-Section-1202-Qualified-Small-Business-Stock.pdf (August 11, 2011) *citing* House of Representatives Report of the Committee on the Budget to Accompany H.R. 2246, Report No. 103-111, 1993-3 C.B. 163 (July 1993), accompanying the Omnibus Budget Reconciliation Act of 1993, which ultimately added Section 1202 to the Code.

[119]IRC § 1202(c)(1).

[120]*Supra,* note 13.

[121]IRC § 1202(c)(3)(B).

If QSB stock in one corporation is exchanged for stock in another corporation through a Section 368 reorganization, or a Section 351 transaction, and the new/acquiring corporation is also a QSB, the stock will continue to be treated as QSB stock.[122] However, if the new/acquiring corporation is not a QSB, then the new stock is treated as QSB stock only to the extent of the gain that would have been recognized at the time of the Section 368 or Section 351 transaction if the original QSB stock had been sold in a taxable transaction.[123]

The QSB stock may also be held by a partnership, LLC, S corporation, regulated investment company, or any common trust fund, and satisfy the original issue requirement.[124] The gain is passed through the entity to the individuals of the partnership. It is noteworthy however, that if QSB stock is held originally by an individual and then transferred to an entity taxed as a partnership, the original issuance requirement will not be met. In order to be eligible to exclude gain from the sale of QSB stock by a partnership:

(1)   The gain must be attributable to the partnership's sale or exchange of stock which is QSB stock in the hands of the partnership.[125]

(2)   Held by the partnership for five or more years.[126]

(3)   The individual taxpayer must have held an interest in the partnership on the date the partnership acquired the QSB stock and at all times thereafter until the partnership disposed of its QSB stock interest.[127]

If the above conditions are met, the taxpayer must treat the gain as a disposition of stock in the corporation issuing the stock disposed of by the partnership, and the taxpayer's basis in the corporation's stock includes the taxpayer's proportionate share of the partnership's adjusted basis in the corporation's stock.[128]

Pension planning considerations are discussed in more detail at Chapter 4 and Chapter 11.

3. QUALIFIED SMALL BUSINESS REQUIREMENT.

In order to be considered a qualified small business, the C corporation must meet the following requirements:

(1)   The aggregate gross assets of such corporation (or any predecessor thereof) at all times on or after the date of the enactment of the Revenue Reconciliation Act of 1993 and before the issuance did not exceed $50,000,000,[129]

---

[122]IRC § 1202(h)(4).
[123]Id.
[124]See generally IRC § 1202(g).
[125]IRC § 1202(g)(2)(A).
[126]Id.
[127]IRC § 1202(g)(2)(B).
[128]IRC § 1202 (g)(1)(B).
[129]IRC § 1202 (d)(1)(A).

(2)   The aggregate gross assets of such corporation immediately after the issuance (determined by taking into account amounts received in the issuance) do not exceed $50,000,000, [130] and

(3)   Such corporation agrees to submit such reports to the secretary and to shareholders as the secretary may require carrying out the purposes of this Section.[131]

Aggregate gross assets means the amount of cash and the aggregate adjusted basis of other property held by the corporation.[132] In computing the aggregate adjusted basis of other property, a special rule applies to property contributed with a built-in gain. The basis of property contributed with a built-in gain, for the purposes of determining the aggregate adjusted basis of other property under Section 1202, is equal to its fair market value at the time of the contribution.[133]

Additionally, for the purpose of determining the aggregate gross assets of a Corporation, all corporations connected with a common parent through more than 50% ownership will be aggregating and considered as one corporation.[134]

4. ACTIVE BUSINESS (ASSETS) REQUIREMENT.

A major hurdle in qualifying for the exclusion of gain under Section 1202 is the active business requirement of Section 1202(e). A corporation will satisfy this requirement if at least 80% of the assets of the corporation are used by the corporation in the active conduct of one or more "qualified trades or businesses."[135] A qualified trade or business is defined by exclusion and means any business other than the following:

(1)   Any trade or business involving the performance of services in the fields of health, law, engineering, architecture, accounting, actuarial science, performing arts, consulting, athletics, financial services, brokerage services, or any trade or business where the principal asset of such trade or business is the reputation or skill of one or more of its employees.[136]

(2)   Any banking, insurance, financing, leasing, investing, or similar business.[137]

(3)   Any farming business (including the business of raising and harvesting trees).[138]

(4)   Any business involving the production or extraction of products of a character with respect to which a deduction is allowable under Sections 613 or 613A.[139]

---

[130]IRC § 1202 (d)(1)(B).
[131]IRC § 1202 (d)(1)(C).
[132]IRC § 1202(d)(2)(A).
[133]IRC § 1202(d)(2)(B).
[134]See IRC § 1202(d)(3).
[135]IRC § 1202(e)(1)(A).
[136]IRC § 1202(e)(3)(A).
[137]IRC § 1202(e)(3)(B).
[138]IRC § 1202(e)(3)(C).
[139]IRC § 1202(e)(3)(D).

(5)   Any business of operating a hotel, motel, restaurant, or similar business.[140]

In determining whether the requirements of an active trade or business is met, any subsidiary corporation shall be disregarded, and the parent corporation is deemed to own a ratable share of the subsidiary's assets and to conduct a ratable share of the subsidiary's activities.[141]

In determining whether 80% of the assets are used in the active conduct of a qualified trade or business, any assets (including cash) held as part of the reasonably required working capital needs of the business are treated as used in the active conduct of such business.[142] Once a corporation has been in existence for more than two years, no more than 50% of the total assets of the corporation can qualify as used in the active conduct of a qualified trade or business by reason of being held as working capital.[143]

A corporation will not satisfy the active trade or business requirement if more than 10% of the corporation's total assets (in excess of its liabilities) are stock or securities in other corporations which are not subsidiaries of such corporation or held as part of the reasonably required working capital of the corporation.[144]

A corporation will also fail the active trade or business requirement if it holds more than 10% of the total value of its assets in real property which is not used in the active conduct of a qualified trade or business.[145] For the purpose of satisfying the active trade or business requirement, the ownership of, dealing in, or renting of real property is not treated as the active conduct of a qualified trade or business.[146] One might conclude that since the statute only mentions the rental of real property, the rental of other business assets, such as equipment and furniture, to a related entity may not cause the corporation to fail the active trade or business requirement. This is discussed in more detail below.

A corporation receiving royalties associated with the production of computer software will satisfy the active trade or business requirement, so long as the royalties are active business computer software royalties which are defined in Section 543(d)(1).[147]

There is limited guidance on the definition of a qualified trade or business specifically related to Section 1202. The IRS stated that a company providing products and services primarily within the pharmaceutical industry was a qualified trade or business even though the company has a close connection to the field of health, and that the company's use of its specific manufacturing assets and intellectual property assets to create value for customers is similar to a car manufacturer.[148] Therefore, the activities of this company did not fall within the meaning of Section 1202(e)(3) as the performance of services in the health industry. The ruling does not provide much guidance but does go to show that just because a company is in a field similar to the ones enumerated in

---

[140]IRC § 1202(e)(3)(E).
[141]IRC § 1202(e)(5)(A).
[142]IRC § 1202(e)(6).
[143]IRC § 1202(e)(6)(B).
[144]IRC § 1202)(e)(5)(B).
[145]IRC § 1202(e)(7).
[146]*Id.*
[147]IRC § 1202(e)(8).
[148]PLR 201436001.

Section 1202(e)(3) it does not mean that the company cannot be a qualified trade or business. The IRS has also stated that a company that did not diagnose or recommend treatment, but whose sole function was to provide laboratory reports to healthcare providers and to summarize the results was not a trade or business involving performance of services in the health field or where the principal asset is the reputation or skill of its employees.[149] These Private Letter Rulings are also discussed in Chapter 9.

The policy behind Section 1202(e)(3) seems to be to exclude companies that offer value to customers primarily in the form of services.[150]

A similar list of trades and businesses appear under Treasury Regulation 1.448-1T(e)(4), which limits the use of the cash method of accounting. Although this is a different Code Section, the following definitions may provide input on how the IRS or the courts may interpret the list of trades or businesses under Section 1202:

1.   The performance of services in the field of health means the provision of medical services by physicians, nurses, dentists, and other similar healthcare professionals. The performance of services in the field of health does not include the provision of services not directly related to a medical field, even though the services may purportedly relate to the health of the service recipient. For example, the performance of services in the field of health does not include the operation of health clubs or health spas that provide physical exercise or conditioning to their customers.

2.   The performance of services in the field of the performing arts means the provision of services by actors, actresses, singers, musicians, entertainers, and similar artists in their capacity as such. The performance of services in the field of the performing arts does not include the provision of services by persons who themselves are not performing artists (e.g., persons who may manage or promote such artists, and other persons in a trade or business that relates to the performing arts). Similarly, the performance of services in the field of the performing arts does not include the provision of services by persons who broadcast or otherwise disseminate the performances of such artists to members of the public (e.g., employees of a radio station that broadcasts the performances of musicians and singers). Finally, the performance of services in the field of the performing arts does not include the provision of services by athletes.

3.   The performance of services in the field of consulting does not include the performance of services other than advice and counsel, such as sales or brokerage services, or economically similar services. For purposes of the preceding sentence, the determination of whether a person's services are sales or brokerage services, or economically similar services, shall be based on all the facts and circumstances of that person's business. Such facts and circumstances include, for example, the manner in which the taxpayer is compensated for the services provided (e.g., whether the compensation for the services is contingent upon the consummation of the transaction that the services were intended to affect).

---

[149]PLR 201717010.
[150]*See* PLR 201436001.

The Tax Court Memorandum decision of *Owen v. Commissioner* also provides some guidance on the definition of a qualified trade or business.[151] In this case, Mr. Owen was seeking to defer recognition of capital gains via Section 1045 by rolling over the gain from qualified small business stock into another qualified small business stock.[152] Despite the Commissioner's argument that Mr. Owen's business was not a qualified small business because the principal asset of the company was Mr. Owen's skill, the Court held that it was a qualified small business, specifically stating that:

> *While we have no doubt that the success of [the business] is properly attributable to Mr. Owen and Mr. Michaels, the principal asset of the companies was the training and organization structure; after all, it was the independent contractors, including Mr. Owen and Mr. Michaels in their commission sales hats, who sold the policies that earned the premiums, not Mr. Owen in his personal capacity.[153]*

Ultimately the exchange did not qualify for a rollover under Section 1045 because the active business requirements required under Section 1202(c)(2) were not met.[154]

As a result of failing to meet the requirements of Section 1202, Mr. Owen was subject to the additional 20% accuracy-related penalty of Section 6662(a) and interest on the amount of the underpayment.[155] Mr. Owen attempted to avoid this penalty by claiming reliance on a qualified professional.[156] In order to satisfy this exception, the taxpayer must show that (1) the adviser was a competent professional who had sufficient expertise to justify reliance, (2) the taxpayer provided the necessary and accurate information to the adviser, and (3) the taxpayer actually relied in good faith on the adviser's judgment.[157] The Court ruled that while Mr. Owen was provided with competent advice he failed to actually follow that advice, and thus was subject to the penalties.[158]

This Tax Court Memorandum, similar to the PLRs mentioned above, also shows that just because a company is in a field similar to the ones enumerated in Section 1202(e)(3), it does not mean that the company cannot be a qualified trade or business. The case also confirms that the corporation cannot be a mere shell company holding large amounts of cash. While the corporation can hold some cash as working capital, it must also have other assets engaged in some active business. It is unclear what mix of assets and working capital (cash) will be considered reasonable by the courts, as Owen Commissioner saved that question for another time.[159]

Congress intended that qualified small business companies must be legitimate businesses, as opposed to being "shell companies" or companies that merely provide services such as consulting, or accounting. Therefore, it is important that a company intending to qualify as a small business

---

[151] *See generally*, T.C. Memo. 2012-21.
[152] *Id.*
[153] *Id.* at 17.
[154] *See* IRC § 1045(b)(1) which states that in order to be eligible for a rollover under § 1045 the stock must be qualified small business stock as defined in § 1202(c).
[155] *Owen*, at 20.
[156] *Id.*
[157] *Id.* at 19.
[158] *Id.* at 20.
[159] *Id.* at 18.

under Section 1202 be a bona fide independent separate business and not a "dummy management company" that does not provide independent services and is not considered an independent trade or business. It will be even more helpful if a company intending to qualify as a small business under Section 1202 has multiple customers and purchasers of products, other than only one or more companies affiliated within the same family.

5. FIVE YEAR HOLDING PERIOD REQUIREMENT.

In general, the holding period of QSB stock begins on the day the stock was originally issued. If qualified small business stock is received by gift, inheritance, or from a partnership, the holding period will include the period the stock was held by the donor, decedent, or partnership.[160] The holding period of stock exchanged in a Section 351 or Section 368 transaction tax on to the original holding period so long as the stock received in the exchange is qualified small business stock.[161]

The five-year holding period requirement will not be satisfied if the taxpayer has an offsetting short position on the qualified small business stock unless:

1.   The stock was held by the taxpayer for more than 5 years as of the first day the short position was taken, and

2.   The taxpayer elects to recognize gain as if the stock was sold on the first day of the short position for its fair market value.[162]

Example:

> Jim purchased qualified small business stock on January 1, 2010 for $100. On January 2, 2015 when the fair market value of the stock was $500, Jim took a short position in the stock. For the purposes of calculating the exclusion under Section 1202, there would be a hypothetical sale of the stock and Jim would have a gain of $400, all of which would be excluded under Section 1202.

Jim's basis would increase to $500 and any subsequent gain on the stock would not be eligible for the Section 1202 exclusion.

A taxpayer is considered to have an offsetting short position if the taxpayer or the taxpayer's relative (within the meaning of Section 267 or Section 707(b)) have:

(1) Made a short sale of substantially identical property,[163]

(2) Acquired an option to sell substantially identically property at a fixed price,[164] or

---

[160] *Supra,* note 13 *citing* IRC § 1202(f)(2).
[161] IRC § 1202(h)(4)(A).
[162] IRC § 1202(j).
[163] IRC § 1202(j)(2)(A).
[164] IRC § 1202(j)(2)(B).

(3) The taxpayer has entered into another transaction which substantially reduces the risk of loss from holding the qualified small business stock.[165]

6. CALCULATING THE AMOUNT OF THE EXCLUSION UNDER SECTION 1202.

Section 1202 has been amended multiple times, so the amount of gain a taxpayer can exclude depends on when the stock was acquired. Originally 50% of the "eligible gain" could be excluded, and Section 57(a) would treat 7% of the amount excluded as a preference item for alternative minimum tax purposes. The Section 1202 exclusion was then increased to 75%,[166] before the Path Act made the exclusion 100% permanently and eliminated the alternative minimum tax preference item.[167] Therefore, the applicable percentages are as follows:

Section 1202 Stock Gain Exclusion Percentage

Date	Capital Gains Exclusion	AMT Applicable
Acquired 8/11/1993 - 2/17/2009	50%	YES
Acquired 2/18/2009 - 9/27/2010	75%	YES
Acquired after 9/27/2010	100%	NO

Although potentially 100% of the "eligible gain" can be excluded, Section 1202 provides a ceiling rule that limits that maximum of "eligible gain." The amount of gain eligible for exclusion cannot exceed the greater of:

(1) $10,000,000 reduced by the amount of gain taken into account in prior taxable years and attributable to dispositions of stock issued by such corporation,[168] or

(2) ten times the aggregate adjusted basis of qualified small business stock issued by the corporation and disposed of by the taxpayer during the taxable year.[169]

It is important to note that the ceiling rule is applied shareholder-to-shareholder on a per-issuer basis; therefore, it is possible for a single taxpayer to exclude amounts greater than the ceiling if the taxpayer has multiple investments in small businesses.[170]

---

[165] IRC § 1202(j)(2)(C).
[166] IRC § 1202(a)(3).
[167] IRC § 1202(a)(4).
[168] IRC § 1202(b)(1)(A).
[169] IRC § 1202(b)(1)(B).
[170] *See* IRC § 1202(b).

Additionally, for the purposes of determining the amount of eligible gain, Section 1202(i)(1)(B) provides that when property is contributed in exchange for qualified small business stock, the basis of the stock in the hands of the taxpayer in no event shall be less than the fair market value of the property exchanged. Practically speaking, this means that if built-in-gain property is contributed in exchange for stock, the amount of built-in-gain is not an "eligible gain" and only the subsequent appreciation in the qualified small business stock will be an "eligible gain" excludable under Section 1202.

Below are some examples of how the exclusion is calculated under Section 1202.

Example: - Cash in Exchange for Qualified Small Business Stock Under Ceiling Rule:

Jim contributes $500,000 in exchange for stock in a qualified small business. Over five years later Jim sells the stock for $6,500,000. Jim would have the following tax ramifications:

Amount Realized	$	6,500,000
Less: Basis	$	(500,000)
Potential Gain	$	6,000,000

Ceiling Rule Calculations

Greater of:	$	
1202(b)(1)(A) Amount	$	10,000,000
1202(b)(1)(B) Amount (10x adjusted basis)	$	5,000,000
Ceiling	$	10,000,000

With a $10,000,000 ceiling, the entire $6,000,000 gain is eligible for Section 1202 exclusion.

Jim's Capital Gain if Acquired 8/11/1993 - 2/17/2009

Potential Gain	$	6,000,000
Capital Gain Exclusion Amount		50%
Amount of Exclusion	$	(3,000,000)
Recognized Gain	$	3,000,000

Jim's Capital Gain if Acquired 2/18/2009 - 9/27/2010

Potential Gain	$	6,000,000
Capital Gain Exclusion Amount		75%
Amount of Exclusion	$	(4,500,000)
Recognized Gain	$	1,500,000

Jim's Capital Gain if Acquired After 9/27/2010

Potential Gain	$	6,000,000
Capital Gain Exclusion Amount		100%
Amount of Exclusion	$	(6,000,000)
Recognized Gain	$	--

For stock acquired prior to September 27, 2010, 7% of the excluded amount will be included as an item of tax preference for the purposes of calculating the alternative minimum tax. Jim would have to include $210,000 as a preference item if acquired between August 11, 1993 and February 17, 2009, and $105,000 as a preference item if acquired between February 17, 2009 and September 27, 2010. The excluded amount for stock acquired after September 27, 2010 is not included as an item of tax preference.

Example: - **Cash in Exchange for Qualified Small Business Stock Over Ceiling Rule:**

Jim contributes $1,500,000 in exchange for stock of a qualified small business. After five years, Jim sells the stock for $18,000,000. Jim's tax ramifications would be as follows:

Amount Realized	$	18,000,000
Less: Basis	$	(1,500,000)
Potential Gain	$	16,500,000

Ceiling Rule Calculations

Greater of:		
1202(b)(1)(A) Amount	$	10,000,000
1202(b)(1)(B) Amount (10x adjusted basis)	$	15,000,000
Ceiling	$	15,000,000

With a $15,000,000 ceiling, $1,500,000 is not eligible for Section 1202 exclusion.

Jim's Capital Gain if Acquired 8/11/1993 - 2/17/2009

Potential Gain	$	16,500,000
Ceiling Limitation	$	15,000,000
Capital Gain Exclusion Amount		50%
Amount of Exclusion	$	(7,500,000)
Recognized Gain	$	9,000,000

Jim's Capital Gain if Acquired 2/18/2009 - 9/27/2010

Potential Gain	$	16,500,000
Ceiling Limitation	$	15,000,000
Capital Gain Exclusion Amount		75%
Amount of Exclusion	$	(11,250,000)
Recognized Gain	$	5,250,000

Example: - **Built-in-Gain Property in Exchange for Qualified Small Business Stock:**

> Jim contributes property with a fair market value of $5,000,000 and a basis of $2,500,000 in exchange for enough stock of a qualified small business to satisfy the control requirements of Section 351. Section 351 permits the formation of a corporation by the various shareholders contributing property in exchange for the corporation's stock without, in many instances, recognizing gain, so long as the contributors are in control of the corporation which is defined as 80% of the combined voting power of all classes of stock entitled to vote, and 80% of the total number of shares of all other classes of stock. Jim sold the stock more than five years later for $10,000,000. Jim's tax ramifications would be as follows:

Amount Realized	$	10,000,000
Less: Basis	$	(2,500,000)
Potential Gain	$	7,500,000

Note: - Jim's basis in the stock would be $2,500,000 under Section 358. This Section generally provides that the contributor receives a basis in stock equal to the basis of the property contributed. However, for purposes of Section 1202 calculations, Jim's basis cannot be less than fair market value of the contributed property. The built-in gain is not eligible for the Section 1202 exclusion.

The remainder of the gain is eligible for exclusion under Section 1202 and is covered under the ceiling rule of Section 1202(b).

Amount Realized	$	10,000,000
Less: Basis	$	(5,000,000)
Potential Gain	$	5,000,000

Jim's Capital Gain if Acquired 8/11/1993 - 2/17/2009

Potential Gain	$	7,500,000
Built-in Gain	$	2,500,000
Capital Gain for 1202 Exclusion	$	5,000,000
Capital Gain Exclusion Amount		50%
Amount of Exclusion	$	(2,500,000)
Recognized Gain	$	5,000,000

Jim's Capital Gain if Acquired 2/18/2009 - 9/27/2010

Potential Gain	$	7,500,000
Built-in Gain	$	2,500,000
Capital Gain for 1202 Exclusion	$	5,000,000
Capital Gain Exclusion Amount		75%
Amount of Exclusion	$	(3,750,000)
Recognized Gain	$	3,750,000

Jim's Capital Gain if Acquired After 9/27/2010

Potential Gain	$	7,500,000
Built-in Gain	$	2,500,000
Capital Gain for 1202 Exclusion	$	5,000,000
Capital Gain Exclusion Amount		100%
Amount of Exclusion	$	(5,000,000)
Recognized Gain	$	2,500,000

B. POTENTIAL USES OF A SECTION 1202 QUALIFIED SMALL BUSINESS

1. POTENTIAL INVESTMENT FOR CLIENT.

A client looking for an alternative investment could use Section 1202 to escape capital gains. This is the original purpose of Section 1202, to encourage investment in startups and small businesses. While these types of investments may carry more risk than traditional investments, clients will be rewarded if they hold the stock for more than five years with no capital gains tax on liquidation. In particular, after the 2017 Tax Act, more taxpayers may benefit from creating C corporations because of the low 21% tax rate in lieu of creating pass-through entities and trying to secure the Section 199A 20% deduction.

If a client wanted to cash in on his or her position and lock in the gains before the end of five years, Section 1045 could be used to roll over the gain into a new qualified small business, in which case it would be deferred until the client wanted to liquidate it. In order to satisfy the requirements of Section 1045, the stock must have been held for 60 days and rolled into a new qualified small business within 60 days.

2. TO TAKE ADVANTAGE OF ADDITIONAL DEDUCTIONS GRANTED TO C CORPORATIONS.

C corporations are able to deduct expenses to some degree for disability insurance premiums,[171] certain health insurance benefits, group term life insurance up to $50,000 per employee, long term care premiums, and other fringe benefits. Such expenses are not deductible in many circumstances with respect to S corporations. If the requirements of Section 1202 can be met to prevent double taxation, it may make sense to set up a business as a C corporation in order to take advantage of the additional deductions granted to C corporations.

A C corporation could also be created to perform the management functions of the business, while an S corporation (or other flow-through entity) is used for the operating side of the business. It is unclear if a management company will meet the requirements of Section 1202, as discussed below, but this type of structure would allow the business as a whole to take advantage of deductions afforded to C corporations, while avoiding double taxation for at least the operating side of the business. In addition, C corporations owned by individuals not related to the owners of an S corporation that pays the C corporation for management services or products may be able to have a separate pension plan if not subject to the affiliated service group, leased employee, and other Section 414 aggregation rules.

The Internal Revenue Code Section 414(n) further requires that certain "leased employees" be considered to be employees of the person or entity that they work for.

Pension planning considerations are discussed in more detail at Chapter 4 and Chapter 11.

---

[171] As a result, the employee would have to include disability insurance benefits in his or her gross income if the benefits were ever paid.

3. **1202 MANAGEMENT COMPANY.**

Clients with companies in a high-income tax bracket may be able to set up a Section 1202 qualified small business to manage their company and pay deductible fees and other expenses to the Section 1202 company. When the Section 1202 company is liquidated, the client would escape double taxation because all of the capital gains would be excluded.

It is unclear if these management companies will satisfy the requirements of an active trade or business under Section 1202. What is clear is that the management company cannot be a dummy management company that does engage in at least some sort of trade or business. One such business could be the rental of equipment, furniture, and other business assets. The management company cannot rent the land/building where the office is located, as the rental of real property is specifically excluded in Section 1202. However, Section 1202 makes no mention of other property; therefore, it is possible that the rental of property other than real property could satisfy the active trade or business requirement. Several authorities have applied a loose interpretation of the statute and stated that just because a company is engaged in a trade or business similar or related to one specifically enumerated in Section 1202(e) does not mean that it is not a qualified small business.[172] The courts may conclude that the rental of equipment, furniture and other business assets, while related to the rental of real property is not exactly the rental of real property, and therefore satisfies the requirements of Section 1202(e). It is important to realize that this is a risky position as currently there is no authority blessing this type of arrangement.

Example:

> Jim has a medical practice with net taxable income of $300,000. Jim decides to create a Section 1202 management company that will provide management and other back office services to his medical practice for $50,000 a year. Assuming this is reasonable payment for such services, the medical practice would have a $50,000 deduction and net income of $250,000, and a Section 1202 company may reinvest. As a result in the recent change in tax law which implements a flat tax of 21% on all C corporations, there would be no immediate income tax savings available for Jim; however if the Section 1202 company was able to reinvest the profits in an active trade or business, the Section 1202 company could eventually be sold tax-free and provide Jim with significant tax savings by reason of avoiding capital gains tax on the sale.

It is also noteworthy that under the new Section 199A, which provides a 20% deduction for flow-through income if certain requirements are met, that certain specified service trades or business are not eligible for the deduction if income exceeds $207,500 for single taxpayers or trusts, or $415,000 for married filer (a phase-out that begins to apply at the $157,500 or $315,000 income level). These Specified Service Trades or Businesses are the same businesses listed in paragraph (D)(1) of the Requirements Section, with the exception of architects and engineers. A Section 1202 management company may be used to reduce the Specified Service Trade or

---

[172] *See generally Owen*; PLR 201436001.

Business income below the limits described above or used to facilitate income being taxed at the 21% corporate income tax level, which is less than the effective rate of 29.6% that would apply to non-specified service flow-through entities. Similar to the above, the profits of the Section 1202 company could be reinvested in an active trade or business and later sold tax-free.

C.   PERSONAL HOLDING COMPANY CONSIDERATIONS

Any C corporation, including a Section 1202 company, may be subject to the Personal Holding Company tax, which would in most cases outweigh the benefits from being taxed as a Section 1202 Company. The Personal Holding Company tax imposed by Internal Revenue Code Section 543 applies if (1) the corporation is owned more than 50% by five or fewer individual shareholders ("Stock Ownership Test"), and (2) 60% of the corporation's income is derived from personal holding company sources ("Gross Income Test").

Generally, personal holding company income sources (with certain exceptions) include:[173]

1.   Dividends, interest, royalties (note that mineral, oil, or gas royalties or copyright royalties and active business computer software royalties have their own separate tests described below in order to be considered personal holding company income), and annuity income;

       A.   Interest does not include interest received on judgments, tax refunds, and condemnation rewards.

2.   Rents, but only if either of the following tests are met:

       A.   Adjusted rental income (generally defined as rental income less deductions for depreciation, interest and taxes associated with the rented property) is less than 50% of the adjusted ordinary gross income of the company. This is referred to as the 50% test.

       B.   Other personal holding company income (i.e. the sum of dividends paid, dividends considered to be paid, and consent dividends) exceeds 10% of the ordinary gross income. This is referred to as the 10% test.

3.   Mineral, oil, and gas royalties, as well as certain copyright royalties. It is noteworthy that no exception exists for royalties received on patents, trademarks, and other intellectual property assets;

4.   Produced film rents;

5.   Use of corporate property by shareholder;

6.   Personal service contracts; and

7.   Estates and trusts.

---

[173] *See* IRC § 543(a).

Therefore, rent received by a company will be considered personal holding company income if the adjusted rental income is less than 50% of the adjusted ordinary gross income of the company and other personal holding company income exceeds 10% of ordinary gross income.

For example, if a corporation has $40,000 of income from the sale and manufacture of products and $35,000 of rental income after allowable deductions, then the rental income would be considered personal holding company income because of the 50% test. Note however, that in this example the company would not be considered a personal holding company because 60% of its adjusted ordinary gross income does not come from personal holding company sources.

By second example, if the corporation's adjusted rental income after allowable deductions was $90,000, and the company also received royalties of $9,000, then rent would not be included as personal holding company income, because neither the 50% test nor the 10% test is satisfied.

As a result of these two tests, it is very difficult to avoid personal holding company tax by using rental income to shelter other personal holding company income, since $9 of gross income from rents must be generated to shelter every $1 of other personal holding company income.[174]

Copyright royalties and mineral, oil, and gas royalties are also only considered to be personal holding company income if the 50% test or the 10% test described above is met.

In addition there is a third test for copyright royalties and mineral, oil, and gas royalties which treats such royalties as personal holding company income if total deductions under Section 162 (trade or business expresses), other than those for compensation for personal services rendered by shareholders, equal or exceed 15% of adjusted ordinary gross income.

Also, personal holding company income includes personal service contract income, which is defined as amounts received pursuant to a contract under which the corporation is to furnish personal services if:[175]

A.   A person other than the corporation has the right to designate the individual to perform the services; or if the individual who is performing the services is designated under a legal agreement between the parties, and

B.   25% or more of the outstanding stock is owned by the individual who is performing, designated to perform, or may be designated to perform the services, or parties related thereto.

It is noteworthy that income from professional service S corporations will not be personal service contract income so long as the contract with the client does not specifically state that the owner will personally perform the services.

As a result of the above, a company that holds intellectual property assets and has income that only consists of royalty payments for the use of the intellectual property will likely be considered a personal holding company and taxed at a 20% rate on its undistributed income each year. This is

---

[174] Richard C. Fung, BNA Portfolio 797-4th: Personal Holding Companies, Detailed Analysis, E. Personal Holding Company Income (PHCI), Section 2.b.2.
[175] *See* IRC § 543(a)(7).

in addition to the 21% corporate income tax that would also apply, for a combined federal tax rate of 36.8% if all income is retained in the company. This will usually outweigh any benefit of Section 1202 status.

If the company also engaged in management of a related business or providing marketing or other similar services, so that income attributable to royalties received for the use of the intellectual property does not exceed 60% of the company's gross income, then the personal holding company tax would not apply, and the company would also qualify for Section 1202.

D.   DOWNSIDE/RISKS ASSOCIATED WITH SECTION 1202 COMPANY PLANNING

As with any potential tax avoidance opportunity, planners must be cognizant of risks that can be associated with these situations. The IRS might attempt to deny deductions for payments made by an S corporation to a related company, pension plan qualification could potentially be lost if affiliated service group, leased employee, and other rules are not followed, deductions may be lost if non-discrimination and associated rules for health insurance and other fringe benefits are not followed, and other risks can result from clients and other advisors not following proper formalities that can be laid out by the planner.

The court in *Owen* noted that payments made from one company to another for purported services or for other purposes must be supported by substantive consideration and must be under some contract or similar agreement between the parties.[176] Thus, legal agreements, and substantive rights and responsibilities must be real, legitimate, and substantive.

In addition, applicable insurance agencies and carriers should be consulted to help assure that liability and casualty insurance arrangements can be structured to provide proper coverage, and third parties who contract with one or more of the entities may need to be notified and possibly consent to altered arrangements.

Clients may also be subject to penalties and interest if gain is excluded under Section 1202 and the C corporation is later found to not have met the necessary requirements. Penalties may be avoided if an exception to Section 6662 is met, such as reliance on the advice of a qualified tax professional. However, the *Owen* case discussed above shows that the requirements of this exception may be hard to satisfy.

E.   ROYALTY COMPANY CONSIDERATIONS

In addition to the above Personal Holding Company Tax concerns, it is unclear whether rights to assets that produce royalties, other than computer software royalties described below, are considered to be assets used in the active conduct of a trade or business.

Under Section 1202(e)(8), rights to computer software which produced active business computer software royalties (within the meaning of Section 543(d)(1)) are treated as an asset used in the active conduct of a trade or business, as further defined below.

---

[176] *Owen*, at 10.

It is unclear whether rights to assets that produce other royalties are considered to be assets used in the active conduct of a trade or business, and the authors know of no authority that discusses this. If so, a C corporation could be set up to own and develop the rights to the software and receive royalty payments and avoid capital gains recognition on the sale of stock. The IRS may take the position that since no other type of royalties are mentioned in the statute that the rights to these assets are not considered as used in the active conduct of a trade or business, and thus not eligible for Section 1202 treatment.

Active Business Computer Software Royalties are defined under Section 543(d) as royalties received by any corporation in connection with the licensing of computer software that meet the following requirements, which are discussed in more detail below:

1.   Received by a corporation actively engaged in the computer software business,

2.   Constitute at least 50% of the total ordinary gross income of the corporation,

3.   Deductions under Sections 162, 174, and 195 must equal or exceed 25% of the corporation's ordinary gross income, and

4.   Dividends must equal or exceed excess of personal holding company income over 10% of ordinary gross income.

F.   RECEIVED BY A CORPORATION ACTIVELY ENGAGED IN THE COMPUTER SOFTWARE BUSINESS

The first requirement that the royalties must be received by a corporation actively engaged in the computer software business is met if the royalties are received by:

1.   A corporation engaged in the active conduct of the trade or business of developing, manufacturing, or producing computer software, AND

2.   Are attributable to computer software which is developed, manufactured, or produced by the corporation or the corporation is directly related to a trade or business developing manufacturing or producing computer software.

G.   DEDUCTIONS UNDER SECTIONS 162, 174, AND 195 MUST EQUAL OR EXCEED 25% OF THE CORPORATION'S ORDINARY GROSS INCOME

The third requirement is met if the deductions under Sections 162, 174, and 195 equal or exceed 25% of gross income for the taxable year, or the average of the deductions equal or exceed 25% of the average gross income of the corporation over a 5-year period. Deductions under Sections 162, 174, and 195 include all trade or business expenses, compensation, depreciation, research and development, and start up expenditures.

Deductions allowable under multiple Sections cannot be counted twice for the purpose of applying the test.[177] Additionally, compensation paid to principal shareholders is disregarded for the

---

[177] IRC § 542(d)(4)(B).

purposes of applying this test.[178] Principal shareholders are the five largest shareholders of the corporation (by value), but do not include individuals owning less than 5% of the stock of the corporation.[179]

H. DIVIDENDS MUST EQUAL OR EXCEED EXCESS OF PERSONAL HOLDING COMPANY INCOME OVER 10% OF ORDINARY GROSS INCOME

Personal Holding Company Income is defined as income from dividends, interest, rents, mineral, oil, and gas royalties, software royalties, and copyright royalties. For purposes of this test, Personal Holding Company Income does not include interest income if the corporation's software business is less than five years old, and active business software royalties. The Bloomberg BNA portfolio[180] on Personal Holding Companies has an example similar to the example below. The authors thank Bloomberg BNA for blazing the trail on calculation demonstrations.

Example:

> ABC Corp. is a C corporation with $200,000 of gross income, attributable to the following: (1) $110,000 from computer software royalties' income, (2) $40,000 from interest income, and (3) $50,000 from rental income. The royalty income will not be deemed to be Personal Holding Company Income if ABC is classified as an active trade or business and meets the three other requirements under Section 543(d) described above. ABC's software royalties constitute over 50% of gross income ($110,000 / $200,000 = 55%), so ABC must also (1) ensure that the sum of deductions under Sections 162, 174, and 195 exceed 25% of gross income, and (2) ensure that dividends paid exceed the excess of Personal Holding Company Income over 10% of gross income ($200,000 x 10% = $20,000). However, for the purposes of the dividend requirement under Section 543(d), both interest and royalty income are excluded from Personal Holding Company Income, which would consist only of $50,000 of rental income. Accordingly, ABC must pay $30,000 in dividends ($50,000 - $20,000 = $30,000) so that ABC's royalty income will not be Personal Holding Company Income, and ABC will not be classified as a Personal Holding Company.

If the above requirements are met and the appropriate dividend is paid, the rights to the computer software can be considered to be an asset used in an active trade or business for purposes of Section 1202. If ABC does not pay the dividends, all of its income will be Personal Holding Company Income, and it will be taxed as a Personal Holding Company. The rights will not be considered an asset used in the active conduct of a trade or business for purposes of Section 1202.

---

[178] IRC § 543(d)(4)(C).

[179] *Id.*

[180] *Richard C. Fung*, 797-4th T.M. at IV.E.1.c(4) (BNA), *Personal Holding Companies.*

If ABC only received income from software royalties, then ABC would not be required to pay a dividend due to the fact that all of the software royalty is excluded for purposes of this test, assuming that the above requirements are met.

•

CHAPTER 9.
PART ONE--ADDITIONAL SECTION 199A RULES

As earlier described, Section 199A allows for a deduction of up to 20% of QBI/flow-through income that is properly reported by a taxpayer from ownership of a flow-through entity.

Example:

> A single taxpayer owns an S corporation law firm that generates $85,000 in flow-through income. Her personal Taxable Income does not exceed $157,500. Her Section 199A deduction is $17,000 ($85,000 x 20%), which is claimed on her personal Form 1040 tax return. Based upon her 2018 highest tax bracket of 22%, this $17,000 deduction saves $3,740 in taxes ($17,000 x 22%).

Here are more terms that readers should be aware of:

A. QUALIFIED BUSINESS INCOME ("QBI")

This is flow-through income reported during the taxable year, which can be from S corporations, entities taxed as partnerships, and trades or businesses owned by individuals and reported on the Form 1040 Schedule C (for businesses) and Schedule E (for rental activities). Trusts may own and operate businesses or rental activities that produce QBI. LLCs with a single owner that are disregarded may own and operate trades or businesses so that the income goes on the Schedule C or E of the owner's Form 1040.

K-1 reported income is the amount that determines QBI from an S corporation or entity taxed as a partnership. Therefore, this measurement for Section 199A purposes is not affected by whether the income is actually distributed or whether W-2 wages are paid to the taxpayer or otherwise. The Schedule C or E tax reported income determines the QBI from a sole proprietorship or single number disregarded entity.

Section 199A excludes the following items from QBI:

1. short- and long-term capital gains and losses,

2. dividends, income equivalent to a dividend, or payment in lieu of dividends, received from foreign corporations (as described in 954(c)(1)),

3. interest income that is not allocable to the trade or business,

4. gain or loss from commodities transactions and foreign currency gains,

5. income, gain, deductions, or loss from notional principal contracts[181],

---

[181] Under Treasury Regulation 1.446-3(c)(1)(i), a notional principal contract is a financial instrument that provides

6.   amounts received from an annuity which is not received in connection with the trade or business, and

7.   any deduction or loss that is allocable to the above 6 items in this list.[182]. Additionally, QBI is not intended to include compensation paid by an entity to the taxpayer-owner who would have a deduction from the net income of the entity, and specifically does not include:

> (A)   "reasonable compensation paid to the taxpayer by any qualified trade or business of the taxpayer for services rendered with respect to the trade or business,"

> (B)   "any guaranteed payment described in Section 707(c) paid to a partner for services rendered with respect to the trade or business," and

> (C)   any payment to a partner who was not acting in the capacity of a partner with respect to services rendered to the trade or business.[183]

While the Final Regulations provide that an individual who was an employee and becomes an independent contractor will be presumed to, nevertheless, be considered an employee for Section 199A purposes, some advisors have warned that the "reasonable compensation" exclusion discussed above could enable the IRS to recharacterize legitimate independent contractor income as being "reasonable compensation" for services rendered. The authors do not believe that the IRS will have this ability as long as the income is received from a party other than the taxpayer, even if it is a related party controlled by the taxpayer or under common control by the taxpayer as long as the arrangement is at arm's-length. The Preamble to the Final Regulations states that reasonable compensation will not be expanded beyond its traditional application to wages paid to an owner of an S corporation and that an individual who was formerly characterized as an employee will have the burden of proving the conversion to independent contractor status should be respected. There is significantly more discussion on employee versus independent contractor and associated issues in Chapter 11.

Independent contractors must also be aware that the IRS has the authority to recharacterize contractors as employees, based upon the relationship between the worker and the employer. Such a determination may cause serious penalties to be incurred on top of owing unpaid employment taxes. This could negatively impact pension planning, since employees must generally be included in pension plans, notwithstanding that the employer may have attempted to treat them as independent contractors for reporting purposes.

Example:

> Jack Legal has a sole proprietorship law firm that has $90,000 of income on Schedule **C of his Form 1040. His rental activity generates $30,000 a year,

---

for the payment of amounts by one party to another at specified intervals calculated by reference to a specified index upon a notional principal amount in exchange for specified consideration or a promise to pay similar amounts. Notional principal contracts include interest rate swaps, currency swaps, basis swaps, interest rate caps, interest rate floors, commodity swaps, equity swaps, equity index swaps, and similar agreements.

[182] IRC §§ 199A(c)(3)(i)-(vi).

[183] Treas. Reg. §§ 1.199A-3(b)(2)(ii)(H)-(J).

> and he receives a salary of $30,000 a year. Jack has no other income. His QBI
> for the taxable year is $120,000, consisting of the $90,000 of law firm income
> and $30,000 of rental income.

Accordingly, Jack is eligible to claim a deduction of $24,000 ($120,000 x 20%). This would apply the same way if his law practice were in an S corporation or under a partnership that he owns with a spouse, who has separate income not exceeding $165,000 so that their total combined income is less than $315,000 and they can file a joint tax return.

QBI will be considered income for the purpose of computing taxable income and the Section 199A deduction. QBI does not include long- or short-term capital gain or losses. This can have a significant impact on planning for certain individuals. For example, capital gains, interest, and dividends from an investment portfolio will not be considered as QBI, although they are considered income for the purposes of computing net income to determine if the $157,500 or $315,000 thresholds apply.

1.   SECTION 1231 PROPERTY PLANNING.

The characterization of gain of or losses from Section 1231 property applies in a consistent manner for purposes of Section 199A. Section 1231 property is defined as property used in a trade or business that (1) is subject to Section 167 depreciation held for more than one year, and (2) real property used in the trade or business held for one year.[184]

All Section 1231 property gains and losses are netted. If the result is a net gain, then such gain is taxed as a long-term capital gain, and if the result is a net loss, then such loss is treated as an ordinary loss. QBI does not include any "item of short-term capital gain, short-term capital loss, long-term capital gain, or long-term capital loss."[185] The Section 1231 property could therefore be used as Qualified Property to help eliminate limitations on the Section 199A deduction, and the gain on that property will be taxed at the more favorable capital gains rates, which peak at 20%.

It is important to note that the netting of Section 1231 property is done at the individual level and not at the entity level, which has led to confusion as to how RPEs should report Section 1231 items on K-1s to their individual owners. Rachael Jaeckel, of the IRS Large Business and International Division, speaking on a May 30, 2019 webinar unofficially indicated that the IRS is looking at making changes to the K-1 instructions to provide guidance on reporting of these items, and that "for now partnerships and S Corporations shouldn't include the Section 1231 items in qualified business income it's reporting to investors."[186] Section 1231 items should therefore be reported

---

[184] IRC § 1231(b)(1). Real property under § 1231(b)(1) is subject to more restrictions than other property, which simply must be held for 1 year and depreciable under § 167. § 1231 property that is also real property must not (1) be includible in inventory, (2) be held primarily for sale to customers in the ordinary course of the trade or business, (3) "patent, invention, model or design (whether or not patented), a secret formula or process, a copyright, a literary, musical, or artistic composition, a letter or memorandum, or similar property," held by the taxpayer described in § 1221(a)(3), or (4) be a publication of the U.S. Government which is received from the U.S. government other than at the price offered for sale to the public and held by a taxpayer described by § 1221(a)(5).
[185] IRC § 199A(c)(3)(B)(i).
[186] Yauch, IRS to Clarify Some Reporting Instructions for 199A, Tax Notes June 10, 2019.

and separately listed on K-1s issued to owners of S Corporations and partnerships, and should only be included as qualified business income after the netting of other Section 1231 items at the individual level if appropriate.[187]

Taxpayers should be aware, however, that losses on Section 1231 property may ultimately lead to a decreased deduction under Section 199A. Also, if a taxpayer is above the high- earning thresholds, and Section 1231 property could be sold for a loss, then such loss could be used to reduce the taxpayer's income to below the high-earning thresholds in order to avoid the application of the Wage and Qualified Property Test.

The Preamble to the Proposed Regulations provides as follows:

"Section 1231 provides rules under which gains and losses from certain involuntary conversions and the sale of certain property used in a trade or business are either treated as long-term capital gains or long-term capital losses, or not treated as gains and losses from sales or exchanges of capital assets. Section 199A(c)(3)(B)(i) excludes capital gains or losses, regardless of whether those items arise from the sale or exchange of a capital asset. The legislative history of Section 199A provides that QBI does not include any item taken into account in determining net long-term capital gain or net long-term capital loss. Conference Report page 30. Accordingly, Final Regulation Section 1.199A-3(b)(2)(ii)(A) clarifies that, to the extent gain or loss is treated as capital gain or loss, it is not included in QBI. Specifically, if gain or loss is treated as capital gain or loss under Section 1231, it is not QBI. Conversely, if Section 1231 provides that gains or losses are not treated as gains and losses from sales or exchanges of capital assets, Section 199A(c)(3)(B)(i) does not apply and thus, the gains or losses must be included in QBI (provided all other requirements are met)."

Chart 9 – Section 1231 Summary Chart

Below is a chart that demonstrates how the netting system under Section 1231 works:

Net Gain of 1231 Property:		Net Loss of 1231 Property:	
Property	**Gain/Loss**	**Property**	**Gain/Loss**
Property 1	$5,000	Property 1	$ (5,000)
Property 2	$ (5,000)	Property 2	$5,000
Property 3	$5,000	Property 3	$ (5,000)
Net Gain	$5,000	Net Loss	$ (5,000)
Taxed as Long-Term Capital Gain		Treated as Ordinary Loss	

---

[187] *Id.*

2. ALTERNATIVE MINIMUM TAX.

The alternative minimum tax ("AMT") is a "government safety net tax" imposed upon individual taxpayers, trusts and estates who would otherwise pay very little or no income tax because of certain tax deductions that are called "preference items." The Section 199A deduction is not considered to be an AMT preference item, and the deduction is therefore taken on QBI under both the regular tax and AMT systems.

For example, under the regular tax system, interest earned on certain state and local municipal bonds is excluded from taxable income, but this can be a "preference item" for AMT purposes so that some tax is paid if the taxpayer has enough regular or otherwise excluded income based upon the thresholds and calculations described below.

Therefore, if an individual had $300,000 of K-1 income from an S corporation, and therefore received a $60,000 Section 199A deduction, this would reduce the alternative minimum taxable income base by $60,000, so Section 199A planning still saves money for taxpayers who are subject to the alternative minimum tax and does not complicate the alternative minimum tax calculation.

To go into more detail, the amount subject to alternative minimum tax is called the alternative minimum taxable income ("AMTI"), which is calculated by taking the taxpayer's otherwise applicable taxable income and adding back the adjustments and preference items found in Sections 56 through 58,[188] which includes among other items, the standard deduction amount ($12,000 for single taxpayers and $24,000 for married couples filing jointly), as well as any excess of itemized deductions over the standard deduction, and state and local taxes.[189]

Additionally, there is an exemption amount deducted from the AMTI of $24,600 for trusts and estates, $70,300 for single filer taxpayers, $54,700 for spouses filing separately, and $109,400 for joint filers and surviving spouses.[190] This number is tied to inflation and is subject to a phase-out at $1,000,000 for joint filing taxpayers and surviving spouses, $500,000 for single filers, and $75,000 for trusts and estates.

As stated above, Section 199A states that QBI is determined without regard to the adjustments to taxable income under the alternative minimum tax for the purposes of calculating AMTI. In other words, the Section 199A deduction is determined the same way, regardless of whether the taxpayer is liable for alternative minimum tax. Additionally, Section 55 states that AMTI starts with taxable income (post-Section 199A income) and does not explicitly list Section 199A as an adjustment, which means that taxpayers will not have to subtract the Section 199A deduction as an adjustment.

---

[188] IRC § 55(c). This section uses taxable income reduced by the foreign tax credit under § 27(a) and does not include increases in tax found in § 45(e)(11)(C), § 49(b), § 50(a), § 42(j), or § 42(k).

[189] IRC § 55(b)(1)(A). Note that the threshold for the tax brackets is $175,000, but IRC § 55(d)(3) ties this number to inflation based on the cost-of-living adjustment in § 1(f)(3), which for 2018 makes the threshold amount $191,500.

[190] IRC § 55(d).

Taxable Income v. Alternative Minimum Taxable Income

Item Included in Taxable Income	Included in Alternative Minimum Taxable Income?
Standard Deduction	Not Allowed
State and Local Taxes	Not Allowed
Depreciation Deductions	Allowed (Some Restrictions Apply/Subject to Different calculation Method)
Itemized Medical Expenses	Allowed (To the extent exceeding 10% of Adjusted Gross Income)
Intangible Drilling Costs	Allowed (Some Restrictions Apply)*
Gain/Loss From Sale or Exchange of Property	Allowed
Section 199A Deduction	Allowed
Mortgage Interest Payment Deduction	Allowed (Except upon home equity loans)
Net Operating Losses	Allowed (but may not exceed 90% of AMTI)

Since taxpayers may have to determine separate depreciation deductions for AMT purposes, and keep appropriate records to permit that, consider the duplicative accounting efforts that might have to be made:

(1)   Regular income tax depreciation or expense calculations.

(2)   Depreciation for accounting not tax purposes. Since significant assets may be expensed immediately small businesses that use outside financing may have to prepare financial statements reflecting the value of the assets that were expensed for income tax purposes.

(3)   AMT depreciation (and hence basis) calculations.

(4)   UBIA calculations of qualified property for the Section 199A tangible property calculation.

3. **QUALIFIED PROPERTY.**

Under Section 199A, Qualified Property is defined as "tangible property of a character subject to … depreciation under Section 167."[191] Qualified property additionally is required to be (1) "held by, and available for use in, the qualified trade or business at the close of the taxable year," (2) "used at any point during the taxable year in the production of QBI," and (3) "the depreciable period for which has not ended before the close of the taxable year."[192]

4. **UNADJUSTED BASIS IMMEDIATELY AFTER ACQUISITION OF QUALIFIED PROPERTY ("UBIA").**

The Final Regulations added the term UBIA, which is defined as the cost basis of the property on the date that it is placed into service, without regard to any adjustments to the property's basis by normal depreciation deductions which are allowable and a taxpayer's election to immediately expense the property under Section 179, or to take bonus depreciation under Section 168(k).

B. **SPECIFIED SERVICE TRADES OR BUSINESSES**

As mentioned above, these are trades and businesses that cannot qualify for Section 199A when the individual taxpayer, estate, or trust that is receiving income from the flow-through entities has taxable income exceeding the $207,500/$415,000 thresholds and are subject to a phase-out if income is between the Section 199A income thresholds ($157,500-$207,500/$315,000-$415,000). The Specified Service Trades or Businesses are the same as are listed under the Section 1202 company discussion above as items (1) through (11), which are as follows:

(1) Health,

(2) Law,

(3) Accounting,

(4) Actuarial Science,

(5) Performing Arts,

(6) Consulting,

(7) Athletics,

(8) Financial Services,

(9) Brokerage Services,

(10) Investing, Trading, or Dealing in Securities, Partnership Interests, or Commodities, and

---

[191] Treas. Reg. § 1.199A-2(c)(1)(i).
[192] Id.

(11)   Any business where the principal asset is the reputation or skill of one or more of its employees or owners.

Example:

> If Jack receives $500,000 in flow-through income from his legal practice, then Jack cannot claim the deduction for income from the law firm because his taxable income exceeds the maximum $415,000 level at which any Section 199A deduction is phased-out. His rental activity income may still qualify for Section 199A, but only if he can satisfy the Wage/Property Test described below. If the rental were the building in which his law practice operated, that too would be disqualified under the Final Regulations.

It is noteworthy that bankers, insurance agents (including life insurance agents), architects and engineers will not be considered to be SSTBs under the Final Regulations, but real estate closing agents, mortgage brokers and lobbyists will be.

It is noteworthy that Internal Revenue Code Section 448, which defines the term "qualified personal service corporations," has definitions of certain service businesses and rulings and case law that may apply by analogy, but not directly, under Section 199A. These references are provided in the book but will not be as directly precedential as the present Final Regulations and future case law that arises directly under Section 199A. Prior case law and letter rulings under Section 1202 will have more precedential value since the language of Section 199A refers to the Section 1202 definitions.

Chart 10 – Sections 448, 1202, & 199A Comparison Chart

Here is a chart that shows the similarity in language between Sections 448, 1202, and 199A.

Section 448(d)(2):	Section 1202(e)(3)	Section 199A(d)(2)
"(2) QUALIFIED PERSONAL SERVICE CORPORATION "The term 'qualified personal service corporation' means any corporation— "(A) substantially all of the activities of which involve the performance of	**"(3) QUALIFIED TRADE OR BUSINESS** "For purposes of this subsection, the term 'qualified trade or business' means any trade or business other than— "(A) any trade or business involving the performance of services in the fields of health, law, engineering, architecture, accounting,	**"(2) SPECIFIED SERVICE TRADE OR BUSINESS** "The term 'Specified Service Trade or Business' means any trade or business— "(A) which is described in section 1202(e)(3)(A) (applied without regard to the words 'engineering, architecture,') or which would be so described if the term 'employees or

Section 448(d)(2):	Section 1202(e)(3)	Section 199A(d)(2)
services in the fields of health, law, engineering, architecture, accounting, actuarial science, performing arts, or consulting, ..."	actuarial science, performing arts, consulting, athletics, financial services, brokerage services, or any trade or business where the principal asset of such trade or business is the reputation or skill of 1 or more of its employees ..."	owners' were substituted for 'employees' therein, or "(B) which involves the performance of services that consist of investing and investment management, trading, or dealing in securities (as defined in section 475(c)(2)), partnership interests, or commodities (as defined in section 475(e)(2))."

The following sections discuss specific professions, and whether some or all of the functions will be considered as Specified Service Trades or Businesses ("SSTBs"):

C.   ARCHITECTS AND ENGINEERS

The definition for Specified Service Trades or Businesses in Section 199A refers to Section 1202(e)(3), which lists architects and engineers. Section 199A includes an explicit exclusion for these two professions from SSTB taint. Some advisors had expressed concern that these professions may be brought back in as an SSTB under the catchall provision where the principal asset is the reputation or skill of one or more of its employees or owners, however in one of the few breaks provided by the Final Regulations, the IRS applied this catchall narrowly, as discussed in more detail below.

Further, the Final Regulations specifically state that "services within the fields of architecture and engineering are not treated as consulting services."[193]

D.   LAW

The Final Regulations define the performance of services in the field of law as "...the performance of legal services by individuals such as lawyers, paralegals, legal arbitrators, mediators, and similar professionals performing services in their capacity as such. The performance of services in the field of law does not include the provision of services that do not require skills unique to the field of law, for example, the provision of services in the field of law does not include the provision of services by printers, delivery services, or stenography services."

Law firms commonly furnish services that are separate and apart from the practice of law.

These services include acting as trustee, personal representative or executor, issuing title insurance, providing expert witness testimony, and providing clients with management and non- legal clerical services. Many patent law firms provide engineering services as part of the patent application and

---

[193] 1.199A-5(b)(2)(vii).

design work that they do. Practitioners have speculated that many law firms would benefit from segregating income and expenses arising from non-legal services. Unfortunately, the Final Regulations as discussed in more detail in Chapter 14 have a significant impact on planning involving the segregation of the components of an SSTB. These restrictions are based on common ownership (50% of more) of an SSTB and its ancillary services and provide that to the extent that property and services are provided back to the SSTB, the ancillary services will be also be treated as SSTB income.

It is not certain whether each of the separate "trades or businesses" which are SSTBs would need to have "separable books and records," but this would certainly be suggested.

Chart Based Upon Regulations Under Section 199A

Activity	Includes	Does Not Include
Law	The provision of "legal" services by lawyers, paralegals, legal arbitrators, mediators, and similar professionals in their capacity as such. Please note that in most states, mediators do not need to be licensed lawyers.	The provision of services that do not require skills unique to the field of law, for example, the provision of services in the field of law does not include the provision of services by printers, delivery services, or stenography services. Excluding delivery services is of no help and demonstrates the broad all-encompassing view the Final Regulations have taken of Specified Service Trades or Businesses. There is no discussion as to whether trustee and executor and executrix, title insurance and other services that do not require a law license are considered to be legal services.

E.   HEALTH

The Final Regulations define the performance of services in the field of health as "…the provision of medical services by individuals such as physicians, pharmacists, nurses, dentists, veterinarians, physical therapists, psychologists, and other similar healthcare professionals performing services in their capacity as such. The performance of services in the field of health does not include the provision of services not directly related to a medical services field, even though the services provided may purportedly relate to the health of the service recipient. For example, the performance of services in the field of health does not include the operation of health clubs or health spas that provide physical exercise or conditioning to their customers, payment processing, or the research, testing, and manufacture and/or sales of pharmaceuticals or medical devices."

The Proposed Regulations had the following phrase in the language that is underlined below, which gave hope that medical professionals who were not giving direct patient care could be excluded from being considered as health professionals:

> *"[T]he field of health means the provision of medical services by individuals such as physicians……and other similar healthcare professionals performing services in*

*their capacity as **such who provide medical services directly to a patient (service recipient)**."*

The Final Regulations removed the above underlined words, and the commentary in the Preamble to the Final Regulations includes the following statement:

> *"The Treasury and the IRS [therefore determined] that proximity to patients is not a necessary component of providing services in the field of health."*

This chapter will discuss if and when a person or entity is engaged in the "field of health" under the definition of a Specified Trade or Business by analyzing the Final Regulations, previous interpretations under Internal Revenue Code Section 1202, and also how similar definitions have been applied in the past under Internal Revenue Code Section 448.

F.   FURTHER DISCUSSION AND EXAMPLES USED IN FINAL REGULATIONS IN THE FIELD OF HEALTH

The Regulations provide four new examples which are intended to give guidance with respect to this but are based on scenarios that are very unusual or impossible because of medical regulations where no employee or agent of a given entity has any contact that would be considered as medical services provided for a particular patient.

1.   PHARMACISTS.

Under the first new example, a board-certified pharmacist has a full-time job but also works part-time as needed as an independent contractor for a small medical facility in a rural area. The part-time pharmacist works at the facility and receives and reviews orders from physicians who are providing medical care at the facility, makes recommendations on dosing and alternative medications, performs inoculations, checks for drug interactions, and fills pharmaceutical orders for patients receiving care at the facility. The example concludes that this part-time pharmacist is engaged in the field of health.

It is surprising that the drafters of the Final Regulations would assume that a pharmacist would not be treated as an employee of the facility based on the circumstances. This example may be used as evidence that it is possible to treat a part-time professional working on the premises of the employer, following the schedule, and using the equipment and amenities of the office, as an independent contractor. The case and statutory law is not supportive of this, unless it can be shown that a substantial number of similarly situated pharmacists are paid as independent contractors under substantially similar circumstances.

The Preamble to the Final Regulations indicates that the "manufacture and/or sales of pharmaceuticals and medical devices" by a retail pharmacy is not by itself a trade or business performing services in the field of health, but some services provided by a retail pharmacy through a pharmacist are in the field of health if "in their capacity [they] provide medical services directly to a patient (service recipient)."

If and when an independent contractor pharmacist, or entity providing pharmacists and similar professionals, works for a retail pharmacy, the separate functions of the pharmacist and the time spent associated therewith should be analyzed in order to determine whether some or all of the pharmacist-related income is Qualified Business Income. Filling prescriptions does not seem to be a health function but talking to doctors and patients about the prescriptions does, and it may not be legally possible to separate these functions and thus satisfy state and federal law, Medicare, Medicaid, and other applicable requirements.[194]

In fact, the law requires that pharmacies provide counseling about the medications. They are obliged to review drug interactions, contraindications based on diagnoses, and the pharmacist, under FDA rules, is obligated to determine whether or not the prescriptions seem reasonable when dispensing controlled substances. The pharmacy has obligations beyond filling prescriptions, and pretty much any type of pharmacy always has to have a pharmacist on the premises.

2. RESIDENTIAL RETIREMENT HOME.

A second example added in the Final Regulations involves an entity that operates a residential facility for the elderly that provides housing, meals, laundry services, and entertainment. The entity also contracts with local professional healthcare organizations to provide residents with a range of medical and health services, including skilled nursing, physical and occupational therapy, speech pathology, medical social services, medications, medical supplies and equipment used in the facility, ambulance transportation and dietary counseling.

The facility receives all of its income from residents for residential services, and any health and medical services are billed directly by the healthcare providers. The example concludes that the facility does not perform services in the field of health.[195]

Similarly situated facilities in the real-world normally have employees who check daily or more frequently to assure that residents take their medications, and also take vital signs (blood pressure, pulse rate, and temperature) daily and log these statistics in a medical chart maintained by the facility. This is probably a small enough function for the facility that it can be considered to be incidental, and not cause the facility to be considered as providing health services, but this not clear from the example.

3. SURGERY CENTERS.

The third example added in the Final Regulations provides that a company that operates day surgery centers, and does not employ physicians, nurses or medical assistants, does not perform services in the field of health, even though it presumably provides medical equipment, medical supplies and support staff other than physicians, nurses and medical assistants.

The entity in the example enters into agreements with other professional medical organizations, or directly with individual medical professionals, to perform the procedures and provide all medical care. As a practical matter, the vast majority of ambulatory surgery centers ("ASC"'s) provide all nursing personnel, as discussed below, allow doctors to bring their patients in for procedures, and

---

[194] Treas. Reg. 1.199A-5(b)(3)(i).
[195] Treas. Reg. 1.199A-5(b)(3)(ii).

then charge a separate procedure fee, with the doctor charging a "procedure fee" and taking care of all physician services before and after the procedure at the doctor's own office.

The example is consistent with this in providing that patients are only billed by the entity for the facility costs relating to their procedure and are billed separately by the healthcare professionals or their affiliated organization for the "actual costs of the procedure conducted by the physician and medical support team."

The vast majority of ambulatory surgical centers directly hire the nurses and medical assistants who have direct physical contact and care responsibilities for the patients and are compensated as part of the facility fee.

It would not be practical for ambulatory surgical centers to require doctors who perform procedures to bring their own nurses and medical assistants, and many ambulatory surgical centers hire anesthesiologists or contract with anesthesia companies and bill patients, directly or indirectly, for the services of anesthesiologists and/or nurse anesthetists. This can be a large part of an ASC's bottom line income.

The Preamble to the Final Regulations indicates that several commentators were asked for clarification regarding when two separate activities would generally be viewed separately and seems to indicate that such facilities can qualify to not be considered as Specified Service Trades or Businesses because medical personnel can be hired as independent contractors, and thus be considered to not be providing medical services or assisting physicians in medical services. This may apply to emergency centers, urgent care centers, and surgical centers where the non-SSTB owners or operators provide use of the real estate, equipment, furniture, and amenities "but do not provide treatment or diagnostic care to service recipients." The example discussed above was a "fact pattern that the Treasury Department and the IRS do not believe is a trade or business providing services in the field of health."

The restructuring of surgery centers as the result of the Final Regulations may involve establishing nursing and personal care service companies that would hire the patient management staff of the ambulatory surgical center, and any anesthesiologists or nurse anesthetists who have been performing services at the center. Additionally, if surgery centers choose to contract with an anesthesiologist or a nurse anesthetist, the relationship can be restructured by reassigning the anesthesiologist's benefits, which would allow the facility to bill under its own tax ID and Medicare numbers.

There will doubtlessly be violations of the federal and some state anti-kickback statutes, and other laws, if and when surgery centers are paid directly or indirectly by anesthesiologists, anesthetists or anesthesia entities for the right to perform anesthesia services at the facility.

While ambulatory surgical centers (ASCs) are able to directly employ anesthesia personnel, indirect employment can be problematic, as indicated in the Office of Inspector General Advisory Opinion No. 12-06 and the Anti-Kickback Statute.

Emergency rooms and urgent care centers will have the same issues. The vast majority, if not all, emergency rooms and urgent care centers directly employ (at least in substance) nursing and other direct patient contact personnel and will have to change their economic and patient care models if they require medical groups or other third parties to provide these personnel as independent contractors or otherwise.

It is noteworthy that in Revenue Ruling 72-203, the IRS ruled that:

Physicians who engage in the pursuit of an independent medical practice in which they offer their services to the public are generally independent contractors and not employees. However, if the requisite control and supervision over a physician exist with respect to services performed for another, he is an employee rather than an independent contractor.

In determining whether the requisite control and supervision exist, the IRS looks at the following primary factors:

(1)   The degree to which such individual has become integrated into the operating organization of the person or firm for which the services are performed.

(2)   The substantial nature, regularity, and continuity of his work for such person or firm.

(3)   The authority vested in or reserved by such person or firm to require compliance with its general policies.

(4)   The degree to which the individual under consideration has been accorded the rights and privileges which such person or firm has created or established for its employees generally. [196]

In applying these factors to a radiologist, four physicians, and physical therapists (collectively referred to as the "Workers"), the IRS advised in TAM 9443002 that the Workers were all employees of a hospital and noted the following:

(1)   The Workers had no investment in the business.

(2)   The Workers expended no money or effort to generate work.

(3)   Managerial skill and know-how to play no role in their ability to increase earnings.

(4)   The Workers only performed services for the hospital and did so on a continual basis.

(5)   The Workers were supplied with staff and equipment by the hospital, were guaranteed a minimum salary and had to comply with the rules and policies of the hospital. [197]

ASCs will need to be careful about those relationships, and if they are going to keep a portion of an independent contractor's revenues, the facility should be able to justify not only why, but also

---

[196] Revenue Ruling 72-203.
[197] TAM 9443002.

that it is for fair market value and does not vary with the volume or value of referrals of patients that are referred to or from the ASC.

4. TESTING BUSINESSES.

The fourth new example involves the "only provider" of a patented test that is used to detect a particular medical condition, which is found to be not providing services in the field of health. This entity accepts test orders only from healthcare professionals and has no patient contact. Its employees do not diagnose, treat or manage any aspect of medical care. Only the manager of the testing operations has an advanced medical degree and no other employees are healthcare professionals, although they are well-educated technical professionals who each receive more than a year of a specialized training in what the company does. The company analyzes results from testing and provides its clients, the medical professionals, with a report summarizing the findings. It does not discuss results or the patient's diagnosis or treatment with any healthcare provider or patient and is not informed as to the resulting diagnosis or treatment.

This example provides unrealistic guidance for the majority of testing and similar operations, which typically include a statistical or charted summary with the test results for each patient to indicate whether the test findings are within normal and abnormal ranges, in order to assist medical professionals in helping to assure that proper identification and communication can result from the test.

Also, in many fields of testing, it is important that the healthcare professionals be able to call the testing service to request information and guidance from the service or a medical director hired by the service to discuss results that may be abnormal or require special consideration.

Private Letter Ruling 201717010 is discussed below and is consistent with the Final Regulations.

There is further guidance in the discussion in the Preamble to the Final Regulations which describes comments received and the IRS's reaction thereto.

These are as follows:

(a)   **Stem Cell and PRP Injection Therapies**

One commentator argued that gene therapy and stem cell and similar therapies, where products are manufactured or produced from the patient's body and then reinjected or otherwise used, should be treated in the same manner as pharmaceuticals so that their manufacture and production is not considered to be a health service, regardless of whether they take place in a hospital or a separate production facility. The Treasury Department and IRS declined to adopt this recommendation, indicating that it is a question of facts and circumstances that can be different in each situation.

To the knowledge of the authors, stem cell or similar extraction and reinjection therapies, which are becoming popular, are closely associated with physicians who provide them in their offices on an outpatient basis where the doctor examines the patient, handles or oversees the extraction, and handles or oversees the reinjection, which is often done with ultrasound or other x-ray style guidance. It is therefore difficult to see how this could be considered not to be the "provision of medical care services" by individuals, unless the facility equipment and non-medical personnel involved are separate and apart from the medical personnel, and the patient or applicable payor source are separately billed.

(b) **Veterinarians**

There is a lengthy discussion of veterinary medicine and animal health in the history of the characterization thereof as being a health service. Apparently, veterinarians lobbied hard to be excluded, and this was not successful. There was no mention of tree surgeons or psychic healers! The lobbyists for veterinarians obviously tried hard but couldn't save themselves or the vets

(c) **Physical Therapists**

One commentator requested a dividing line between physical therapists and other health-related occupations, noting that physical therapists are paid less than doctors and that Congress initially attempted to exclude physical therapists from being reimbursed Medicare and Medicaid. The Treasury Department and the IRS declined to exclude physical therapists from being healthcare professionals.

(d) **Remote Radiologists and Non-Patient Contact Professionals**

One commenter suggested that services are not performed in the field of health unless "performed directly to a patient." For example, a physician who reads x-rays for another physician, but does not work directly with the patient, would not be performing health services under this example. The Treasury Department and the IRS agreed that proximity to patients is not a necessary component of providing services in the field of health, so the Final Regulations removed the requirement from the Proposed Regulations, which had indicated that medical services had to be provided directly to a patient to be considered as a Specified Service Trade or Business. The Final Regulations did not adopt the suggestion that technicians who operate medical equipment or test samples are not considered to be performing services in the field of health.

This will directly affect the work of radiologists in test centers. It is a very common model for the radiologist to be an independent contractor of the test center. This set up would allow the technicians in the center to conduct the tests and send the date to the radiologist who could potentially be working remotely. Regardless of where the Radiologist is located, these facilities themselves would still be considered healthcare providers. They are heavily regulated by the state and federal government, and the individuals that work in them are all licensed and have higher degrees. The technicians have to use some judgement before sending films to the radiologist because they must determine whether or not the images are diagnostic quality or not, and whether or not they should be retaken.

Private Letter Rulings that were issued under Section 1202 prior to the passage of Section 199A would indicate that health professionals may have activities separate and apart from health-related services, which may include research, laboratory testing, and development of pharmaceuticals. One example of a service that is related to the health field but was held not to be an SSTB in a Private Letter Ruling, was laboratory testing for non-patients. [198] The Private Letter Rulings

---

[198] PLR 201717010 (2017). The ruling stated that, for Section 1202, a company that ran lab reports for healthcare providers, but did not interact with or diagnose patients, would not be a Specified Service Trade or Business.

discussed below were issued well before Section 199A was enacted to provide guidance on the same definition of "the field of health" as under Section 1202 and are reprinted in Exhibit 15 in their entirety. It is important to note that Private Letter Rulings reveal the thinking of the IRS at the time of issuance but may not be relied upon as precedent. It is further possible that all such Private Letter Rulings will not apply to the extent inconsistent with the Final Regulations.

(1)   **PLR 201436001**. In this 2014 ruling, the IRS stated that a company that provided "products and services in connection with the pharmaceutical industry ... did not perform services in the health industry within the meaning of Section 1202(e)(3)." The company helped clients "commercialize experimental drugs" by researching drug formulation effectiveness, testing drugs in clinical trials, and manufacturing drugs, but did not offer services "in the form of individual expertise." The "thrust of Section 1202(e)(3)" is that the value of businesses engaged in listed activities is primarily derived from offering services, whether "those services are the providing of hotel rooms, for example, or in the form of individual expertise (law firm partners)." The company in question deployed "specific manufacturing assets and intellectual property assets to create a value for customers." Also, the Service noted that the pharmaceutical industry is a component of the health industry, but that the company in question did not perform services in the health industry and analogized the company's role in the pharmaceutical industry to that of an automobile parts manufacturer not being in the business of providing services.

(2)   PLR 201717010. In this 2017 ruling, the IRS stated that a company that received medical samples from physicians, ran laboratory testing, and sent reports that merely indicated what level of a specific substance was present in the sample was not considered to be a health service under Section 1202(e)(3). The reports sent by the company did not include diagnosis or treatment information, and the physician would not discuss diagnosis or treatment with the testing company.

Only rarely would patients receive copies of the report directly from the company. The IRS based the ruling upon the fact that the company did not provide diagnosis or treatment to patients or healthcare providers, and that none of the revenue of the company was earned from the medical care of patients. The company would instead direct patients to talk to their healthcare provider.

It is noteworthy that most blood labs provide not only results, but also point out whether they are within the normal or abnormal ranges. This Private Letter Ruling may not apply for conventional blood labs, which do provide such reports. Those labs may consider having an unrelated third-party contractor provide the analysis of when a given patient's results are normal or abnormal, and if the law and applicable Medicare, Medicaid, and insurance carriers would be willing to pay for lab services under these circumstances.

As mentioned above, a company that processed computerized billing claims for hospitals and doctors was found not to be in the field of health in Private Letter Ruling 8927006, which is discussed below under the category of accounting, where it is explained that the company was found not to be in the business of accounting either.

In Tax Court Memorandum 2007-124, a corporation that provided radiation therapy to its patients was deemed to be performing services in the field of health, as was a company that provided ambulance services in a 1992 Advisory Memorandum. The performance of ultrasound services was deemed to be an activity in the field of health, but the 2017 Tax Court Memorandum decisions of *Zia-Ahmadi v. Commissioner*, Tax Court Opinion 2017-39, could be services in the field of health.[199]

The Treasury Regulations for Section 448 provides an analogous definition for businesses performing services in the field of health:

> *"[T]he performance of services in the field of health means the provision of medical services by physicians, nurses, dentists, and other similar healthcare professionals. The performance of services in the field of health does not include the provision of services not directly related to a medical field, even though the services may purportedly relate to the health of the service recipient. For example, the performance of services in the field of health does not include the operation of health clubs or health spas that provide physical exercise or conditioning to their customers."*[200]

Chart Based Upon Regulations Under Section 199A

Activity	Includes	Does Not Include
Health	The provision of medical services by physicians, pharmacists, nurses, dentists, veterinarians, physical therapists, psychologists, and other similar healthcare professionals who provide medical services directly to the patient.	The provision of services not directly related to a medical field, even though the services may purportedly relate to the health of the service recipient. For example, the performance of services in the field of health does not include the operation of health clubs or health spas that provide physical exercise or conditioning to their customers, payment processing, or research, testing and manufacture and/or sales of pharmaceuticals or medical devices where patient care and physician assistants were not provided. Payment processing is quite limited and would not appear to facilitate medical practices dividing off significant practice administrative activities as producing non-Specified Service Trade or Business revenue. Practitioners also need to read these very limited exclusions with consideration to the broad aggregation rules which further limit planning.

5. WHAT ABOUT MARIJUANA GROWING, REFINING AND DISTRIBUTION?

There was probably not much thought given in the legislative process as to whether the Section 199A deduction would apply to income from a company that manufacturers, tests, or sells

---

[199] See *Zia-Ahmadi v. Commissioner*, T.C. Summ. Op. 2017-39. The Tax Court in this case noted two important things: (1) state licensing is not relevant when determining if an employee performs services in an industry; and (2) "'field of health' includes services provided by healthcare professionals that are directly related to a medical field."

[200] Treas. Regs. § 1.448-1T(e)(ii).

marijuana or marijuana products, which are presently illegal under federal law. One question is whether the activity of manufacturing or selling medical marijuana would be considered to be in the field of health. Some commentators have suggested that medical marijuana growers and manufacturers are not likely to be seen as providing health services, because they could be analogized to automobile parts manufacturers consistent with the Private Letter Ruling from 2014 found above. It is unknown whether selling medical marijuana to medical patients will be considered to be a Specified Service Trade or Business, based in part on whether patients receive counseling or assistance in selecting or consuming medical marijuana.

Qualifying for the Section 199A deduction is especially important to marijuana growers, refiners, and distributors because they cannot deduct ordinary business expenses, except for the cost of goods sold, as explained below. The authors believe that marijuana growers, processors, and sellers will be eligible for the Section 199A deduction because Section 280E only disallows deductions for "any amount paid or incurred . . . in carrying on any trade or business [that] . . . consists of trafficking in controlled substances," but does not appear to prevent the 20% deduction for Qualified Business Income.

This rationale relies on the distinction between revenues, gross income, and net income, as displayed in the chart below. Gross income is revenue less the cost of goods sold, and net income is gross income less business expenses. Section 280E prohibits the claiming of deductions for business expenses on gross income. The Tax Court has drawn a sharp line to say that Section 280E does not disallow the deduction for cost of goods sold in a 2007 Tax Court Memorandum decision that has not been challenged.[201] Section 199A affects the net income after business expenditures are deducted and, similar to the cost of goods sold analysis, does not affect gross income.

Additionally, Section 199A is not a deduction for business expenses incurred or amounts paid and does not apply at the business-entity level. Instead, it is a deduction at the individual taxpayer level on Qualified Business Income. Therefore, the authors believe that marijuana company owners can be eligible for Section 199A, assuming other normal requirements are met.

---

[201] *Californians Helping to Alleviate Med. Problems, Inc. v. Commissioner*, 128 T.C. 173, 178 n.4 (2007). "In other words, respondent concedes that the disallowance of sec. 280E does not apply to cost of goods sold, a concession that is consistent with the case law on that subject and the legislative history underlying sec. 280E." *See also Olive v. Commissioner*, 139 T.C. 19 (2012).

Chart 11 – Section 280E Effect Chart

This chart displays the effect of Section 280E on business deductions:

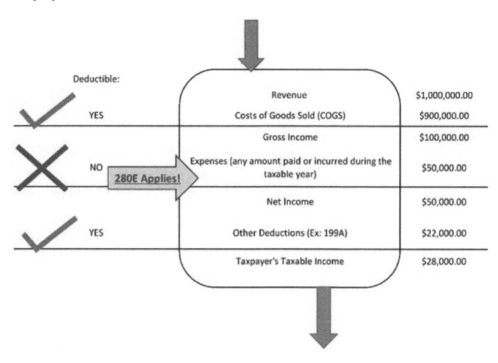

Deductible:

Revenue	$1,000,000.00
Costs of Goods Sold (COGS)	$900,000.00
Gross Income	$100,000.00
Expenses (any amount paid or incurred during the taxable year)	$50,000.00
Net Income	$50,000.00
Other Deductions (Ex: 199A)	$22,000.00
Taxpayer's Taxable Income	$28,000.00

YES
NO — 280E Applies!
YES

G.   ACCOUNTING

The Final Regulations define the performance of services in the field of accounting as "…the provision of services by individuals such as accountants, enrolled agents, return preparers, financial auditors, and similar professionals performing services in their capacity as such."

It is noteworthy that the field of accounting is not limited to traditional accounting services, and includes bookkeeping, tax return preparation, and financial statement preparation. Further, the Preamble to the Final Regulations indicates that even real estate closing agents could be considered to be performing services in the field of accounting, depending upon the facts and circumstances.

PLR 8927006. One of the few Private Letter Rulings on the performance of services in the field of accounting analyzes the definition under Internal Revenue Code Section 448 and may be useful by analogy, when not inconsistent with the Final Regulations. A company that processed computer billing claims for hospitals and doctors and maintained accounts receivables balances with respect to individual patients asked the Service if their business was engaged in the performance of services in the field of accounting or, separately, in the field of health. Relying on an example found in the Regulations for Section 448, the IRS found that a trade or business would not be considered to be engaged in the field of accounting unless it performed audit, financial statement, and tax return preparation services.[202]

This is a much narrower definition of what "accounting services" consists of, and unfortunately, was not adopted by the Final Regulations under Section 199A.

It may be noteworthy, however, the Final Regulations for Section 448, which were issued in 1987, provide the following guidance as to when an entity is engaging in accounting services:

> *"(i) X, a Corporation, is engaged in the business of providing accounting services to its clients. These services consist of the preparation of audit and financial statements and the preparation of tax returns. For purposes of Section 448, such services consist of the performance of services in the field of accounting. In addition, for purposes of Section 448, the supervision of employees directly preparing the statements and returns, and the performance of all administrative and support services incident to such activities (including secretarial, janitorial, purchasing, personnel, security, and payroll services) are the performance of services in the field of accounting.*

> *"(ii) In addition, X owns and leases a portion of an office building. For purposes of this section, the following types of activities undertaken by the employees of X shall be considered as the performance of services in a field other than the field of accounting: (A) services directly relating to the leasing activities, e.g., time spent in leasing and maintaining the leased portion of the building; (B) supervision of employees engaged in directly providing services in the leasing activity; and (C) all administrative and support services incurred incident to services described in (A) and (B). The leasing activities of X are considered the performance of services in a field other than the field of accounting, regardless of whether such leasing activities constitute a trade or business under the Code. If the employees of X spend 95% or more of their time in the performance of services in the field of accounting, X satisfies the function test of paragraph (e)(4) of this section."*

However, the Final Regulations under Section 199A took a much broader view of the accounting industry and specifically included services such as bookkeeping and possibly the preparation of closing statements even though a CPA license is not required. One commenter suggested that "real estate settlement agents" be excluded from the definition. The Treasury declined to adopt this comment and stated in the Preamble to the Final Regulations that "Whether a real estate settlement agent is engaged in the performance of services in the field of accounting depends on the facts and circumstances including the specific services offered and performed by the trade or business."

---

[202] PLR 8927006. *See also* Treas. Reg. § 1.448-1T(e)(5)(vii), Example 1.

Chart Based Upon Regulations Under Section 199A

Activity	Includes	Does Not Include
Accounting	The provision of services by accountants, enrolled agents, return preparers, financial auditors, and similar professionals in their capacity as such accounting is not limited to services requiring state licensure as a certified public accountant (CPA) which includes tax return and bookkeeping services, even though the provision of such services may not require the same education, training, or mastery of accounting principles as a CPA.	Payment processing and billing analysis. The inclusion of bookkeeping services, an activity that does not require the professional training or licensing of a CPA, further illustrates the broad Specified Service Trade or Business view of the Final Regulations.

H.   PERFORMING ARTS

The Final Regulations define the performance of services in the field of performing arts as "the performance of services by individuals who participate in the creation of performing arts, such as actors, singers, musicians, entertainers, directors, and similar professionals performing services in their capacity as such. The definition does not include the provision of services that do not require skills unique to the creation of performing arts, such as the maintenance and operation of equipment or facilities for use in the performing arts. Similarly, it does not include the provision of services by persons who are not involved in the actual performance on stage or otherwise, such as those who broadcast or otherwise disseminate video or audio of performing arts to the public."

The Final Regulations state that broadcasters and the maintenance and operation of facilities where performing arts are performed are not considered to be SSTBs.

By analogy, the Section 448 regulations provide the following guidance on what "engaged in services performed in the field of performing arts" means:

> *"[T]he provision of services by actors, actresses, singers, musicians, entertainers, and similar artists in their capacity as such. The performance of services in the field of the performing arts does not include the provision of services by persons who themselves are not performing artists (e.g., persons who may manage or promote such artists, and other persons in a trade or business that relates to the performing arts). Similarly, the performance of services in the field of the performing arts does not include the provision of services by persons who broadcast or otherwise disseminate the performances of such artists to members of the public (e.g., employees of a radio station that broadcasts the performances of musicians and singers). Finally, the performance of services in the field of the performing arts does not include the provision of services by athletes."[203]*

---

[203] IRC § 1.448-1T(e)(4)(iii).

In a 1994 Technical Advice Memorandum (TAM 9416006), the Service held that a corporation that employs a director of motion pictures and then contracts such director's work out to others was not involved in the performance of services in the field of performing arts under Section 448(d)(2). The Service said that "only persons who perform for an audience will be considered to perform services in the field of performing arts." Simply put, the director's skills did not "involve performing before an audience."

The discussion above mentions that the definition of "performing arts" would not include the activities of a director and presumably backstage hands, makeup artists, camera people, and other professionals who are not themselves "on stage." Unfortunately, the Preamble to the Final Regulations states that the Treasury declined to limit the definition in this manner, and that any individual who is "integral to the creation of the performing arts" would be considered to be in the field of performing arts, and presumably would include directors, editors, stage hands, and others even if they are not "on stage."

The Preamble to the Final Regulations also states that to the extent that a writer is paid for written material that is turned into a performing art (such as a song or screenplay), the writing is performing services in the field of performing arts.

The Final Regulations also contain the following example illustrating that a singer/songwriter is an SSTB:

> A, a singer and songwriter, writes and records a song. A is paid a mechanical royalty when the song is licensed or streamed. A is also paid a performance royalty when the recorded song is played publicly. A is engaged in the performance of services in an SSTB in the field of performing arts within the meaning of Section 199A(d)(2) or paragraphs (b)(1)(v) and (b)(2)(vi) of this Section. The royalties that A receives for the song are not eligible for a deduction under Section 199A.

Chart Based Upon Regulations Under Section 199A

Activity	Includes	Does Not Include
Performing Arts	The performance of services by individuals who participate in the creation of performing arts, such as actors, singers, musicians, entertainers, directors, and similar professionals performing services in their capacity as such.	The provision of services by persons who broadcast or otherwise disseminate video or audio of performing arts to the public. Does not include the performance of services that do not require skills unique to the creation of performing arts, such as maintenance and operation of equipment or facilities used in the performing arts.

I.   CONSULTING

The Final Regulations define the performance of services in the field of consulting as "the provision of professional advice and counsel to clients to assist the client in achieving goals and solving problems. Consulting includes providing advice and counsel regarding advocacy with the intention of influencing decisions made by a government or governmental agency and all attempts to influence legislators and other government officials on behalf of a client by lobbyists and other similar professionals performing services in their capacity as such.

The performance of services in the field of consulting does not include the performance of services other than advice and counsel, such as sales (or economically similar services) or the provision of training and educational courses. For purposes of the preceding sentence, the determination of whether a person's services are sales or economically similar services will be based on all the facts and circumstances of that person's business. Such facts and circumstances include, for example, the manner in which the taxpayer is compensated for the services provided. Consulting also does not include the performance of consulting services embedded in, or ancillary to, the sale of goods or performance of services on behalf of a trade or business that is otherwise not an SSTB (such as typical services provided by a building contractor) if there is no separate payment for the consulting services.

Services "within the fields of architecture and engineering" are not treated as consulting services, and presumably an architect or engineer who provides expert witness testimony would also not be considered a consultant and such income would be eligible for the Section 199A deduction.

> *The Final Regulations specifically included lobbyists in this definition which surprised many commentators. Builders, architects, engineers, and other industries that provide guidance and suggestions before installing products were concerned that this category would taint a portion of the income as being consulting income; however, the Final Regulations include an exception if there was no separate payment for the consulting services. As a result, this may require some businesses to modify their billing practices to incorporate fees for what would otherwise have been separately stated services into the price of the product.*

Further, the Final Regulations specifically exclude architecture and engineering services from being considered "consulting" income.

The Final Regulations include a new example which provides that a temporary employment agency is not considered to be in the field of consulting when compensation to the employees is based on whether the applicants accept employment positions.

The example reads as follows:

> E is an individual who owns and operates a temporary worker staffing firm primarily focused on the software consulting industry. Business clients hire E to provide temporary workers that have the necessary technical skills and experience with a variety of business software to provide consulting and advice regarding the proper selection and operation of software most appropriate for

the business they are advising. E does not have a technical software engineering background and does not provide software consulting advice herself. E reviews resumes and refers candidates to the client when the client indicates a need for temporary workers. E does not evaluate her clients' needs about whether the client needs workers and does not evaluate the clients' consulting contracts to determine the type of expertise needed. Rather, the client provides E with a job description indicating the required skills for the upcoming consulting project. E is paid a fixed fee for each temporary worker actually hired by the client and receives a bonus if that worker is hired permanently within a year of referral. E's fee is not contingent on the profits of its clients. E is not considered to be engaged in the performance of services in the field of consulting within the meaning of Section 199A(d)(2) or (b)(1)(vi) and (b)(2)(vii) of this Section.

Two other examples in the Final Regulations related to the field of consulting are as follows:

Efficiency Consulting Example

D is in the business of "Efficiency Consulting" services that assist unrelated entities in making their personnel structures more efficient. D studies its client's organization and structure and compares it to peers in its industry. D then makes recommendations and provides advice to its client regarding possible changes in the client's personnel structure, including the use of temporary workers. D does not provide any temporary workers to its clients and D's compensation and fees are not affected by whether D's clients used temporary workers to its clients and D's compensation and fees are not affected by whether D's clients used temporary workers. D is engaged in the performance of services in an SSTB in the field of consulting within the meaning of Section 199A(d)(2) or paragraphs (b)(1)(vi) and (b)(2)(vii) of this Section.

Flat Fee Software Sales and Design and Implementation Services

F is in the business of licensing software to customers. F discusses and evaluates the customer's software needs with the customer. The taxpayer advises the customer on the particular software products it licenses. F is paid a flat price for the software license. After the customer licenses the software, F helps to implement the software. F is engaged in the trade or business of licensing software and not engaged in an SSTB in the field of consulting within the meaning of Section 199A(d)(2) or paragraphs (b)(1)(vi) and (b)(2)(vii) of this Section.

Treas. Reg. Section 448-1T may be applied by analogy for the field of consulting and states that:

"[T]he performance of services in the field of consulting means the provision of advice and counsel. The performance of services in the field of consulting does not include the performance of services other than advice and counsel, such as sales or brokerage services, or economically similar services. For purposes of the preceding sentence, the determination of whether a person's services are sales or brokerage services, or economically similar services, shall be based on all the facts and circumstances of that person's business. Such facts and circumstances include, for example, the manner in which the taxpayer is compensated for the services provided (e.g., whether the compensation for the services is contingent upon the consummation of the transaction that the services were intended to effect)."

There are ten examples under Treasury Regulation Section 1.448-T(e)(4)(iv) that can be useful in determining if and when a service is considered to be consulting.[204] The discussion and the examples themselves are as follows:

(B) Examples. The following examples illustrate the provisions of paragraph (e)(4)(iv)(A) of this section. The examples do not address all types of services that may or may not qualify as consulting. The determination of whether activities not specifically addressed in the examples qualify as consulting shall be made by comparing the service activities in question to the types of service activities discussed in the examples. With respect to a corporation which performs services which qualify as consulting under this section, and other services which do not qualify as consulting, see paragraph (e)(4)(i) of this section which requires that substantially all of the corporation's activities involve the performance of services in a qualifying field.

Example 1.

A taxpayer is in the business of providing economic analyses and forecasts of business prospects for its clients. Based on these analyses and forecasts, the taxpayer advises its clients on their business activities. For example, the taxpayer may analyze the economic conditions and outlook for a particular industry which a client is considering entering. The taxpayer will then make recommendations and advise the client on the prospects of entering the industry, as well as on other matters regarding the client's activities in such industry. The taxpayer provides similar services to other clients, involving, for example, economic analyses and evaluations of business prospects in different areas of the United States or in other countries, or economic analyses of overall economic trends and the provision of advice based on these analyses and evaluations. The taxpayer is considered to be engaged in the performance of services in the field of consulting.

---

[204] Treas. Reg. § 1.448-1T(e)(4)(iv).

Example 2.

A taxpayer is in the business of providing services that consist of determining a client's electronic data processing needs. The taxpayer will study and examine the client's business, focusing on the types of data and information relevant to the client and the needs of the client's employees for access to this information. The taxpayer will then make recommendations regarding the design and implementation of data processing systems intended to meet the needs of the client. The taxpayer does not, however, provide the client with additional computer programming services distinct from the recommendations made by the taxpayer with respect to the design and implementation of the client's data processing systems. The taxpayer is considered to be engaged in the performance of services in the field of consulting.

Example 3.

A taxpayer is in the business of providing services that consist of determining a client's management and business structure needs. The taxpayer will study the client's organization, including, for example, the departments assigned to perform specific functions, lines of authority in the managerial hierarchy, personnel hiring, job responsibility, and personnel evaluations and compensation. Based on the study, the taxpayer will then advise the client on changes in the client's management and business structure, including, for example, the restructuring of the client's departmental systems or its lines of managerial authority. The taxpayer is considered to be engaged in the performance of services in the field of consulting.

Example 4.

A taxpayer is in the business of providing financial planning services. The taxpayer will study a particular client's financial situation, including, for example, the client's present income, savings and investments, and anticipated future economic and financial needs. Based on this study, the taxpayer will then assist the client in making decisions and plans regarding the client's financial activities. Such financial planning includes the design of a personal budget to assist the client in monitoring the client's financial situation, the adoption of investment strategies tailored to the client's needs, and other similar services. The taxpayer is considered to be engaged in the performance of services in the field of consulting.

Example 5.

A taxpayer is in the business of executing transactions for customers involving various types of securities or commodities generally traded through organized exchanges or other similar networks. The taxpayer provides its clients with economic analyses and forecasts of conditions in various industries and businesses. Based on these analyses, the taxpayer makes recommendations regarding transactions in securities and commodities. Clients place orders with the taxpayer to trade securities or commodities based on the taxpayer's recommendations. The taxpayer's compensation for its services is typically based on the trade orders. The taxpayer is not considered to be engaged in the performance of services in the field of consulting. The taxpayer is engaged in brokerage services. Relevant to this determination is the fact that the compensation of the taxpayer for its services is contingent upon the consummation of the transaction the services were intended to effect (i.e., the execution of trade orders for its clients).

Example 6.

A taxpayer is in the business of studying a client's needs regarding its data processing facilities and making recommendations to the client regarding the design and implementation of data processing systems. The client will then order computers and other data processing equipment through the taxpayer based on the taxpayer's recommendations. The taxpayer's compensation for its services is typically based on the equipment orders made by the clients. The taxpayer is not considered to be engaged in the performance of services in the field of consulting. The taxpayer is engaged in the performance of sales services. Relevant to this determination is the fact that the compensation of the taxpayer for its services is contingent upon the consummation of the transaction the services were intended to effect (i.e., the execution of equipment orders for its clients).

Example 7.

A taxpayer is in the business of assisting businesses in meeting their personnel requirements by referring job applicants to employers with hiring needs in a particular area. The taxpayer may be informed by potential employers of their need for job applicants, or, alternatively, the taxpayer may become aware of the client's personnel requirements after the taxpayer studies and examines the client's management and business structure. The taxpayer's compensation for its services is typically based on the job applicants, referred by the taxpayer to the clients, who accept employment positions with the clients. The taxpayer is not considered to be engaged in the performance of services in the field of consulting. The taxpayer is involved in the performance of services economically similar to brokerage services. Relevant to this determination is the fact that the compensation of the taxpayer for its services is contingent upon the consummation of the transaction the services were intended to effect (i.e., the hiring of a job applicant by the client).

Example 8.

The facts are the same as in Example 7, except that the taxpayer's clients are individuals who use the services of the taxpayer to obtain employment positions. The taxpayer is typically compensated by its clients who obtain employment as a result of the taxpayer's services. For the reasons set forth in Example 7, the taxpayer is not considered to be engaged in the performance of services in the field of consulting.

Example 9.

A taxpayer is in the business of assisting clients in placing advertisements for their goods and services. The taxpayer analyzes the conditions and trends in the client's particular industry, and then makes recommendations to the client regarding the types of advertisements which should be placed by the client and the various types of advertising media (e.g., radio, television, magazines, etc.) which should be used by the client. The client will then purchase, through the taxpayer, advertisements in various media based on the taxpayer's recommendations. The taxpayer's compensation for its services is typically based on the particular orders for advertisements which the client makes. The taxpayer is not considered to be engaged in the performance of services in the field of consulting. The taxpayer is engaged in the performance of services economically similar to brokerage services. Relevant to this determination is the fact that the compensation of the taxpayer for its services is contingent upon the consummation of the transaction the services were intended to effect (i.e., the placing of advertisements by clients).

Example 10.

A taxpayer is in the business of selling insurance (including life and casualty insurance), annuities, and other similar insurance products to various individual and business clients. The taxpayer will study the particular client's financial situation, including, for example, the client's present income, savings and investments, business and personal insurance risks, and anticipated future economic and financial needs. Based on this study, the taxpayer will then make recommendations to the client regarding the desirability of various insurance products. The client will then purchase these various insurance products through the taxpayer. The taxpayer's compensation for its services is typically based on the purchases made by the clients. The taxpayer is not considered to be engaged in the performance of services in the field of consulting. The taxpayer is engaged in the performance of brokerage or sales services. Relevant to this determination is the fact that the compensation of the taxpayer for its services is contingent upon the consummation of the transaction the services were intended to effect (i.e., the purchase of insurance products by its clients).

It is unclear from the above example and the Regulations as to whether fee-for-service life insurance income will qualify as being income from the sale of insurance under Section 199A. It is ironic that commissioned income is often criticized, while fee-for-service revenues are less commonly criticized but may be taxed less advantageously.

Chart Based Upon Regulations Under Section 199A

Activity	Includes	Does Not Include
Consulting	The provision of professional advice and counsel to clients to assist the client in achieving goals and solving	The performance of services other than advice and counsel. This determination is made based on all

Activity	Includes	Does Not Include
	problems...includes providing advice and counsel regarding advocacy with the intention of influencing decisions made by a government or governmental agency and all attempts to influence legislators and other government officials on behalf of a client by lobbyists and other similar professionals performing services in their capacity as such.	the facts and circumstances of a person's business. Does not include the performance of services in the field of consulting services embedded in, or ancillary to, the sale of goods or performance of services on behalf of a trade or business.

J. ATHLETICS

The Final Regulations define the performance of services in the field of athletics as:

> *The performance of services by individuals who participate in athletic competition such as athletes, coaches, and team managers in sports such as baseball, basketball, football, soccer, hockey, martial arts, boxing, bowling, tennis, golf, skiing, snowboarding, track and field, billiards, and racing. The performance of services in the field of athletics does not include the provision of services that do not require skills unique to athletic competition, such as the maintenance and operation of equipment or facilities for use in athletic events. Similarly, the performance of services in the field of athletics does not include the provision of services by persons who broadcast or otherwise disseminate video or audio of athletic events to the public. Fees that are paid to the athletic organization for the right to broadcast in audio and video will be SSTB income; but a separate business that pays such fees to the SSTB, employs commentators and makes a profit from broadcasting, it will not be an SSTB, although the "performers" who act as commentators are providing SSTB services.*

Commentators suggested that the performance of services in the field of athletics be limited to athletes and the athletes' personal service companies. The Treasury declined to adopt this comment and stated that the trade or business of owning a sports team or professional sports club would be considered an SSTB, including ticket sales and broadcast rights. The Preamble does discuss that a sports team may operate more than one trade or business and states that concession services generally would not be considered an SSTB. As a result, owners of athletic teams will want to make sure that concession stand and merchandise sales, maintenance and operation of equipment and facilities are separated from ticket sale and broadcast right revenues if they are profitable.

The Final Regulations also include the following example:

C is a partner in Partnership, which solely owns and operates a professional sports team. Partnership employs athletes and sells tickets and broadcast rights for games in which the sports team competes. Partnership sells the broadcast rights to Broadcast LLC, a separate trade or business. Broadcast LLC solely broadcasts the games. Partnership is engaged in the performance of services in an SSTB in the field of athletics within the meaning of Section 199A(d)(2) or paragraphs (b)(1)(vii) and (b)(2)(viii) of this Section. The tickets sales and the sale of the broadcast rights are both the performance of services in the field of athletics. C is a passive owner in Partnership and C does not provide any services with respect to Partnership or the sports team. However, because Partnership is engaged in an SSTB in the field of athletics, C's distributive share of the income, gain, deduction, and loss with respect to Partnership is not eligible for a deduction under Section 199A. Broadcast LLC is not engaged in the performance of services in an SSTB in the field of athletics.

Chart Based Upon Regulations Under Section 199A

Activity	Includes	Does Not Include
Athletics	Is most similar to the field of performing arts provides that the term "performance of services in the field of athletics" means the performances of services by individuals who participate in athletic competition such as athletes, coaches, and team managers in sports such as baseball, basketball, football, soccer, hockey, martial arts, boxing, bowling, tennis, golf, skiing, snowboarding, track and field, billiards, and racing.	The provision of services that do not require skills unique to athletic competition, such as the maintenance and operation of equipment or facilities for use in athletic events; the provision of services by persons who broadcast or otherwise disseminate video or audio of athletic events to the public. It is noteworthy that an IRS spokesperson indicated that coaches will be considered to be engaged in athletics.

K. ACTUARIAL SCIENCE

The Final Regulations define the performance of services in the field of Actuarial Science as the provision of services by individuals such as actuaries and similar professionals performing services in their capacity as such.

The Preambles to both the Proposed and Final Regulations indicate that "the field of actuarial science does not include the provision of services by analysts, economists, mathematicians, and statisticians not engaged in analyzing or assessing the financial cost of risk or uncertainty of events."

Further, the Preamble to the Final Regulations states that "the mere employment of an actuary does not itself cause a trade or business to be treated as performing services in the field of actuarial science," and that whether a trade or business is providing actuarial services depends upon the particular facts and circumstances.

It is noteworthy that commentators requested that businesses that do not separately bill for actuarial services but employ actuaries, such as when the insurance industry has actuaries determine risk and appropriate rates, would not be considered to be performing services in the field of actuarial science similar to the rule that applies for consulting. The Treasury declined to adopt this comment and stated that "Section 199A looks to the trade or business of performing services rather than the performance of services themselves," and provide in other SSTB definitions that the insurance industry will not be considered an SSTB.

With reference to the above narrow definition of actuarial science under the Final Regulations, it appears that actuaries, who work to analyze patient arrangements and provide pension plans and actuarial reports and similar services associated therewith, will not be considered to be engaged in "actuarial science," but they may be considered to be consultants or practicing in the fields of law/accounting.

Chart Based Upon Regulations Under Section 199A

Activity	Includes	Does Not Include
Actuarial Science	Is based on the ordinary meaning "actuarial science" and provides that the term "performance of services in the field of actuarial science" means payment processing and billing analysis.	The provision of services by analysts, economists, mathematicians, and statisticians not engaged in analyzing or assessing the financial costs of risk or uncertainty of events.

L. FINANCIAL SERVICES

The Final Regulations define performance of services in the field of financial services as the provision of financial services to clients including managing wealth, advising clients with respect to finances, developing retirement plans, developing wealth transition plans, the provision of advisory and other similar services regarding valuations, mergers, acquisitions, dispositions, restructurings (including in Title 11 of the Code or similar cases), and raising financial capital by underwriting, or acting as a client's agent in the issuance of securities and similar services. This includes services provided by financial advisors, investment bankers, wealth planners, retirement advisors, and other similar professionals performing services in their capacity as such. Solely for purposes of Section 199A, the performance of services in the field of financial services does not include taking deposits or making loans but does include arranging lending transactions between a lender and borrower.

The Preamble to the Final Regulations states that insurance, including the commissioned based sale of life insurance, will not be considered an SSTB. The Preamble discusses that the reasoning behind this exclusion is that Section 199A only defines SSTBs as those listed in

Section 1202(e)(3)(A), and insurance is listed under Section 1202(e)(3)(B); so insurance "cannot be considered a financial service for purposes of Section 199A." Based upon this reasoning, it appears that the following industries are not listed in Section 1202(e)(3)(A), but are mentioned in other Sections of Section 1202 and, therefore, presumably are not considered to be SSTBs:

    (1)   Banking, financing, leasing, or other similar business.

    (2)   Farming businesses (including the business of raising or harvesting trees).

    (3)   Oil, gas, coal, and other businesses involving the production or extraction of minerals

    (4)   The operating of a hotel, motel, restaurant, or similar business.

The Preamble to the Final Regulations specifically discusses that the commissioned based sale of life insurance products is not considered to be an SSTB:

> *The Treasury Department and the IRS decline to categorically exclude services provided by insurance agents from the definition of financial services as financial services such as managing wealth, advising clients with respect to finances, and the provision of advisory and other similar services that can be provided by insurance agents. However, the Treasury Department and the IRS note that the provision of these services to the extent that they are ancillary to the <u>commission-based sale of an insurance policy</u> will generally not be considered the provision of financial services for purposes of Section 199A.*

The Final Regulations contain the below examples that provide further guidance for financial planners:

> G is in the business of providing services to assist clients with their finances. G will study a particular client's financial situation, including, the client's present income, savings, and investments, and anticipated future economic and financial needs. Based on this study, G will then assist the client in making decisions and plans regarding the client's financial activities. Such financial planning includes the design of a personal budget to assist the client in monitoring the client's financial situation, the adoption of investment strategies tailored to the client's needs, and other similar services. G is engaged in the performance of services in an SSTB in the field of financial services within the meaning of Section 199A(d)(2) or paragraphs (b)(1)(viii) and (b)(2)(ix) of this Section.

The second example indicates that a franchisor will not be considered to be an SSTB, even if the type of business franchised is an SSTB.

> H is in the business of franchising a brand of personal financial planning offices, which generally provide personal wealth management, retirement planning, and other financial advice services to customers for a fee. H does not provide

financial planning services itself. H licenses the right to use the business tradename, other branding intellectual property, and a marketing plan to third-party financial planner franchisees that operate the franchised locations and provide all services to customers. In exchange, the franchisees compensate H based on a fee structure, which includes a one-time fee to acquire the franchise. H is not engaged in the performance of services in the field of financial services within the meaning of Section 199A(d)(2) or paragraphs (b)(1)(viii) and (b)(2)(ix) of this Section.

Chart Based Upon Regulations Under Section 199A

Activity	Includes	Does Not Include
Financial Services	Limits the definition of financial services to services typically performed by financial advisors and investment bankers and provides that the field of financial services includes the provision of financial services to clients including managing wealth, advising clients with respect to finances, developing retirement plans, developing wealth transition plans, the provision of advisory and other similar services regarding valuations, mergers, acquisitions, dispositions, restructurings (including in Title 11 or similar cases), and raising financial capital by underwriting, or acting as the client's agent in the issuance of securities, and similar services... services provided by financial advisors, investment bankers, wealth planners, and retirement advisors and other similar professionals.	Taking deposits or making loans. Please note that interest earned on notes owed by customers or on notes receivable resulting from the financed sale of products to customers will be included in Section 199A income, but that normal interest income earned on accounts owned by a trade or business will not.

M.   BROKERAGE SERVICES

The Final Regulations define performance of services in the field of brokerage services as services in which a person arranges transactions between a buyer and a seller with respect to securities (as defined in Section 475(c)(2)) for a commission or fee. This includes services provided by stockbrokers and other similar professionals but does not include services provided by real estate or life insurance agents and brokers.

While the definition provided in the Final Regulations specifically excludes real estate agents and brokers, it does not exclude arranging lending transactions between a lender and a borrower. Therefore, a mortgage broker will be considered to be an SSTB.

The Preamble to the Final Regulations also states that the definition of brokers is not solely limited to stockbrokers and includes all services in which a person arranges transactions between a buyer and seller with respect to "securities (as defined in Section 475(c)(2))" for a commission or fee. Section 475(c)(2) defines securities as any:

1. Share of stock in a corporation;

2. Partnership or beneficial ownership interest in a widely held or publicly traded partnership or trust;

3. Note, bond, debenture, or other evidence of indebtedness;

4. Interest rate, currency, or equity notional principal contract;

5. Evidence of an interest in, or a derivative financial instrument in, any security described [above], or any currency, including any option, forward contract, short position, and any similar financial instrument in such a security or currency; and

6. Any position which—

   A. is not a security described [above];

   B. is a hedge with respect to such a security; and

   C. is clearly identified in the dealer's records as being described [above] before the close of the day on which it was acquired or entered into (or such other time as the Secretary may by regulations prescribe).

The Final Regulations contain the following example to illustrate the above:

> J is in the business of executing transactions for customers involving various types of securities or commodities generally traded through organized exchanges or other similar networks. Customers place orders with J to trade securities or commodities based on the taxpayer's recommendations. J's compensation for its services typically is based on completion of the trade orders. J is engaged in an SSTB in the field of brokerage services within the meaning of Section 199A(d)(2) or paragraphs (b)(1)(ix) and (b)(2)(x) of this Section.

1. **INVESTING, TRADING, OR DEALING IN SECURITIES, PARTNERSHIP INTERESTS, OR COMMODITIES.**

Performance of Services That Consist of Investing and Investment Management. The Final Regulations define this SSTB as a trade or business involving the receipt of fees for providing, investing, asset management, or investment management services, including providing advice with respect to buying and selling investments.

The Final Regulations go on to state that this term does not include directly managing real property.

Performance of Services That Consist of Trading. The Final Regulations define this term as the trade or business of trading in securities (as defined in Section 475(c)(2)), commodities (as defined in Section 475(e)(2)), or partnership interests.

Determining whether a person is a trader in securities, commodities, or partnership interests will rely heavily on the relevant facts and circumstances for each individual case and will include the source and type of profit that is associated with engaging in the activity regardless of the fact that a person is trading for their own account, an account for other persons, or a combination of both.

Performance of Services That Consist of Dealing in Securities. The Final Regulations define this term as regularly purchasing securities from and selling securities to customers in the ordinary course of a trade or business or regularly offering to enter into, assume, offset, assign, or otherwise terminate positions in securities with customers in the ordinary course of a trade or business.

Due to several concerns from commentators, the Final Regulations state that the performance of services to originate a loan does not equate to the purchase of a security from the borrower when determining if the lender is dealing in securities.

Performance of Services That Consist of Dealing in Commodities. The Final Regulations define this as regularly purchasing commodities from and selling commodities to customers in the ordinary course of a trade or business or regularly offering to enter into, assume, offset, assign, or otherwise terminate positions in commodities with customers in the ordinary course of a trade or business.[205]

The Preamble to the Final Regulations addresses commentators' concerns over the limitation to this term, and in response, the IRS and the Treasury Department have limited the definition of dealing in commodities to a trade or business that deals in financial instruments or otherwise does not engage in substantial activities with respect to physical commodities, as well as adopting rules that "qualified active sales" of commodities are not taken into account in determining whether a taxpayer is dealing in commodities. A qualified active sale requires a trade or business to both (1) be engaged in the active conduct of a commodities business as a producer, processor, merchant, or handler of commodities and (2) to perform certain activities with respect to those commodities, but only if both of the following requirements are met:

1.   The trade or business directly holds the commodities as inventory or similar property.

---

[205] Under IRC 475(e)(2)(2), "commodity" means:
     (A)   any commodity which is actively traded (within the meaning of section 1092(d)(1));
     (B)   any notional principal contract with respect to any commodity described in subparagraph (A);
     (C)   any evidence of an interest in, or a derivative instrument in, any commodity described in subparagraph (A) or (B), including any option, forward contract, futures contract, short position, and any similar instrument in such a commodity; and
     (D)   any position which –
          (i) is not a commodity described in subparagraph (A), (B) or (C),
          (ii) is a hedge with respect to such commodity, and
          (iii) is clearly identified in the taxpayer's records as being described in this subparagraph before the close of the day on which it was acquired or entered into (or such other time as the Secretary may be regulations prescribe).

This is defined as "property that is stock in trade of the trade or business or other property of a kind that would properly be included in the inventory of the trade or business if on hand at the close of the taxable year, or property held by the trade or business primarily for sale to customers in the ordinary course of its trade or business."

2.   The trade or business "incurs substantial expenses in the ordinary course" of the commodities trade or business, or the commodities trade or business "performs significant activities" with respect to the commodities.

The Final Regulations define the term "incurs substantial expenses in the ordinary course" as directly engaging in one or both of the following activities, not through an agent or independent contractor:

A.   Substantial activities in the production of the commodities, including planting, tending or harvesting crops, raising or slaughtering livestock, or extracting minerals; or

B.   Substantial processing activities prior to the sale of the commodities, including the blending and drying of agricultural commodities, or the concentrating, refining, mixing, crushing, aerating, or milling of commodities.

"Performing significant activities" is defined as:

A.   The physical movement, handling and storage of the commodities, including preparation of contracts and invoices, arranging transportation, insurance and credit, arranging for receipt, transfer or negotiation of shipping documents, arranging storage or warehousing, and dealing with quality claims;

B.   Owning and operating facilities for storage or warehousing; or

C.   Owning, chartering, or leasing vessels or vehicles for the transportation of the commodities.

Hedging transactions entered into in the normal course of a business, such as when farmers and manufacturers contract to be assured that what they receive or pay for a specific commodity will not be a Specified Service Trade or Business.

It is noteworthy that Section 199A defines "commodities" by reference to Internal Revenue Code Section 475(e)(2), which provides that the term "commodity" means:

(1)   any commodity which is actively traded (within the meaning of Section 1092(d)(1));

(2)   any notional principal contract with respect to any commodity described in (1) above;

(3)   any evidence of an interest in, or a derivative instrument in, any commodity described in (1) or (2) above, including any option, forward contract, future

contract, short position, and any similar instrument in such a commodity; and

(4)   any position which-

    (a)   is not a commodity described in (1), (2) or (3) above;

    (b)   is a hedge with respect to such commodity; and

    (c)   is clearly identified in the taxpayer's records as being described in this subsection (4) before the close of the day on which it was acquired or entered into (or such other time as the Secretary may by regulations prescribe).

The Final Regulations deleted the specific exclusion in the Proposed Regulations that applied for farmers and manufacturers that engaged in hedging transactions; however these transactions should be excluded from SSTB status as a qualified active sale since they are entered into in the normal course of the business as discussed above.

Performance of Services That Consist of Dealing in Partnership Interests. The Final Regulations state that this term refers to regularly purchasing and selling partnership interests to customers in the ordinary course of a trade or business or regularly offering to enter into, assume, offset, assign, or otherwise terminate positions in partnership interests with customers in the ordinary course of a trade or business.

Chart Based Upon Regulations Under Section 199A

Activity	Includes	Does Not Include
Brokerage Services	The performance of services in the field of brokerage services includes services in which a person arranges transactions between a buyer and a seller with respect to securities for a commission or fee. This includes services provided by stockbrokers and other similar professionals.	Does not include services provided by real estate agents and brokers, or life insurance agents and brokers
Investment Management	The performance of services that consist of investing and investment management refers to a trade or business involving the receipt of fees for providing investing, asset management, or investment management services, including providing advice with respect to buying and selling investments.	The performance of services of investing and investment management does not include directly managing real property.
Trading Services	The performance of services that consist of trading means a trade or business of trading in securities, commodities, or partnership interests. Whether a person is a trader in securities, commodities, or partnership interests is determined by taking into account all relevant facts and circumstances, including the source and type of profit that is associated with engaging in the activity regardless of whether that person trades for the person's own account, for the account of others, or any combination thereof.	A taxpayer who engages in hedging transactions as part of their business is not considered to be engaged in the trade or business of trading commodities.
Dealing in Securities	The performance of services that consist of dealing in securities means regularly purchasing securities from and selling securities to customers in the ordinary course of a trade or business or regularly offering to enter into, assume, offset, assign, or otherwise terminate positions in securities with customers in the ordinary course of a trade or business.	A taxpayer that regularly originates loans ("lenders") in the ordinary course of a trade or business of making loans but engages in no more than negligible sales of the loans is not dealing in securities.
Dealing in Commodities	The performance of services that consist of dealing in commodities means regularly purchasing commodities from and selling commodities to customers in the ordinary course	A taxpayer who engages in hedging transactions as part of their business (specifically including

Activity	Includes	Does Not Include
	of a trade or business or regularly offering to enter into, assume, offset, assign, or otherwise terminate positions in commodities with customers in the ordinary course of a trade or business.	farming and manufacturing) is not considered to be engaged in the trade or business of trading commodities.

2. BUSINESSES WHERE THE PRINCIPAL ASSET IS THE REPUTATION OR SKILL OF ONE OR MORE OF ITS EMPLOYEES OR OWNERS.

This category of SSTB also comes from Section 1202 and has been significantly reduced in scope by the Final Regulations, which are almost identical to the Proposed Regulations, and generally provide that engineers and architects will never be considered to be under this category.

The Final Regulations define this as any trade or business that consists of any of the following (or any combination thereof):

(A)   Receiving fees, compensation, or other income for endorsing products or services,

(B)   Receiving license fees, compensation, or other income for the use of an individual's image, likeness, name, signature, voice, trademark, or any other symbols associated with the individual's identity,

(C)   Receiving fees, compensation, or other income for appearing at an event or on radio, television, or another media format.

For purposes of (A) through (C) above, the term "fees, compensation, and other income" includes the receipt of a partnership or S corporation ownership and the corresponding distributive share of income therefrom when it is the result of one or more of the categories set forth above.

The Final Regulations provide two examples that provide guidance on when a taxpayer may fall under this category of SSTBs:

Example 1:

L is a well-known chef and the sole owner of multiple restaurants each of which is owned in a disregarded entity. Due to L's skill and reputation as a chef, L receives an endorsement fee of $500,000 for the use of L's name on a line of cooking utensils and cookware. L is in the trade or business of being a chef and owning restaurants and such trade or business is not an SSTB. However, L is also in the trade or business of receiving endorsement income. L's trade or business consisting of the receipt of the endorsement fee for L's skill and/or reputation is an SSTB within the meaning of Section 199A(d)(2) or paragraphs (b)(1)(xiii) and (b)(2)(xiv) of this Section.

Example 2:

M is a well-known actor. M entered into a partnership with Shoe Company, in which M contributed her likeness and the use of her name to the partnership in exchange for a 50% interest in the partnership and a guaranteed payment. M's trade or business consisting of the receipt of the partnership interest and the corresponding distributive share with respect to the partnership interest for M's likeness and the use of her name is an SSTB within the meaning of Section 199A(d)(2) or paragraphs (b)(1)(xiii) and (b)(2)(xiv) of this Section.

There is further guidance in the 2012 Tax Court decision of *Owen v. Commissioner*, which is also discussed in Chapter 8. The IRS argued that Mr. Owen's skills were a principal asset of a company attempting to take the Section 1202 exclusion on the sale of stock, but the Tax Court disagreed, concluding that "the principal asset of the companies was the training and organizational structure" because "the independent contractors, including [the owners] in their commission sales hats, ... earned the premiums" and that the owners in their personal capacities were not the principal asset. Therefore, the company was properly characterized as a qualified trade or business under Section 1202(e)(3). The same result should apply under Section 199A since the definition of Specified Service comes directly from Section 1202(e)(3).

PART TWO –
MANAGING SSTB AND NON-SSTB INCOME AND MULTIPLE TRADES OR BUSINESSES

The Final Regulations Confirm That All General Activities and Assets Typically Associated with the Operation of an SSTB Will Be Considered a Part of the SSTB, with Very Few Exceptions.

For example, a law practice will include the building, personnel, and management of the practice, but may exclude stenography and delivery activities. Copying was not mentioned but would seem to be a possible non-SSTB service, along with trustee and personal representative services, and title insurance work that does not have extensive accounting functions.

A. WHEN AN ENTITY WITH PRIMARILY SSTB INCOME HAS A SMALL AMOUNT OF NON-SSTB INCOME

The Proposed Regulations contained an "incidental" 5% level threshold that was not adopted by the Final Regulations, which now permit any percentage of non-SSTB income to be segregated and not subject to the SSTB limitations if the requirements below can be met.

The Final Regulations provide that any amount of non-SSTB products or services can qualify as non-SSTB income.[206]

In order to treat the non-SSTB activity as being separate and apart from the SSTB, the non-SSTB activity must be a trade or business on its own under Code Section 162, which requires that an activity be carried on regularly and continuously with the intent of making a profit. If the non-SSTB activity can be considered a separate trade or business on its own, then the books and records of the company must be "separable" to enable the non-SSTB activities to qualify for the Section 199A deduction, as discussed in more detail below.

1. THE DE MINIMIS EXCEPTION APPLIES WHEN AN ENTITY WITH MOSTLY NON-SSTB INCOME HAS LESS THAN 10% SSTB REVENUES (5% IF GROSS RECEIPTS EXCEED $25 MILLION).

Under the Final Regulations, an entity having 10% or less in SSTB revenue will not be considered to be an SSTB as long as more than 90% of the entity's gross receipts comes from non-SSTB activities. This is known as the "*de minimis* exception." Under this rule, if gross receipts from the SSTB total less than 10% of the gross receipts of the entity, then the SSTB income can be disregarded and will not cause the entity to be treated as an SSTB. If the annual receipts for the entity are more than $25 million, then this *de minimis* threshold falls to 5%.

For example, if the revenue coming from a consultant, who works for a manufacturer, is less than 10% of the total combined revenue of the manufacturer and the consultant, then the exception

---

[206] Under the Proposed Regulations non-SSTB products or services offered by a company or affiliated entity under common ownership would be considered to be SSTB services unless they exceeded 5% of the revenues of the combined SSTB and non-SSTB.

would apply, and the manufacturing firm would not be treated as engaging in the field of consulting.

If, however, the consulting activity exceeds the 10% *de minimis* threshold, then the consulting revenue would taint all of the manufacturing firm's income because it must be treated as an SSTB unless the consulting part of the business is treated as a separate trade or business as discussed below. This is illustrated in the following example under the Final Regulations:

> Landscape LLC sells lawn care and landscaping equipment and also provides advice and counsel on landscape design for large office parks and residential buildings. The landscape design services include advice on the selection and placement of trees, shrubs, and flowers and are considered to be the performance of services in the field of consulting under paragraphs (b)(1)(vi) and (b)(2)(vii) of this section. Landscape LLC separately invoices for its landscape design services and does not sell the trees, shrubs, or flowers it recommends for use in the landscape design. Landscape LLC maintains one set of books and records and treats the equipment sales and design services as a single trade or business for purposes of Sections 162 and 199A. Landscape LLC has gross receipts of $2 million.
>
> $250,000 of gross receipts is attributable to the landscape design services, an SSTB. Because the gross receipts from the consulting services exceed 10 percent of Landscape LLC's total gross receipts, the entirety of Landscape LLC's trade or business is considered an SSTB.

Even though the majority of the business is derived from a non-SSTB activity, and such activity is separately invoiced, the entire business is treated as an SSTB, because the consulting revenue exceeds 10% of the gross receipts of the entity. This is extremely harsh; and as a result, taxpayers need to carefully examine all aspects of their businesses and activities in order to determine if one or more of its activities or functions need to be separated in order to avoid the SSTB taint.

The chart shown below will be helpful to the reader when reviewing the discussion that follows:

Separating SSTB and Non-SSTB Income

Type of Business	Percentage of SSTB Gross Receipts When Divided by Total Gross Receipts	Are Separable Books and Records Maintained*	Tax Treatment
Mainly Non-SSTB *De minimis* **Rule**	Under 10% of gross receipts, provided that if total gross receipts exceed $25 million, then under 5%.	Does not affect treatment.	All income is treated as non-SSTB income.
Over 10% Non-SSTB (or 5% if total gross receipts exceed $25 million)	Over 10% with gross receipts under $25 million or over 5% with gross receipts over $25 million.	No separable books and records.	All income is treated as SSTB income.
Mainly Non-SSTB	Over 10% with gross receipts under $25 million or over 5% with gross receipts over $25 million.	Books and records are separable.	The taxpayer may treat non-SSTB income as non-SSTB if books and records are "separable."
Mainly SSTB	Does not affect treatment.	If maintained, separable books and records.	All non-SSTB income is treated as non-SSTB income.
Mainly SSTB	Does not affect treatment.	No separable books and records.	All income is treated as SSTB income.

*The Final Regulations can be read to require separate books and records, but most likely separable will be sufficient, as further discussed below.

Discussion

These Regulations are logical and can be adhered to by most taxpayers, but it will not be easy to implement what is required. This will certainly be an inconvenience, if not a significant obstacle, for many businesses.

Although not specifically mentioned in the statute or the Final Regulations, each example that allows taxpayers to separate SSTB and non-SSTB income indicates that the taxpayer in the example maintained separate books and records for non-SSTB and SSTB activities, with no discussion as to whether the books and records were required to have been separately kept, or could have been "separable." The examples that permitted such segregation also made mention that the separate activities were treated as separate businesses by the taxpayer.

Many believe that the drafters of the Regulations thought that the Section 446 Regulations required separate books and records, but then discovered that this was not the case, and did not see the change of the language of the Preamble to match the Final Regulations, which points out that the Internal Revenue Code Section 446 Regulations provide that a trade or business will not be considered as separate and distinct from another trade or business "unless a complete and separable set of books and records is kept for that trade or business," as per the following language in the Final Regulations:

> *The Treasury Department and the IRS also believe that multiple trades or businesses will generally not exist within an entity unless different methods of accounting could be used for each trade or business under §1.446-1(d).* **_Section 1.446- 1(d) explains that no trade or business is considered separate and distinct unless a complete and separable set of books and records is kept for that trade or business_**. *Further, trades or businesses will not be considered separate and distinct if, by reason of maintaining different methods of accounting, there is a creation or shifting of profits and losses between the businesses of the taxpayer so that income of the taxpayer is not clearly reflected.*

In an April 4, 2019 ABA webinar, Audrey Ellis of the Office of Tax Policy of the Treasury apologized for the confusion and stated that separate books and records do not actually have to be maintained as long as they are separable, meaning that an accountant would be able to create separate books and records in the future to verify the proper allocation of income and expenses that was used. The ABA has since requested in a June 27, 2019 comment letter that the provision requiring separate books to be maintained to reflect income and expenses for each rental real estate enterprise under the Revenue Procedure described in Chapter 12 be modified to require that if the enterprise has more than one property, maintaining income and expense information statements separately for each property, which are consolidated, should be sufficient to satisfy the "separable books and records" requirement, because taxpayers typically maintain their books on a property-by-property basis.

As a practical matter, as further discussed below, it seems that until further guidance is issued with respect to this, taxpayers will be safer maintaining separate books and records so that it is clear that the identities of SSTB and non-SSTB activities are separate and well organized.

It is noteworthy that the below described example in the Final Regulations mentions that the non-SSTB activity has separate employees that are not affiliated with the SSTB activity, and that the taxpayer has treated each activity as a separate trade or business in all respects, although these additional formalities do not appear to be required under the Section 446 Regulations cited above. The example reads as follows:

> Animal Care LLC provides veterinarian services performed by licensed staff and also develops and sells its own line of organic dog food at its veterinarian clinic and online. The veterinarian services are considered to be the performance of services in the field of health under paragraphs (b)(1)(i) and (b)(2)(ii) of this

section. Animal Care LLC separately invoices for its veterinarian services and the sale of its organic dog food. Animal Care LLC maintains separate books and records for its veterinarian clinic and its development and sale of its dog food. Animal Care LLC also has separate employees who are unaffiliated with the veterinary clinic and who only work on the formulation, marketing, sales, and distribution of the organic dog food products. Animal Care LLC treats its veterinary practice and the dog food development and sales as separate trades or businesses for purposes of Section 162 and 199A. Animal Care LLC has gross receipts of $3,000,000. $1,000,000 of the gross receipts is attributable to the veterinary services, an SSTB. Although the gross receipts from the services in the field of health exceed 10 percent of Animal Care LLC's total gross receipts, the dog food development and sales business is not considered an SSTB due to the fact that the veterinary practice and the dog food development and sales are separate trades or businesses under Section 162.

Under Section 446 of the Internal Revenue Code, a taxpayer may use different accounting methods for multiple trades or businesses, such as using the cash method of accounting in one business and the accrual method of accounting in another. Alternatively, a taxpayer with a single trade or business may only use one method for accounting. This requirement has been highlighted by several court decisions.

In some cases, it can be fairly easy to determine whether the IRS will consider two businesses as separate and distinct if they are in completely different lines of business. For example, in the 1928 case of *Stern*, the petitioners were partners under the firm name of Stern Brothers that carried on two businesses – one business operated two retail stores and the other business bought and sold coal lands.[207] The Board of Tax Appeals held that the businesses were separate and distinct by reasoning that the two businesses were "wholly different in character."

The determination can be much more difficult, however, when the businesses are similar or different divisions operated primarily for the purposes of transactions between the divisions.

The Courts have used the following factors to determine if a taxpayer has multiple trades or businesses:

1.   Whether the trades or businesses are commonly managed.

2.   Whether the taxpayer holds each trade or business out as a separate trade or business.

3.   Whether separate bank accounts are maintained.

4.   Whether the trades or businesses share common employees.

---

[207] *Stern v. Commissioner*, 14 B.T.A. 838 (1928).

5.   The nature of each trade or business.[208]

In *Peterson Produce Co.*, the District Court determined that the corporate taxpayer was unsuccessful in attempting to use difference accounting methods for different divisions of the corporation.[209] The taxpayer used the accrual method for the feed and hatchery divisions of the poultry corporation and the cash method for the broiler division. The District Court reasoned that the broiler division was not a separate and distinct business from the feed and hatchery divisions. In this case, the feed and hatchery divisions operated almost solely to transfer feed and young chickens to the broiler division at cost. Although the general ledger accounts of the three divisions could be separated, the original and daily entries could not be physically separated. Therefore, the court determined that the separate books and records kept by the taxpayer were not adequate and held that the three divisions were functionally integrated.

On the other hand, the Tax Court came to the opposite conclusion in *Rocco, Inc.* even though the corporation in *Rocco* was essentially trying to accomplish the same objective as the corporation in *Peterson Produce Co.*[210] In Rocco, the corporate taxpayer created a distinct new corporation to run the turkey broiler division completely separate from the chicken broiler division, even though the two divisions transacted with each other, The Tax Court determined that the turkey broiler division and the chicken broiler division were distinct and separate because each business was conducted through a separate entity.

These decisions have lead tax and legal professionals to conclude that entity structure can be very important in determining whether a particular activity can be included as part of a trade or business and multiple entities can result in multiple trades or business.

In an April 11, 2019 Webinar, attorney and author, Steve Gorin, had some practical insights on the matter. As stated by Mr. Gorin:

> As a matter of sound bookkeeping and sound business practices, I highly recommend keeping a separate set of books and records for each business. I would also suggest having separate bank accounts for each separate business to help you track your accounting for each business… You have to be able to show that these really are separate businesses – they may have some interdependencies, but they are being run separately.

Mr. Gorin also provided the following practical example: "If I were going to try to establish my title company as a separate business [from my law firm], I would advertise to the real estate community the ability of my separate title company to provide services for their real estate needs that are completely independent of my law firm services."

---

[208] Ellen Fitzpatrick, *Recent Guidance Raises Long-Standing Issue of What is a Separate Trade or Business*, Tax Adviser (2015).
[209] *Peterson Produce Co. v. United States*, 205 F. Supp. 229 (W.D. Ark. 1962), aff'd, 313 F.2d 609 (8th Cir. 1963).
[210] *Rocco, Inc. v. Commissioner*, 72 T.C. 140 (1979).

While maintaining separate books and records and observing other formalities with respect to separate functions for non-SSTB activities will be somewhat inconvenient and time consuming, the separation of these functions may have other advantages, which may include the following:

1.   *Know Thyself*. Many businesses and professional practices are not aware of what their bottom-line profits (or losses!) are from separate activities and may be happily or unhappily surprised when they find out what the situation is.

Thus, some taxpayers will shut down non-SSTB activities if they are determined to be economic losers or not worth the time, trouble, effort and distraction.

2.   *Know Your Cost*. Many professional practices and businesses become complacent with the overall status quo while their bottom line is healthy, because there are so many other things to attend to.

The analysis required by the regulations may result in useful analysis, discussion, and education with respect to how and why overhead and activities interact in a trade or business.

A common result is to reduce expenses and activities that are not in the best interest of the practice owners.

3.   S*egregating Liability*. The separation of expenses and functions can result in separation of the actual activities and assets used in each separate activity to be held under separate disregarded LLCs in order to insulate the separate assets and activities from creditors.

> For example, a medical practice which provides both primary care and diagnostic imaging may conclude that the primary care practice exposes all assets and activities to significant liability risk, while the diagnostic imaging equipment and activities pose little risk, assuming that tests are read by radiologists who are outside of the practice.

Many times S corporations that are providing medical services will become qualified subchapter S subsidiaries of a new parent S corporation that can be formed to enable the medical practice or business entity to transfer its assets to other subsidiaries of the same new parent company on a tax-free basis to segregate assets and activities for liability insulation and other purposes. This is permitted under Internal Revenue Code Section 368(a)(l)(f) and is often referred to as a "new parent F Reorganization."[211]

In order to avoid having the radiology services be considered to be an SSTB, the practice company could transfer the radiology equipment into a separate subsidiary LLC and the primary care practice might continue to be owned and operated under what would now be referred to as the "parent" entity, or may be placed in a separate subsidiary LLC, if healthcare counsel concludes

---

[211] See Gassman, Crotty and O'Leary, *The Estate Planner's Guide to New Parent F Reorganizations*, Estate Planning Magazine, Volume 35, No. 5, May 2008.

that this is safe from a Medicare, Medicaid or other healthcare law and billing requirements standpoint. An arrangement with a parent company and separate subsidiaries would probably have to have the parent company bill for all Medicare and Medicaid services to comply with applicable healthcare law and Medicare requirements. Many practices have done this with the advice of competent healthcare counsel, based upon a provision in the Stark Regulations which allows a separate subsidiary of a medical practice entity to provide testing services.

As a result, a malpractice claimant would have a difficult time pursuing the radiology equipment, which may be very valuable.

In the above example, it may be best to set up a new parent company that would initially own the original entity, and then set up a new entity owned by the same parent company that would be a "brother / sister company" of the original entity.

The original entity would then transfer the radiology equipment, furniture, and computers associated with the imaging practice so that past liabilities of the practice entity would not cause loss of ownership of the operational LLCs or of the imaging equipment.

Safest to Separate Trades or Businesses into Separate Taxable Entities. In similar but more dramatic situations, the correct strategy will be to move the non-SSTB or SSTB activities and business into a separately taxed entity.

> For example, if a veterinary practice were to also sell dog food, the business of selling dog food could be completely moved into a separately taxed entity apart from the veterinary practice in order to completely avoid any concern over SSTB activity.

In conclusion, thousands of taxpayers having ownership interests in SSTBs need guidance on how to identify what portions of their business are considered to be non-SSTB, and how to accommodate separation of these functions and appropriate cost accounting to be able to identify the separation and comply with the Final Regulations.

While it is unclear whether the IRS will be requiring taxpayers to maintain separate books and records for SSTB and non-SSTB functions, it seems to be safest to actually maintain the separate books and records even though not specifically called for under the Final Regulations, as mentioned in the two examples provided thereunder. As a result, taxpayers should review how these activities can be best owned and accounted for after consultation with their advisors.

This process enables CPAs and legal and other advisors to assist professional practices and other SSTB businesses in accomplishing other objectives that may not have been considered in the past.

While record keeping and cost accounting have their drawbacks, the tax savings, better management and financial information, and liability insulation features may make the process more worthwhile than would initially be thought.

2. **AGGREGATION OF SEPARATE TRADES OR BUSINESSES FOR PURPOSES OF THE WAGE/PROPERTY LIMITATION UNDER THE FINAL REGULATIONS.**

While many commentators expected that the grouping rules of Internal Revenue Code Section 469 would apply, the IRS instead adopted a new set of aggregation rules, which are reasonable and workable. [212]

The Final Regulations generally repeated the Proposed Regulations with few changes.

3. **AGGREGATION REQUIREMENTS TO APPLY WAGES AND/OR QUALIFIED PROPERTY AS BETWEEN SEPARATE TRADES AND BUSINESSES.**

In order to be aggregated under the Final Regulations, the trades or businesses must meet the following requirements:

(a) **50% or More Common Ownership Requirement.**

The same person or group of persons directly or indirectly own 50% or more of each trade or business, although minority owners may aggregate if the 50% or more test is met by other owners (i.e. each owner makes separate decision on what to aggregate). This is further explained below.

(b) **Sections 267(b) and 707(b) Attribution Rules Apply.**

The Section 267(b) and Section 707(b) ownership attribution rules are used and ownership by spouses, as well as children, grandchildren, parents, and siblings, can be attributed to each other. Under the Proposed Regulations, siblings would not have been considered as having been related. [213] In addition, the constructive attribution rules in Section 267(c) and the other provisions of Section 267 regarding attribution will also apply to determine whether the 50% common ownership test is met, although most advisors were not aware of this until it was clarified as a part

---

[212] *See* Gassman, Shenkman, Blattmachr, & Ketron, *Using Multiple Entities to Reduce Income Taxes for Families Owing Personal Service Corporations Under Section 199A and Unique Concerns,* LISI Income Tax Planning Newsletter #136, (March 12, 2018).

The ACIPA recommended that taxpayers who group their activities in accordance with the passive loss rules under Section 469 should also have those groupings be recognized for the purposes of Section 199A. The House Reports originally used Section 469 to govern aggregation rules under Section 199A, but this was removed by the time the Senate considered the bill. Section 469 governs passive activity loss and credit rules and allows the IRS to group certain entities. While some commentators share the view of the AICPA, others believe and the Preamble to the Proposed Regulations stated that the use of Section 469 is inappropriate because it governs the difference between passive and active activities and not separate trades or businesses. Further, Section 469 deals with the taxpayer's involvement in an activity, which is irrelevant for purposes of Section 199A. As a result, the Proposed Regulations and now Final Regulations adopted a new set of aggregation rules, which are surprisingly reasonable, and allow taxpayers owning interests in multiple trades or businesses to aggregate them for the best result where one trade or business may have more wages or qualified property than needed, and others have less.

[213] The Final Regulations addressed commentator's concerns and recommendations by requiring that the same person or group of persons, directly or by attribution through Section 267(b) or 707(b), own 50% or more of each trade or business. The Final Regulations also note that a C corporation may constitute part of this group.

of the April 4, 2019 ABA Webinar described in Chapter 9 and Chapter 13. The inclusion of Section 267(c) causes the constructive ownership of stock held by family members, partners, or by corporations, partnerships, estates, or trusts in which the taxpayer has an ownership or beneficial interest, including double attribution in certain scenarios.

(c) **Majority of Tax Year.**

The ownership existed for a majority of the tax year, including the last day of the taxable year.

(d) **Same Taxable Year.**

The items must be reported on returns within the same taxable year.

(e) **No SSTB Income Allowed**

None of the businesses can be an SSTB; and

(f) **The Two-Out-Of-Three Test**

The aggregated trades or businesses must also satisfy at least two of the following factors:

i) Products or Services Customarily Offered Together. The trade or businesses provide products or services that are the same or customarily offered together;

ii) Common Centralized Business Elements. The trade or businesses share facilities or significant centralized business elements such as personnel, accounting, legal, manufacturing, purchasing, human resources, or information technology resources; and

iii) Operated in Coordination with or Reliance Upon. The trades or businesses are operated in coordination with, or reliance upon, one or more of the businesses in the aggregated group (for example, supply chains interdependencies).

A series of eighteen well-written examples, which can be found below, provide detailed guidance on the aggregation provisions. In addition, Example 11 demonstrates that a taxpayer owning less than 50% of multiple entities can elect to aggregate her interests therein, as long as there are other common taxpayers who own more than 50% of each entity. The minority owner can elect to aggregate even if the other owners do not.

Aggregation will allow wages and Qualified Property to be considered as paid for all of the entities, so that the deduction can be taken for income received from a partnership, S corporation or proprietorship that has little or no wages or Qualified Property if another entity has sufficient wages and Qualified Property for both its own income and the income of affiliates. The examples, which are reproduced below, show that losses from any entity that could be aggregated must be netted against the aggregate profits of other applicable entities, if any aggregation occurs.

The examples indicate that ownership of a sailboat racing team and a marina by separate companies would not be aggregated, but that ownership of a trucking company that delivers lumber and other supplies in one company, operation of a lumber yard in another company, and operation of a construction business that presumably uses lumber and other supplies, can be aggregated.

A new example added in the Final Regulations states that residential and commercial property rental activities cannot be aggregated for purposes of satisfying the Wage/Qualified Property Test, due to the fact that residential and commercial property are not the same type of property and do not otherwise satisfy two of the three aggregation requirements. If a high-income Taxpayer has rental income from both residential property and commercial property that is considered to be a trade or business, then the residential rental activity and the commercial rental activity must be separately tested to see if both satisfy the wage/Qualified Property Test. In addition, hours spent on residential and commercial property must be separately tracked as they cannot be aggregated together for purposes of testing whether the 250-hour safe harbor is met under Notice 2019-7. Comments on the Notice were submitted by the American Bar Association Section of Taxation on June 27, 2019. The comments suggest that the 250-hour requirement be lowered to 120 hours, because the 250-hour requirement "is so high that relatively few taxpayers who use the Safe Harbor will actually need its protection." For more on the ABA's comments to the Notice refer to Chapter 12, Part Two.

Once a taxpayer chooses to aggregate two or more trades or businesses, they must be consistently reported and aggregated for all subsequent taxable years, unless there is a change in facts and circumstance so that a taxpayer's prior aggregation no longer qualifies for aggregation. The implications of all of this to professional advisers can be daunting. In some instances, modeling the various options may be the only way to determine what the actual impact of various decisions might be. Practitioners should be cautious about providing conclusions to clients with specificity without the opportunity to perform the appropriate analysis. The costs of the level of detailed analysis that might be necessary in many instances will often be material.

The Final Regulations also give partnerships, S corporations or other entities (referred to in the Final Regulations as Relevant Pass-Through Entities, or RPEs) owning multiple trades or businesses by direct ownership or subsidiaries the ability to make an aggregation election at the entity level, if the requirements for aggregation are met by the RPE. The election made by the Relevant Pass-Through Entity should be carefully considered, because it will be binding upon all of the individual owners of the Relevant Pass-Through Entity. Although individual owners include trades or businesses that are aggregated by the Relevant Pass-Through Entity, such owners can aggregate additional trades or businesses with the Relevant Pass-Through Entity's aggregation, assuming that the other requirements for aggregation are met.

While making such an election can simplify tax reporting for the partners or S corporation owners, it can also cause loss of Section 199A tax savings by eliminating aggregation options that an individual partner or S corporation owner would otherwise have.

In the example that follows, Taxpayer A has a food business and also owns 60% of a partnership that operates both a movie theater and a food business, and may elect to aggregate his personally owned food business with the food business of the partnership, due to the fact that they are the same type of products and services and share centralized business elements. On the other hand, if the partnership makes an aggregation election to combine the movie theater with the partnership's food business (since they are operated in coordination with each other and share centralized business elements), then the individually owned food service cannot be aggregated with the combined movie theater and food business due to the fact that the individually owned food business is not considered the same type of product or service as the combined movie theater and food operations, and therefore the requirements for aggregation cannot be met.

The example in the Final Regulations reads as follows:

Example:

(i) Facts:

> PRS1, a partnership, directly operates a food service trade or business and owns 60% of PRS2, which directly operates a movie theater trade or business and a food service trade or business. PRS2's movie theater and food service businesses operate in coordination with, or reliance upon, one another and share a centralized human resources department, payroll, and accounting department. PRS1's and PRS2's food service businesses provide products and services that are the same and share centralized purchasing and shipping to obtain volume discounts.

(ii) Analysis:

> PRS2 may aggregate its movie theater and food service businesses. Paragraph (b)(1)(v) of this Section is satisfied because the businesses operate in coordination with one another and share centralized business elements. If PRS does aggregate the two businesses, PRS1 may not aggregate its food service business with PRS2's aggregated trades or businesses. Because PRS1 owns more than 50% of PRS2, thereby satisfying paragraph (b)(1)(i) of this section, PRS1 may aggregate its food service businesses with PRS2's food service business if PRS2 has not aggregated its movie theater and food service businesses. Paragraph (b)(1)(v) of this Section is satisfied because the businesses provide the same products and services and share centralized business elements. Under either alternative, PRS1's food service business and PRS2's movie theater cannot be aggregated because there are no factors in paragraph (b)(1)(v) of this Section present between the businesses.[214]

---

[214] Treas. Reg. §1.199A-4(d), Example 15.

Lawyers who are drafting or updating entity arrangements may wish to have the documents prohibit the entity from making an aggregation election without the consent of all, or substantially all, of the owners or may additionally provide that no officer, manager, or director will have a fiduciary duty to aggregate or to not aggregate.

The other examples from the Final Regulations are reproduced below and provide significant guidance on the types of trades and businesses that can be aggregated:

> *The following examples illustrate the principles of this section. For purposes of these examples, assume the taxpayer is a United States citizen, all individuals and RPEs use a calendar taxable year, there are no ownership changes during the taxable year, all trades or businesses satisfy the requirements under Section 162, all tax items are effectively connected to a trade or business within the United States within the meaning of Section 864(c), and none of the trades or businesses is an SSTB within the meaning of §1.199A-5. Except as otherwise specified, a single capital letter denotes an individual taxpayer.*

Example 1:

(i) Facts:

> A wholly owns and operates a catering business and a restaurant through separate disregarded entities. The catering business and the restaurant share centralized purchasing to obtain volume discounts and a centralized accounting office that performs all of the bookkeeping, tracks and issues statements on all of the receivables, and prepares the payroll for each business. A maintains a website and print advertising materials that reference both the catering business and the restaurant. A uses the restaurant kitchen to prepare food for the catering business. The catering business employs its own staff and owns equipment and trucks that are not used or associated with the restaurant.

(ii) Analysis:

> Because the restaurant and catering business are held in disregarded entities, A will be treated as operating each of these businesses directly and thereby satisfies paragraph (b)(1)(i) of this section. Under paragraph (b)(1)(v) of this section, A satisfies the following factors: paragraph (b)(1)(v)(A) of this Section is met as both businesses offer prepared food to customers; and paragraph (b)(1)(v)(B) of this Section is met because the two businesses share the same kitchen facilities in addition to centralized purchasing, marketing, and accounting. Having satisfied paragraphs (b)(1)(i) through (v) of this section, A may treat the catering business and the restaurant as a single trade or business for purposes of applying §1.199A-1(d).

Example 2:

(i) Facts:

Assume the same facts as in Example 1 of paragraph (d)(1) of this section, but the catering and restaurant businesses are owned in separate partnerships and A, B, C, and D each own a 25% interest in each of the two partnerships. A, B, C, and D are unrelated.

(ii) Analysis:

Because under paragraph (b)(1)(i) of this Section A, B, C, and D together own more than 50% of each of the two partnerships, they may each treat the catering business and the restaurant as a single trade or business for purposes of applying §1.199A-1(d).

Example 3:

(i) Facts:

W owns a 75% interest in S1, an S corporation, and a 75% interest in PRS, a partnership. S1 manufactures clothing and PRS is a retail pet food store. W manages S1 and PRS.

(ii) Analysis:

W owns more than 50% of the stock of S1 and more than 50% of PRS thereby satisfying paragraph (b)(1)(i) of this section. Although W manages both S1 and PRS, W is not able to satisfy the requirements of paragraph (b)(1)(v) of this Section as the two businesses do not provide goods or services that are the same or customarily offered together; there are no significant centralized business elements; and no facts indicate that the businesses are operated in coordination with, or reliance upon, one another. We must treat S1 and PRS as separate trades or businesses for purposes of applying §1.199A-1(d).

Example 4:

(i) Facts:

E owns a 60% interest in each of four partnerships (PRS1, PRS2, PRS3, and PRS4). Each partnership operates a hardware store. A team of executives oversees the operations of all four of the businesses and controls the policy decisions involving the business as a whole. Human resources and accounting are centralized for the four businesses. E reports PRS1, PRS3, and PRS4 as an aggregated trade or business under paragraph (b)(1) of this Section and reports PRS2 as a separate trade or business. Only PRS2 generates a net taxable loss.

(ii) Analysis.

E owns more than 50% of each partnership thereby satisfying paragraph (b)(1)(i) of this section. Under paragraph (b)(1)(v) of this section, the following factors are satisfied: paragraph (b)(1)(v)(A) of this Section because each partnership operates a hardware store; and paragraph (b)(1)(v)(B) of this Section because the businesses share accounting and human resource functions. E's decision to aggregate only PRS1, PRS3, and PRS4 into a single trade or business for purposes of applying §1.199A-1(d) is permissible. The loss from PRS2 will be netted against the aggregate profits of PRS1, PRS3, and PRS4 pursuant to §1.199A-1(d)(2)(iii).

Example 5:

(i) Facts:

Assume the same facts as Example 4 of paragraph (d)(4) of this section, and that F owns a 10% interest in PRS1, PRS2, PRS3, and PRS4.

(ii) Analysis.:

Because under paragraph (b)(1)(i) of this Section E owns more than 50% of the four partnerships, F may aggregate PRS 1, PRS2, PRS3, and PRS4 as a single trade or business for purposes of applying §1.199A-1(d), provided that F can demonstrate that the ownership test is met by E.

Example 6:

(i) Facts:

D owns 75% of the stock of S1, S2, and S3, each of which is an S corporation. Each S corporation operates a grocery store in a separate state. S1 and S2 share centralized purchasing functions to obtain volume discounts and a centralized accounting office that performs all of the bookkeeping, tracks and issues statements on all of the receivables, and prepares the payroll for each business. S3 is operated independently from the other businesses.

(ii) Analysis:

D owns more than 50% of the stock of each S corporation thereby satisfying paragraph (b)(1)(i) of this section. Under paragraph (b)(1)(v) of this section, the grocery stores satisfy paragraph (b)(1)(v)(A) of this Section because they are in the same trade or business. Only S1 and S2 satisfy paragraph (b)(1)(v)(B) of this Section because of their centralized purchasing and accounting offices. D is only able to show that the requirements of paragraph (b)(1)(v)(B) of this Section are satisfied for S1 and S2; therefore, D only may aggregate S1 and S2 into a single trade or business for purposes of §1.199A-1(d). D must report S3 as a separate trade or business for purposes of applying §1.199A-1(d).

Example 7:

(i) Facts:

Assume the same facts as Example 6 of paragraph (d)(6) of this Section except each store is independently operated and S1 and S2 do not have centralized purchasing or accounting functions.

(ii) Analysis:

Although the stores provide the same products and services within the meaning of paragraph (b)(1)(v)(A) of this section, D cannot show that another factor under paragraph (b)(1)(v) of this Section is present. Therefore, D must report S1, S2, and S3 as separate trades or businesses for purposes of applying §1.199A-1(d).

Example 8:

(i) Facts:

G owns 80% of the stock in S1, an S corporation and 80% of LLC1 and LLC2, each of which is a partnership for Federal tax purposes. LLC1 manufactures and supplies all of the widgets sold by LLC2. LLC2 operates a retail store that sells LLC1's widgets. S1 owns the real property leased to LLC1 and LLC2 for use by the factory and retail store. The entities share common advertising and management.

(ii) Analysis:

G owns more than 50% of the stock of S1 and more than 50% of LLC1 and LLC2 thus satisfying paragraph (b)(1)(i) of this section. LLC1, LLC2, and S1 share significant centralized business elements and are operated in coordination with, or in reliance upon, one or more of the businesses in the aggregated group. G can treat the business operations of LLC1 and LLC2 as a single trade or business for purposes of applying §1.199A-1(d). S1 is eligible to be included in the aggregated group because it leases property to a trade or business within the aggregated trade or business as described in §1.199A-1(b)(14) and meets the requirements of paragraph (b)(1) of this section.

Example 9:

(i) Facts:

Same facts as Example 8 of paragraph (d)(8) of this section, except G owns 80% of the stock in S1 and 20% of each of LLC1 and LLC2. B, G's son, owns a majority interest in LLC2, and M, G's mother, owns a majority interest in LLC1. B does not own an interest in S1 or LLC1, and M does not own an interest in S1 or LLC2.

(ii) Analysis:

Under the rules in paragraph (b)(1) of this section, B and M's interest in LLC2 and LLC1, respectively, are attributable to G and G is treated as owning a majority interest in LLC2 and LLC1; G thus satisfies paragraph (b)(1)(i) of this section. G may aggregate his interests in LLC1, LLC2, and S1 as a single trade or business for purposes of applying §1.199A-1(d). Under paragraph (b)(1) of this section, S1 is eligible to be included in the aggregated group because it leases property to a trade or business within the aggregated trade or business as described in §1.199A- 1(b)(14) and meets the requirements of paragraph (b)(1) of this section.

Example 10:

(i) Facts:

F owns a 75% interest and G owns a 5% interest in five partnerships (PRS1-PRS5). H owns a 10% interest in PRS1 and PRS2. Each partnership operates a restaurant and each restaurant separately constitutes a trade or business for purposes of Section 162. G is the executive chef of all of the restaurants and as such he creates the menus and orders the food supplies.

(ii) Analysis:

F owns more than 50% of the partnerships thereby satisfying paragraph (b)(1)(i) of this section. Under paragraph (b)(1)(v) of this section, the restaurants satisfy paragraph (b)(1)(v)(A) of this Section because they are in the same trade or business, and paragraph (b)(1)(v)(B) of this Section is satisfied as G is the executive chef of all of the restaurants and the businesses share a centralized function for ordering food and supplies. F can show the requirements under paragraph (b)(1) of this Section are satisfied as to all of the restaurants. Because F owns a majority interest in each of the partnerships, G can demonstrate that paragraph (b)(1)(i) of this Section is satisfied. G can also aggregate all five restaurants into a single trade or business for purposes of applying §1.199A-1(d). H, however, only owns an interest in PRS1 and PRS2. Like G, H satisfies paragraph (b)(1)(i) of this Section because F owns a majority interest. H can, therefore, aggregate PRS1 and PRS2 into a single trade or business for purposes of applying §1.199A-1(d).

Example 11:

(i) Facts:

H, J, K, and L own interests in PRS1 and PRS2, each a partnership, and S1 and S2, each an S corporation. H, J, K, and L also own interests in C, an entity taxable as a C corporation. H owns 30%, J owns 20%, K owns 5%, and L owns 45% of each of the five entities. All of the entities satisfy 2 of the 3 factors under paragraph (b)(1)(v) of this section. For purposes of Section 199A the taxpayers report the following aggregated trades or businesses: H aggregates PRS1 and S1 together and aggregates PRS2 and S2 together; J aggregates PRS1, S1 and S2 together and reports PRS2 separately; K aggregates PRS1 and PRS2 together and aggregates S1 and S2 together; and L aggregates S1, S2, and PRS2 together and reports PRS1 separately. C cannot be aggregated.

(ii) Analysis.

Under paragraph (b)(1)(i) of this section, because H, J, and K together own a majority interest in PRS1, PRS2, S1, and S2, H, J, K, and L are permitted to aggregate under paragraph (b)(1) of this section. Further, the aggregations reported by the taxpayers are permitted, but not required for each of H, J, K, and L. C's income is not eligible for the Section 199A deduction and it cannot be aggregated for purposes of applying §1.199A-1(d).

Example 12:

(i) Facts:

L owns 60% of PRS1, a partnership, a business that sells non-food items to grocery stores. L also owns 55% of PRS2, a partnership, which owns and operates a distribution trucking business. The predominant portion of PRS2's business is transporting goods for PRS1.

(ii) Analysis:

L is able to meet paragraph (b)(1)(i) of this Section as the majority owner of PRS1 and PRS2. Under paragraph (b)(1)(v) of this section, L is only able to show the operations of PRS1 and PRS2 are operated in reliance of one another under paragraph (b)(1)(v)(C) of this section. For purposes of applying §1.199A-1(d), L must treat PRS1 and PRS2 as separate trades or businesses.

Example 13:

(i) Facts:

C owns a majority interest in a sailboat racing team and also owns an interest in PRS1 which operates a marina. PRS1 is a trade or business under Section 162, but the sailboat racing team is not a trade or business within the meaning of Section 162.

(ii) Analysis:

C has only one trade or business for purposes of Section 199A and, therefore, cannot aggregate the interest in the racing team with PRS1 under paragraph (b)(1) of this section.

Example 14:

(i) Facts:

Trust wholly owns LLC1, LLC2, and LLC3. LLC1 operates a trucking company that delivers lumber and other supplies sold by LLC2. LLC2 operates a lumber yard and supplies LLC3 with building materials. LLC3 operates a construction business. LLC1, LLC2, and LLC3 have a centralized human resources department, payroll, and accounting department.

(ii) Analysis:

Because Trust owns 100% of the interests in LLC1, LLC2, and LLC3, Trust satisfies paragraph (b)(1)(i) of this section. Trust can also show that it satisfies paragraph (b)(1)(v)(B) of this Section as the trades or businesses have a centralized human resources department, payroll, and accounting department. Trust also can show is meets paragraph (b)(1)(v)(C) of this Section as the trades or businesses are operated in coordination, or reliance upon, one or more in the aggregated group. Trust can aggregate LLC1, LLC2, and LLC3 for purposes of applying §1.199A-1(d).

Example 15:

(i) Facts:

PRS1, a partnership, directly operates a food service trade or business and owns 60% of PRS2, which directly operates a movie theater trade or business and a food service trade or business. PRS2's movie theater and food service businesses operate in coordination with, or reliance upon, one another and share a centralized human resources department, payroll, and accounting department. PRS1's and PRS2's food service businesses provide products and services that are the same and share centralized purchasing and shipping to obtain volume discounts.

(ii) Analysis:

PRS2 may aggregate its movie theater and food service businesses. Paragraph (b)(1)(v) of this Section is satisfied because the businesses operate in coordination with one another and share centralized business elements. If PRS does aggregate the two businesses, PRS1 may not aggregate its food service business with PRS2's aggregated trades or businesses. Because PRS1 owns more than 50% of PRS2, thereby satisfying paragraph (b)(1)(i) of this section, PRS1 may aggregate its food service businesses with PRS2's food service business if PRS2 has not aggregated its movie theater and food service businesses. Paragraph (b)(1)(v) of this Section is satisfied because the businesses provide the same products and services and share centralized business elements. Under either alternative, PRS1's food service business and PRS2's movie theater cannot be aggregated because there are no factors in paragraph (b)(1)(v) of this Section present between the businesses.

Example 16:

(i) Facts:

PRS1, a partnership, owns 60% of a commercial rental office building in state A, and 80% of a commercial rental office building in state B. Both commercial rental office building operations share centralized accounting, legal, and human resource functions. PRS1 treats the two commercial rental office buildings as an aggregated trade or business under paragraph (b)(1) of this section.

(ii) Analysis:

PRS1 owns more than 50% of each trade or business thereby satisfying paragraph (b)(1)(i) of this section. Under paragraph (b)(1)(v) of this section,

PRS1 may aggregate its commercial rental office buildings because the businesses provide the same type of property and share accounting, legal, and human resource functions.

Example 17:

(i) Facts:

S, an S corporation owns 100% of the interests in a residential condominium building and 100% of the interests in a commercial rental office building. Both building operations share centralized accounting, legal, and human resource functions.

(ii) Analysis:

S owns more than 50% of each trade or business thereby satisfying paragraph (b)(1)(i) of this section. Although both businesses share significant centralized business elements, S cannot show that another factor under paragraph (b)(1)(v) of this Section is present because the two building operations are not of the same type of property. S must treat the residential condominium building and the commercial rental office building as separate trades or businesses for purposes of applying §1.199A-1(d).

Example 18:

(i) Facts:

M owns 75% of a residential apartment building. M also owns 80% of PRS2. PRS2 owns 80% of the interests in a residential condominium building and 80% of the interests in a residential apartment building. PRS2's residential condominium building and residential apartment building operations share centralized back office functions and management. M's residential apartment building and PRS2's residential condominium and apartment building operate in coordination with each other in renting apartments to tenants.

(ii) Analysis:

PRS2 may aggregate its residential condominium and residential apartment building operations. PRS2 owns more than 50% of each trade or business thereby satisfying paragraph (b)(1)(i) of this section. Paragraph (b)(1)(v) of this Section is satisfied because the businesses are of the same type of property and share centralized back office functions and management. M may also add its residential apartment building operations to PRS2's aggregated residential condominium and apartment building operations. M owns more than 50% of each trade or business thereby satisfying paragraph (b)(1)(i) of this section. Paragraph (b)(1)(v) of this Section is also satisfied because the businesses operate in coordination with each other.

The Final Regulations contain additional examples on the calculation of the Section 199A deduction when a taxpayer has ownership in multiple trades or businesses, and the effect of aggregating as opposed to separately calculating the Section 199A deduction independently for each trade or business. The Examples are as follows:

Example 1:

Example 1 - (A) F, an unmarried individual, owns as a sole proprietor 100 percent of three trades or businesses, Business X, Business Y, and Business Z. None of the businesses hold qualified property. F does not aggregate the trades or businesses under §1.199A-4. For taxable year 2018, Business X generates $1 million of QBI and pays $500,000 of W-2 wages with respect to the business. Business Y also generates $1 million of QBI but pays no wages. Business Z generates $2,000 of QBI and pays $500,000 of W-2 wages with respect to the business. F also has $750,000 of wage income from employment with an unrelated company. After allowable deductions unrelated to the businesses, F's taxable income is $2,722,000.

(B) Because F's taxable income is above the threshold amount, the QBI component of F's section 199A deduction is subject to the W-2 wage and UBIA of qualified property limitations. These limitations must be applied on a business-by-business basis. None of the businesses hold qualified property, therefore only the 50% of W-2 wage limitation must be calculated. Because QBI from each business is positive, F applies the limitation by determining the lesser of 20% of QBI and 50% of W-2 wages for each business. For Business X, the lesser of 20% of QBI ($1,000,000 x 20 percent = $200,000) and 50% of Business X's W-2 wages ($500,000 x 50% = $250,000) is $200,000. Business Y pays no W-2 wages. The lesser of 20% of Business Y's QBI ($1,000,000 x 20% = $200,000) and 50% of its W-2 wages (zero) is zero. For Business Z, the lesser of 20% of QBI ($2,000 x 20% = $400) and 50% of W-2 wages ($500,000 x 50% = $250,000) is $400.

(C) Next, F must then combine the amounts determined in paragraph (B) of this example and compare that sum to 20% of F's taxable income. The lesser of these two amounts equals F's section 199A deduction. The total of the combined amounts in paragraph (B) is $200,400 ($200,000 + zero

+ 400). Twenty percent of F's taxable income is \$544,400 (\$2,722,000 x 20%). Thus, F's section 199A deduction for 2018 is \$200,400.[215]

Example 2:

Example 2 - (A) Assume the same facts [as Example 1 above], except that F aggregates Business X, Business Y, and Business Z under the rules of §1.199A-4.

(B) Because F's taxable income is above the threshold amount, the QBI component of F's section 199A deduction is subject to the W-2 wage and UBIA of qualified property limitations. Because the businesses are aggregated, these limitations are applied on an aggregated basis. None of the businesses holds qualified property, therefore only the W-2 wage limitation must be calculated. F applies the limitation by determining the lesser of 20% of the QBI from the aggregated businesses, which is \$400,400 (\$2,002,000 x 20%) and 50% of W-2 wages from the aggregated businesses, which is \$500,000 (\$1,000,000 x 50%). F's section 199A deduction is equal to the lesser of \$400,400 and 20% of F's taxable income (\$2,722,000 x 20% = \$544,400).

Thus, F's section 199A deduction for 2018 is \$400,400.[216]

4. SEPARATING OUT THE AGGREGATION RULES UNDER SECTION 199A.

Many complicated rules apply under Section 199A, and the complexity is increased for high earner taxpayers (an individual or trust with more than \$157,500 or a married couple with more than \$315,000 of taxable income, as adjusted for inflation) because qualified business income from a Specified Service Trade or Business or from any trade or business that does not pay sufficient wages and/or have sufficient "Unadjusted Basis" in the trade or business will be limited as to deductibility.

These include if and when separate leasing or other activities can be combined to be prominent enough to be an "active trade or business," special rules with respect to non-triple net leases, and if and when wages and Qualified Property can be aggregated. They also include if and when SSTB and non-SSTB businesses can be considered to be separable within a single entity.

In many situations, individual taxpayers and trusts are involved with multiple trades and businesses, which may be aggregated to allow wages or Qualified Property from one or more entities to be allocated among all aggregated entities so that an entity or entities not having

---

[215] Treas. Reg. § 1.199A-1(d)(4), Example 7.
[216] Treas. Reg. § 1.199A-1(d)(4), Example 8.

sufficient wages or Qualified Property can benefit from excess wages or Qualified Property of others.

There are multiple types of Aggregation/combination rules that can apply in tax planning, and they are easy to confuse:

A.   What entities and functions can be combined to determine if one or more businesses are active enough to meet the definition of an "active trade or business," which is needed to be eligible to make a Section 199A deduction, or losses under Section 162?

B.   What kinds of leased property can be combined with other leased property to meet the 250-hour Safe Harbor that was made available under IRS Notice 2019-7 for leased property under Section 199A?

C.   When separate entities or activities can be aggregated for purposes of sharing wages and Qualified Property for a high-income taxpayer when there is common ownership.

The term "aggregation" has a specific technical meeting under the Section 199A Final Regulations, and generally should only be used when referring to the aggregation of the wages and qualified property of multiple entities for purposes of satisfying the Wage and Qualified Property Test.

These three aggregation/combination rules are described below.

A.   **Combining Businesses to Satisfy the Active Trade or Business Test.** No Section 199A deduction will be available for passive investments or activities that do not meet the Section 162 definition of an "active trade or business."

An individual, trust, S corporation, or partnership may own multiple trades or businesses or have multiple rental properties or other activities that would not be considered to be active or entrepreneurial enough to qualify separately as a "trade or business," but which may meet the definition of an "active trade or business" when considered as a group.

Under this "Aggregation" rule, the question is whether the separate activities can be considered to be one activity for purposes of determining whether there is sufficient entrepreneurial risk and sufficient activities to qualify as an "active trade or business."

The level and volume of activity is measured at the level of the owner and operator of the activity, which is known as the Relative Pass-Through Entity ("RPE") when owned and operated by an entity taxed as an S corporation or a partnership.

For example, an individual trustee of a trust may spend 10 hours a year on average with respect to rental services and may have an employee and also one or two contractors who themselves spend 20 hours a year on average on each property.

If this were one or two properties, the IRS might not consider this to be sufficient to be considered a "trade or business," but with 10 properties combined at the individual level, this may well surpass what is needed to establish an active trade or business under these rules.

On the other hand, if the individual or trust owns 10 separate S corporations or partnerships which each owns and operates a separate property, then these cannot be combined for purposes of determining whether the properties and activities are considered to be active trades or businesses, simply because the Final Regulations issued by the Internal Revenue Service on February 4th do not permit this.

If instead the 10 separate S corporations or partnerships contribute their respective properties to a single commonly owned LLC or other entity, then all of the activities could be combined to determine if an active trade or business exists. The LLC could be taxed as a partnership and issue K-1s reporting income to each owner entity.

The following charts illustrate the above:

Combination of Multiple Entities for Active Trade or Business Measurement Purposes

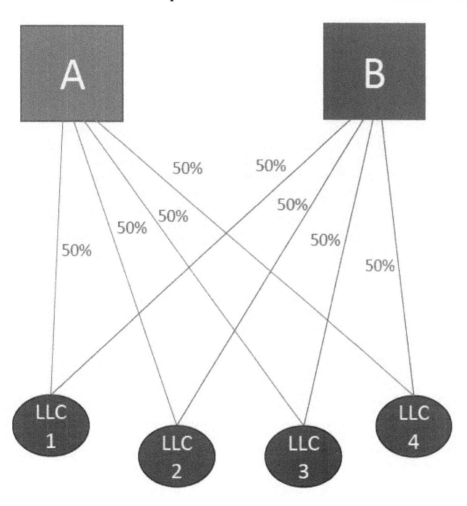

Each LLC must separately rise to the
level of a Trade or Business

Combination of Multiple Entities for Active Trade or Business Measurement Purposes (Continued)

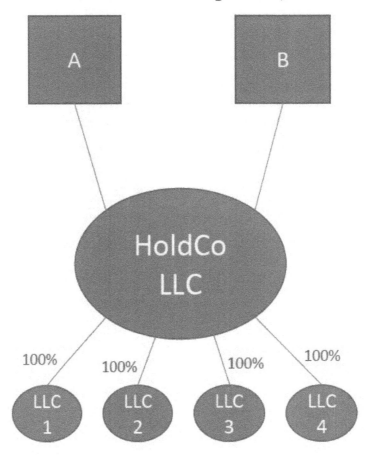

Activities of LLCs can be
combined to determine if HoldCo
is a Trade or Business.

It is noteworthy that many advisors and return preparers consider LLCs wholly owned as tenants by the entireties, or otherwise jointly owned by spouses, as disregarded single member LLCs, as applies in community property states. Before the passage of Section 199A there was little risk in the event that the IRS reclassified the LLC as a partnership, as the penalty for failure to file a partnership return would not normally apply due to the safe harbor provided under Rev. Proc. 84-

35.[217] If two spouses owned multiple LLCs as tenants by the entireties with each LLC holding a separate property, then a reclassification of the LLC as a partnership would also result in the loss of the spouses' ability to combine the activities of each LLC for purposes of qualifying for Section 199A, and instead each LLC would have to rise to the level of a trade or business on its own to qualify. It may therefore be safest to have the LLC owned partly by one spouse and a disregarded grantor trust so that charging order protection can apply, and the LLC is clearly treated as disregarded for income tax purposes.

The Management Company Solution. If the ten separate S corporations or partnerships cannot be combined and each separate property does not rise to the level of a trade or business, then a management company may be established to manage the properties for an arm's-length management fee, and may be considered to be a trade or business that is eligible for Section 199A. The management company could be responsible for negotiating leases, making repairs and handling maintenance at the properties, seeking out tenants, and performing other services related to the rental of properties, which can certainly qualify as a trade or business under Section 162 if it is reasonably active. This was discussed briefly in a May 2, 2019 ALI webinar with Jerry August and a Treasury official who seemed to give a "nod" to the concept when it was discussed.

One limitation of a management company is that it can only charge arm's-length management fees, so there will still normally be profit at the leasing entity level that will be even less likely to qualify for the Section 199A deduction when the entity does not "manage for itself." The concepts that apply when related parties provide services for each other include IRC Sections 269A and 482, are discussed at length in LISI Income Tax Planning Newsletter No. 136, entitled Using Multiple Entities to Reduce Income Taxes for Families Owning Personal Service Corporations Under Section 199A and Unique Concerns. The article points out that it is common in the health care industry for arm's-length management companies to charge fees equal to the entire net income of an applicable business when the medical professionals execute long-term employment agreements with non-competition covenants that transport their personal goodwill to the management company. This may be possible to some extent with a real estate management arrangement.

Triple Net Leases with Related Party Tenants May Be Considered As Active. A triple net lease can be considered to be an active trade or business if the tenant is a related party engaged in an active trade or business under an entity taxed as a proprietorship, S corporation or partnership, and the landlord and the tenant are considered to be commonly owned under the attribution rules described in Chapter 12, Part Two. Therefore, the tenant must be a commonly controlled Relevant Pass-Through Entity or individual sole proprietor for this to apply.

B.   **250 Hour Safe Harbor for Non-Triple Net Leases.** IRS Notice 2019-7 provides a safe harbor for when a landlord who has an active (not triple net) lease arrangement can be sure of being considered to be an active trade or business. This Proposed Revenue Procedure requires at least 250 hours per year of activity by the landlord and agents of the landlord in specified modes of activity, which must be contemporaneously memorialized and fall into categories of functions

---

[217] See Gassman and Ketron, *Yes, It is Usually Safe to Consider an LLC Owned as TBE as Disregarded for Income Tax Purposes.*

that would not include buying and selling the rental properties, travel to or from the rental properties, or reviewing financial statements.

Most advisors feel that the Proposed Revenue Procedure is not helpful, because virtually any taxpayer that would qualify under the Revenue Procedure would have qualified without its assistance.

IRS Notice 2019-7 and the ABA's comments on the Notice are discussed in more detail in Chapter 12, Part Two.

Similar Properties Under Revenue Notice 2019-7. IRS Notice 2019-7 provides that taxpayers can either (a) treat each non-triple net lease property owned by an individual or Relevant Pass-Through Entity separately; or (b) treat all similar properties as a single enterprise. The Notice does not discuss what is considered to be a similar property, with the exception of stating that residential and commercial property cannot normally be treated as part of the same enterprise. It therefore appears that all rental activity related commercial properties held by an individual or a Relevant Pass-Through Entity can be combined for the purpose of determining whether the 250-hour safe harbor is met. Because the word "similar" is open to many interpretations, the ABA proposed in June 2019 that it be defined or eliminated altogether.

Residential and Commercial Property Cannot Normally Be Combined. Residential and commercial property cannot be combined for purposes of determining whether there is an active trade or business; therefore, residential and commercial property must be tested separately to determine if the 250 hours required under the safe harbor is met. It is unclear if residential and commercial property may be combined if they are significantly interrelated, such as if a store and the apartment above the store are rented to the same tenant, or a building has both retail and commercial space and is wholly owned by the landlord. The Notice simply states that commercial and residential property may not be part of the same enterprise and the authors are not aware of any other guidance on this issue. The ABA argues in their June 2019 comments to the Notice that the "fundamental activities carried on by a taxpayer holding rental properties, whether commercial, residential, or mixed-use, are essentially the same," and that the rule should be clarified to allow for commercial and residential real estate in the same enterprise.

C.   **Combining Wages and Qualified Properties.** Unrelated to whether an activity is an active trade or business, taxpayers may elect to aggregate commonly controlled entities for purposes of combining the Wages and Qualified Property of each entity in applying the Wage/Qualified Property Test under Section 199A if certain requirements are met, as further discussed in Chapter 9, Part Two.

The implications of all of this to professional advisers can be daunting. In some instances, modeling the various options may be the only way to determine what the actual impact of various decisions might be. Practitioners should be cautious about providing conclusions to clients with specificity without the opportunity to perform the appropriate analysis. The costs of the level of detailed analysis that might be necessary in many instances will often be material.

5. **REALLOCATION OF PAYMENTS BETWEEN RELATED TAXPAYERS.**

There are two important Code Sections that give the IRS power to control allocations and payments between related parties: Section 269A and Section 482. The payments between related companies in exchange for services, assets, licensing rights, are referred to as "transfer pricing."

Section 269A is reproduced below and gives the IRS the authority to reallocate income and expenses, or even completely disregard a personal/professional service corporation if both (1) substantially all of the services of the "personal service corporation" are performed by "employee-owners" of the personal service corporation, who own more than 10%, of one other entity, and (2) the principal purpose of the corporation is to avoid income tax. A professional service company under this statute is a corporation whose principal activity is the performance of personal services and such services are substantially performed by employee-owners. The statute reads as follows:

"(a) GENERAL RULE If—

(1)   substantially all of the services of a personal service corporation are performed for (or on behalf of) 1 other corporation, partnership, or other entity, and

(2)   the principal purpose for forming, or availing of, such personal service corporation is the avoidance or evasion of Federal income tax by reducing the income of, or securing the benefit of any expense, deduction, credit, exclusion, or other allowance for, any employee-owner which would not otherwise be available, then the Secretary may allocate all income, deductions, credits, exclusions, and other allowances between such personal service corporation and its employee- owners, if such allocation is necessary to prevent avoidance or evasion of Federal income tax or clearly to reflect the income of the personal service corporation or any of its employee-owners.

(b)   DEFINITIONS For purposes of this section—

(1)   PERSONAL SERVICE CORPORATION

The term "personal service corporation" means a corporation the principal activity of which is the performance of personal services and such services are substantially performed by employee-owners.

(2)   EMPLOYEE-OWNER

The term "employee-owner" means any employee who owns, on any day during the taxable year, more than 10 percent of the outstanding stock of the personal service corporation. For purposes of the preceding sentence, Section 318 shall apply, except that "5 percent" shall be substituted for "50 percent" in Section 318(a)(2)(C).

(3)   RELATED PERSONS

All related persons (within the meaning of Section 144(a)(3)) shall be treated as 1 entity."

Section 482 allows the IRS to reallocate income, deductions, credits or allowances between trades or businesses to prevent the evasion of taxes or to clearly reflect income of these businesses. The determinative factor in this Section is that these trades or businesses must be "owned or controlled directly or indirectly by the same interests." Relationships between related entities are respected only if substantially similar arrangements would have been entered into by unrelated third parties.

Section 269A gives the IRS more discretion than Section 482 by allowing the IRS to completely disregard the company, and reallocate all of its income, even if transactions are at arm's-length. Accordingly, a taxpayer who wants to be as safe as possible would want to conform to conduct that would prevent Section 269A from applying.

The following article that was originally posted as Leimberg's Income Tax Planning Email Newsletter Archive Message 136 has more detail on the reallocation of income as well as a thorough look at the assignment of income doctrine and these two Code Sections[218]

6. TREATMENT OF LOSSES

The Final Regulations take a netting approach, so that a taxpayer who has a loss from one trade or business, but a net gain when all of them are netted together, must apportion the net loss among the trades or businesses relative to the amount of gain for each such trade or business. The Wage and Qualified Property of the trade or business producing the net loss are not considered when applying the Wage/Property limitation unless an election is made to aggregate the trades or businesses.

Example:

> John has three businesses, Business A produces $1,000,000 of QBI, Business B produces $500,000 of QBI, and Business C has a $600,000 net loss. Unless an election is made to aggregate the trades or businesses, the $600,000 loss will be allocated two-thirds to Business A, reducing Business A's QBI to $600,000 ($1,000,000 - $400,000), and one-third to Business B, reducing Business B's QBI to $300,000 ($500,000 - $200,000). John would then apply the Wage/Property Limitation separately to Business A and Business B to determine John's Section 199A deduction.

In the Congressional Reports on Section 199A, the Senate gave an example of a taxpayer with $20,000 of flow-through income from one company but $50,000 in losses from another company

---

[218] Letter from Karen G. Sowell, Chair, New York State Bar Association Tax Section, to David Kautter, Acting Commissioner, I.R.S., and William Paul, Principal Deputy Chief Counsel, I.R.S. (March 23, 2018) (on file with NYSBA-Tax Section). *See also* New York State Bar Association Tax Section, *Report on Section 199A*, Report No. 1392 (March 23, 2018), https://www.nysba.org/Sections/Tax/Tax_Section_Reports/Tax_Section_Reports_2018/1392_Report.ht ml.

in year one. The example stated that the taxpayer would not be allowed to take a deduction for that year and would have a $30,000 loss carry forward to the next year.[219] This was also stated in the Preamble to the Proposed Regulations, and not discussed in the Preamble to the Final Regulations.

The Final Regulations also contain examples on the effect of aggregation when one or more trades or businesses owned by the taxpayer report a net loss. As discussed above, when a taxpayer's trade or business has a net loss and an aggregation election is not made, such loss must offset positive QBI from the taxpayer's other trades or businesses in proportion to the relative amounts of QBI from the other trades or businesses. If an aggregation election is made, then the QBI from all trades or businesses must be netted together to determine the taxpayer's total QBI.

In the event that the taxpayer's combined QBI amount produces a net loss, regardless of whether an aggregation election is made, the loss is carried over to the following tax year, and is treated as a net loss from a separate trade or business in the next tax year, and the Wages/Qualified Property will not carry over to the next tax year. The examples in the Final Regulations are as follows:

Example 1:

(A) Assume the same facts as [the above examples] except that for taxable year 2018, Business Z generates a loss that results in ($600,000) of negative QBI and pays $500,000 of W-2 wages. After allowable deductions unrelated to the businesses, F's taxable income is $2,120,000. Because Business Z had negative QBI, F must offset the positive QBI from Business X and Business Y with the negative QBI from Business Z in proportion to the relative amounts of positive QBI from Business X and Business Y. Because Business X and Business Y produced the same amount of positive QBI, the negative QBI from Business Z is apportioned equally among Business X and Business Y. Therefore, the adjusted QBI for each of Business X and Business Y is $700,000 ($1 million plus 50% of the negative QBI of $600,000). The adjusted QBI in Business Z is $0, because its negative QBI has been fully apportioned to Business X and Business Y.

(B) Because F's taxable income is above the threshold amount, the QBI component of F's section 199A deduction is subject to the W-2 wage and UBIA of qualified property limitations. These limitations must be applied on a business-by-business basis. None of the businesses hold qualified property, therefore only the 50% of W-2 wage limitation must be calculated. For Business X, the lesser of 20% of QBI ($700,000 x 20% = $140,000) and 50% of W-2 wages ($500,000 x 50% = $250,000) is $140,000. Business Y pays no W-2 wages. The lesser of 20% of Business Y's QBI ($700,000 x 20% = $140,000) and 50% of its W-2 wages (zero) is zero.

---

[219] This specific example from Congressional Reports can be found on the first page of Appendix 10.

(C) F must combine the amounts determined in paragraph (B) of this example and compare the sum to 20% of taxable income. F's section 199A deduction equals the lesser of these two amounts. The combined amount from paragraph (B) of this example is $140,000 ($140,000 + zero) and 20% of F's taxable income is $424,000 ($2,120,000 x 20%). Thus, F's section 199A deduction for 2018 is $140,000. There is no carryover of any loss into the following taxable year for purposes of section 199A.[220]

Example 2:

(A) Assume the same facts as [Example 1 above], except that F aggregates Business X, Business Y, and Business Z under the rules of §1.199A-4.

(B) Because F's taxable income is above the threshold amount, the QBI component of F's section 199A deduction is subject to the W-2 wage and UBIA of qualified property limitations. Because the businesses are aggregated, these limitations are applied on an aggregated basis. None of the businesses holds qualified property, therefore only the W-2 wage limitation must be calculated. F applies the limitation by determining the lesser of 20% of the QBI from the aggregated businesses ($1,400,000 x 20% = $280,000) and 50% of W-2 wages from the aggregated businesses ($1,000,000 x 50% = $500,000), or $280,000. F's section 199A deduction is equal to the lesser of $280,000 and 20% of F's taxable income ($2,120,000 x 20% = $424,000). Thus, F's section 199A deduction for 2018 is $280,000. There is no carryover of any loss into the following taxable year for purposes of section 199A.[221]

Example 3:

(A) Assume the same facts as [Example 1 and 2 above], except that Business Z generates a loss that results in ($2,150,000) of negative QBI and pays $500,000 of W-2 wages with respect to the business in 2018. Thus, F has a negative combined QBI of ($150,000) when the QBI from all of the businesses are added together ($1 million plus $1 million minus the loss of ($2,150,000)). Because F has a negative combined QBI for 2018, F has no section 199A deduction with respect to any trade or business for 2018. Instead, the negative combined QBI of ($150,000) carries forward and will be treated as negative QBI from a separate trade

---

[220] Treas. Reg. § 1.199A-1(d)(4), Example 9.
[221] Treas. Reg. § 1.199A-1(d)(4), Example 10.

or business for purposes of computing the section 199A deduction in the next taxable year. None of the W-2 wages carry forward. However, for income tax purposes, the $150,000 loss may offset F's $750,000 of wage income (assuming the loss is otherwise allowable under the Code).

(B) In taxable year 2019, Business X generates $200,000 of net QBI and pays $100,000 of W-2 wages with respect to the business. Business Y generates $150,000 of net QBI but pays no wages. Business Z generates a loss that results in ($120,000) of negative QBI and pays $500 of W-2 wages with respect to the business. F also has $750,000 of wage income from employment with an unrelated company. After allowable deductions unrelated to the businesses, F's taxable income is $960,000. Pursuant to paragraph (d)(2)(iii)(B) of this section, the ($150,000) of negative QBI from 2018 is treated as arising in 2019 from a separate trade or business. Thus, F has overall net QBI of $80,000 when all trades or businesses are taken together ($200,000) plus $150,000 minus $120,000 minus the carryover loss of $150,000). Because Business Z had negative QBI and F also has a negative QBI carryover amount, F must offset the positive QBI from Business X and Business Y with the negative QBI from Business Z and the carryover amount in proportion to the relative amounts of positive QBI from Business X and Business Y. Because Business X produced 57.14% of the total QBI from Business X and Business Y, 57.14% of the negative QBI from Business Z and the negative QBI carryforward must be apportioned to Business X, and the remaining 42.86% allocated to Business Y. Therefore, the adjusted QBI in Business X is $45,722 ($200,000 minus 57.14% of the loss from Business Z ($68,568), minus 57.14% of the carryover loss ($85,710). The adjusted QBI in Business Y is $34,278 ($150,000, minus 42.86% of the loss from Business Z ($51,432) minus 42.86% of the carryover loss ($64,290)). The adjusted QBI in Business Z is $0, because its negative QBI has been apportioned to Business X and Business Y.

(C) Because F's taxable income is above the threshold amount, the QBI component of F's section 199A deduction is subject to the W-2 wage and UBIA of qualified property limitations. These limitations must be applied on a business-by-business basis. None of the businesses hold qualified property, therefore only the 50% of W-2 wage limitation must be calculated. For Business X, 20% of QBI is $9,144 ($45,722 x 20%) and 50% of W-2 wages is $50,000 ($100,000 x 50%), so the lesser amount is $9,144. Business Y pays no W-2 wages. Twenty percent of Business Y's QBI is $6,856 ($34,278 x 20%) and 50% of its W-2 wages (zero) is zero, so the lesser amount is zero.

(D) F must then compare the combined amounts determined in paragraph (C) of this example to 20% of F's taxable income. The section 199A deduction equals the lesser of these amounts. F's combined amount from paragraph (C) of this example is $9,144 ($9,144 plus zero) and 20% of F's taxable income is $192,000 ($960,000 x 20%). Thus, F's section 199A deduction for 2019 is $9,144. There is no carryover of any negative QBI into the following taxable year for purposes of section 199A.[222]

Example 4:

(A) Assume the same facts [Examples 1, 2 and 3 above] except that F aggregates Business X, Business Y, and Business Z under the rules of §1.199A-4. For 2018, F's QBI from the aggregated trade or business is ($150,000). Because F has a combined negative QBI for 2018, F has no section 199A deduction with respect to any trade or business for 2018. Instead, the negative combined QBI of ($150,000) carries forward and will be treated as negative QBI from a separate trade or business for purposes of computing the section 199A deduction in the next taxable year. However, for income tax purposes, the $150,000 loss may offset taxpayer's $750,000 of wage income (assuming the loss is otherwise allowable under the Code).

(B) In taxable year 2019, F will have QBI of $230,000 and W-2 wages of $100,500 from the aggregated trade or business. F also has $750,000 of wage income from employment with an unrelated company. After allowable deductions unrelated to the businesses, F's taxable income is $960,000. F must treat the negative QBI carryover loss ($150,000) from 2018 as a loss from a separate trade or business for purposes of section 199A. This loss will offset the positive QBI from the aggregated trade or business, resulting in an adjusted QBI of $80,000 ($230,000 - $150,000).

(C) Because F's taxable income is above the threshold amount, the QBI component of F's section 199A deduction is subject to the W-2 wage and UBIA of qualified property limitations. These limitations must be applied on a business-by-business basis. None of the businesses hold qualified property, therefore only the 50% of W-2 wage limitation must be calculated. For the aggregated trade or business, the lesser of 20% of QBI ($80,000 x 20% = $16,000) and 50% of W-2 wages ($100,500 x 50% = $50,250) is $16,000. F's section 199A deduction equals the lesser of that amount ($16,000) and 20% of F's taxable income ($960,000 x 20% = $192,000). Thus, F's section 199A deduction for 2019 is $16,000. There is no carryover of any negative QBI into the following taxable year for purposes of section 199A.[223]

---

[222] Treas. Reg. § 1.199A-1(d)(4), Example 11.
[223] Treas. Reg. § 1.199A-1(d)(4), Example 12.

7. ASSIGNMENT OF INCOME.

The Assignment of Income Doctrine was first developed in 1930 by the Supreme Court in the case of *Lucas v. Earl.*[224] Under this doctrine, a taxpayer's right to receive income from services rendered must be taxed to the taxpayer who earned the income and not to another person or entity who was assigned the right to receive income.

At its inception, the Supreme Court solved the issue before them – preventing individuals from assigning income to lower their taxable income. However, this doctrine has further developed in professional sports cases where athletes working for a sports team were not permitted to consider income to have passed through a company owned by the athlete (a "loan-out" entity) unless formal documentation confirmed that the sports team was paying the athlete's company, which was in turn paying the athlete, and that the athlete's company, and not the sports team, had the power to direct the athlete's actions.[225]

One of the earlier cases that involved professional service companies ("PSCs"), a professional athlete, and the assignment of income doctrine was *Johnson v. Commissioner*. The Court noted that looking at employment contracts alone does not determine the earner of income.[226] The Court made its final determination as to who was the earner of the income by applying a two-prong control test. Under this test, "a professional service company controls the service and receives revenues, and earns income, if: (1) The service-provider is an employee of the professional service company, and the company has the right to direct and control him or her in a meaningful sense; and (2) the PSC and the service-recipient have a contract or similar indicium recognizing the controlling position of the PSC."[227]

Athletes are not the only ones who have struggled with the assignment of income doctrine.

Victor Borge, a well-known musical and comedy genius, was one of the first entertainers to use a "loan-out company" where he was an employee of the company, and the company was paid by concert halls and otherwise for his "loan out of services."[228] The IRS assessed significant additional taxes by reallocating the income between Mr. Borge and his closely held company.

In 1958, the highest individual tax rate was 91% and the highest corporate rate tax was only 52%. The bad news was that the Tax Court upheld the IRS's assertion of reallocating income under Internal Revenue Code Section 482, which still exists, but the good news was that Mr. Borge still came out far better under the IRS proposed allocation than he would have if he had not used the

---

[224] *Lucas v. Earl*, 281 U.S. 111 (1930).

[225] *Sargent v. Commissioner*, 929 F.2d 1252 (8th Cir. 1991).

[226] *Johnson v. Commissioner*, 698 F. 2d 372 (1982).

[227] *See Leavell v. Commissioner*, 104 T.C. 140, 182 (Tax 1995) discussing the application of the two-prong control test which evolved from case law.

[228] It was Victor Borge who said "the difference between a violin and a viola is that a viola burns longer." *Borge v. Commissioner*, 405 F.2d 673 (2d Cir. 1968).

loan-out company.[229] The court noted that such an arrangement should be respected only if the taxpayer would have entered into a similar arrangement with unrelated third parties.

The Service may invoke Section 482 to distribute, apportion or allocate income or deductions among two or more "organizations, trades or business" in order to prevent evasion of taxes or clearly to reflect income when the organizations, trades or businesses are owned or controlled by the same interests. It is the reality of the control which is decisive for Section 482 purposes, not the form or mode of exercise of control.[230] Note that this standard, that such an arrangement should be respected only if the taxpayer would have entered into a similar arrangement with unrelated third parties, would be a fair standard to apply under an IRC Section 199A analysis of SSTB vs. non-SSTB income. If a tainted professional practice would pay $X to an unrelated landlord for comparable space, there should be no reason that same amount of rent cannot be treated as non-SSTB income. However, it remains to be seen whether this logic will prevail. Applying IRC Section 469 definitions of trade or business and aggregation rules might well prevent this.

The Doctrine became more taxpayer friendly after the 1981 case of *Keller v. Commissioner*, where the Tenth Circuit Court of Appeals in review of a Tax Court decision held that a medical doctor could have revenues and expenses attributable to his traditional medical practice taxed under his professional corporation, which was therefore able to provide him with employee benefits on a tax advantaged basis.[231] Importantly, the PSC also presumably paid him reasonable compensation commensurate with what an arm's-length arrangement between unrelated parties would be.[232]

This case was followed by the enactment of IRC Section 269A in 1970, which provides that the IRS can reallocate income and expenses, or completely disregard a PSC where substantially all of the services of the company are performed for one other entity, and the principal purpose of the company is to avoid income tax. This statute does not prevent professional service companies from being used to provide services to multiple patients, clients or customers, but if the company is providing personal services that are substantially performed by employees who own more than 10% of the stock of the company, the IRS has plenary power to reallocate or even disregard the company.

Specifically, the definition of a professional service company under Section 269A is as follows:

> "means a corporation the principal activity of which is the performance of personal services, which are substantially performed by employee-owners."[233]

An employee-owner is "any employee who owns more than 10% of the outstanding stock of the personal service corporation on any day during the taxable year. For purposes of the preceding sentence, the Section 318 relationship attribution rules apply, except that '5 percent' is substituted for '50 percent' in Section 318(a)(2)(C)."[234] Thus, if the IRS audits a PSC doing work on behalf

---

[229] The predecessor to Section 482 of the Internal Revenue Code was enacted in 1918.

[230] Treas. Reg. § 1.482-1(a)(3). Note that for 199A purposes the 20% deduction must be calculated for each trade or business, which would seem to lend planning to challenge under Section 482.

[231] *Keller v. Commissioner*, 723 F.2d 58, 58 (10th Cir. 1983).

[232] *Id.*

[233] 26 U.S.C. § 269A (b).

[234] *Id.*

of one customer, it can reallocate income between the PSC and whatever entity it primarily performs services for, unless the PSC is structured to not have any 10% or greater owner or relative thereof act as an employee of the company.[235]

The setting of payments between related entities in exchange for services rendered, assets leased, licensing rights and for products sold is called "transfer pricing." The IRS regularly uses its transfer pricing reallocation powers under Section 482 when auditors have concluded that payments were more or less than arm's-length and to the tax advantage of the taxpayer.[236] Section 269A gives the IRS more power than does Section 482 in that it enables the IRS to reallocate all payments/income between related entities and not just those that do not satisfy the arm's-length test; therefore, it is preferable to structure the related entity so that Section 269A does not apply, as discussed above.

The IRS may allocate or impute the income received by the corporation to its employee-owner under Sections 269A and 482 in order to put the employee-owner on a tax parity with uncontrolled taxpayers. The IRS can raise the argument that the employee-owner is taxable on the income paid to his or her corporation for personal services he or she rendered to another entity under the assignment of income doctrine because the employee- owner was able to control, and possibly

---

[235] 26 U.S.C. § 269A – Personal service corporations formed or availed of to avoid or evade income tax.

    (a)   General rule.--If--

           (1)   substantially all of the services of a personal service corporation are performed for (or on behalf of) 1 other corporation, partnership, or other entity, and

           (2)   the principal purpose for forming, or availing of, such personal service corporation is the avoidance or evasion of Federal income tax by reducing the income of, or securing the benefit of any expense, deduction, credit, exclusion, or other allowance for, any employee-owner which would not otherwise be available, then the Secretary may allocate all income, deductions, credits, exclusions, and other allowances between such personal service corporation and its employee-owners, if such allocation is necessary to prevent avoidance or evasion of Federal income tax or clearly to reflect the income of the personal service corporation or any of its employee-owners.

    (b)   Definitions.--For purposes of this Section—

           (1)   Personal service corporation.--The term "personal service corporation" means a corporation the principal activity of which is the performance of personal services and such services are substantially performed by employee-owners.

           (2)   Employee-owner.--The term "employee-owner" means any employee who owns, on any day during the taxable year, more than 10 percent of the outstanding stock of the personal service corporation. For purposes of the preceding sentence, Section 318 shall apply, except that "5 percent" shall be substituted for "50 percent" in Section 318(a)(2)(C).

           (3)   Related persons.--All related persons (within the meaning of Section 144(a)(3)) shall be treated as 1 entity.

[236] 26 U.S.C. § 482 – Allocation of income and deductions among taxpayers.

In any case of two or more organizations, trades, or businesses (whether or not incorporated, whether or not organized in the United States, and whether or not affiliated) owned or controlled directly or indirectly by the same interests, the Secretary may distribute, apportion, or allocate gross income, deductions, credits, or allowances between or among such organizations, trades, or businesses, if he determines that such distribution, apportionment, or allocation is necessary in order to prevent evasion of taxes or clearly to reflect the income of any of such organizations, trades, or businesses. In the case of any transfer (or license) of intangible property (within the meaning of Section 936(h)(3)(B)), the income with respect to such transfer or license shall be commensurate with the income attributable to the intangible. For purposes of this Section, the Secretary shall require the valuation of transfers of intangible property (including intangible property transferred with other property or services) on an aggregate basis or the valuation of such a transfer on the basis of the realistic alternatives to such a transfer, if the Secretary determines that such basis is the most reliable means of valuation of such transfers.

manipulate, the characterization of income and expenses as between the related parties.[237] As noted in FSA 1992-11162, "...the enactment of Section 269A was not intended to preclude the Service from reallocating income under Section 482."[238]

Management companies for medical and dental practices, according to one author's experience, commonly receive profits that can represent 30-35% of the total entity income when the professionals have "sold their good will" and have entered into long-term, arm's-length employment agreements that require them to work for less than normal compensation, in order to allow the management company to receive profits. This is common for publicly-traded companies and venture capital firms when permitted by state law for medical doctors, dentists, veterinarians, and other professionals.

With reference to setting up a separate management company that can receive arm's-length management fees from a professional practice, it can be helpful to have a key individual who is integral to management operations invest to own a small percentage of the management entity, and to participate in negotiations and oversight of that entity, to help assure that economic arrangements occur at arm's-length, after taking into account compensation arrangements that enable the management company to receive profits. This may also be a good way to encourage key employees to "think like owners," and become more involved to enhance the bottom-line of an affiliated entity. Finally, having equity owned by a key person in one of the ancillary businesses may break an identity of ownership between the SSTB and non-SSTB. A practical issue with providing such equity is terminating the equity arrangement if the relationship is not successful or if it is not desired after 2025 when Section 199A is scheduled to sunset.

8. APPLICATION TO TRUSTS AND ESTATES.

As discussed in depth in Chapter 13 and also Chapter 14, trusts and estates may be permitted to take the Section 199A deduction on income from a Specified Service Trade or Business in situations where the grantor of the trust or other family members may be over the threshold that otherwise applies.

Under these rules, individual taxpayers and trusts having less than $157,500/$315,000 of taxable income can deduct Section 199A flow-through income from a trade or business without regard to the kind of services rendered and whether the Wage/Property Limitation is met.

Taxpayers having more than the $207,500/$415,000 of taxable income can only qualify for the 20% deduction if the flow-through income is not from an SSTB and meets the Wage/Property Limitation. Taxpayers with taxable income between $157,500-$207,500 if not married filing jointly, or between $315,000-$415,000 if filing jointly, will have a limited deduction for income

---

[237] FSA 1992-11162 (Nov. 16, 1992).

[238] *See* Proposed Treas. Reg. §1.269A-1(f) ("Nothing in Section 269A or the Regulations thereunder, including the safe harbor provided in paragraph (c) of this Section, precludes application with respect to personal service corporations or their employee-owners of any other Code Section (e.g., Sections 61 or 482) or tax law principle (e.g., assignment of income doctrine) to reallocate or reapportion income deductions, credits, etc., so as to reflect the true earner of income")."

derived from (1) SSTB; and (2) Non-SSTB income where the Wage/Property Limitation discussed below is not met.

If separating the income thresholds saves taxes overall, married couples can file separately and have two separate $157,500-$207,500 thresholds. The income threshold for a separately taxed trust or estate is also $157,500, with the phase-out occurring between $157,500 - $207,500. As discussed in Chapter 13, there are many planning opportunities that may apply to separately taxed trusts.

Chart 12 – 2018 Specified Service Trade or Business Income Deductibility Thresholds Chart

The chart below shows how SSTBs may qualify for the 20% deduction:

2018 Personal taxable income thresholds	Specified Service Trade or Businesses (including law, health, and accounting)	Non-Specified Service Trade or Businesses
LESS than $315,000 joint filers / $157,500 single filers or separately-taxed trust	Eligible for the 20% deduction; not subject to the Wage/Property Test	Eligible for the 20% deduction; not subject to the Wage/Property Test
MORE than $415,000 joint filers / $207,500 single filers	**Not eligible for the 20% deduction**	**Eligible for the 20% deduction; subject to the Wage/Property Test**
BETWEEN $315,000-$415,000 joint filers / $157,500 – $207,500 single filers	**Eligible for a portion of the 20% deduction based upon ratable phase-out**	**Eligible for the 20% deduction; subject to the Wage/Property Test based upon ratable phase- in**

Chart 12 A – 2019 Specified Service Trade or Business Income Deductibility Thresholds Chart

The chart below shows how SSTBs may qualify for the 20% deduction:

2019 Personal taxable income thresholds	Specified service businesses (including law, health, and accounting)	Non-Specified Service Trade or Businesses
LESS than $321,400 joint filers / $160,700 single filers or separately-taxed trust	Eligible for the 20% deduction; not subject to the Wage/Property Test	Eligible for the 20% deduction; not subject to the Wage/Property Test

2019 Personal taxable income thresholds	Specified service businesses (including law, health, and accounting)	Non-Specified Service Trade or Businesses
MORE than $421,400 joint filers / $210,700 single filers	Not eligible for the 20% deduction	**Eligible for the 20% deduction; subject to the Wage/Property Test**
BETWEEN $321,400-$421,400 joint filers / $160,700 – $210,700 single filers	**Eligible for a portion of the 20% deduction based upon ratable phase-out**	**Eligible for the 20% deduction; subject to the Wage/Property Test based upon ratable phase- in**

Example:

> Suzy Lawyer and her spouse have combined marital taxable income of under $315,000, which includes $200,000 of Suzy's K-1 income received from a legal practice which is an S corporation. Suzy Lawyer and her spouse can receive a deduction of $40,000 ($200,000 x 20%) on their personal income tax return.

Example:

> Suzy Lawyer and her spouse, from above, had $355,000 of taxable income in 2018, which included $190,000 of flow-through income from the couple's law firm. The $190,000 will qualify for Section 199A, but since their taxable income exceeds $315,000, the deduction will be partially phased out. The couple's Section 199A deduction for 2018 is $22,800 on their personal Form 1040 tax return ($190,000 x 20% x (1-40%); 40% is derived from dividing the amount by which taxable income exceeds $315,000 by $100,000 ($355,000 – $315,000)/ $100,000). Suzy and her spouse lost nearly half of their deduction because their income was $40,000 over the $315,000 threshold; causing loss of $15,200 of the deduction ($38,000 – $22,800). In Suzy's bracket (32%), this will cost her $4,864 in tax savings ($15,200 x 32%).

Example:

> Jack Legal owns a law firm as a sole proprietor, is a partner in a glass factory, owns and conducts a rental activity, and has income of over $500,000 a year with his spouse. They file jointly and will not qualify for Section 199A on the law firm income. They may qualify for the Section 199A deduction on the rental activity and glass factory income, if the Wage/Property Test is met.

If Jack and his spouse were to give ownership of the rental activity and the glass factory to their two lower income children, the children may be able to qualify for Section 199A for the income they receive from those entities. This will hold true, without any limitations, if the children have less than $157,500 each of taxable income. Even with the Kiddie Tax, each child's tax rate would not exceed 29.6%. It is noteworthy that the Kiddie Tax was changed effective January 1, 2018, so that children under the age of 19 and "full-time students" under the age of 24 will be taxed on unearned income at the progressive brackets that apply to complex trusts, but only if such child's earned income does not exceed one-half of the "support" provided to such child during the tax year. Support is defined under Treasury Regulations Section 1.152-1(a)(1) to include food, shelter, clothing, medical and dental care, education, and other similar items. Support also includes the payment of real estate and personal property insurances, medical insurance, and items such as housekeeping services, laundry and dry cleaning, babysitters, child care, vitamins, toys, bicycle repairs, telephones, televisions, book club costs, hairstyling and haircuts, pets, entertainment, wedding expenses, vacations, gifts, and charitable contributions by or on behalf of such individual.[239]

Educational expenses do not include amounts received as scholarships. There are conflicting views as to whether distributions from Section 529 Plans count as "support," and the IRS has not formally or informally addressed this in any guidance.

Some practitioners take the position that since the student is taxed on non-qualified distributions (distributions not used for educational expenses) from 529 Plans, the payments from such plans should be considered as contributed by the student for his or her own support, and therefore not included in the calculation of whether the child's earned income exceeds one-half of his or her support.

Other practitioners note that since the parent is the owner of the account and can change the beneficiary, it should be considered as support provided by the parent, and thus included in the calculation of whether one-half of the child's support exceeds his or her earned income.

The rate brackets are as follows:

---

[239] Maule, 513 T.M., Family and Household Transactions.

Chart 13 – 2018 Complex Trust/Kiddie Tax Brackets Chart

Unearned Taxable Income	Applicable Kiddie Tax Rate	Capital Gain Income	Applicable Kiddie Tax Rate
$0-$2,550	10%	$0-$2,600	0%
$2,551-$9,150	24%	$2,661-$12,700	15%
$9,151-$12,500	35%	$12,700+	20%
$12,500+	37%		

Chart 13 A – 2019 Complex Trust/Kiddie Tax Brackets Chart

Unearned Taxable Income	Applicable Kiddie Tax Rate	Capital Gain Income	Applicable Kiddie Tax Rate
$0-$2,600	10%	$0-$2,600	0%
$2,551-$9,300	24%	$2,661-$12,700	15%
$9,151-$12,750	35%	$12,700+	20%
$12,750+	37%		

If the Kiddie Tax applies, then these children also reach the 3.8% Net Investment Income Tax threshold on passive income at $12,500, which means that passive income above $12,500 will be subject to the 3.8% Medicare tax.

Detail on the Wage/Property Test. This test must be met for a high-income taxpayer to be eligible for the Section 199A deduction on income from any given trade or business activity. The taxpayer's deduction will be limited by not having enough wages paid by or Qualified Property owned or used by the flow-through entity, or a combination of the two. The test will yield an amount to allow some or all of the otherwise applicable 20% deduction based upon the greater of the following:

> *Wage Test.* 50% of the taxpayer's pro rata share of W-2 wages paid to any and all employees of the flow-through entity or Schedule C or E activity, including wages paid to the owners of an S corporation[240] or

---

[240] IRC § 199A(f)(1)(A)(iii). Notes that each partner in a partnership or shareholder in an S corporation shall be treated as having wages and Unadjusted Basis in Qualified Property equal to each person's "allocable share."

Property Test. The sum of (a) 25% of the taxpayer's pro rata share of W-2 wages paid to employees, and (b) the taxpayer's pro rata share of 2.5% of the original basis of qualified depreciable property owned by the flow-through entity and used in the production of flow-through income.

If the greater of the above two amounts is less than 20% of the taxpayer's QBI, then the taxpayer's deduction will be limited, as discussed below. If one of these two values is greater than 20% of the taxpayer's QBI, then the deduction will not be limited.

Further, the taxpayer may only count the W-2 wages and Qualified Property in proportion to their interest in the entity. For example, a 25% owner of an entity would only be able to count 25% of the wages paid by the entity, and the taxpayer's Wage Test outcome would be one-fourth of what it would be if they had 100% ownership.

A useful rule of thumb is that a taxpayer should always use the 50% Wage Test unless their share of Qualified Property is greater than 10 times their share of wages. This is because once a taxpayer's Qualified Property is equal to 10 times their share in wages, 25% of wages and 2.5% of Qualified Property will total 50% of wages. This renders the outcomes of the Wage Test and the Property Test the same, and any increase in Qualified Property beyond this point makes the Property Test the greater value.

For example, if someone had $10,000 in wages paid, and $100,000 in Qualified Property, the results of the two tests (Wage Test - $5,000; Property Test - $5,000) are the same and the taxpayer might as well use the Wage Test. But if the taxpayer were to acquire any more in Qualified Property, they should use the Property Test.

Example:

> Jack and his spouse have taxable income over $415,000, and own the glass factory and also the rental activity, with each giving them flow-through income of $100,000. The glass factory has no depreciable assets and would have to pay at least $40,000 in wages to qualify. The rental activity has no employees that receive wages and will need to have at least $800,000 in Qualified Property to allow the full deduction ($800,000 times 2.5% is $20,000). They cannot deduct any part of the law firm income under Section 199A.

If the glass factory has $500,000 in Qualified Property then it would only have to pay $30,000 in wages to qualify for the full Section 199A deduction. If the rental activity has only $200,000 of Qualified Property, then it would have to pay $60,000 in wages to receive the full deduction under the combined Wage/Qualified Property Test, but would only have to pay $40,000 in wages if relying solely on the Wage Test. As discussed above, a taxpayer in this situation is better off relying solely on the Wage Test to satisfy the limitation.

Most taxpayers with more than $207,500/$415,000 in taxable income can satisfy the Wage Test by paying W-2 wages of at least 28.57% of the net profits of the flow-through entity, while real estate companies relying solely on UBIA of Qualified Property will need to assure that 2.5% of their UBIA in Qualified Property is worth at least 8 times the taxpayer's QBI. For example, if a taxpayer has $1,000,000 of QBI, then the taxpayer will need UBIA of $8,000,000 in order to avoid the deduction being limited by the Wage/Property Test.[241] Qualified property does not include any asset that has been held by the trade or business for the greater of (1) its depreciable life, or (2) ten years. Commercial buildings placed into service after 1986 have a depreciable life of 39 years, although components of buildings that qualify for faster "component depreciations" typically have a 5- to 7-year life. Generally, equipment has a 5- or 7-year life. As a result, the UBIA of non-residential real property may be used to satisfy the Property Test for up to 39 years, while the UBIA of segregated building components and equipment may be used for only 10 years.

Business owners with significant amounts of Qualified Property will be able to take lower salaries, and thus pay less in employment taxes, without sacrificing their Section 199A deduction. Taxpayers using Qualified Property to take lower salaries will need to keep an eye on the length of time the property has been placed into service so that the Section 199A deduction will not be inadvertently limited or lost. Real estate that is no longer countable as qualified property for Section 199A purposes may be ideal for donation to a private foundation that can actively support a charitable cause to enable the owner to receive a charitable deduction based upon the full fair market value of the property, while retaining the ability to continue to control and operate the property while using the property, or income therefrom, for charitable purposes in satisfaction of the applicable rules.[242]

Many businesses that pay independent contractors or service agencies will need to convert the individuals providing the services to employees in order to pay wages and satisfy the Wage/Property Test and claim a Section 199A deduction on flow-through income, after weighing the other costs of employment status, which will usually include most, if not all, of the following:

(1) employment taxes, which are summarized at Charts 3 and 4 in Chapter 4,

(2) unemployment insurance,

(3) workers compensation costs,

(4) limited liability resulting from having workers compensation in place,

(5) pension considerations,

(6) health insurance considerations,

(7) other employee benefits,

(8) right to work laws, and

(9) the doctrine of *respondeat superior* — an employer is responsible for the negligence

---

[241] With $1,000,000 of QBI, the taxpayer's deduction would be equal to $200,000. 2.5% of $8,000,000 is equal to $200,000.

[242] *See* Alan Gassman & Thomas Ellwanger, *Don't Overlook the Benefits—Tax and Otherwise—of Private Operating Foundations*, 34 Tax Mgmt. Est. Gifts & Tr., J., 250 (November 12, 2009).

of an employee working within the scope of employment.

In addition, an independent contractor may have his or her own pension plan, tax benefits, including a possible Section 199A deduction, and other considerations that would make employment more or less desirable.

Simply put, a taxpayer who has taxable income exceeding the $207,500/$415,000 threshold who is in a Specified Service Trade or Business cannot qualify for the Section 199A deduction for such Specified Service Trade or Business income. For example, a lawyer who has more than $207,500/$415,000 in 2018 could not claim the 20% deduction on his or her law firm income.

Lawyers who are high-income taxpayers may get a deduction from non-law firm income, contingent upon the results of the Wage/Property Test for each separate flow-through entity.

As noted above, single filers, and trusts with income between $157,500 and $207,500 ($315,000 and $415,000 for joint filers), who are owners of Specified Service Trade or Businesses will have their Section 199A deductions phased-out as their income exceeds the $157,500 for single filers or $315,000 for joint filers. Additionally, every taxpayer seeking a 199A deduction with taxable income above the $157,500/$315,000 thresholds will be subject to the Wage/Property Test.

For non-specified service owners, if the taxpayer's taxable income is over $207,500/$415,000 (single filer/joint filers), the taxpayer's deduction will be the lesser of (1) 20% of the taxpayer's QBI, and (2) the greater of (A) the Wage Test (50% of W-2 wages), and (B) Qualified Property test (25% of wages plus 2.5% of the taxpayer's basis in depreciable assets).

It is important to note that flow-through income from a Specified Service will be subject to both the phase-in of the Wage/Property Test requirements, and the phase-out of the overall deduction as the taxpayer's taxable income exceeds the $157,500/$315,000 thresholds until completely phased-out at the $207,500/$415,000 thresholds.

Example:

> If Joe Smith's law firm, taxed as a partnership, gives him flow-through income of $800,000, his widget factory entity (not a Specified Service) gives him flow-through income of $150,000, and his rental activity earns him $50,000, then he can qualify for a tax deduction based on 20% of the $150,000 from the widget factory entity as long as it pays W-2 wages of at least $60,000 per year, and he can qualify for a 20% deduction on the real estate activity income as long as it has Qualified Property with an original cost basis of at least $400,000 ($10,000 / 2.5%) that is either still within its depreciable life, or no more than 10 years has passed since it was placed into service.

In the next year, Joe's title company might manage the law firm and charge $50,000 per year as arm's-length management fees. This would reduce the law firm income by $50,000 and would increase the title company's income and Section 199A deduction by $10,000 (assuming that the title company is paying sufficient wages), thus saving $3,700 in income taxes.

As a result of the above, owners of Specified Service Trades or Businesses will seek to identify and maximize sources of income that will be eligible for the 20% Section 199A deduction to the extent that this is feasible.

Those who wish to master the concept and implications of taxpayers in the Phase-out rules can review the deeper discussion found in Chapter 10.

CHAPTER 10.
PHASE-IN AND PHASE-OUT RULES

Most readers will not spend long on this chapter, but advisors need to understand how the deduction applies for those clients with income between $157,500-$207,500 for single filers or $315,000-$415,000 for joint filers, particularly with respect to the interaction that these rules will have when a high earner taxpayer has Specified Service Trade or Business Income and insufficient wages associated therewith. Also, those with clients who cannot pay more in wages, or acquire additional Qualified Property, or who are engaged in a Specified Service will need to know how to calculate a deduction that is subject to phase-in of the Wage/Property limitation or is partially phased-out.

The reader may wish to review charts 15 and 16, which appear at the end of this chapter, before proceeding further.

The degree to which a taxpayer's deduction is subject to the phase-in or phase-out is determined by their taxable income, while their flow-through income is only considered to the extent it affects the taxpayer's taxable income.

The calculation will become very complicated when the taxpayer is between the thresholds and there is an SSTB that does not have sufficient wages or qualified property that would otherwise allow the maximum deduction.

Chart 14 – Phase-In/Phase-Out Wage and Property Chart

This chart explains how phasing applies to the income levels in Section 199A:

	$0-$157,500 (single filers)/$0-$315,000 (joint filers)	$157,500-$207,500 (single filers)/ $315,000-$415,000 (joint filers)	$207,500+ (single filers)/$415,000+ (joint filers)
Non-Specified Service Trades or Businesses (only subject to Phase- In)	Full Deduction: No limits from Wage/Property Test	Phase-In Zone: Wage/Property Test is phased-in as income exceeds lower income thresholds	Fully Phased-In: Wage/Property Test is fully phased-in for
Non-Specified Services Specified Service Trades or Businesses (subject to Phase- In and Phase-Out)	Full Deduction: No limits from Wage/Property Test; no limitation from being a Specified Service	Phase-In/-Out Zone: Wage/Property Test is phased-in, and deduction for Specified Service income starts being phased-out, as income exceeds lower income thresholds	Fully Phased-Out: No deduction under any circumstances for Specified Service income.

Taxpayers with taxable income below the lower-income thresholds ($157,500 for single filers or $315,000 for joint filers) generally will not be subject to phasing or other restrictions on their deduction.

Taxpayers with taxable income above the lower-income thresholds ($157,500/$315,000) but below the higher-income thresholds ($207,500 for single filers or $415,000 for joint filers) will be subject to both a phase-in on the Wage/Property Limitation and a phase-out of their deduction if the flow-through income is derived from a Specified Service.

Taxpayers with taxable income above the higher-income thresholds ($207,500/$415,000) will be subject to a fully phased-in Wage/Property Limitation, and the deduction for flow-through income from Specified Services will be completely phased-out, meaning no deduction will be available.

How phasing works in calculating a deduction is described below. The definitions of phasing-in and phasing-out will also be reviewed in this chapter.

It is noteworthy that REIT dividends are not reduced by the Wage/Property Limitation or the SSTB Limitation, and as a result, REITS in the Phase-Out Zone can ignore these calculations. Publicly Traded Partnership income is subject to the phase-out, but not the phase-in.[243]

Specifically, as the taxpayer's taxable income exceeds the lower-income thresholds ($157,500 for single filers, $315,000 for joint filers), the limitation imposed by the Wage/Property Test is phased-in and the deduction for flow-through income associated with Specified Services is phased-out. The authors refer to the degree a taxpayer's deduction is subject to the phase-in and phase-out under Section 199A as the amount the taxpayer is in the Phase-Out Zone, which is how much either limitation can reduce the taxpayer's overall deduction. For example, a taxpayer who is 75% in the Phase-Out Zone (either single with $195,000 or married with $390,000) and the owner of an SSTB has an SSTB deduction that is reduced by 75%, so that 25% of the deduction remains (a deduction of 5% of QBI in lieu of 20%) by the phase-out, but the taxpayer's deduction can also be further reduced by the Wage/Property Limitation.

The taxpayer is in the Phase-Out Zone by the amount that the taxpayer's taxable income is between the lower-income and higher-income thresholds, such that a joint filer with $315,000 of taxable income is 0% Phased and a joint filer with $415,000 of taxable income is 100% Phased.

The technical calculation to determine the amount the taxpayer is in the Phase-Out Zone is determined by (1) subtracting the taxable income by the lower-income threshold ($157,500 if a single filer/$315,000 if a joint filer), and then (2) dividing that by the difference between the higher- and lower-income thresholds ($50,000 if a single filer/$100,000 if a joint filer).

For example, if John was a joint filer with taxable income of $365,000, he would be 50% in the Phase-Out Zone, because his taxable income is halfway between $315,000 and $415,000, and as a result, John's deduction can, at most, be cut in half assuming he was not in a Specified Service. The same result would occur if John was a single filer with taxable income of $182,500, which is

---

[243] The phase-in of the Wage/Property Limitation is applied before REIT dividends and Publicly Traded Partnership income are added to the taxpayer's deduction, so they are excluded from Wage and Qualified Property restrictions.

halfway between the $157,500 and $207,500 thresholds. If John was 25% in the Phase-Out Zone, his deduction can only be reduced by 25%.

However, calculating how much a taxpayer is in the Phase-Out Zone would not be quite as fun as finding a math trick to figure out the amount using one less step.

1. PHASE-IN SHORTCUT.

An easier way to determine the amount by which a joint filer is in the Phase-Out Zone is to take the difference between taxable income and the lower threshold ($315,000) and start the tens' place of the result in the Phase-Out Zone percentage with the number at the ten thousands' place of the result. Then, the subsequent numbers will be from the thousands' place, hundreds' place, and so on.

For example, a taxpayer with a taxable income of $356,000 is 41% in the Phase-Out Zone ($356,000 - $315,000 = $41,000), a taxpayer with a taxable income of $316,000 is 1% in the Phase-Out Zone, because there is no value in the ten thousands' place ($316,000 – $315,000 = $1,000), and a taxpayer with a taxable income of $315,001 is .001% in the Phase-Out Zone.

For single filers, subtract the $157,500 threshold amount from taxable income, multiply the result by 2, and start the percentage the same way as a joint filer, with the number in the ten thousands' place. For example, a single filer with a taxable income of $182,500 is 50% in the Phase-Out Zone ($182,500 - $157,500 = $25,000 x 2 = $50,000), and a single filer with $207,400 in taxable income would be 99% in the Phase-Out Zone ($207,000 - $157,500 = $49,500 x 2 = $99,000).

2. PHASE-IN (THE WAGE/PROPERTY LIMITATION).

As a taxpayer's taxable income exceeds the lower-income threshold ($157,500/$315,000), the Wage/Property Test is phased-in, which means that the taxpayer's deduction can be subject to a limitation.

For example, a joint filer with only half of the wages they need to overcome the limitation would be subject to no reduction at $315,000 of taxable income; a 25% reduction at $365,000, when the test is 50% phased-in; and a 50% reduction (representing the fact that the taxpayer only has half of the wages needed) at $415,000, when the test is fully phased-in.

The Wage/Property Tests are composed of two parts:

(i) *Wage Test*. This is the taxpayer's pro rata share (proportional to his/her ownership interest in the entity) of 50% of W-2 wages paid by the entity.

(ii) *Property Test*. This is the taxpayer's pro rata share (proportional to his/her ownership interest in the entity) of 2.5% of the entity's UBIA in qualified depreciable property, plus 25% of W-2 wages paid by the entity.

The greater value of these two tests is always the one used in Section 199A calculations. The taxpayer's deduction will be limited if the greater outcome of the Wage/Property Limitation is less than the taxpayer's tentative deduction, or 20% of their flow-through income. This determination is made on an entity-by-entity basis, so the Wages and Qualified Property from Entity 1 will be compared with the flow-through income from Entity 1, and the same goes for all other entities unless the entities are aggregated under the Final Regulations.

In order to calculate a deduction that has been limited by the phase-in, three values must be calculated: (1) the amount by which the taxpayer is in the Phase-Out Zone, (2) the greater outcome of the Wage/Property Test, and (3) the taxpayer's tentative deduction (20% of flow- through income).

Once these are known, there are three steps to calculate the taxpayer's limited deduction:

(1)   Subtract the greater outcome of the Wage/Property Tests above from the tentative deduction (20% of flow-through income),

(2)   multiply the value of Step 1 above by the amount the taxpayer is in the Phase-Out Zone, and

(3)   subtract the result of Step 2 from the taxpayer's tentative deduction.

Voilà! The Section 199A deduction is calculated, which is the result of Step 3. This may seem complicated, so consider the examples below that illustrate each step.

John Taxpayer is a joint filer with $365,000 in taxable income and makes $100,000 from owning a flow-through business that pays $20,000 in wages and holds no Qualified Property. Because his tentative deduction ($100,000 x 20% = $20,000) is larger than the greater outcome of the Wage/Property Test ($20,000 in W-2 wages x 50% = $10,000), we know his deduction will be limited.

The first thing to do is to calculate how far John is in the Phase-Out Zone. To do this, subtract his taxable income from the lower threshold for joint filers, which would be $50,000 ($365,000 - $315,000) and either divide that value by $100,000, or use our Phasing Trick from above, but the result is the same: John is 50% in the Phase-Out Zone. With this consideration taken care of, here are the steps to calculate John's deduction:

(1)   Subtract the greater outcome of the Wage/Property Test ($20,000 x 50% = $10,000) from John's tentative deduction ($100,000 x 20% = $20,000), with the result being $10,000.

(2)   Multiply the value from Step 1 ($10,000) by the amount that the taxpayer is in the Phase-Out Zone (50%), with the result being $5,000.

(3)   Subtract the result from Step 2 ($5,000) from the taxpayer's tentative deduction ($20,000), with the result being $15,000 ($20,000 - $5,000) which is John's Section 199A deduction.

The following chart explains this calculation:

Value/Step	$
Flow-through Income	$100,000
Tentative Deduction (20% of above)	$20,000
Greater outcome of Wage/Property Test* *(50% of Wages or 25% of Wages plus 2.5% of Qualified Property)	$10,000
Result of Step 1* *(subtract Tentative Deduction by Greater outcome of Wage/Property Tests)	$10,000
Amount in Phase-Out Zone *(In John's case – ($365,000 - $315,000)/$100,000)	50%
Result of Step 2* *(multiply Step 1 value by the amount Phased)	$5,000
Result of Step 3 / 199A Deduction* *(subtract Step 2 from Tentative Deduction)	**$15,000**

Here is a slightly more complicated example: A joint-filer taxpayer, with 100% ownership of an S corporation, reports $200,000 of flow-through income and has a taxable income of $340,000. If the company pays only $30,000 in wages, there will be a limitation of the taxpayer's deduction, but because the taxpayer's taxable income is below the higher-income threshold, the Wage/Property Limitation is only partially phased-in.

First, find the amount by which the taxpayer is in the Phase-Out Zone, which is 25% ($340,000 - $315,000 = $25,000). Next, follow the steps of the calculation:

(1)   Subtract the greater Wage/Property Test value ($30,000 x 50% = $15,000) from the taxpayer's tentative deduction ($200,000 x 20% = $40,000), with the result being $25,000 ($40,000 - $15,000).

(2)   Multiply the value of Step 1 ($25,000) by the amount by which the taxpayer is in the Phase-Out Zone (25%), with the result being $6,250 ($25,000 x 25%).

(3)   Subtract the result of Step 2 ($6,250) from the taxpayer's tentative deduction ($40,000), with the result being $33,750 ($40,000 - $6,250).

Here is the calculation displayed visually:

Value/Step	$
Flow-through Income	$200,000
Tentative Deduction (20% of above)	$40,000
Greater outcome of Wage/Property Test* *(50% of Wages or 25% of Wages plus 2.5% of Qualified Property)	$15,000
Result of Step 1* *(subtract Tentative Deduction by Greater outcome of Wage/Property Tests)	$25,00
Amount in Phase-Out Zone * (In John's case – ($340,000 - $315,000) / $100,000)	25%
Result of Step 2* *(multiply Step 1 value by amount Phased)	$6,250
Result of Step 3 / 199A Deduction* *(subtract Step 2 from Tentative Deduction)	**$33,750**

For those with a taxable income above the higher-income thresholds ($207,500 for single filers/$415,000 for joint filers), the taxpayer's income will simply be the lesser of the following two values:

(1)   The taxpayer's tentative deduction, or 20% of their flow-through income, or

(2)   The greater outcome of the Wage/Property Tests.

3.   PHASE-OUT (THE SPECIFIED SERVICE LIMITATION).

SSTBs under Section 199A are subject to a phase-out on the deduction for flow-through income derived from these businesses. This means that like the phase-in from above, the taxpayer loses a greater part of their deduction as their taxable income exceeds the lower-income thresholds. Unlike the phase-in from above, however, this reduction is guaranteed, and nothing can be done to stop the limitation on the taxpayer's deduction other than to lower the taxpayer's taxable income.

The statute provides that this phase-out reduces the number of qualified items of income, gain, deduction, and loss (also known as QBI); the amount of wages; and the amount of Qualified Property a taxpayer can claim. Section 199A states that Publicly Traded Partnership income includes "qualified item[s] of income, gain, deduction, and loss," which means that this income will be reduced by the phase-out.

A limited deduction based on the phase-out is calculated in the following way: The taxpayer's deduction is reduced by the amount by which the taxpayer is in the Phase-Out Zone, such that a taxpayer who is 60% in the Phase-Out Zone would only be eligible to claim 40% of the full 20% deduction, or a deduction of 8% of flow-through income. Here are some further examples:

Joint filers with $365,000 of taxable income are 50% in the Phase-Out Zone ($365,000 - $315,000 = $50,000) on Specified Service income and their deduction will be cut in half, assuming their deduction is not also limited by the Wage/Property Limitation.

A joint filer with $375,000 of taxable income who receives $100,000 of flow-through income from an SSTB that pays sufficient wages to not be subject to the Wage/Property Limitation will receive only 40% of the normal deduction. The taxpayer is 60% in the Phase-Out Zone ($375,000 – $315,000 = $60,000), and therefore the taxpayer's deduction is reduced from $20,000 ($100,000 x 20%) to $8,000 ($20,000 x 40%).

A single filer who owns a law firm and has a taxable income of $200,000 and receives $100,000 from the firm will be limited by the SSTB Limitation. This taxpayer is 85% in the Phase-Out Zone ($200,000 - $157,500 = $42,500 x 2 = $85,000) and will only be eligible for 15% of the taxpayer's normal deduction, which would have been $20,000, but this is reduced to $3,000 ($20,000 x 15%).

For those wondering how the phase-in and phase-out interact, the authors have included the following discussion:

Explanation: As per the discussion above, the results of the Wage/Property Test can go one of two ways: (1) 20% of the QBI is less than the Wage/Property Limitation amount, in which case the phase-in will not apply, or (2) 20% of QBI is greater than the Wage/Property Limitation amount, so the phase-in will apply. As a refresher, the Wage/Property Limitation amount is the greater of (1) 50% of W-2 wages, or (2) the sum of 2.5% of Qualified Property plus 25% of wages.

As stated above, the SSTB Limitation reduces the amount of wages; and the amount of Qualified Property a taxpayer can claim. As a result, if the taxpayer is 50% in the Phase-Out Zone, the taxpayer can only count 50% of the wages paid and 50% of the UBIA in Qualified Property.

Example:

> For example, Richard files jointly with his spouse, and has a taxable income of $385,000, $250,000 of which is flow-through income from his law firm taxed as a partnership. As a result, Richard's deduction will first be reduced by the amount that Richard is in the Phase-Out Zone, which is 70% ($385,000 - $315,000/$100,000). Richard's deduction will therefore be reduced by $35,000 (70% x $50,000), and his tentative Section 199A deduction will be $15,000 ($50,000 x (1 - 70%)).

If Richard's law firm has no qualified assets and pays $120,000 in W-2 wages, then the wages allocated to Richard would be reduced by the amount he is in the Phase-Out Zone (70%) since the wages were paid by an SSTB, and therefore Richard has $36,000 of wages. Richard would "pass" the Wage/Property Limitation because 50% of W-2 wages ($18,000 = $36,000 x 50%) is greater than his tentative deduction of $15,000, and his deduction is not further reduced by the Wage/Property Limitation.

Example:

> We have the same scenario, but Richard's law firm only paid $80,000 in wages. Again the deduction is first reduced by the SSTB Limitation by the amount that Richard is in the Phase-Out Zone, which is 70% ($385,000 - $315,000 / $100,000). Richard's deduction will therefore be reduced by $35,000 (70% x $50,000), and his tentative Section 199A deduction will be $15,000 ($50,000 x (1 - 70%)).

The wages allocated to Richard would be reduced by the amount he is in the Phase-Out Zone (70%) since the wages were paid by an SSTB, and therefore Richard has $24,000 of wages. Since 50% of Richard's wages, after reduction for the SSTB Limitation ($12,000 = $24,000 x 50%) is less than his tentative deduction, Richard's deduction is further reduced by the Wage/Property Limitation. To calculate the reduction, first take the proportion that Richard's taxable income exceeds the threshold amount ($385,000 – $315,000)/$100,000 = 70%) and apply the result to the difference between Richard's tentative deduction and the Wage/Property Limitation amount (($15,000 - $12,000) x 70% = $2,100). Richard's deduction is reduced by that amount ($15,000 – $2,100 = $12,900). Richard's final Section 199A deduction after applying both the SSTB Limitation and the Wage/Property Limitation is $12,900.

As a reminder, Specified Service Trades or Businesses are trades or businesses engaged in the performance of services in the fields of (1) health, (2) law, (3) accounting, (4) actuarial science, (5) performing arts, (6) consulting, (7) athletics, (8) financial services, (9) brokerage services, (10) investing, trading, or dealing in securities, partnership interest, or commodities, and (11) any business where the principal asset is the reputation or skill of one or more of its employees.

The Final Regulations also contain the following examples to illustrate the phase in and phase out calculation rules:

Example 1:

> (A) B and C are married and file a joint individual income tax return. B is a shareholder in M, an entity taxed as an S corporation for Federal income tax purposes that conducts a single trade or business. M holds no qualified property. B's share of the M's QBI is $300,000 in 2018. B's share of the W-2 wages from M in 2018 is $40,000. C earns wage income from employment by an unrelated company. After allowable deductions unrelated to M, B and C's taxable income for 2018 is $375,000. B and C are within the phase-in range because their taxable income exceeds the applicable threshold amount, $315,000, but does not exceed the threshold amount plus $100,000, or $415,000. Consequently, the QBI component of B and C's section 199A deduction may be limited by the W-2 wage and UBIA of qualified property limitations but the limitations will be phased in.

(B) Because M does not hold qualified property, only the W-2 wage limitation must be calculated. In order to apply the W-2 wage limitation, B and C must first determine 20% of B's share of M's QBI. Twenty percent of B's share of M's QBI of $300,000 is $60,000. Next, B and C must determine 50% of B's share of M's W-2 wages. Fifty percent of B's share of M's W-2 wages of $40,000 is $20,000. Because 50% of B's share of M's W-2 wages ($20,000) is less than 20% of B's share of M's QBI ($60,000), B and C must determine the QBI component of their section 199A deduction by reducing 20% of B's share of M's QBI by the reduction amount.

(C) B and C are 60% through the phase-in range (that is, their taxable income exceeds the threshold amount by $60,000 and their phase-in range is $100,000). B and C must determine the excess amount, which is the excess of 20% of B's share of M's QBI, or $60,000, over 50% of B's share of M's W-2 wages, or $20,000. Thus, the excess amount is $40,000. The reduction amount is equal to 60% of the excess amount, or $24,000. Thus, the QBI component of B and C's section 199A deduction is equal to $36,000, 20% of B's $300,000 share M's QBI (that is, $60,000), reduced by $24,000. B and C's section 199A deduction is equal to the lesser of 20% of the QBI from the business as limited ($36,000) or (ii) 20% of B and C's taxable income ($375,000 x 20% = $75,000). Therefore, B and C's section 199A deduction is $36,000 for 2018.[244]

Example 2:

(A) Assume the same facts [as Example 1 above], except that M is engaged in an SSTB. Because B and C are within the phase-in range, B must reduce the QBI and W-2 wages allocable to B from M to the applicable percentage of those items. B and C's applicable percentage is 100% reduced by the percentage equal to the ratio that their taxable income for the taxable year ($375,000) exceeds their threshold amount ($315,000), or $60,000, bears to $100,000. Their applicable percentage is 40%. The applicable percentage of B's QBI is ($300,000 x 40% =) $120,000, and the applicable percentage of B's share of W-2 wages is ($40,000 x 40% =) $16,000. These reduced numbers must then be used to determine how B's section 199A deduction is limited.

(B) B and C must apply the W-2 wage limitation by first determining 20% of B's share of M's QBI as limited by paragraph (A) of this example. Twenty percent of B's share of M's QBI of $120,000 is $24,000. Next, B and C must determine 50% of B's share of M's W-2 wages. Fifty percent of B's share of M's W-2 wages of $16,000 is

---

[244] Treas. Reg. §1.199A-1(d)(4), Example 5.

$8,000. Because 50% of B's share of M's W-2 wages ($8,000) is less than 20% of B's share of M's QBI ($24,000), B and C's must determine the QBI component of their section 199A deduction by reducing 20% of B's share of M's QBI by the reduction amount.

(C) B and C are 60% through the phase-in range (that is, their taxable income exceeds the threshold amount by $60,000 and their phase-in range is $100,000). B and C must determine the excess amount, which is the excess of 20% of B's share of M's QBI, as adjusted in paragraph (A) of this example or $24,000, over 50% of B's share of M's W-2 wages, as adjusted in paragraph (A) of this example, or $8,000. Thus, the excess amount is $16,000. The reduction amount is equal to 60% of the excess amount or $9,600. Thus, the QBI component of B and C's section 199A deduction is equal to $14,400, 20% of B's share M's QBI of $24,000, reduced by $9,600. B and C's section 199A deduction is equal to the lesser of 20% of the QBI from the business as limited ($14,400) or 20% of B's and C's taxable income ($375,000 x 20% = 75,000). Therefore, B and C's section 199A deduction is $14,400 for 2018.[245]

---

[245] Treas. Reg. §1.199A-1(d)(4), Example 6.

Chart 15 – Phase-Out Zone Chart

This illustration shows the amount the taxpayer is in the Phase-Out Zone at certain amounts of taxable income. It also demonstrates the proportion of the deduction that can be limited by the Wage/Property Limitation that increases with the taxpayer's taxable income. In the final row, this chart displays the maximum deduction for a taxpayer on the flow-through income of a Specified Service. Keep in mind that if the taxpayer failed to pay sufficient wages or acquire Qualified Property for the Wage/Property Limitation, their deduction may be limited further.

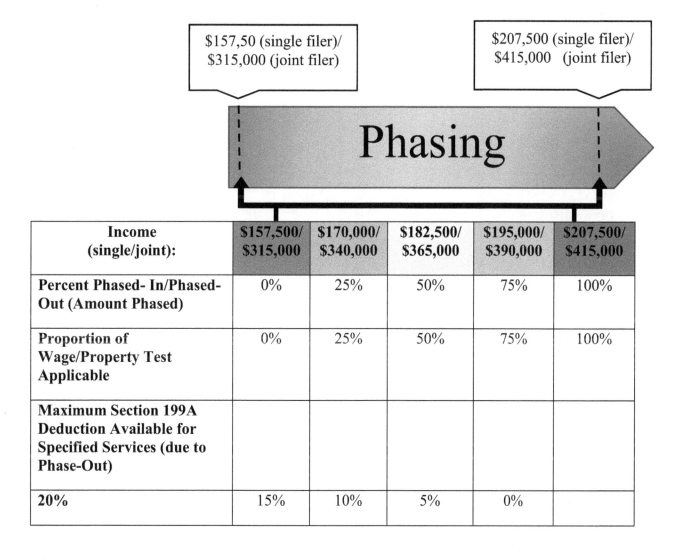

Income (single/joint):	$157,500/ $315,000	$170,000/ $340,000	$182,500/ $365,000	$195,000/ $390,000	$207,500/ $415,000
Percent Phased- In/Phased-Out (Amount Phased)	0%	25%	50%	75%	100%
Proportion of Wage/Property Test Applicable	0%	25%	50%	75%	100%
Maximum Section 199A Deduction Available for Specified Services (due to Phase-Out)					
20%	15%	10%	5%	0%	

Chart 16 – Section 199A Phase-Out Calculations Chart

For this chart, assume the taxpayer is a joint filer who owns an S corporation. The taxpayer's taxable income is listed at the top of the chart and the left column shows if the business is a Specified Service, the flow-through income derived from the business, the W-2 wages paid by the business and the Qualified Property owned by the business. If Qualified Property is not listed in the left column, assume it is $0. The resulting percentage in the right five columns is what remains of the 20% Section 199A deduction. A full deduction is 20%, and the deduction reduced by half would be 10%.

Scenario:	$315,000	$340,000	$365,000	$390,000	$415,000
Specified Service Income - $100,000 Wages - $60,000	20%	15%	10%	5%	0%
Specified Service Income - $100,000 Wages - $0	20%	11.25%	5%	1.25%	0%
Non-Specified Service Income - $100,000 Wages - $60,000	20%	20%	20%	20%	20%
Non-Specified Service Income - $100,000 Wages - $0	20%	15%	10%	5%	0%
Non-Specified Service Income - $100,000 Wages - $20,000 Property - $600,000	20%	20%	20%	20%	20%
Non-Specified Service Income - $100,000 Wages - $10,000 Property - $200,000	20%	17.5%	15%	12.5%	10%

CHAPTER 11.
SECTION 199A STRATEGIES

There are a great many strategies and planning techniques available to maximize the Section 199A deduction, although some of these were curtailed by the Final Regulations. Strategies are discussed throughout this book, but readers may wish to use this chapter as a checklist and for review.

The following is a condensed list of practical applications of Section 199A to reduce tax liability:

1.   Take a passive, income-earning activity and make it into a "trade or business."

As discussed in Chapter 14, the Final Regulations provide that the definition of "trade or business" will be based upon the case law under Section 162, which focuses on the profit motive of the activity. For rental activities to be considered active, landlords may have to provide management services for tenants, and take affirmative steps to demonstrate an intention to acquire more properties or other indicia of an active trade or business. Additionally, the Final Regulations provide that leasing to a related party trade or business will also be considered a trade or business under Section 199A, regardless of whether the two trades or businesses are aggregated.

As a reminder, no cut and dry definition exists for the term "trade or business" in the Code; however, Supreme Court rulings have required that trades or businesses engage in an income-producing activity (1) with continuity and regularity, and (2) for the purpose of profit to qualify.

2.   When high-income taxpayers have trade or business flow-through income, but not sufficient wages or Qualified Property under the activity to receive a full deduction:

A.   Consider paying wages to the taxpayer or the taxpayer's spouse. While doing so may increase employment taxes for the taxpayer, the payment of a sufficient amount of wages and/or having sufficient Qualified Property can allow taxpayers to qualify for the full, or at least a greater, deduction under Section 199A.

B.   If the entity is a partnership, wages cannot be paid directly to a partner under the "guaranteed payment" rules described in Chapter 4, but the individual partner could transfer his or her partnership interest to an S corporation that would become the partner, so that wages could be paid by the partnership to the individual taxpayer and count for Section 199A purposes.

C.   Taxpayers may also consider purchasing another business that pays significant wages or has significant qualified property that can be aggregated with the taxpayer's other businesses in order to qualify for the Section 199A deduction. The Final Regulations do not contain any anti-abuse rules that would prevent this type of acquisition, even if purchased for the primary purpose of helping the taxpayer qualify for the Section 199A deduction. This may be worthwhile, even for a nominally profitable business. For example, a taxpayer with $1,000,000 a year of Section 199A flow-through income from a business having no wages or qualified property could receive a $200,000 tax deduction, saving $74,000 a year in taxes by buying another business that can be aggregated with the existing business, if the new business breaks even but pays at least $400,000 of wages, or the business may pay $200,000 in wages and have $6,000,000 worth of qualified property, or pay nothing in wages and have $8,000,000 worth of qualified property to allow for the full $200,000 deduction.

D.   If the activity is on a Schedule C, E or F of the individual tax return and is owned by one spouse, then wages can be paid to the non-owner spouse, even if they file a joint return.

E.   A business with insufficient wages might purchase a building or other assets for use in the business so that 2.5% of the acquisition cost, plus 25% of wages paid to employees and employee-owners by the entity, would become available as an annual Section 199A deduction for the taxpayer. However, the Final Regulations state that Qualified Property purchased within 60 days of the end of the taxable year and disposed of within 120 days will not be counted for the Property Test if (1) the trade or business does not use the property for at least 45 days prior to disposition, or (2) the principal purpose of the acquisition and disposition was for a reason other than increasing the Section 199A deduction.

F.   Most pension plan contributions and employee health cost expenses can be included in the definition of wages. Pension planning is further discussed below and in Chapter 4.

3.   When a high-income taxpayer owns an SSTB (like a CPA firm or medical practice) or has Qualified Business Income from a trade or business that has insufficient wages or Qualified Property to permit the deduction:

A.   Reduce the taxpayer's taxable income by:

(1)   Consider a defined benefit, cash balance, or other pension plan to reduce the taxpayer's taxable income. The limits imposed by the Wage/Property Tests and Specified Services are based on taxable income thresholds, as described in Chapter 10. Therefore, it is wise to consider every opportunity to reduce taxable income, but for certain individuals, it may not be realistic to decrease earnings below the income thresholds of Section 199A.

(2)   Give part ownership of one or more trades or businesses to other family members, separately taxed trusts, or charitable entities, so that the remaining income of the taxpayer is under the lower-income thresholds ($157,500 if single or $315,000 if married filing jointly). Trusts can receive up to $157,500 from any flow-through business and qualify for the full 20% deduction, and this planning can be done for each separate trust. This holds true even if the flow-through entity is a Specified Service, pays no wages, and holds no Qualified Property. For more on trusts, see Chapter 13 of this book.

(3)   Have one or more of the trades or businesses purchase significant immediately depreciable assets under Sections 179 or 168(k). Section 179 and Section 168(k) do not apply to real property; however, these Sections can apply for improvements to real property.

Section 179 allows taxpayers to deduct up to $1,000,000 of the cost of Qualified Property placed into service for a trade or business, with a Phase-Out limitation if the value of the property acquired during the year exceeds $2,500,000. Depreciation under Section 179 is subject to a host of limitations, and land and buildings cannot be expensed under this method. The Tax Cuts and Jobs Act added the ability to take a Section 179 depreciation deduction on Section 1245 property and certain qualified improvements to buildings, as discussed in subsection (iv) below. [246]

For example, a construction company with more than $1,000,000 of net income could purchase new equipment for $1,000,000, and expense the entire cost thereof in the year that the equipment is placed in service. That equipment can continue to be treated as Qualified Property for ten years. Section 179 cannot be used to create a loss; if the company otherwise had $500,000 of taxable income for the year, it can only deduct $500,000 from the purchase of the new equipment.

It is noteworthy that the Section 179 deduction cannot be taken by estates or a Complex Trust, or by a beneficiary of a Complex Trust that receives distributable net income from a non-grantor trust along with an allocable share of deductions, as reported on a K-1 form; however, the trust or beneficiary can claim bonus depreciation under Section 168(k), which is often identical to the Section 179 deduction, as discussed below.

Under Section 168(k), taxpayers can write off 100% of the cost of new and used Qualified Property, and these rules allow taxpayers to create losses with the depreciation. The statute defines Qualified Property as having a recovery period of 20 years or less, certain depreciable software, water utility property, and "qualified improvement property."[247] Taxpayers can expense the full cost of the Qualified Property that was acquired and placed into service after September 27, 2017 and before January 1, 2023.

It is important to consider that if a company depreciates Qualified Property in one year under Sections 179 or 168(k), it may still be considered as Qualified Property for the longer of (1) its depreciable life; or (2) 10 years after being placed into service. Also, remember that Qualified Property and wages are inseparable from their entity, and each trade or business will need

---

[246] IRC § 1245 property includes tangible and intangible personal property of a business, such as oil and gas storage tanks, silos, blast furnaces, basic oxygen furnaces, structures that are essentially machinery or equipment, refrigerators, display racks, as well as patents and copyrights.
[247] IRC § 168(k)(2)(A).

to pay more in wages or acquire more Qualified Property for the taxpayer to receive a full 20% deduction on each entity's flow-through income unless the aggregation rules apply.

Taxpayers should also consider whether taking accelerated depreciation is appropriate, as the deduction may reduce income by too much in the year of acquisition, and the taxpayer's Section 199A deduction may be limited by the 20% of taxable income limitation. In addition, the taxpayer may be better off taking normal depreciation deductions to reduce income by a smaller amount each year if this would still allow the taxpayer to stay below the threshold limitation, rather than accelerating the deduction and only being below the threshold limitation in the first year.

(4)   Consider improving property that is already owned. The Final Regulations state that improvements to property will be considered a separate asset.[248] Generally under Section 168(i), the recovery period of improvements is the depreciable life of the property being improved upon and begins when the improvement is placed into service.[249]

Further, certain improvements made to commercial property can qualify for the Section 179 depreciation deduction, as mentioned above, and include such things as roofs, heating, ventilation, air-conditioning, fire protection and alarms, and security systems and other qualified improvement property as defined in Section 168(e)(6), which reads as follows:

168(e)(6) Qualified Improvement Property

(A)   In general --

The term "qualified improvement property" means any improvement to an interior portion of a building which is nonresidential real property if such improvement is placed in service after the date such building was first placed in service.

(B)   Certain improvements not included – Such term shall not include any improvement for which the expenditure is attributable to

(i)   the enlargement of the building,

(ii)   any elevator or escalator, or

(iii)   the internal structural framework of the building.

---

[248] IRC § 263(a) reads: "No deduction shall be allowed for— (1) Any amount paid out for new buildings or for permanent improvements or betterments made to increase the value of any property or estate. …" (emphasis added).
[249] IRC § 168(i)(6).

(5)   Work less and have responsibilities handled by other family members who may be in lower tax brackets.

(6)   File separately from a high-earning spouse, or better yet, marry someone with net operating losses ("NOLs").

(7)   Donate to charity. Remember to bunch charitable contributions in a single year so that the itemized deductions will exceed the standard deduction. The standard deduction in 2019 is $12,400 for single filers and $24,800 for married joint filers.

A married individual donating $10,000 to charity each year would be better off donating $30,000 every third year to save $1,924 in tax liability, assuming a 37% income tax bracket. This example does not include the deduction of medical expenses, state and local taxes, and mortgage interest, and these considerations may change whether and when an individual decides to itemize.

(8)   Consider reducing taxable income by investing in oil and gas arrangements.

Under Section 263, an individual taxpayer who directly owns an interest in an oil or gas well may expense the Intangible Drilling Costs.[250] These are costs associated with developing and maintaining the operations of a well that do not have a salvage value, and generally include labor (wages), fuel, repairs, hauling, supplies, surveying land, and the clearing of land related to drilling, etc.[251] The Intangible Drilling Costs that can be expensed immediately are listed in Treas. Reg. 1.612-4(a).[252]

To deduct Intangible Drilling Costs, investors must have a "working interest" in the oil and/or gas well activity.[253] Therefore, investors cannot hold their investment interest under an entity that limits their liability (such as a limited partner in a limited liability partnership[254]); otherwise their ownership will be deemed to be a passive activity, and they will not be eligible for the Intangible Drilling Cost deduction. Working interests are determined without regard to indemnification agreements, stop loss arrangements, and insurance policies.[255]

Oil and gas well rights cannot be counted as Qualified Property for

---

[250] Treas. Reg. § 1.612-4.

[251] *Id.* In general, IDCs are "all expenditures made by an operator … incident to and necessary for the drilling of wells and the preparation of wells for the production of oil or gas."

[252] Treas. Reg. § 1.612-5(c)(1) enumerates Intangible Drilling Costs that cannot be immediately expensed.

[253] Treas. Reg. § 1.469-1T(e)(4)(i).

[254] Being a general partnership in a limited partnership would still allow for a deduction of IDCs under Treas. Reg. § 1.469-1T(e)(4)(v)(A)(1).

[255] Treas. Reg. § 1.469-1T(e)(4)(v)(B).

the Wage/Property Limitation under Section 199A, because they are "depletable" assets and not depreciable.[256] Depletable assets cannot be expensed like Intangible Drilling Costs.[257] The depletion deduction is based upon a percentage of revenues derived from oil and gas production without reference to whether the deduction taken over the lifetime of the well is more or less than the non-deductible costs associated therewith. The deduction is given to taxpayers with economic interest in an oil and/or gas well.[258] A depletion deduction is the larger of a cost method or percentage method of calculation.[259] However, these calculations are beyond the scope of this book.

A person who buys oil and gas well interests can take depletion on their capital investments in the wells in the above manner. Additionally, the Supreme Court ruled that taxpayers who lease oil and gas wells can be given control of the resources and considered to have been an economic interest.[260] Lessees may therefore be eligible for a depletion deduction on their capital investment, and lessors may be eligible for a depletion deduction on royalties received.[261]

4.   When income is from an SSTB and the taxpayer cannot reduce their taxable income below the $207,500/$415,000 limits:

A.   See Section 3 above with respect to transferring part ownership of the entity to one or more different taxpayers.

B.   Establish separate non-commonly controlled S corporations or partnerships to provide arm's-length services to the SSTB, and have such entities pay sufficient wages or purchase sufficient Qualified Property to allow for reasonable profits therefrom to qualify for the Section 199A deduction. If common control exists, then the anti-abuse rules under the Final Regulations will likely deny the Section 199A deduction in most circumstances, as described in Chapter 9.

C.   Increasing the rent paid to another entity from an SSTB in which the taxpayer has ownership, but does not have more than 50% common ownership with the SSTB, including the related party attribution and constructive ownership rules, will reduce the income of the SSTB and increase the rent income, which may be deductible

---

[256] IRC § 611(a) (noting that an interest in an oil and gas well is a depletable asset). Depletable assets, as defined under IRC § are usually non-renewable natural resources like nickel, coal, and oil.

[257] T.A.M. 201448020 (November 11, 2014).

[258] An economic interest in oil and gas wells is established through operating interests and royalties under IRC § 614 and Treas. Reg. § 1.614-1(a)(2). These economic interests include operating and non-operating interests (such as royalties). An operating interest is given to those working to extract resources from wells and non-operating interests include royalties from oil and gas well leases.

[259] For the cost method, *see* Treas. Reg. § 1.611-2. For the percentage method, *see* IRC § 613.

[260] G.C.M. 22730, 1941-1 C.B. 214 (noting that those who lease regarding oil and gas wells do not sell their economic interest, but the lessee gains an economic interest by "assuming the obligation to develop and operate the property").

[261] *See Palmer v. Bender*, 287 U.S. 551 (1933).

under Section 199A. Keep in mind that this could cause additional sales tax or other issues under state law.

5.   Have an arm's-length S corporation, C corporation, or partnership provide management, marketing, intellectual property, equipment leasing, or other services with a reasonable profit margin that can be taxed at S corporation rates and qualify for the Section 199A deduction, further reducing the tax liability. Not only will having intellectual property, management, and assets in separate entities be better for income tax purposes, but this positioning will also be superior from a creditor protection standpoint.

The Final Regulations state that a trade or business with 50% or more common related party ownership with an SSTB will also be considered an SSTB, if the other trade or business provides its property or services to the SSTB, however, only the portion of products or services provided to the SSTB will be considered SSTB income.

The Final Regulations provide the following examples:

Example 1:

Law Firm is a partnership that provides legal services to clients, owns its own office building and employs its own administrative staff. Law Firm divides into three partnerships. Partnership 1 performs legal services to clients. Partnership 2 owns the office building and rents the entire building to Partnership 1. Partnership 3 employs the administrative staff and through a contract with Partnership 1 provides administrative services to Partnership 1 in exchange for fees. All three of the partnerships are owned by the same people (the original owners of Law Firm). Because Partnership 2 provides all of its property to Partnership 1, and Partnership 3 provides all of its services to Partnership 1, Partnerships 2 and 3 will each be treated as an SSTB under paragraph (c)(2) of this Section.

Example 2:

Assume the same facts as in Example 1 of this paragraph (c)(2), except that Partnership 2, which owns the office building, rents 50 percent of the building to Partnership 1, which provides legal services, and the other 50 percent to various unrelated third-party tenants. Because Partnership 2 is owned by the same people as Partnership 1, the portion of Partnership 2's leasing activity related to the lease of the building to Partnership 1 will be treated as a separate SSTB. The remaining 50 percent of Partnership 2's leasing activity will not be treated as an SSTB.

The following charts illustrate the above:

Green = Non-SSTB Income
Red = SSTB Income

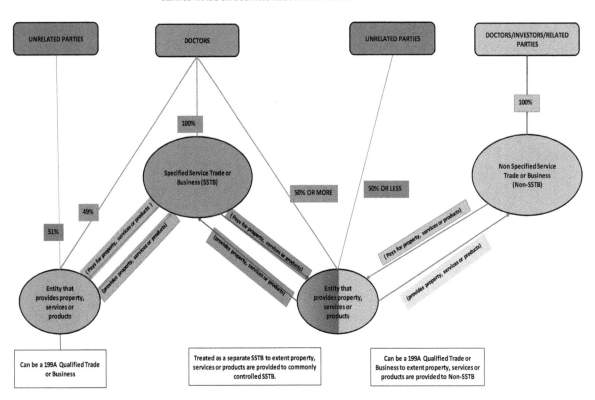

SERVICE TRADE OR BUSINESS ILLUSTRATION CHART

Many taxpayers will attempt to avoid this by avoiding 50% or more related party ownership. For example, if a medical practice is owned 1/3 each by three doctors, one doctor and his family may own a management company, another may own a billing company, and the third may own a factoring company. The income that they receive from these separate companies would not be SSTB income.

A chart illustrating the above is as follows:

Chart 17 – Non-SSTB Company Chart

Doctor 2
Doctor 1
Doctor 3
Doctor 1
Doctor 3

33 1/3%

100%
100%
100%

33 1/3%
33 1/3%

Management or
Real Estate,
LLC

Doctor 1
Medical
Practice

Doctor 2
Medical
Practice

Doctor 3
Medical
Practice

Provides management, marketing, and billing services to
the doctors' three separate practices.

Can be a Section 199A Qualified Trade or Business.

1.   Additionally, business owners can consider sale and leaseback transactions with real estate and equipment as a way to lower taxable income by making deductible lease payments while continuing to use the property. Keep in mind that doing this will remove the Qualified Property from the flow-through business, and if the sale is made to a related party, certain rules with respect to related arm's-length transactions and payments to related entities can apply.

2.   Restructure entities owned as partnerships to reduce guaranteed payments and increase partnership profits received by partners to enhance eligibility for the Section 199A deduction, as discussed in Chapter 4 and Chapter 9.

3.   Getting married or divorced can be helpful or harmful for Section 199A deduction purposes, depending upon the circumstances.

For example, an individual who has under $157,500 of income might marry an individual who has several times that amount,[262] and will lose the Section 199A deduction on SSTB income if a joint tax return is filed.

---

[262] Tax planning aside, it is often a good idea to marry someone having multiple times your earnings, even if you have to pay more taxes.

Chart 18 – Marital Considerations Chart

The following chart summarizes some of the important financial considerations for those contemplating marriage as a financial option:

Consideration	Single Status	Married Status
Sale of a primary residence (Section 121(b))	Capital gain is excluded up to $250,000	Capital gain is excluded up to $500,000
Federal estate tax exemption	Can only shield assets up to $11.4 million from estate, gift, and generation-skipping tax	Can shield assets up to $22.8 million from estate, gift, and generation-skipping tax
Marital Tax Penalty and Bonuses	High-earning individuals may be better separate from a financial standpoint	Two high-earning individuals who get married may be subject to an increase in tax; one high-earner and one low-earner getting hitched may create tax savings
Medicare surtax threshold (additional 0.9% tax above the threshold)	$200,000 per person threshold	$250,000 per married couple threshold (a $150,000 threshold loss)
Tax on Social Security benefits	Can earn up to $25,000 and not be taxed on Social Security benefits	Can earn up to $32,000 and not be taxed on Social Security benefits
Transferability of assets upon death	Subject to estate tax if decedent is over $11,400,000 exemption amount on death	Surviving spouse can receive assets tax-free upon the death of the first spouse
Social Security survivorship benefits	Unmarried children under 18 can receive benefits; possibly parents where the deceased provided at least half of their parent's support	Spouses can receive partial benefits if they are under retirement age, and may be eligible for 100% of the deceased's benefit if they have reached retirement age

Consideration	Single Status	Married Status
Government and Employer Pension Plan survivorship benefits	No surviving spouse benefits if not married	Potentially eligible for survivorship benefits
Transferability of assets upon divorce	N/A	Tax-free passing of assets upon divorce
Ability to roll over an IRA on the death of a spouse	Cannot treat it as one's own IRA; cannot make continued contributions to the IRA	Allowed to roll over the IRA upon death without a tax hit; can treat the IRA as the surviving spouse's own; can continue to make contributions to the IRA
Net operating losses (NOL)	Cannot transfer to others	If losses are accumulated during marriage, they can be used against the joint income of the couple. If they are accumulated while single, it may be possible for one spouse to hire the NOL spouse and pay them a wage, which would be deductible depending on how large the NOLs are
Related Party Losses (Section 167(e))	Can take the losses on the sale to another individual	Can take the losses on the sale to his spouse
Medical and Nursing Expenses (to the extent they exceed 10% of Adjusted Gross Income)	May not be able to be claimed because of too high income (where the expenses fall under 10% of adjusted gross income) or too low, where much of a potential deduction is wasted	Large medical expenses are more likely to impact the marital income, and may save thousands in taxes[263]

---

[263] Gene and John are single taxpayers in 2018. If Gene has $130,000 of adjusted gross income and $10,000 of medical expenses, he cannot itemize his medical costs. If John has $20,000 of income, but $50,000 of medical expenses. John may only deduct the medical expenses that exceed 7.5% of his adjusted gross income, meaning John could claim $48,500 of expenses ($20,000 x 7.5% = $1,500; $50,000 minus $1,500 = $48,500). John can deduct $20,000 but loses nearly $28,500 of an itemized deduction because it is limited to his adjusted gross income. If Gene and John were to marry, with an adjusted gross income of $150,000 and medical expenses of $60,000, the couple would be able to take advantage of their full medical deduction, which would be $48,750 ($150,000 x 7.5% = $11,250; $60,000 minus $11,250 = $48,750), making their taxable income $101,250 ($150,000 minus $48,750).

Consideration	Single Status	Married Status
Sharing Capital Loss Carryforward (the excess of $3,000 is carried forward into future years)	N/A	An unmarried individual with loss carryforward from capital losses can marry someone with capital gains, and use the loss carryforward to reduce their capital gains liability
Tax Brackets	Enters the highest bracket of 37% at $500,000 of taxable income	Enters the highest bracket of 37% at $600,000 of taxable income
Standard deduction	Able to claim a $12,000 standard deduction	Able to claim a $24,000 standard deduction or two $12,000 standard deductions if filing separately

4.   Defer payment of wages to a subsequent tax year if the business will not generate sufficient Qualified Business Income to use those wages in a way that maximizes the Section 199A deduction, such as if the business might not have sufficient wages to allow for the full Section 199A deduction in subsequent years.

5.   Pay off loans to eliminate interest expense in order to qualify for a larger deduction or maintain debt if interest expenses will reduce income below the high earner thresholds. Taxpayers who pay down debt to enhance the Section 199A deduction may wish to put related party debt into place to have less equity at risk to creditors in business and investment operations. As of August 2019, related party debt can be as low as 1.90% compounded semi-annually, if the loan is a demand loan or for a term of three years or less, 1.86% compounded semi-annually if for a term of more than three years, but not more than 9 years, and 2.32% compounded semiannually if for more than nine years without having interest imputed under Internal Revenue Code Section 7872 low interest loan rules.[264]

6.   Convert wage income into trade or business income by becoming a Schedule C independent contractor or operating an S corporation that owns a trade or business. The Final Regulations provide that a former employee will be presumed to be in the trade or business of performing services as an employee that will not qualify for Section 199A purposes. This presumption continues for three years after the employee becomes an independent contractor but can be overcome by appropriate evidence and documentation that the individual is no longer appropriately classified as an employee. The Final Regulations make this transition somewhat difficult, but not impossible. Individuals who are presently classified and treated as employees may elect to pay 80% of the federal income tax otherwise incurred upon their net employment income by satisfying the criteria of being classified and paid as an independent contractor instead

---

Overall, their marital decision has saved them $11,700 in income tax ($48,750 x 24% = $11,700).

[264] See Hesch, Gassman, Denicolo, *Interesting Interest Questions: Interest Rates for Intra-Family Transactions*, Estates Gifts and Trusts Journal, Vol. 36, No. 2 , March 10, 2011.

of an employee. The above planning technique is only available for true independent contractors; thus, employee relationships will be viewed as "sticky" and not easy to change or adapt.

A good many employers will welcome the opportunity to no longer contribute 7.65% in employment taxes on the first $128,400 (or $132,900 for 2019) per year of salary (the Social Security Tax cap), plus worker's compensation, unemployment taxes, state payroll taxes, and expenses associated with payroll tax compliance. 7.65% is the combined Social Security and Medicare tax rates, which are 6.2% and 1.45%, respectively. On salaries in excess of $128,400, ($132,900 for 2019) the employer will save 1.45% of Medicare tax.

This strategy can be especially useful for taxpayers below both Section 199A thresholds, who will be able to claim their 20% deduction regardless of Specified Service status or wages paid and Qualified Property held. Therefore, below-threshold business owners should focus on reducing other tax liabilities like the employment tax.

> The Final Regulations include an example where a lawyer employed by Law Firm 1 leaves and forms Law Firm 2 with several associates from Law Firm 1 who all have taxable income below the threshold amount. Law Firm 2 provides services for Law Firm 1 in a contractual relationship and the lawyers are generally providing the same services that they were previously providing directly to Law Firm 1. The Final Regulations state that the lawyer will be presumed to be in the trade or business of performing services as an employee, and thus her income from Law Firm 2 will not qualify for the Section 199A deduction unless she can prove that she is truly an independent contractor as to Law Firm 1.

The Final Regulations provide that this presumption can be rebutted by providing the IRS with "records, such as contracts or partnership agreements that provide sufficient evidence to corroborate the individual's status as a non-employee"

A second example, which was added under the Final Regulations provides guidance on how the presumption can be rebutted and reads as follows:

> F is a financial advisor employed by a financial advisory firm, Advisory Firm, a partnership for Federal tax purposes, as a fulltime employee and is treated as such for federal employment tax purposes. F has taxable income below the threshold amount. Advisory Firm is a partnership and offers F the opportunity to be admitted as a partner. F elects to be admitted as a partner to Advisory Firm and is admitted as a partner to Advisory Firm. As a partner in Advisory Firm, F shares in the net profits of Advisory Firm, is obligated to Advisory Firm in ways that F was not previously obligated as an employee, is no longer entitled to certain benefits available only to employees of Advisory Firm and has materially modified his relationship with Advisory Firm. F's share of net profits is not subject to a floor or capped at a dollar amount. F is presumed (solely for purposes of Section 199A(d)(1)(B) and paragraphs (a)(3) and (d) of this Section)

to be in the trade or business of performing services as an employee with respect to the services F provides to Advisory Firm. However, F is able to rebut the presumption by showing that F became a partner in Advisory Firm by sharing in the profits of Advisory Firm, materially modifying F's relationship with Advisory Firm, and otherwise satisfying the requirements under federal tax law, regulations, and principles (including common-law employee classification rules) to be respected as a partner.

On the other hand, the S corporation or independent contractor arrangements must be carefully considered with reference to the following:

1.   The possible loss of medical insurance benefits when a person is not employed and cannot qualify to be included on a group medical insurance plan,

2.   401(k) employer matching,

3.   Making sure that health insurance will cover on-the-job injuries and understanding the cost of worker's compensation insurance or the risk of not having lifetime support benefits if the taxpayer cannot work because of an employment- related injury, and

4.   Loss of unemployment compensation if and when terminated.

The distinction between independent contractors and employees has long been examined but is worth reviewing here. An employee-employer relationship normally exists "when the person for whom services are performed has the right to control and direct the individual who performs the services, not only as to the result to be accomplished by the work, but also as to the details and means by which that result is accomplished."[265] An independent contractor is typically someone "who is entrusted to undertake a specific project but who is left free to do the assigned work and to choose the method for accomplishing it." [266]

For many years, the IRS used a 20 common law factor test to determine if an individual is an employee, including the right to terminate employment, whether the worker is required to bring their own tools and materials, whether there are set work hours, and whether work is completed on an employer's premises.[267] In 1996, the IRS reworked this test into three major categories:

1.   Behavioral control,

2.   Financial control, and

3.   Relationship of the parties.[268]

---

[265] Treas. Reg. § 31.3121(d)-1.

[266] Black's Law Dictionary, 9th Ed. (2009). Additionally, the work of an independent contractor generally does not create liability for the person hiring the contractor.

[267] *Rev. Rul. 87-41.*

[268] Department of the Treasury, Internal Revenue Service, *Independent Contractor or Employee? Training*

In reality, the 20 common law factors can be plugged into the above three categories as follows, so nothing significant really changed in 1996:

Chart 19 - 3 Factors / 20 Factors Combination Chart

	Common Law Test Factor	Behavioral Control	Financial Control	Relationship of the Parties
1	Compliance with instructions	X		
2	Training	X		
3	Integration	X		
4	Services rendered personally	X		
5	Hiring, supervision, and paying assistants	X		
6	Set hours to work	X		
7	Full time required	X		
8	Doing work on employer's premises	X		X
9	Order or sequence test	X		
10	Oral or written reports	X		
11	Payment by the hour, week, or month		X	
12	Payment of business and/or traveling expenses		X	
13	Furnishing tools and materials		X	
14	Significant investment		X	
15	Realization of profit or loss		X	

Materials, Training 3320-102 (1996), available at https://www.irs.gov/pub/irs- utl/emporind.pdf. The IRS lists the facts that illustrate if there is a right to direct or control work under each category. For behavioral control, this is instructions or training; for financial control, this is significant investments, unreimbursed expenses, method of payment, etc.; and for relationship of the parties, this is intent of the parties/written contracts, employee benefits, terms regarding each category. For behavioral control, this is instructions or training; for financial control, this is significant investments, unreimbursed expenses, method of payment, etc.; and for relationship of the parties, this is intent of the parties/written contracts, employee benefits, terms regarding discharge/termination, and regular business activity.

	Common Law Test Factor	Behavioral Control	Financial Control	Relationship of the Parties
16	Making services available to the general public		X	
17	Continuing relationship			X
18	Working for more than one firm at a time			X
19	Right to discharge			X
20	Right to terminate			X

Further, under Internal Revenue Code Section 3121 the following categories of workers will be treated as employees, notwithstanding that they would normally be considered as independent contractors under the traditional tests:[269]

1.   An agent-driver/commission-driver engaged in distributing meat, vegetables, bakery, or beverage products, or laundry or dry-cleaning services;

2.   A full-time life insurance salesman;

3.   A home-worker using material furnished by the person employing their services if such material must be returned to the employer; or

4.   A traveling or city salesman.

Real estate agents are classified as "statutory non-employees," and can be treated as independent contractors if the following three requirements under Section 3508 are met: [270]

1.   The agent must be licensed,

2.   Substantially all (at least 90%)[271] of compensation for the services performed is directly related to commissions rather than fixed salary or hours worked, and

3.   The services of the agent are performed pursuant to a written contract that states that the agent will not be treated as an employee for federal tax purposes.

---

[269] IRC § 3121. If they also meet the following three elements, they will be classified as employees: (A) the service contract states or implies that substantially all of the services are to be performed by them, (B) they do not have a substantial investment in the equipment or property used to perform the services, and (C) the services are performed on a continuing basis for the same payer.
[270] IRC § 3508(b)(1).
[271] Prop. Reg. § 31.3508-1(d)(1).

In the same statute, "direct sellers" are also defined as statutory non-employees if they meet the following three requirements:

1. Such person must be engaged in the trade or business of—

    A. Selling consumer products in the home or otherwise than in a permanent retail establishment,

    B. Selling consumer products on a buy-sell basis, a deposit- commission basis, or any similar basis allowed by regulations for resale in the home or otherwise than in a permanent retail establishment, or

    C. Delivering or distribution of newspapers or shopping news (including any services directly related to such trade or business),

2. Substantially all compensation for the performance of these services is directly related to sales or other output (including the performance of services) rather than the number of hours worked, and

3. The services performed pursuant to a written contract that says that the person shall not be treated as an employee for federal tax purposes.

    a. Special Rules for Certain Life Insurance Agents. Life insurance agents who work for independent agencies are not treated as Statutory Employees, unless the agency itself writes products primarily for one life insurance company, as explained in the following chart and the explanation below.

Employee v. Statutory Employee v. Independent Contractor

CATEGORY	EMPLOYEE	STATUTORY EMPLOYEE	INDEPENDENT CONTRACTOR
Definition	Individual worker who follows explicit instructions of the employer as a traditional employee.	Individual worker classified as Independent Contractor under traditional tests but treated as a "Statutory Employee" under Internal Revenue Code Section 3121(d)*.	Individual worker who is not an employee / not required to follow the instructions of the employer and compensation causes risk to be allocated to the contractor.
Are compensation payments treated as wages for the Wage/Qualified Property Test?	YES	NO	NO
Is income received by the individual Section 199A	NO	YES	YES

CATEGORY	EMPLOYEE	STATUTORY EMPLOYEE	INDEPENDENT CONTRACTOR
"Qualified Business Income"?		(If an active trade or business and other requirements are met).	(If an active trade or business).
Employer withholds income taxes.	YES	NO	NO
Employer withholds Social Security and Medicare taxes.	YES (And employer pays one-half of FICA).	YES (But all FICA comes from Statutory Employee's share).	NO
Are professional/employment related expenses deductible on Schedule C (above the line)?	NO	YES	YES

* See also Treasury Regulation 3121(d)-1(d)(3)(ii), Revenue Ruling 69-287 and Private Letter Ruling 9242003.

Life insurance agents who are Independent Contractors are treated differently under the employment tax rules, pursuant to Internal Revenue Code Section 3121(d) and Treasury Regulation 31.3121(d)-1(d)(3)(ii) (and as verified by Revenue Ruling 69-287 and Private Letter Ruling 9242003), which defined certain Independent Contractors as "Statutory Employees" for the purposes of assuring that employers withhold Social Security and Medicare taxes that are paid into the system.

Under this statute, a full-time life insurance sales agent who is otherwise treated as an independent contractor will be subject to this definition and these requirements, if his or her principal business activity is selling life insurance or annuity contracts, or both, primarily for one life insurance company, and all three of the following conditions are met:

1.   The service contract states or implies that substantially all of the services are to be performed personally by the individual.

2.   The individual does not have a substantial investment in the equipment and property used to perform the services (other than his or her automobile or other "transportation facilities.")

3.   The services are performed on a continuing basis for the same employer.

The above was confirmed in Private Letter Ruling 9242003, where an individual selling life insurance on a commissioned basis was found to be classified as an Independent Contractor and Statutory Employee, so that the employer would pay Social Security taxes, but the life insurance agent would be solely responsible for unemployment taxes and income tax withholding.

If the life insurance sales person is an Independent Contractor under the normal tests, then his or her income will qualify for the Section 199A deduction as non-SSTB income, as long as it is appropriately documented as being separate and apart from income derived as an employee, and any income derived from being an investment broker or advisor, which is an SSTB activity. The separate, or separable, books and records requirement described in Chapter 9 will apply under these circumstances.

A. **INDEPENDENT CONTRACTOR SAFE HARBOR STATUTE FOR REASONABLE BASIS ASSOCIATED WITH LONG STANDING PRACTICE OF SIGNIFICANT SEGMENT OF INDUSTRY**

Many advisors are not aware of the safe harbor statute under Section 530 of the Revenue Act of 1978 which allows employers to treat certain individuals as independent contractors, notwithstanding that they would otherwise be considered as employees, where the following requirements are met:

1. **THE EMPLOYER MUST HAVE A "REASONABLE BASIS" FOR TREATING THE WORKER AS AN INDEPENDENT CONTRACTOR.**

One statutorily-provided reasonable basis a taxpayer can rely on is a "long- standing practice of a significant segment of the industry" that the taxpayer is engaged in,[272] which is presumed when more than 25% of the industry in the geographical area where the employer is located is engaged in a similar practice of worker classification.[273]

The employer must have treated the worker as an independent contractor, and not as an employee, in the past.

2. **THE EMPLOYER HAS FILED ALL FEDERAL TAX RETURNS ON A BASIS CONSISTENT WITH INDEPENDENT CONTRACTOR CLASSIFICATION.[274]**

Relief under the safe harbor statute is not available where the worker provides services as an engineer, computer programmer, systems analyst, drafter, or other "similarly skilled worker engaged in work similar thereto."[275]

The safe harbor statute will apply only up through the time when an audit occurs, but once the IRS reclassifies the status of a given employer's employees, the safe harbor will no longer apply with respect to any employee who has been reclassified by the IRS upon audit.

Additionally, the IRS voluntary compliance settlement program (VCSP) enables employers to request reclassification of their workers to avoid an audit. To be eligible for this program, taxpayers must have consistently treated the workers they seek to reclassify as non-employees for the past three years, must have filed Form 1099s for these workers, and must not currently be under

---

[272] § 530(a)(2)(C) of the Revenue Act of 1978, Pub. L. No. 95-600.

[273] *Id.* at §530(e)(2)(B). This does not preclude a finding of a significant segment engaged in a practice of classifying workers as employees/independent contractors when less than 25% of the taxpayer's industry does so. Additionally, the geographic area that a court decides to use can also have a large impact on the availability of safe harbor relief.

[274] § 530 of the Revenue Act of 1978.

[275] *Id.* at § 530(d).

employment tax audit. [276] Taxpayers can apply by filing a Form 8952, which includes an agreement to pay some employment taxes under reduced rates for workers at issue for the most recent tax year.[277]

3. PENSION PLAN CONCERNS WITH RESPECT TO INDEPENDENT CONTRACTORS.

It is noteworthy that an individual treated as an independent contractor may have to be retroactively included in a pension plan, if and when recharacterized as an employee, except when the pension plan provisions define eligible employees to not include independent contractors who have been reclassified as common law employees.[278]

It is important for tax advisors to let clients know that they should assure that their pension plan documents include such a provision.

Even Microsoft did not have the appropriate pension language needed to avoid these penalties. In the case of *Vizcaino v. Microsoft Corporation*, the Ninth Circuit Court of Appeals held that Microsoft had to pay benefits to misclassified workers under its 401(k) plan.

In doing so, the Ninth Circuit determined that the broad terminology of this provision extended eligibility to the misclassified workers once they had been recharacterized as common law employees. The court quoted a magistrate judge from the lower court who stated that Microsoft "could easily have accomplished the limitation it now urges through the use of more explicit language."[279]

The excellent BNA Portfolio on this subject notes that *Vizcaino* begs the question of whether ERISA, and the similar language of Section 401(a) requires all employees to be covered under a qualified pension plan, or whether an employer can designate eligible employees, within reason.[280] The case law and regulations[281] indicate that the answer is yes.[282] In one of the worksheets in their portfolios, BNA provides a sample 401(k) provision that excludes leased employees.[283]

---

[276] Taxpayers who were previously under audit must have complied with the results of the audit and not be currently contesting the outcome in court.

[277] The reduced rates are set forth in IRC § 3509(a).

[278] *Vizcaino v. Microsoft Corporation*, 97 F.3d 1187, (9th Cir. 1997).

[279] *Id.*

[280] Bianchi, 399-3rd T.M. at III.B.5 (BNA), *Employee Benefits for the Contingent Workforce*.

[281] §401(b)(1) requires the plan not be discriminatory in favor of highly compensated employees. §401(a)(26) requires that a plan has a participation of the lesser of (1) 50 employees, or (2) 40% of all employees. The test also found that §401(k)(3)(A)(ii) should lead to the same result because the equation only considers <u>eligible employees.</u>

[282] Treas. Reg. § 1.401(a)-(3)d states that conditions that are not based on age and service conditions in §410(a) and this would include exclusion based on compensation or whether an employee is salaried.

[283] Bortz, Mason, and Raish, 358-4th T.M. (BNA), *Cash or Deferred Arrangements*. This would enable the employer to exclude employees who were thought to be independent contractors in previous years and prevent misclassified employees from being able to sue for being improperly excluded from pension plans. While this sample provision from BNA does not exclude reclassified workers from being eligible for the current plan, *Vizcaino* and Treasury Regulations for Section 410(b) appear to enable an employer to exclude "individuals who have been reclassified as common law employees" from a pension plan without disqualifying the plan because of prohibited age or length-of-service requirements. This will not, however, protect the plan from disqualification based on the non-discrimination minimum participation requirements of Section 401 and minimum coverage requirements of Section

4. BEWARE OF THE AFFILIATED SERVICE GROUP RULES.

Additionally, careful consideration must be given to the affiliated service group rules under Section 414(m) and the employee leasing rules under Section 414(n) before concluding that a pension plan can be set up that would not have to cover the employees of the original employer.

The affiliated service group rules are highly expansive, and often take taxpayers and their advisors by surprise. The Code has strict rules that preclude the favoring of highly-compensated employees for pensions, health plans, and other fringe benefits. Catastrophic results may occur with the reclassification of affiliated service groups as employees, such as the loss of the qualified status of pension plans and deductions for the company's health insurance and employee benefits.

Section 414(m) defines an affiliated service group as a service organization ("the first organization") and one or more of (1) any service organization that is a shareholder or partner of the first organization, and regularly performs services for the first organization or with the first organization for third-parties; or (2) any other organization if a "significant portion" of the business is the performance of services typically done by employees, and greater than 10% of the interest in the service organization is held by highly compensated employees.

> For example, Jane Lawyer is a partner at the law firm Jane, Jessica, & John, P.A., and wants to set up a management company for her law firm. The partners decide to let Jane own the company, which will provide management services to the law firm for a fee. Because Jane is a highly compensated employee under Section 414(m) and owns more than 10% of the management company, it will be classified as an affiliated service group under part (2) of the definition above. This may endanger the law firm's pension plan qualification if the management company employees are excluded from participation; however, if the partners established a single qualified plan for both companies' employees to contribute to, the classification as an affiliated service group would not be as dire as in the first scenario.

5. LIABILITY EXPOSURE FOR MISCLASSIFYING WORKER.

In addition, incorrectly classified workers may have causes of action against their employers and affiliates for loss of unemployment compensation, worker's compensation, medical insurance rights, and other benefits that they would have received as employees but were deprived of. There have been a number of national class action suits presently being waged against "employers" such as Uber, Lyft, and FedEx, and many state or local class action suits against strip bars, restaurants, and residential construction companies in an attempt to claim compensation for these benefits. Arbitration clauses in agreements signed by independent contractors may prevent them from joining in class action lawsuits.[284]

410(b).

[284] *Epic Systems Corp. v. Lewis*, No. 16-285 (2018).

The employer's share of the 7.65% employment taxes paid on an employee's wages is tax deductible to the employer, and may therefore only cost the employer 6.04%, assuming that the employer is a C corporation in the 21% bracket (79% of 7.65% is 6.04%). If the employer is an S corporation, whose earnings flow-through to an individual taxed at the highest individual bracket, the rate would be 4.82% (63% of 7.65% is 4.82%). The employee must also pay 7.65% of their wages in employment tax but receives no deduction for the payment. To see the employment tax rates broken down, refer to Charts 3 and 4 in Chapter 4 of this book.

An independent contractor who reports his or her income on Schedule C of the Form 1040 Income Tax Return will be required to pay the 12.47% self-employment tax (7.45% employee's share and 4.82% employer's share if they are in the highest individual bracket), composed of the Social Security tax plus the Medicare tax that would have been paid one-half by the employer.

If the taxpayer wants to use an S corporation to avoid employment tax by receiving K-1 income/dividends in lieu of wages or lieu of being an independent contractor, then the arrangement must be at arm's-length, whereby the taxpayer's S corporation earns and receives the income, and pays the taxpayer/owner a reasonable salary, which will be subject to wage taxes, and other expenses described above.

If the taxpayer has a high income (over $207,500 if single or $415,000 if married filing jointly for the 2018 tax year), then the ratio of wages to S corporation K-1 income will need to be 4/14ths (28.57%) to qualify all of the K-1 income as being deductible under Section 199A but cannot be lower than the amount that constitutes reasonable compensation for the services provided.

> For example, if the high-income taxpayer's S corporation has $200,000 of net income before wages, then it would need to have $57,140 in wages paid to the taxpayer and other employees for the taxpayer to be able to qualify the remaining $142,860 for the full 20% deduction.

Assuming that the taxpayer is married with $410,000 of total taxable income for the 2018 tax year (after reduction for itemized expenses or the standard deduction and pension plan contributions), then the tax savings under Section 199A on $100,000 of K-1 income will be $6,700, given that the taxpayer and his or her spouse will be in the 35% tax bracket on $10,000 of this income and the 32% tax bracket on the other $10,000.

Alternatively, a true independent contractor arrangement may result in greater tax savings if the contractor is able to establish a qualified retirement plan that might otherwise not be available if the taxpayer remains an employee of the original employer.

The following examples and planning opportunities in the Section 199A arena should be of use should be of use to planners:

B. PLANNING OPPORTUNITY #1 - TRANSFER OWNERSHIP TO FAMILY MEMBERS BELOW THRESHOLD AMOUNTS

Many high earner taxpayers have ownership interests in directly owned businesses and entities taxed as partnerships and S corporations, which constitute Specified Service Trades or Businesses, including health, law, accounting and consulting.

A taxpayer's Section 199A deduction on income from a Specified Service Trade or Business will begin to be limited if the taxpayer's 2019 taxable income exceeds $160,700 if single, or $321,400 if married filing jointly, and will be completely eliminated if the taxpayer's 2019 taxable income exceeds $201,700 if single, or $421,400 if married filing jointly.

Although the deduction will be limited or completely eliminated for high earners, part ownership in these entities may be held by related individuals who have less than $160,700 if single or $321,400 if married filing jointly, so that income from a Specified Service Trade or Business can qualify for the deduction.

This can include the children, grandchildren, and the parents - and possibly even the grandparents - of the professional.

When state law does not allow the ownership of such interests by non-licensed professionals, it will be possible to establish a management company that will provide arm's-length management services to the Specified Service Trade or Business and receive reasonable revenues to generate a reasonable profit, which may commonly be approximately 15% of what the bottom line income of the Specified Service Trade or Business and salaries of owners of the Specified Service Trade or Business have been in the past.

This "Management Services Organization" ("MSO") may provide marketing, personnel, intellectual property, IT, and associated services, and should be adequately capitalized and should employ managerial and other workers directly to be a legitimate separate entity.

In addition, the Management Services Organizations or a different parallel entity may provide the factoring of accounts receivable for the Specified Service Trade or Business, and may become the owner of the goodwill of the Specified Service Trade or Business, if the professional who owns the business and has significant personal goodwill executes a long-term employment agreement with non-competition covenants in the same manner as is commonly used in the physician, dental and veterinary medicine industries where venture capital, publicly traded companies, hospitals and other entities purchase personal goodwill for significant consideration in exchange for the right to receive a significant portion of the former practice income by charging management and use fees that may typically range in the 35% to 40% of otherwise applicable bottom line income.

The transfer of personal goodwill and execution of non-competition covenants will be considered to be a gift by the professional to the Management Services Organizations entity that can provide income and financial stability for family members, while also protecting the assets of a professional practice from potential future creditors.

C. PLANNING OPPORTUNITY #2 - MANAGEMENT SERVICES ORGANIZATIONS WITH LESS THAN 50% COMMON OWNERSHIP PROVIDING PROPERTY OR SERVICES TO SSTBS

Before the Proposed Regulations were published, many planners were expecting to be able to form Management Services Organizations like the ones described above, and to have these Management Services Organizations owned in whole or in large part by the high earner professional and his or her spouse as a non-Specified Service Trade or Business. Management Services Organizations are common in the medical industry, and typically provide management, billing, and related services to medical practices and businesses that would otherwise manage themselves. Typically, Management Services Organizations receive management fees, and are often owned by independent management companies who may purchase the goodwill of a medical business and its professionals, and also receive long-term employment agreements with non-competition covenants in exchange for the payment of significant amounts.

Unfortunately, the Final Regulations considered entities that have 50% or more common family ownership, and which perform services for each other as a Specified Service Trades or Businesses, even where the Management Services Organizations entity does not provide any professional services directly to patients, clients or other third parties.

The Proposed Regulations provided that a Management Services Organizations having at least 50% common ownership, and which provided 80% or more of its property or services to the SSTB, would be considered to be aggregated and a part of the SSTB, and thus not eligible for the Section 199A deduction if the owner's taxable income exceeded the threshold amounts.

The Final Regulations simplify this by providing that a Management Services Organizations entity that provides property or services to an SSTB with 50% or more common ownership will be treated as a separate SSTB, but only to the extent that such property or services are provided to the SSTB. If property or services are provided to entities that are less than 50% commonly owned, regardless of whether they are SSTBs or not, then the income attributable to such activities will not be treated as SSTB income.

As the result of this limitation, some Specified Service Trades or Businesses may contract to have Management Services Organizations services provided by companies which are owned 49% or less by the family members of the Specified Service Trade or Business owners.

A possible arrangement would be to have a talented management person or entrepreneur own 2% or more of a Management Services Organizations which is owned 49% or less by a group of doctors, lawyers, accountants or other professionals, or family members thereof, who own the professional practices that the Management Services Organizations will manage and provide services for.

The income received by the high earner professional taxpayers and spouses, as well as other family members, should not be considered to be SSTB income under the Final Regulations, so long as the substance of the Management Services Organizations organization is at arm's-length.

There are limitations to having such service organization arrangements apply in professional service organizations. These are discussed in great depth in an article entitled Using Multiple

Entities to Reduce Income Taxes for Families Owning Personal Service Corporations Under Section 199A and Unique Concerns that was written by the authors and published in LISI Income Tax Planning Newsletter #136 (March 12, 2018).

It is important to note that the 50% common ownership test is measured based upon the common ownership between the two entities and is not simply a 50% test for one owner. For example, if three doctors equally own a medical practice and a Management Services Organizations that provides services to the medical practice, then the common ownership test is satisfied, notwithstanding the fact that no doctor individually owns more than 50% of either entity, since the entities are 100% commonly owned.

However, if the three doctors each owned their own separate practice and established an MSO that was equally owned by the three doctors, then the common ownership would not exceed 50%, and the Management Services Organizations would not be considered an SSTB. A reasonable management fee can then be paid to the Management Services Organizations in exchange for the Management Services Organizations managing the three doctors' practices and qualify for the Section 199A deduction.

Application of the Attribution Rules Under Sections 267 and 707

Below, we explain how the anti-abuse rules under the Section 199A Final Regulations work, and what planning opportunities still exist in this arena. For example, the Final Regulations appear to allow an individual who owns less than 50% of an SSTB to own 100% of a management, billing, or other "cracked and packed entity" that will yield Non-SSTB income, even after application of the attribution rules under Sections 267 and 707.

For example, if A, B, and C are equal 33 1/3% each partners in a partnership that is an SSTB, and A has a separate entity owned solely by A, or by A and other parties unrelated to B and C, then the separate entity would not be treated as more than 50% commonly owned, and thus could earn non-SSTB income from servicing the SSTB. The separate entity could be owned by A individually, by a disregarded LLC owned 100% by A, or taxed as a partnership or S corporation.

In order to determine whether the 50% common ownership test is satisfied, one must first understand the attribution rules under Sections 267(b) and 707(b).

Section 267 disallows losses from the sale or exchange of property between related parties, and provides that the following persons and entities are considered to be related:

1.   Members of a family, as defined in subsection 267(c)(4), which includes only brothers and sisters (whether by whole or half -blood), spouses, ancestors, and lineal descendants without reattribution.

For example, a mother and daughter will be considered to be related parties, but the mother's second husband, who is not the father of the daughter, will not be considered to be related to his step-daughter, and the daughter's husband who is not otherwise related to the mother will not be considered to be related to his mother-in-law.

2.   An individual and a corporation more than 50% in value of the outstanding stock of which is owned, directly or indirectly, by or for such individual, as further described below where we discuss the constructive ownership rules of Section 267(c).

3.   Two corporations which are members of the same controlled group, as defined in IRC Sections 267(f) and 1563(a).

4.   A grantor and a fiduciary of any trust.

5.   A fiduciary of a trust and a fiduciary of another trust, if the trusts have the same grantor.

6.   A fiduciary and a beneficiary of the same trust.

7.   A fiduciary of a trust and a beneficiary of another trust, if the trusts have the same grantor or grantors.

8.   A fiduciary of a trust and a corporation owned more than 50%, directly or indirectly, by or for the trust or by or for a person who is a grantor of the trust.

9.   A person and a charitable organization that is subject to Section 501, including Section 501(c)(3) are related if the charity is controlled directly or indirectly by such person, or by members of the family of such person, as described in IRC Section 267(b)(9).

10.   A corporation and a partnership if the same persons own—

        A.   More than 50% in value of the outstanding stock of the corporation; and

        B.   More than 50% of the capital interest, or the profits interest, in the partnership.

11.   An S corporation and another S corporation if the same persons own more than 50% in value of the outstanding stock of each corporation.

12.   An S corporation and a C corporation, if the same persons own more than 50% in value of the outstanding stock of each corporation.

13.   An executor of an estate and a beneficiary of such estate (except with respect to a sale or exchange in satisfaction of a pecuniary bequest).

Section 267(c) states that for purposes of applying Section 267(b), the below enumerated four "second stage" attribution rules apply. It is not entirely clear whether Section 267(c) will apply for purposes of testing under Section 199A, since Section 199A and the Final Regulations do not mention Section 267(c), but an IRS attorney who helped draft the Final Regulations has indicated that Section 267(c) will apply.

The Section 267(c) rules can be somewhat complicated, and are set forth below, with bracketed comments and helpful charts and examples:

Rule 1. "Stock owned, directly or indirectly, by or for a corporation, partnership, estate, or trust shall be considered as being owned proportionately by or for its shareholders, partners, or beneficiaries."

Example 1 – As illustrated below, ABC Partnership is equally owned by A, B and C, and in turn owns 60% of X Corporation. A, B and C will each be treated as owning 20% of X Corporation (their 1/3rd share of the corporation owned by the partnership).

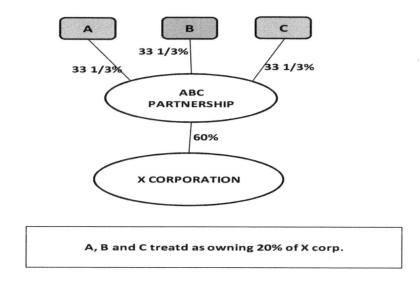

This Attribution Rule 1 is "reattributed" for purposes of this Section, as further discussed in Rule 4, Part I, below.

Rule 2. An individual will be considered to be the owner of stock that is owned, directly or indirectly, by or for his family.

Example 2 – As illustrated below, A owns 60% of ABC Partnership, and X, who is A's spouse, owns 60% of XYZ Partnership. A will be treated as also owning 60% of XYZ Partnership, and X will be treated as owning 60% of ABC Partnership.

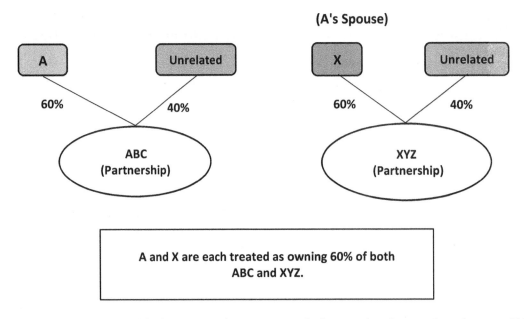

(A's Spouse)

A and X are each treated as owning 60% of both ABC and XYZ.

Example 3 – As illustrated below, A and X, are married to each other and each own 40% of DEF Partnership. They will therefore each be treated as owning their own 40% and the spouse's 40%, and therefore a total of 80% of DEF Partnership after application of the attribution rules.

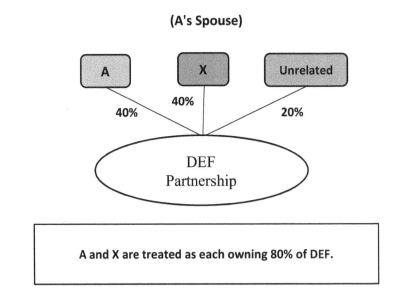

(A's Spouse)

A and X are treated as each owning 80% of DEF.

This Attribution Rule 2 is not "reattributed," as described in Section 4, Part 2, below.

Rule 3. An individual owning (other than by the application of [Rule] 2 above) any stock in a corporation shall be considered as owning the stock owned, directly or indirectly, by or for his partner in a partnership.

Example 4 – As illustrated below, A and B are partners in Partnership A, in any percentage, no matter how small, and are not otherwise related. A and B each own 30% of X Corporation, and 40% of X Corporation is owned by unrelated parties. A is treated as owning the shares of B in X Corporation, and B is treated as owning the shares of A in X Corporation. As a result, A and B are both treated as owning 60% of X Corporation, and X Corporation.

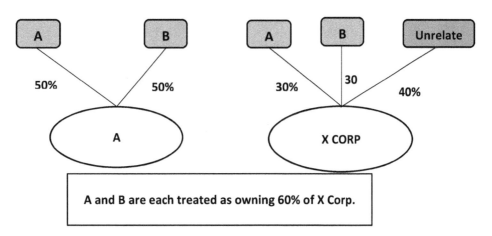

This Attribution Rule 3 is not "reattributed," as described in Section 4, Part 2, below.

Rule 4 – Part 1 and Part 2. Under Section 267(c), there are really two separate rules, which address "double attribution," and read as follows:

Rule 4 - Part 1. Stock constructively owned by a person by reason of the application of [Rule] 1 [above] shall, for the purpose of applying [Rule] 1, 2, or 3, be treated as actually owned by such person.

What this means, for example, is that if someone is considered to be the owner of stock because he or she owns stock or partnership interests in an entity that in turn owns another entity, then such person will be considered to own such interest directly and will be subject to all constructive ownership rules.

Example 5 – As illustrated below, A, B and C are equal 33 1/3% each owners of ABC Partnership, which in turn owns 60% of X Corporation. A and B also have 50% each ownership in DEF Partnership. As a result of Part 1 of Rule 4 described above, A and B are treated as each owning 20% of X directly, and therefore A's ownership of X is treated as constructively owning B's stock in C, and B is treated as constructively owning A's stock in X under Rule 3.

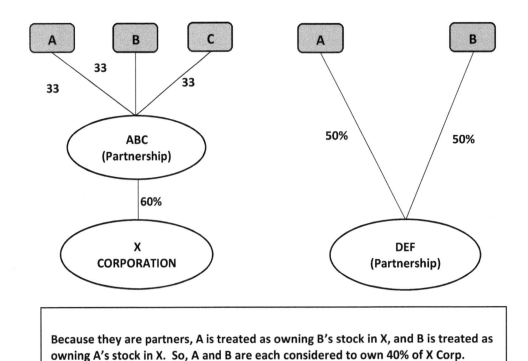

Because they are partners, A is treated as owning B's stock in X, and B is treated as owning A's stock in X. So, A and B are each considered to own 40% of X Corp.

Rule 4 - Part 2. [But] **stock constructively owned by an individual by reason of the application of [number] 2 or 3 shall not be treated as owned by him for the purpose of again applying either of such paragraphs in order to make another the constructive owner of such stock.**

Stated differently, if ownership is attributed to an individual by reason of ownership by a family member (Rule 2) or because of a partnership relationship (Rule 3), then such ownership will not again be attributed to another party under Rules 1, 2 and 3 above. This is commonly referred to as double attribution. Therefore, if ownership is attributed to an individual by reason of numbers 2 and 3 above, such ownership cannot be reattributed to another under the other attribution rules.

Example 6 – As illustrated below, assume the same facts as Example 5 above, except that X (A's spouse) owns 50% of DEF Partnership. A will be treated as constructively owning 50% of DEF, however A will not be treated as also constructively owning B's stock in X due to the fact that A does not actually have an ownership interest in DEF since such ownership cannot be reattributed under Part 2 of Rule 4. In addition, B will not be treated as constructively owning A's ownership of X stock since A's constructive ownership of DEF cannot be reattributed to B under Part 2 of Rule 4.

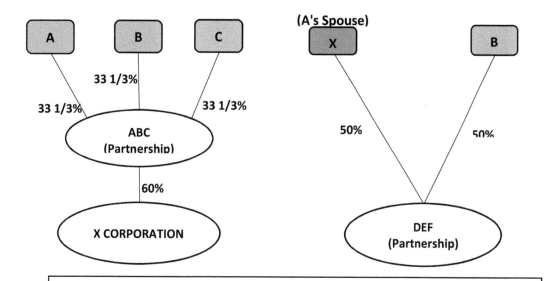

A is treated as owning 50% of DEF, but B's ownership in X Corp stock is not reattributed to A by reason of being treated as a constructive owner of DEF. A's ownership of X Corp will also not be attributed to B. A and B are only treated as owning 20% each of X Corp.

The same limitation on double attribution will also apply if ownership is attributed to another by reason of partner-to-partner attribution under Rule 3 above. This is illustrated by the following example:

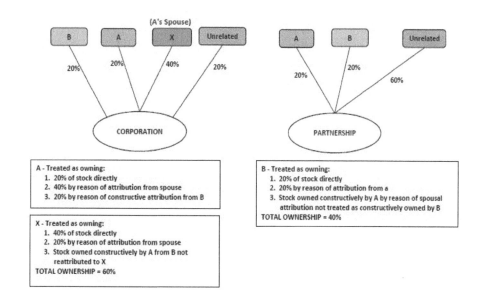

Confused Yet? Hold on tight. We are just about there, with simplified examples to follow.

Section 707(b) applies for purposes of determining attribution between partners and partnerships. Under Section 707(b), a partner and a partnership will be considered as related if a person owns, directly or indirectly, more than 50% of the capital interest, or the profits interest, in such partnership, and two partnerships will be considered related if the same persons own, directly or indirectly, more than 50% of the capital interests or profits interests in both partnerships.

In applying the above, Section 707(b)(3) states that the ownership of the partnership will be determined in accordance with the rules for constructive ownership provided in Section 267(c), other than by application of Section 267(c)(3). Section 267(e)(3) states that for purposes of determining ownership of a partnership, the principles of Section 267(c) will apply, except that:

1.   Section 267(c)(3) (Rule 3 above) will not apply; and

2.   Interests owned (directly or indirectly) by or for a C corporation will be considered as owned by or for any shareholder only if such shareholder owns (directly or indirectly) 5% or more in value of the stock of such corporation.

As a reminder, Section 267(c)(3) states that "An individual owning any stock in a corporation shall be considered as owning the stock owned, directly or indirectly, by or for his partner."

Since Section 267(c)(3) does not impute ownership to partnerships, the ownership of one partner or multiple partners will not be attributable to other partners under Sections 707 or 267.

As mentioned above, different attribution rules apply with respect to Section 199A ownership of a corporation than for partnerships and can have a dramatic effect on the treatment of an entity that provides services to an SSTB. This is best explained through the use of the following examples:

Example 8 – A owns 60% of ABC Law Partnership (an SSTB), and the remaining 40% is owned equally by B and C who are unrelated to A. A, Z (the office manager) and other unrelated parties own 33 1/3% each of X Corporation, an S corporation that provides management services to the law firm. A and Z also each have 50% ownership interest in AZ, LLC a separate unrelated entity that invests in real estate ventures.

At first glance, it appears that X Corporation does not trigger the 50% common ownership threshold because there is not 50% common ownership of either entity. However, under Section 267(c)(3), because A and Z are partners, A is treated as owning the shares of Z in X Corporation, and Z is treated as owning the shares of A in X Corporation. As a result, A and Z are treated as owning 66 2/3% of X Corporation, and therefore ABC and X Corporation would trigger the 50% common ownership test (A owns 60% of ABC and 66 2/3% of X Corporation), and any income from X would be considered SSTB income to its shareholders. If they were not partners in a separate partnership, then this attribution would not apply.

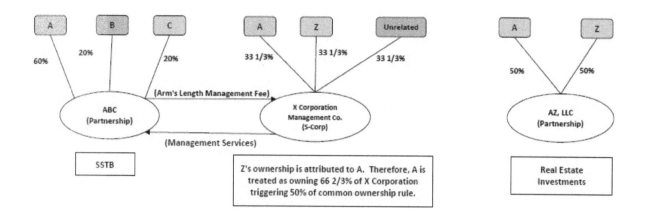

Example 9 – Assume the same facts as the above example, except that X Corporation is a partnership.

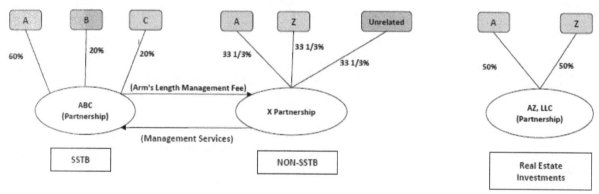

Since Section 267(c)(3) does not apply for purposes of determining ownership in a partnership, the 50% common ownership requirement is not triggered, and therefore X will not be considered related, and the income earned by X will be non-SSTB income that can qualify for the Section 199A deduction, notwithstanding whether the individual owners are high income taxpayers.

Examples 8 and 9 show that entity selection can be an important factor in Section 199A planning. An SSTB owner may prefer that the management company servicing the SSTB be taxed as an S corporation so that wages can be paid from the management company to the owner in order to satisfy the wage/property test; however, checking the box and electing S corporation status can be a trap for the unwary and convert what would have been an unrelated entity eligible for the Section 199A deduction, because it is taxed as a partnership into a related entity that is not eligible for the Section 199A deduction.

What if in examples 8 and 9 above, only A owned the management company?

Example 10 – A, B and C each own 33 1/3% of XYZ Partnership. A owns 100% of a separate entity that provides management services for ABC Partnership. Neither Section 707(b) nor Section 267(b) are applicable because A's interest in ABC Partnership is not more than 50% and A's ownership in the management entity is not attributed to B and C.

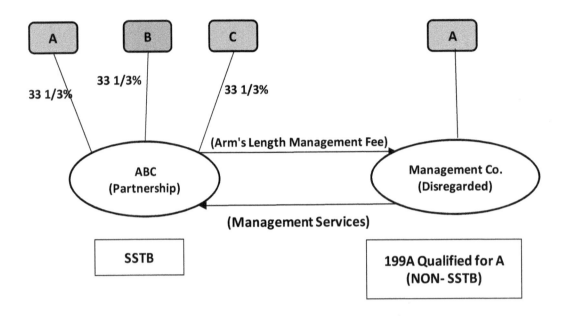

In this scenario, A's ownership of the management company would not be attributed to B or C under Section 267(c)(3), and therefore the management company would not be considered a related party and A's income from the management company would qualify for the Section 199A deduction, regardless of whether the management company is taxed as a partnership or S corporation.

It is noteworthy that there is no minimum ownership required under 267(c)(3) for the partner-to-partner attribution rules to apply. Therefore, if B or C owned just 1% of the management company that was taxed as an S corporation then A's ownership would be attributed to B and C, and the management company and the law firm would be considered as more than 50% commonly controlled.

Although at first glance Treas. Reg. 1.199A-5(c)(2) appears to end "crack and pack" planning, a thorough understanding of the attribution rules of Sections 267 and 707 reveal that many planning opportunities still exist.

Individuals owning SSTBs who have less than a 50% ownership therein can set up a management company that is owned 100% by the SSTB owner, or by trusts for their children and spouses, and income earned by the management company will be considered Non-SSTB income.

In addition, it may be possible for three equal partners in an SSTB to set up multiple entities so that each partner can break off a portion of the SSTB into a Non-SSTB entity. For example, if A B and C are equal owners of ABC Law Firm, A could set up a management company, B could set up a billing company, and C could set up a marketing company. ABC law firm could pay an arm's-length fee to each of the three separate companies, and the income earned by the management company, billing company, and marketing company may be considered Non-SSTB income.

The IRS may try to combine the three companies together through a substance over form argument, in which event the combined companies would be considered more than 50% commonly owned, and thus not eligible for the deduction; however properly structured arm's -length arrangements should withstand an IRS challenge.

Based upon the above, "crack and pack" planning is still available for those who can navigate Sections 267 and 707.

D. ENTITY SELECTION

Section 199A is a new, important factor in determining what entity is best suited to own or operate property and activities.

The chart below provides the primary 13 factors that can be considered from a choice of entity standpoint for planning with the new tax law.

While most pass-through entities (companies and LLCs taxed as S corporations, partnerships, or disregarded) will not change as the result of Section 199A, this will not always be the case, for the following reasons:

Chart 20 – Section 199A and Related Factors with Respect to Entity Selection Chart

Issue/Factor	Sole Proprietorship	Partnership	S corporation	C corporation
Tax Rates	Owners are taxed at individual rates for salary and income of the company	Owners are taxed at individual rates for salary and income of the company	Owners are taxed at individual rates for salary and income of the company	Entity taxed for income at 21%; - shareholders taxed for dividends and distributions
Double Taxation	No	No	No	Dividends or distributions taxed separately
Availability of Section 199A deduction	Available (depending on limitations)	Available (depending on limitations)	Available (depending on limitations)	Cannot qualify for Section 199A
Accumulated Earnings	Taxed to owner as reported on their Form K-1, regardless of whether distributions are made	Taxed to owner as reported on their Form K-1, regardless of whether distributions are made	Taxed to owner as reported on their Form K-1, regardless of whether distributions are made	Taxed at 21% corporate rate; beware of accumulated earning tax issues
Guaranteed payments	N/A	Excluded from QBI; Not	N/A	N/A

Issue/Factor	Sole Proprietorship	Partnership	S corporation	C corporation
		considered to be W- 2 wages		
Owner provides services (reasonable compensation issues)	Self-Employed (no W-2 wages); currently not subject to reasonable compensation	Self-Employed (no W-2 wages); currently not subject to reasonable compensation rules	W-2 Wages are excluded from QBI and subject to reasonable compensation rules	W-2 Wages are subject to reasonable compensation rules
Business is a Specified Service Trade or Business	Eligible if owner's taxable income is under lower-income thresholds; limited if in between lower- and higher-income thresholds; lost if taxable income is greater than higher-income thresholds	Eligible if owner's taxable income is under lower-income thresholds; limited if in between lower- and higher-income thresholds; lost if taxable income is greater than higher-income thresholds	Eligible if owner's taxable income is under lower-income thresholds; limited if in between lower- and higher-income thresholds; lost if taxable income is greater than higher-income thresholds	N/A
High Income earner as owner	May be limited if Wage/Property Hurdle is not met	May be limited if Wage/Property Hurdle is not met	May be limited if Wage/Property Hurdle is not met	N/A
Employees (W-2 Wages)	Consider impact on Wage/Property Limitation; adjust if necessary	Consider impact on Wage/Property Limitation; adjust if necessary	Consider impact on Wage/Property Limitation; adjust if necessary	N/A
Independent contractors	Hurts in application of Wage/Property Hurdle; compensation not considered W-2 wages	Hurts in application of Wage/Property Hurdle; compensation not considered W-2 wages	Hurts in application of Wage/Property Hurdle; compensation not considered W-2 wages	N/A
Qualified property basis	Consider impact on Wage/Property Hurdle; adjust if necessary	Consider impact on Wage/Property Hurdle; adjust if necessary	Consider impact on Wage/Property Hurdle; adjust if necessary	N/A
State and local tax deductions	Deduction Limited	Deduction Limited	Deduction Limited	Fully Deductible
Medical expenses and	N/A	N/A	N/A	Premiums and medical

Issue/Factor	Sole Proprietorship	Partnership	S corporation	C corporation
plans deductions				reimbursement plans are deductible

CHAPTER 12.
PART ONE -- ACTIVE TRADE OR BUSINESS REQUIREMENTS

Section 199A does not define the words "trade or business," and the Code references such term in more than 400 sections.[285] The Final Regulations followed the Proposed Regulations and apply the definition of trade or business under Section 162.

A. CODE DEFINITIONS

It is noteworthy that the Code defines trade or business in several sections, somewhat inconsistently,[286] including the following:

1. ### TREAS. REG. § 301.7701-1[287]:

    "A separate entity exists for federal tax purposes if co-owners of an apartment building lease space and in addition provide services to the occupants either directly or through an agent. Nevertheless, a joint undertaking merely to share expenses does not create a separate entity for federal tax purposes. For example, if two or more persons jointly construct a ditch merely to drain surface water from their properties, they have not created a separate entity for federal tax purposes."

    2. ### SECTION 165:

    "For an individual to be engaged in a trade or business, the individual must be engaged in an activity for the primary purpose of producing income or profit and must be involved in the activity with continuity and regularity.

    The determination of whether a taxpayer is carrying on a trade or business requires an examination of the facts of each case.

    For instance, a taxpayer who offers goods and services for sale is generally considered to be engaged in a trade or business. However, the offering of goods and services is not an absolute prerequisite to satisfying the trade or business test, and this factor, by itself, does not raise an otherwise unqualified activity to the level of a trade or business." [288]

---

[285] May Beth Hallissey Musco, *The Supreme Court Gambles on the Definition of Trade or Business: Commissioner v. Groetzinger*, 61 St. John's L. Rev. 643 (1987) (noting that, in 1986, the IRC used the term in 492 subsections), available at https://scholarship.law.stjohns.edu/cgi/viewcontent.cgi?article=2043&context=lawreview.

[286] Lee Grant University Tax Education Foundation, Inc., Chapter 4: Trade or Business, National Income Tax Workbook (2015) (noting that most references to "trade or business" refer back to IRC § 162, which does not define the term), http://taxworkbook.com/files/2015/09/Trade-or-BusinessWEB.pdf.

[287] Treas. Reg. § 301.7701-1 affects IRC § 7701 that governs entity classification rules, also known as check-the-box regulations.

[288] *Groetzinger*, 480 US 23 (1987). *See also* Individual Tax Answer Book by Terence M. Myers and Dorinda D. DeScherer, Q 6:3.

3. TREAS. REG. § 1.446-1[289]:

(a) **Two or More Distinct Trades or Businesses.**

"Where a taxpayer has two or more separate and distinct trades or businesses, a different method of accounting may be used for each trade or business... For example, a taxpayer may account for the operations of a personal service business on the cash receipts and disbursements method and of a manufacturing business on an accrual method, provided such businesses are separate and distinct and the methods used for each clearly reflect income. The method first used ... must be consistently followed thereafter."

(b) **Separable Books and Records.**

"No trade or business will be considered separate and distinct for purposes of this paragraph unless a complete and separable set of books and records is kept for such trade or business."

(c) **Not Separate and Distinct.**

"If, by reason of maintaining different methods of accounting, there is a creation or shifting of profits or losses between the trades or businesses of the taxpayer (for example, through inventory adjustments, sales, purchases, or expenses) so that income of the taxpayer is not clearly reflected, the trades or businesses of the taxpayer will not be considered to be separate and distinct."

4. TREAS. REG. § 1.469-4(B)(1) 290:

"A 'trade or business activity' is one that involves the conduct of a trade or business, is conducted in anticipation of the start of a trade or business or involves certain research or experimental expenses. A trade or business activity cannot be a rental activity, or an activity treated as incidental to an activity of holding property for investment."

5. TREAS. REG. §1.1411-5(B)(3) EX. 1291:

"The IRS concluded that the rental of a commercial building by an unmarried individual to another entity did not involve the conduct of a trade or business because the unmarried individual was "not involved in the activity of the commercial building on a regular and continuous basis."

---

[289] Treas. Reg. § 1.446-1 affects IRC § 446 that governs methods of accounting.
[290] Treas. Reg. § 1.469-4 affects IRC § 469 that governs passive activity losses and credits.
[291] Treas. Reg. § 1.1411-5 affects IRC § 1411 that governs the application of the Net Investment Income Tax.

6. TREAS. REG. §1.469-4(C)(2) 292:

"[W]hether activities constitute an appropriate economic unit and, therefore, may be treated as a single activity depends upon all the relevant facts and circumstances. A taxpayer may use any reasonable method of applying the relevant facts and circumstances in grouping activities," which include (1) the similarities and differences in types of trades or businesses, (2) the extent of common control, (3) the extent of common ownership, (4) geographical location, and (5) interdependencies between or among the activities."

In 1987, the Supreme Court determined that a trade or business must be "activity with continuity and regularity and that the taxpayer's primary purpose for engaging in the activity must be for income or profit." in order to satisfy the definition under Treasury Regulation Section 301.7701-1 which is quoted above.[293]

In this decision, Justice Blackmun noted that the term trade or business is not defined anywhere in the Code. "We accept the fact that to be engaged in a trade or business, the taxpayer "must be involved in the activity with continuity and regularity and that the taxpayer's primary purpose for engaging in the activity must be for income or profit. A sporadic activity, a hobby, or an amusement diversion does not qualify." It seems that the most important factors are that (1) the taxpayer's purpose for engaging in said activity must be for profit or income, and (2) the taxpayer must engage in said activity with continuity and regularity.

The Proposed Regulations included two examples regarding rental activities and assume that these are trades or businesses, while stating that the landlord "manages" the real estate. Although these examples were not under the trade or business definition Section, and were meant to provide guidance on the calculation of the Section 199A deduction for taxpayers with taxable income above the threshold amount, the Final Regulations stated that "For purposes of these examples, unless indicated otherwise, assume that all of the trades or businesses are trades or businesses as defined in paragraph (b)(13) of this Section..."

These examples were changed in the Final Regulations to remove the references to land in both examples, and the Preamble to the Final Regulations indicated that the first example was intended to provide a simple illustration of how the calculation would work if a taxpayer lacked sufficient W-2 wages or UBIA of qualified property to claim the deduction while the second example was to build on the fact pattern by adding UBIA of qualified property to the facts.

A comparison of the two examples, which show the words deleted to avoid confusion, is as follows:

Example 1: D, an unmarried individual, operates a business as a sole proprietorship. The business generates $1,000,000 of QBI in 2018. Solely for purposes of this example, assume that the business paid no wages and holds no qualified property for use in the business. After allowable deductions unrelated to the business, D's total taxable income for 2018 is $980,000. Because D's taxable income exceeds the applicable threshold amount, D's section 199A deduction is subject to the W-

---

[292] *Supra*, note 243.
[293] *Commissioner v. Groetzinger*, 480 U.S. 23 (1987).

2 wage and UBIA of qualified property limitations. D's section 199A deduction is limited to zero because the business paid no wages and held no qualified property.

Example 2: Assume the same facts as in Example 1 of this paragraph (d)(4), except that D holds qualified property with a UBIA of $10,000,000 for use in the trade or business. D reports $4,000,000 of QBI for 2020. After allowable deductions unrelated to the business, D's total taxable income for 2020 is $3,980,000. Because D's taxable income is above the threshold amount, the QBI component of D's section 199A deduction is subject to the W-2 wage and UBIA of qualified property limitations. Because the business has no W-2 wages, the QBI component of D's Section 199A deduction will be limited to the lesser of 20% of the business's QBI or 2.5% of its UBIA of qualified property. Twenty percent of the $4,000,000 of QBI is $800,000. Two and one-half percent of the $10,000,000 UBIA of qualified property is $250,000. The QBI component of D's section 199A deduction is thus limited to $250,000. D's section 199A deduction is equal to the lesser of (i) 20% of the QBI from the business as limited ($250,000) or (ii) 20% of D's taxable income ($3,980,000 x 20% = $796,000). Therefore, D's Section 199A deduction for 2020 is $250,000.

B. ARE YOU A "TRADE" OR "BUSINESS"?

The Courts have primarily focused on two factors in this area to determine if there is a "trade or business":

1. Whether there is a profit motive, and

2. The scope of the activities performed.

As noted in an April 16, 2018 BNA Tax & Accounting Center Article, the Committee Reports from the Revenue Act of 1980 are useful in understanding Congress' intention on what rental business is considered active:

> *"Further, in the case of rental activities, there must be significant furnishing of services incident to the rentals to constitute an active business (within the meaning of Section 162) rather than an investment. Thus, a rental activity is not considered to be an active trade or business solely because deductions attributable to it are allowable in computing adjusted gross income (Section 62(5)). In general, the operation of an apartment complex, an office building, or a shopping center would constitute an active trade or business."* [294]

Additionally, case law is helpful in this area.

1. NEIL V. COMMISSIONER, 46 B.T.A. 197 (1942):

The collection of rent does not involve sufficient management activity to constitute a trade or business. In this case, the petitioner owned rental real estate in Philadelphia which was completely "handled by the tenant." She claimed that this ownership constituted the "carrying on of business." The Tax Court analogized that because mere ownership of stocks and bonds that accumulate in

---

[294] *See* James M. Kehl, *§199A Gets an Update Three Months After Its Enactment*, 59 Tax Mgmt. Mem. (BNA) No. 115 (April 16, 2018), (citing S.Rept 96-1036 on Pub. L. No. 98-605).

value does not amount to a trade or business, neither should ownership of rental property. Similarly, mere ownership of a patent without exploiting should not constitute a trade or business.

2. *CURPHEY V. COMMISSIONER*, 73 T.C. 766 (1980):

The Tax Court held that the taxpayer's efforts in finding new tenants, supplying furnishings, and making the units ready for new tenants "were sufficiently systematic and continuous to place him in the business of real estate rental."

3. *DEAMODIO V. COMMISSIONER*, 34 T.C. 894 (1960):

A taxpayer that contracts with various real estate firms to collect rent from properties, make repairs, and acquires tenants is considered to be engaged in a trade or business because the activities carried on by his agents are considerable, continuous, and regular, and are beyond the scope of mere ownership of property.

Further discussion on the trade or business requirement is as follows, which is derived from LISI Newsletter 175, "When is Rental Real Estate a "Trade or Business" Under 199A?"

> Section 199A points to Section 162 for the definition of a "trade or business," however, even looking past the repetition of the phrase "trade or business," Section 162 does not provide a clear definition either. Section 162 states that expenses can be deducted when they are incurred for a legitimate and active trade or business. Section 199A of the Act modifies the Section 162 definition of what constitutes "trades and businesses" by excluding "the trade or business of performing services as an employee and 'specified service' trades or businesses ("SSTBs"). SSTBs involve the performance of services in law, accounting, financial services, and several other enumerated fields, or when the business's principal asset is the reputation or skill of one or more owners or employees." Thus, the 199A definition of "trade or business" begs the question: who actually qualifies as a trade or business for the 199A deduction?
>
> We do know that a taxpayer owning SSTBs is not eligible for the Section 199A deduction if the taxpayer's taxable income exceeds the threshold amounts, and that services as an employee are excluded. Those two concepts are also fraught with nuance and uncertainty but will not be addressed in this article. Rather, this article will explore the remaining territory of what is a business for 199A other than these two special situations, with a focus on how a real estate trade or business is defined for purposes of applying 199A.
>
> While the definition of a "trade or business" under Section 162 and case law is complex and in many cases quite fact specific, the analysis is much more complicated. Even apart from the SSTB and employee exclusions, the 199A Regulations include a range of other comments affecting the definition of what is a trade or business for purposes of 199A.
>
> The question of whether a taxpayer is engaging in a trade or business is an issue of fact that requires analysis of the scope of activities that the taxpayer is engaged in,

either personally or through an agent. The new Final Regulations state that: "Whether an activity rises to the level of a Section 162 trade or business, however, is inherently a factual question…accordingly, the Treasury Department and the IRS have concluded that the factual settings of various trades or businesses varies so widely that a single rule or list of factors would be difficult to provide in a timely and manageable manner and would be difficult for taxpayers to apply."

We will start by reviewing how the Courts have defined the term "trade or business" in order to give the Internal Revenue Code definitions some context, particularly since many of these cases are cited by the new Regulations.

C.   CASE HISTORY DEFINING "TRADE OR BUSINESS"

The Supreme Court has been faced with the task of defining a "trade or business" in tax context multiple times over the last century. Going back to 1911, the Court in *Flint v. Stone Tracey* used the Bouvier Dictionary to broadly define a business as "that which occupies the time, attention and labor of men for the purpose of a livelihood or profit."[295] In 1935, the U.S. Supreme Court provided a limitation to the definition by distinguishing between an active trade and an investor.[296] In *Snyder v. Commissioner,* the Court determined that an investor seeking to merely increase his personal holdings was not engaged in a trade or business,[297] however, Justice Brandeis also stated that a taxpayer who made his livelihood from buying and selling on the stock exchange would be a trade or business.[298] This was the first of many instances where the activity level of the taxpayer is a deciding factor in whether the definition of a "trade or business" applies.

Not long after *Snyder*, the Court was faced with two "trade or business" cases in one year which centered upon estate preservation. In the 1941 *Higgins v. Commissioner* case, also cited in the new Final Regulations, the Supreme Court stated that determining whether a taxpayer is 'carrying on a business' "requires an examination of the facts in each case" therefore highlighting that this is a factual determination.[299] In *Higgins* specifically, the Court determined that a taxpayer managing and preserving his own estate did not qualify as carrying on a business.[300] Additionally, in City Bank Farmers *Trust v. Helvering*, the Supreme Court used the same analysis to determine that asset conservation and maintenance by way of estate or trust efforts is not a trade or business.[301]

These cases highlight the Supreme Court's ongoing struggle in deciding whether a certain activity qualifies as a trade or business without a succinct definition from Congress or its agencies. In its 1987 sentinel case *Commissioner v. Groetzinger*, a case cited in the new Regulation, the U.S. Supreme Court laid out a definition for what qualifies as a trade or business that is still good law.[302] In *Groetzinger*, the Court determined that a full-time gambler who wagered for himself alone was

---

[295] *Flint v. Stone Tracy Co.*, 220 U.S. 107 (1911).
[296] *Snyder v. Commissioner*, 295 U.S. 134 (1935).
[297] Id.
[298] Id.
[299] *Higgins v. Commissioner*, 312 U.S. 212 (1941).
[300] Id. at 217.
[301] *City Bank Farmers Trust Co. v. Helvering*, 313 U.S. 121 (1941).
[302] *Commissioner v. Groetzinger*, 480 U.S. 23 (1987).

engaged in a "trade or business" within the meaning of the applicable Internal Revenue Code.[303] The Court rejected the previously used 'goods and services' test reasoning that almost every activity could potentially satisfy the test leading to litigation over the meaning.[304]

The Court held that to be engaged in a trade or business:

1.   The taxpayer's involvement must be continuous and regular; and

2.   The primary purpose of the activity must be for income or profit.[305]

The Court cautioned future courts to examine the facts of each case, refusing to create a bright line rule, and highlighted that it is the responsibility of Congress to make changes or revisions to this Court's interpretation of the definition.[306] While it is true that Congress has the ultimate responsibility to define "trade or business" as used in its rules and Proposed Regulations, they have not done so. In fact, the new Final Regulations cite back to the two definitional requirements in *Groetzinger*, so it follows that the best definition or test available still comes from the Supreme Court in *Groetzinger*.

It is important to keep in mind that the Supreme Court only hears a select number of cases. The majority of disputes related to tax matters are heard by the Tax Court. The Tax Court has held that, beyond the definition provided in *Groetzinger*, the threshold test for deduction of income expenses under Section 162 is twofold: (1) whether the primary purpose and intention of the taxpayer was to make a profit,[307] and (2) the level of activity involved. Along with the new Final Regulations, the IRS also released a Notice that included a safe harbor for real estate activities related to the level of activity necessary to qualify as a trade or business. This safe harbor will be discussed further below.

By way of illustration, if a taxpayer loses money by participating in a hobby, the taxpayer cannot receive benefits of income tax deductions by calling the hobby a trade or business. In the 1988 U.S. Tax Court case of *Seebold v. Commissioner*, a married couple decided to breed horses to add to their retirement income.[308] In this case, the court explicitly placed greater weight on the objective factors showing the couple's intent to profit rather than simply their statement of intent.[309] For example, they worked hard to learn the subject area, sought advice from experts in the field, used a veterinarian for the purpose of breeding, and consulted an accountant.[310] Moreover, Mrs. Seebold eventually quit her job to work on the breeding farm full time.[311]

The Tax Court determined that this level of activity met the threshold in that the primary purpose and intention of the Seebolds was to incur a profit, regardless of the loss they sustained when they

---

[303] Id.
[304] Id.
[305] Id.
[306] Id.
[307] *Seebold v. Commissioner*, 55 T.C.M. 723 (1988).
[308] Id.
[309] Id.
[310] Id.
[311] Id.

first started, and the Seebolds' horse breeding qualified as a trade or business.[312] As a result, in addition to the *Groetzinger* test, taxpayers must also be able to show that the primary purpose and intent of the activity is to incur a profit, and the taxpayer bears the burden of proving they meet this threshold before benefitting from the Section 199A deduction.

In certain tax cases not related to the Section 199A deduction, taxpayers may have wanted to avoid being labeled as a trade or business in order to avoid paying additional taxes as a trade or business. In *Bennett v. Commissioner*, two partners leased equipment to site organizations allowing people to play a form of lottery called Keno under the company name of Lucky Keno ("Lucky").[313] The partners both reported their business income from Lucky but did not report self-employment tax.[314] The partners argued that they did not have to pay the self-employment tax because Lucky was a passive owner of the equipment and not actively engaged in trade or business.[315] The Tax Court disagreed, stating that the partners oversimplified their role.[316] Lucky's name was on all of the Keno advertisements and Lucky controlled the funds and distributed them to the winners, municipalities, the state, and the site organizations.[317] Therefore, Lucky was not a passive owner, and the partners were required to pay self-employment taxes because they owned a trade or business.[318]

---

[312] Id.

[313] *Bennett v. Commissioner*, 83 T.C.M. 1429 (2002).

[314] Id.

[315] Id.

[316] Id.

[317] Id.

[318] Id.

PART TWO –APPLIED TO REAL ESTATE

There are several factors that taxpayers may wish to document if there is any uncertainty as to whether their real estate involvement may qualify as a trade or business.

A.   QUALIFYING FOR TRADE OR BUSINESS STATUS

Real estate investors attempting to qualify for trade or business status could pursue and corroborate the following:

1.   Save internet research on real estate rental matters to corroborate work done in an effort to educate him/herself on the subject.

2.   Document consultations with experts, e.g. saving emails and other correspondence.

3.   Hire professional experts, including CPAs, and save all bills and payments thereto.

4.   Maintain time records.

5.   Prepare a financial plan to reflect the need for income to support the argument that the intent is to earn a profit.

As illustrated above, taking proactive steps to corroborate intent at the time activities and actions are completed may be a prudent way to prepare for the possibility of a future challenge.

Even without a definitive test, passive ownership of a rental property has most often been found to not be enough to qualify as a trade or business, although active management of such a property historically has been viewed as a trade or business. Since qualifying as a trade or business is based on a question of fact, the line distinguishing passive ownership and active ownership can easily become blurry.

B.   FOUR FACTORS COURTS USE TO DETERMINE TRADE OR BUSINESS STATUS

The new Final Regulations do provide four factors that have been used by courts for years to determine whether a real estate venture qualifies as a trade or business.[319]

1.   TYPE OF PROPERTY.

First, the IRS will consider the type of property owned and/or managed by the taxpayer (i.e. commercial, residential, condominium, or personal).

---

[319] *See also* Tony Nitti, IRS Provides Guidance On 20% Pass-Through Deduction, But Questions Remain, FORBES (Aug. 9, 2018), https://www.forbes.com/sites/anthonynitti/2018/08/09/irs-providesguidance-on-20-pass-through-deduction-but-questionsremain/#7cf566562ff8.

2. NUMBER OF RENTAL PROPERTIES.

Second, the court will consider the number of properties rented out by the taxpayer.

3. INVOLVEMENT OF OWNER OR AGENT.

Third, and what seems to be most important, the court will consider the day to day involvement of the owner or agent.

4. TYPE OF RENTAL.

Fourth, the court will consider the type of rental (i.e. triple net lease, traditional lease, short term lease, or long-term lease).

C.   PROACTIVE STEPS

Based upon the above, taxpayers seeking to qualify might take the following proactive steps:

1.   LIKELIHOOD PROPERTY WILL QUALIFY.

When making a new investment, consider the likelihood that the type of property being considered will qualify if this is not inconsistent with overall goals. For example, purchasing a commercial property is more likely to qualify then renting a vacation home, and purchasing multiple properties may be more favorable than having one large property with one tenant.

2.   DOCUMENT DAILY ACTIVITIES.

This can be done with a calendar program or perhaps an Excel spreadsheet. Even documenting simple and easily overlooked items may be useful to "fill-out" the documentation and demonstrate a more regular involvement, such as providing the dates on which supplies are purchased, the dates on which internet research is conducted, and the dates in which emails are sent to an agent, prospective tenant, repair contractor, and so on. This can also be helpful in the event that the taxpayer wishes to qualify under the 250-hour safe harbor.

3.   KNOWLEDGEABLE COUNSEL.

Taxpayers should be certain that the real estate attorney drafting and negotiating the lease understands the implications. It may be possible to charge a higher rent and leave property tax, insurance, and other expenses to be paid for by the owner. That might not meaningfully impact the economics of the transaction, but it may impact the potential characterization of the transaction for Sections 162 or 199A trade or business characterization.

In the 1946 case *Hazard v. Commissioner*, the Tax Court ruled that even one single family rental was a trade or business.[320] The Internal Revenue Service has since adopted the same reasoning and the rule still stands in most jurisdictions.[321] It would therefore be reasonable for the IRS to

---

[320] *Hazard v. Commissioner*, 7 T.C. 372 (T.C. 1946).
[321] The Second Circuit decided in *Grier v. US* that "broader activity" on the part of the owner was needed in order for a rental to constitute a trade or business.

continue to follow the *Hazard* standard with regards to 199A deductions and allow single family or single property rentals to qualify as a trade or business, however, much case law has shown that simply renting the property alone is not enough. As noted above, if the taxpayer has options when purchasing a new real estate investment, such as structuring a more sustainable investment for QBI purposes, doing so may be feasible. Practically speaking, how much change will a taxpayer tolerate for the amount of the deduction?

In *Neill v. Commissioner*, the 1942 Tax Court ruled that the mere collection of rent without any other activity was not enough to constitute a trade or business.[322] In *Hendrickson v. Commissioner*, the Tax Court ruled that a passive investment in an oil gas well where the owner simply purchased the lease and collected income from it did not qualify as a trade or business.[323] Therefore, while it is possible for a rental business to constitute a "trade or business," simply owning the business and collecting money is not enough. Even so, as indicated above, it may not be difficult for taxpayers to document a quantum of activity, modify lease terms, etc. to support the active trade or business characterization.

Based on the relevant case law, in order to qualify as engaging in a trade or business, the taxpayer must have some active role in running the rental. In *Schwarcz v. Commissioner*, the Tax Court determined that a landlord owning, managing, and operating apartment buildings was engaging in a trade or business.[324] Interestingly, the owner could do so through an agent and would still qualify.[325] While most or all rental activities can be handled through an agent, having the owner personally visit and inspect the property at least once a month (even if from the outside so as not to disturb a tenant) to take photos that can be stored to prove the dates and actuality of the inspections may be prudent to help support the taxpayer's position.

In order to qualify for the deduction, the trade or business must be an "active trade or business" as defined under Internal Revenue Code Section 162. For further discussion, please see the blog one of the authors wrote entitled "Does Rental Income Qualify for the New 20% Section 199A Deduction."

D.   ACTIVITIES OF AGENTS CAN BE COUNTED TOWARDS LEVEL OF ACTIVITY

Based upon the following discussion, the activities of an employee, contractor, management company, or any combination thereof can be considered to be activities of the taxpayer for purposes of determining whether an investment or business arrangement meets the definition of an active "trade or business" under Section 162. We believe this will apply if the taxpayer is ultimately responsible for the risks of the trade or business and may be rewarded with profits in a typical entrepreneurial manner.

For example, an individual owning five rental houses who pays a manager by the hour or based upon a percentage of rent to interview tenants, have leases signed, collect rents, and supervise

---

[322] *Neill v. Commissioner*, 46 B.T.A. 197 (1942).
[323] *Hendrickson v. Commissioner*, 78 T.C.M. 322 (1999).
[324] *Schwarcz v. Commissioner*, 24 T.C. 733 (1955).
[325] Id. See also *Elek v. Commissioner* which states that having an agent actively manage and maintain the rental property does not disqualify the owner from engaging in a trade or business.

repairs is still in the business of renting, notwithstanding that she delegates these functions to someone who the landlord will be responsible for if they don't get the job done.

This is supported by several court decisions, going back to the 1953 *Gilford v. Commissioner* decision from the Second Circuit.[326] The Gilford sisters (and some other family) owned eight buildings in Manhattan which were rented out as dwelling units. The Gilfords hired a real estate firm to manage the properties and pay each owner his or her share of the net income from the properties.

In determining that the Gilfords were engaged in a trade or business, the court reasoned that while the owners did not necessarily manage the buildings, "an appreciable amount of time and work was necessarily required on the part of the managing agent" and that "if such management was a 'trade or business,' the petitioner was so engaged although she acted only through an agent." Therefore, because the agent worked under the control of the Gilfords, the court determined that they were engaging in a trade or business through the agent.

The Tax Court follows this decision in the 1986 case of *Whyte v. Commissioner* by stating that "It is well settled that where an agent is acting on behalf of an owner in managing a business, the owner is still considered to be engaged in a trade or business."[327]

On the other hand, if the property management company guarantees that a minimum rent amount will be received, that expenses will not exceed a certain percentage, or that there will be a guaranteed net income, then the result can be different. If the owner (or agent) does not work with the rental property regularly, systematically, and continuously, the IRS can conclude that the rental property is a passive investment as opposed to a trade or business and thus would be disqualified from the Section 199A deduction.

A common situation that seems to be in a gray area is when individuals buy condominium units, time shares, or co-ops that are part of a "rental pool" arrangement where the owner does nothing but receive periodic reports of rental income and expenses. In this situation, the owner is not seen by renters or the general public as being an independent business, but still has the risk of loss if rentals are not sufficient to pay expenses.

Tax Court decisions have gone both ways in these situations. For example, in the 1997 Tax Court decision of *Murtaugh v. Commissioner*, a married couple owned a 25% time share, or about three months per year, in two condominium units.[328] The couple used a management company as their agent to rent and maintain the units. The Tax Court used the reasoning from *Gilford* to determine that the couple's ownership was considered a business for tax purposes.

Also, a federal court in *Grier v. United States* came to the same conclusion with respect to treating an agent's efforts as being the efforts of the property owner, although the court found that twelve

---

[326] *Gilford v. Commissioner*, 201 F.2d 735 (2d Cir. 1953).
[327] *Whyte v. Commissioner*, Docket Nos. 7953-83, 7954-83.1These cases were consolidated pursuant to an Order of this Court dated September 30, 1985., 1986 Tax Ct. Memo LEXIS 114 (T.C. Sep. 29, 1986) affd. 852 F.2d 306 (7th Cir. 1988).
[328] *Murtaugh v. Commissioner*, Docket No. 5181-95, 1997 Tax Ct. Memo LEXIS 381 (T.C. July 9, 1997).

years of renting a single house to the same tenant did not arise to being an active business.[329] In this case, Mr. Grier inherited a house and rented it out to a single tenant for a twelve year period. The District Court was willing to aggregate the efforts of Mr. Grier and his agent, but nevertheless concluded that their combined activities of renting a single house to a single tenant did not rise to the level of being considered an active trade or business. Mr. Grier did not have to re-rent the house because the same tenant stayed there for twelve years and there were no regularly needed employees for maintenance or repair. Therefore, the IRS and the court determined that Mr. Grier's ownership of the home constituted an investment rather than a business.

However, now you know that you don't have to fire your agents in order to qualify!

E.   APPLICATION TO TRIPLE NET LEASES

In a triple net lease, the tenant usually agrees to pay rent and utilities, plus the three "nets" – real estate taxes, building insurance, and maintenance. However, there is often confusion as to what qualifies as a triple net lease. The following definitions should be helpful:

Triple Net Lease – Lease agreement under which the tenant agrees to pay all expenses of operating the property and any common area maintenance that might apply, including real estate taxes, building insurance, and maintenance on the property, while the landlord is responsible for structural repairs. Also known as a "fully net lease".

Absolute Triple Net Lease – is sometimes considered a type of "triple net lease," but requires the tenant to pay all expenses, including *structural and roof* maintenance repairs in addition to real estate taxes, building insurance, and maintenance on the property. Also known as an "absolute net lease".

Double Net Lease – Lease agreement under which the tenant agrees to pay for property taxes and insurance payments for the building, in addition to rent, but not repairs.

Single Net Lease – Lease agreement under which tenant agrees to pay property taxes, in addition to rent.

Gross Lease – Lease agreement under which the tenant agrees to pay a flat rate to encompass all costs of ownership, such as taxes, insurance, and utilities. Also known as a "full service gross lease".

Using the *Groetzinger* test, a triple net landlord will normally not qualify as having a trade or business because, while owning the property for the purpose of making a profit would meet the second prong of the test, the involvement of the landlord is not typically continuous and regular enough to meet the first prong.

The Proposed Regulations under Section 199A offered two examples of real estate leases that qualify as a trade or business. In the first example, an individual who owns and manages land leased to airports for parking lots qualified as a Section 162 business. The management aspect of the owner is the likely reason why this example qualified as a trade or business. It is unclear how

---

[329] *Grier v. United States*, 120 F. Supp. 395 (D. Conn. 1954).

this example could apply practically because if the land is leased to airports, there is not much management left for the owner to handle. In the second example, the owner developed the same land to build parking structures and then leased the parking structures to the airports. It is noteworthy that in those prior examples the dollar value of costs incurred by the owner were insignificant in relation to the rental income involved, yet those examples skirted the trade or business issue and merely assumed without further indication that they qualified. Despite this, relevant case law would suggest that these expenses would not qualify as trade or business deductions.

To alleviate the confusion, the new Final Regulations have removed all references to land in both of these examples. The Preamble to the Final Regulations states that the examples "were not intended to imply that the lease of the land is, or is not, a trade or business for the purposes of Section 199A beyond the assumption in the examples."

Along with the new Final Regulations, the IRS also released a special notice (Notice 2019-7) to provide "notice of a proposed revenue procedure detailing a proposed safe harbor under which a rental real estate enterprise may be treated as a trade or business solely for the purpose of Section 199A."

Under the new safe harbor, rental real estate may be treated as a trade or business for the purposes of Section 199A alone as long as the following criteria are met:

1.   Separate books and records are maintained for each rental activity (or the combined enterprise if grouped together);

2.   Two hundred and fifty (250) hours or more of "rental services" are performed per year for the activity (or combined enterprise); and

3.   The taxpayer maintains contemporaneous records, including time reports or similar documents, regarding the hours of all services performed, a description of all services performed, the dates on which such services are performed, and who performed the services.[330]

4.   The taxpayer includes a statement on the return, **under penalties of perjury**, that the taxpayer satisfies the above requirements of the safe harbor.

To this end, taxpayers should consider the following:

1.   Be certain to maintain separate books and records. If the taxpayer uses Quicken or a similar program to track records, he/she may want to set up a new account for this.

2.   If the taxpayer has commingled rental income and expenses in his/her personal checking account, then set up a new separate account for the business.

3.   If the taxpayer has used one account for all rental properties then, unfortunately, separate bank accounts should be created.

---

[330] Toni Nitti, *supra.*

4.   The taxpayer should maintain a calendar and also a supporting file of saved emails, internet research, photos saved with date/time stamp, etc. to show ongoing involvement and corroborate that actions were taken supporting the hours tracked.

It is noteworthy that the recordkeeping requirement only applies for taxable years beginning after January 1, 2019. As a result, taxpayers relying upon the safe harbor for the 2018 tax year do not have to provide records of time spent on the real estate activities.[331]

IRS Notice 2019-7 provides that real estate rented or leased under a triple net lease is not eligible under the safe harbor, even though a taxpayer who has an active business of entering into and selling triple net leases may still be considered to be sufficiently active to qualify as a trade or business under the case law.

For the purposes of the Section 199A deduction, a triple net lease is defined very broadly to include leases that would not typically be called "triple net" by landlords and tenants. In a normal triple net lease, the tenant pays all of the taxes, maintenance and insurance, although there are many types of "triple net leases," including an absolute triple net lease, an absolute net lease, a fully net lease, and others.[332] The Notice would require that any lease where a tenant pays any portion of the taxes, maintenance and insurance be a triple net lease, based upon the following language from the Revenue Procedure: "a triple net lease includes a lease agreement that requires the tenant or lessee to pay taxes, fees, and insurance, and to be responsible for maintenance activities for a property in addition to rent and utilities."[333]

The definition seems to leave open the ability to avoid triple net lease status by having a tenant be responsible for some portion of the maintenance, taxes, fees, insurances and other expenses that would normally be payable by a landlord.

In the June 27, 2019 commentary letter to Notice 2019-7, sent by the Tax Section of the ABA, this is described as follows:

> *For purposes of the Proposed Revenue Procedure, a 'triple net lease' **includes** a lease agreement that requires the tenant or lessee to pay taxes, fees, and insurance, and to be responsible for maintenance activities for a property in addition to rent and utilities, or a lease agreement that requires the tenant or lessee to pay a portion of the taxes, fees, and insurance, and to be responsible for maintenance activities allocable to the portion of the property rented by the tenant.*

The ABA appropriately points out that in order to have a triple net lease, the tenant should be required to pay *all* taxes, operating expenses, maintenance and insurance, as opposed to having some portion of what the total obligation would normally be under a true triple net lease.

---

[331] Internal Revenue Service Notice 2019-7.
[332] *Brenner v. Amerisure Mut. Ins. Co.*, 893 N.W.2d 193 (Wis. 2017).
[333] Internal Revenue Service Notice 2019-7.

The Tax Section letter indicates that a triple net lease may include a situation where the landlord only has to repair and replace foundations and exterior walls and roofs, if the tenant is responsible for all other normal triple net lease expenses, which appears to be a very reasonable concession.

As the result of this situation, many landlords will be well advised to offer significant rent reductions to tenants who are willing to pay for some part of one or more items, so that the landlord can fit within the safe harbor to reduce the effective tax rate on taxable income from 37% to 29.6%, in addition to whatever may be saved in state income taxes and state sales taxes as a result of such adjustments. The safe harbor cannot be used by taxpayers who rent their personal residences out for part of the year (e.g. Airbnb or VRBO rentals).

The safe harbor requires that any entity must own the real estate directly or through another disregarded entity (such as a single member LLC).

Additionally, for the years 2018 through 2022, 250 or more hours of rental services must be performed to qualify a property for the safe harbor in a calendar year. This includes time spent by owners, employees, agents and independent contractors as owners, which can include management and maintenance companies who have personnel who keep and provide such contemporaneous records. However, time spent by computers that have artificial intelligence will not apply.

Negotiating and executing leases, advertisement to rental lease properties, and verifying information contained in tenant applications will be included in the definition of rental services, as will collecting rent and supervising employees and independent contractors. Rental services do not include time spent on items that would typically be handled by a consultant with an MBA or similar degree rather than by a real estate developer, such as financial or investment management activities, arranging financing, studying or reviewing financial statements or reports on operations, or planning, managing, or constructing long-term capital improvements to properties.

Each individual taxpayer, estate or trust can elect to treat each separate property as a separate enterprise, or all similar properties as a single enterprise, for the purposes of applying safe harbor rules, except that commercial and residential real estate cannot be considered as part of the same enterprise and triple net real estate cannot be part of a combined enterprise for testing purposes because they "are not eligible for the safe harbor."

Further, separate books and records must be maintained to reflect the income and expenses for each property, and contemporaneous records must be created which include time reports, logs or similar documents which will report the hours of all services performed, the description of all services performed, the dates on which such services are performed and who performed such services.

A more detailed discussion of the safe harbor which follows is derived from the author's LISI newsletter #170, which concerned "one particular harbor":

> **Wastin' Away Again --**
> **In One Particular Harbor**
>
> **"The sea (and 199A) is in my veins"**
> **I've had enough tax advisors' refrain**
> **And "I'm just glad I don't [rent out] a trailer"**

Many thanks to Jimmy Buffett for use of the lyrics to the song, One Particular Harbour,[334] which tells the story of a sailor who finds the ideal destination after many voyages. Some people wish the drafters of the Regulations had taken a "slow boat to China" at Mr. Buffett's suggestion.[335]

Real estate investors have been looking for such a harbor since Section 199A was passed in December of 2017, particularly with respect to if and when leasing activities would be considered as an active trade or business under the statute.

The IRS and Treasury Department have now defined "one particular harbor" in a way that allows a great many landlords to moor their boats into and relax, knowing that they will receive the Section 199A deduction. It is hard to fathom that just four days ago there was so much less clarity than today for those who are able to have at least 250 hours a year spent on legitimate rental activities.

The new tax law passed in December of 2017 includes a provision that allows a deduction of up to 20% for an individual, a trust, or an estate that has income, or receives income, through a partnership or S corporation organization that is a "trade or business" as defined under certain parts of the Internal Revenue Code. The Proposed Regulations that were released over the summer gave little guidance on if and when a rental real estate arrangement would be considered as an "active trade or business" for purposes of qualifying for the deduction, and case law guidance in this area is not very thorough.

The IRS released new Proposed Regulations that clarify many aspects of Section 199A and also, a special notice (Notice 2019-7), which provides tentative guidance and a request for comments on the sole subject of if and when a rental activity will be considered as an active trade or business. It is generally understood in the tax law community that a proposal like this can be relied upon, and that the eventual final Notice will be at least as taxpayer-friendly, and possibly friendlier, than what this new proposed safe harbor provides.

---

[334] Jimmy Buffett, One Particular Harbour, on One Particular Harbour (MCA Records 1983).

[335] (I'd Like to Get You) On a Slow Boat to China, originally published by Frank Loesser in 1948, as recorded on Jimmy Buffett's album, Somewhere Over China (MCA Records 1982).

It is important to keep in mind that real estate investors can still rely upon the case law, and there will be situations where the safe harbor will not apply in "shelter[ing] you from the wind. "[336] While the case law gives the taxpayer a strong degree of certainty, please do not try to "do this at home" because you will not be "safe within."[337] We have made this post as easy to understand as possible, but unless you are a skilled tax lawyer, CPA, or tax advisor, there is a chance that you may find yourself capsized or run aground.

The first thing we see is that the Notice provides that real estate rented or leased under a triple net lease is not eligible under the safe harbor even though a taxpayer who has an active business of entering into and selling triple net leases may still qualify under the case law.

The Notice defines a triple net lease to include an agreement that requires the tenant to pay taxes, fees, and insurance, and to be responsible for maintenance in addition to rent and utilities, and includes lease agreements that require the tenant to pay common area maintenance expenses, which are where a tenant pays for its allocable portion of the rented property's taxes, fees, insurance, maintenance activities, which are normally paid by the landlord.

The definition seems to leave open the ability to avoid triple net lease status by having the tenant be responsible for some portion of the maintenance, taxes, fees, insurances, and other expenses that would normally be payable by a landlord, and many landlords will be well-advised to offer significant rent reductions to tenants who are willing to pay for some part of one or more items, so that the landlord can fit within the safe harbor to reduce the effective tax rate on taxable income from 37% to 29.6%, in addition to whatever may be saved in state income taxes and state sales taxes as a result of such adjustments.

In addition, the safe harbor cannot be used by taxpayers (including an owner or beneficiary of a relevant pass-through entity) who rent their personal residences out for any part of the year. The safe harbor coins a new phrase, which is the "Rental Real Estate Enterprise." This phrase is defined as an ownership interest in real estate that is rented and may consist of one or more properties.

An individual relying upon the safe harbor, or a partnership or S corporation entity that owns the applicable interest in the real estate, the income from which may qualify for the Section 199A deduction, must own the real estate directly or through another entity that is disregarded for income tax purposes, like a "single member LLC." A tax lawyer or other advisor should be consulted if the individual or the entity taxed as an S corporation or partnership does not directly own the applicable real estate to see if the disregarded entity rules will apply.

Each individual taxpayer, estate, or trust can elect to treat each separate property as a separate enterprise, or all similar properties as a single enterprise, for

---

[336] Buffet, supra note 1.
[337] Ltd.

purposes of applying the safe harbor rules, except that commercial and residential real estate cannot be considered as part of the same enterprise for testing purposes, and, of course, triple net leased real estate and real estate used as a residence by the taxpayer cannot qualify for the safe harbor.

As to each separate enterprise, the following requirements must be satisfied during each year to allow the income from the enterprise to be eligible for the safe harbor:

Separate books and records are maintained to reflect the income and expenses for each enterprise. This may require taxpayers who keep separate records for each separate property to also keep aggregate records if the properties are going to be considered to be grouped as a single enterprise.

Contemporaneous records, including time reports, logs, or similar documents are kept regarding the hours of all services performed, the description of all services performed, and the dates upon which the services were performed, as well as who performed the services with respect to tax years beginning January 1, 2019. This requirement will not apply for 2018 tax returns for fiscal year taxpayers for years that end prior to December 31, 2019.

> *"I used to rule my world from a pay phone*
> *Ships out on the sea*
> *But now times are rough*
> *And I got too much stuff (including paperwork)*
> *Can't explain the likes of me"*[338]

For 2018 through 2022, 250 or more hours of rental services must be performed to qualify the property for the safe harbor. Rental services include time spent by owners, employees, agents, and independent contractors of the owners, which can include management and maintenance companies, who have personnel who keep and provide the above-mentioned contemporaneous records. Time spent by computers that have artificial intelligence capability will not apply here, so taxpayers may elect to use low cost offshore call rooms and similar workers to effectuate many tasks that may add up to meet the time requirement (250 hours divided by 52 weeks is 4.8 hours a week or approximately 21 hours each month). This may involve providing tenants with additional services that can be provided by inexpensive call center employees, such as scheduling periodic inspections, insect treatments, insurance renewals and the condition of building systems, and also monitoring and reporting on such reporting items, and engaging in satisfaction surveys and other conversations with tenants, which will be a boom for offshore servicing centers and tenants and landlords who can enjoy these services.

The term "rental services" does not include arranging for financing or investing, buying property, studying and reviewing financial statements or reports, planning,

---

[338] *Id.*

managing or constructing long-term capital improvements, or time spent traveling to and from real estate.

Aside from the above exclusions, rental services that are included within the 250 hours of time required are as follows:

Advertising to rent or lease the properties;

Negotiating and executing leases;

Verifying information contained in tenant applications;

Collecting rent;

Daily operation, maintenance, and repair;

Management of the real estate;

Purchase of materials; and

Supervision of employees and independent contractors.

> *"Where it all ends I can't fathom my friends*
> *If I knew I might toss out my anchor*
> *So I cruise along always searchin' for songs*
> *Not a lawyer a thief or a banker"[339]*

The time is now to reach out to clients who have rental properties, convert triple net leases to be able to qualify under the statute, and make sure that clients, or their employees and agents, are spending at least 250 hours a year doing the right things.

While at it, we can explain what entities clients should have their real estate in, determine if they have sufficient Unadjusted Basis immediately after acquisition (UBIA) of their qualified properties, and talk to them about other planning opportunities.

Unfortunately, this safe harbor will not allow taxpayers with small boats to navigate successfully unless they can justify how 250 hours a year were spent on their properties. We are sure that commentators will request that the IRS allow for fewer hours when there are only one or two properties involved.

The Notice is to apply for taxable years ending after December 31, 2017 and can be relied upon until the final Revenue Procedure is published.

Surprisingly, the Notice specifically excludes triple net leases as ineligible for the safe harbor! This does not prevent the taxpayer from arguing that the real estate enterprise should qualify as a

---

[339] Buffett, supra note 322.

trade or business under the Section 162 definition if there are other considerations at play.[340] Although it is important to remember that both the Final Regulations and relevant case law say that qualifying under Section 199A involves a factual case-by-case analysis, triple net lease arrangements will most likely need to be altered in order to qualify.[341] Practitioners should consider the structure of the ownership of the triple net leased properties and the aggregation rules. It may be possible to alter the structure, e.g. have all separate non-qualifying LLCs restructured into disregarded entities so that they can be aggregated for this test.

While the regulations and safe harbor are brand new and case law is scant, one Revenue Ruling has addressed the issue regarding whether a triple net lease specifically qualifies as a trade or business. Under Section 871, there are special rules for the taxation of nonresident aliens who are engaged in trade and business in the United States. This could be used as a potential argument for meeting the Section 162 definition of trade or business, nonetheless, Revenue Ruling 73-522, 1973-2 C.B. 226 stated that a rental under a net lease is not considered a trade or business for the purposes of Section 871.

The question of whether a triple net lease can constitute a trade or business was also raised with regard to withdrawal liability under the Multiemployer Pension Plan Amendments Act (MPPAA) in the 2001 7th Circuit U.S. Court of Appeals case of *Central States, Southeast and Southwest Areas Pension Fund v. Fulkerson*.[342] Thomas and Dolly Fulkerson owned several triple net leases and were also shareholders of Holmes Freight Lines, Inc. (Holmes) when it became bankrupt.[343] As a creditor, Central States used the MPPAA of 1980 to calculate the withdrawal liability of Holmes.[344] Under the MPPAA, all "trades or businesses" are treated as one employer.[345] Under that theory, the Fulkerson's leasing business and Holmes were under the common control of the Fulkersons, and the leasing business was thereby pulled in to help pay the remainder of what was owed to Central States.[346] Because the leasing business was unincorporated, the Fulkersons became personally liable.

The MPPAA, like the IRC, uses the term "trade or business" but does not define it. Therefore the appellate court affirmed the Supreme Court's test in *Groetzinger*, reasoning that the test comports with the common meaning and can be used generally.[347] In order to meet the first prong of the *Groetzinger* test, the taxpayer's involvement must be continuous and regular. Since the leases were triple net leases, Mr. Fulkerson only spent about five hours per year involved with the properties.[348] The properties were purchased with the intent of pure investment. The court held that the "mere holding of leases for ten years by shareholder was not such continuous and regular activity as to constitute a trade or business, for purpose of imputing withdrawal liability to

---

[340] Id.

[341] The specific requirements for this safe harbor are discussed further in the article: "One Particular Harbor: New Regulatory Guidance on If and When a Rental Real Estate Activity Can Qualify for the 20% Section 199A Deduction." LISI Income Tax Planning Newsletter #170 (January 21, 2019) at http;//www.leimbergservices.com.

[342] *C. States, S.E. and S.W. Areas Pension Fund v. Fulkerson*, 238 F.3d 891 (7th Cir. 2001).

[343] Id.

[344] Id.

[345] Id.

[346] Id.

[347] Id.

[348] Id.

company."[349] A similar ruling today would probably be upheld with regards to Section 199A, even with the new safe harbor, due to the 250-hour requirement. Practitioners should also be mindful of the special rules in the final Regulations as to these matters of aggregation.

In the 7th Circuit U.S. Court of Appeals case of *Central States v. Personnel*, the court reached the opposite decision with similar facts as *Fulkerson*.[350] In *Personnel*, the defendant was held responsible for withdrawal of liability because the defendant was much more frequently engaged in activities related to leasing, such as buying and selling multiple properties annually and advertising.[351] The court concluded that this conduct was both regular and continuous.[352]

Based on the reasoning in these cases along with the new Final Regulations, it is clear that: (1) the *Groetzinger* test is still applicable and used by courts to determine whether an activity is a trade or business, and (2) courts truly use activity level of the taxpayer as a deciding factor. Based on the relevant case law as well as the new safe harbor provision, it seems as though the courts and the IRS are really looking for some degree of activity/time spent working with the enterprise or legal responsibility of risk on part of the taxpayer. In order to show that, an owner of a triple net lease can do a few things to increase their level of activity with the rental such as: take on responsibility for maintenance, participate in tenant management, participate in advertisement initiatives, and be more active in pursuing new leases or selling leases. Also consider the additional suggestions mentioned above.

Qualified Property must be owned by the taxpayer or the entity taxed as a partnership or an S corporation on the last day of the taxable year to be considered in the UBIA calculation.

It is also noteworthy that this rule applies to the end of the tax year and not necessarily the calendar year. Therefore, if a business sells all of its assets and closes its tax year the same day, the assets will be considered as owned on the last day of the tax year and the UBIA of such assets may be used.

A developer selling three properties from one entity might therefore sell one property on the last day of the calendar year and the last property on the first day of the following year so that 2.5% of the last property's Unadjusted Basis will count for Section 199A purposes.

Many real estate developers have wisely kept their respective properties in separate taxable entities for purposes of separating and insulating for liability and financial segregation.

A real estate investor who has parcels that he has purchased for resale may or may not have sufficient activities to rise to the level of satisfying the "active trade or business" requirement.

Nevertheless, it may be best for this investor to be considered a "passive nondealer" so that he is not subject to ordinary income tax and can pay capital gains tax on the sale.

---

[349] Id.
[350] *C. States, S.E. and S.W. Pension Fund v. Personnel, Inc.*, 974 F.2d 789 (7th Cir. 1992).
[351] Id.
[352] Id.

The IRS takes the position that a taxpayer who has purchased and held real estate for the primary purpose of reselling it will be considered a "dealer" and will thus be subject to ordinary income tax when the property is sold.

Is it possible that a "dealer" would not have been active enough to qualify as an "active trade or business" under Section 162?

Certainly, someone who has purchased real estate with the intention of selling it would satisfy the first prong of Section 162, being that there is an active entrepreneurial risk being taken.

The person who buys a property and puts a "For Sale" sign on it is not necessarily "actively engaged" in a trade or business and may therefore not qualify for Section 199A treatment.

Any analysis of Section 199A application to real estate must include consideration of whether the Passive Loss Rules apply to a particular situation and what their impact will be on Section 199A planning.

Under the passive loss rules, taxable losses are incurred when rent and any other income derived from real estate is less than the combined deductions for operational expenses, depreciation, and interest expense.

Further, a person, partnership or S corporation that is not "active" and has a passive loss from real estate cannot use the loss against other income, but instead will separately track the loss and wait for it to be released when the property that caused the loss becomes profitable from a tax standpoint or is sold.

When the property is sold, the loss is released and is applied like a net operating loss carryforward.

A person or entity that is generating passive losses that cannot be used because of the passive loss rules will not be impacted by the Section 199A deduction, because the losses will not be increased or decreased because Section 199A would only apply if there was positive taxable income from an active trade or business.

Since the passive losses are "trapped" in the year when the losses occur, they will not reduce a taxpayer's taxable income for Section 199A calculation purposes.

Normally, losses from the conduct of a rental activity will reduce a taxpayer's taxable income, which may reduce the Section 199A deduction that the taxpayer can qualify for.

For example, a taxpayer who earns a $12,000 salary and has one business that generates $100,000 of taxable income from an active business, who also has a $20,000 loss from a rental activity that he or she spends considerable time and effort working on, may have the 199A deduction be limited to 20% of $80,000, if these are the only sources of income in the taxable year.

The above assumes that the $20,000 loss that results in large part because of depreciation and interest expenses associated with the rental activity will be taken as losses on the tax return in the year in which they are incurred.

Under the Passive Loss Rules, however, the net loss coming from a rental arrangement that may be considered to be "active" under the Section 162 "Trade or Business" rules but "inactive" under the Section 469 "Passive Loss Rules" will not reduce taxable income for Section 199A measurement purposes until the taxable year when these passive losses are released upon the sale of the property.

When pre-2018 passive losses are released, they will not be considered to be losses that reduce Qualified Business Income under Section 199A because the Section 199A rules only began to apply in 2018.

On the other hand, passive losses released from 2018 and thereafter will reduce the taxable income of the applicable taxpayer for purposes of applying the 20% of taxable income limitation.

For example, if the taxpayer described above had $12,000 of salary income, $100,000 of Qualified Business Income, and sold a property that released $30,000 of suspended losses from 2018 and $40,000 of suspended losses from 2017, then the Qualified Business Income deduction for that single taxpayer would not exceed 20% of $70,000 ($14,000) for the subject year.

The question of whether a taxpayer's trade or business related activities are sufficiently "active" under Sections 162 and 199A is separate and apart from the question as to whether the Passive Loss Rules apply to prevent net losses from real estate rental activities to be used to reduce a taxpayer's taxable income in a given year.

In some situations, the taxpayer may be better off by having losses considered to be passive so that the losses will not reduce the taxpayer's Section 199A deduction. Such losses can be released in later tax years to offset income when the income tax rates may be much higher, and Section 199A may no longer be available.

CHAPTER 13.
USING TRUSTS FOR SECTION 199A PLANNING

The Final Regulations issued on January 18, 2019, and reissued February 4, 2019, impose many of the same limitations and rules for trusts that were initially published in the Proposed Regulations, and there is much to know.

To summarize briefly, the Final Regulations provide that Complex Trusts formed or funded for a primary purpose of avoiding income tax under Section 199A will be aggregated with the Grantor or Grantors for purposes of the $157,500 or $315,000 thresholds, with no discussion or example as to whether income that may be distributed by the trust to a beneficiary would also be aggregated.

On an April 4, 2019 ABA webinar, Treasury Department lawyers declined to comment on whether income distributed by a Complex Trust to a beneficiary would also be aggregated for purposes of determining the threshold of the trust and the beneficiary receiving the distribution, so time will tell whether this is the case.

The Final Regulations also implement the disallowance of multiple brackets when multiple trusts are formed by the same Grantor or Grantors to benefit the same group of beneficiaries under IRC Section 643(f), take out much of the detail and examples that had provided taxpayer guidance, and no longer delineate some safe areas of practice previously provided in the Final Regulations.

The Final Regulations further require that Electing Small Business Trusts will have only one $157,500 threshold for both the S corporation and the non-S corporation portions thereof.

The trust rules leave many Section 199A and multiple trust planning avenues open for those who have an understanding of the new rules and the different varieties of trusts and tax planning vehicles associated therewith, which are covered under this chapter.

This chapter begins with a basic discussion of the different types of trusts and trust arrangements commonly involved in Section 199A and associated planning, followed by a more in-depth discussion and specific planning strategies that can be applied.

Irrevocable trusts will be key entities for Section 199A planning and have already been implemented by many taxpayers. Because of the strong stance taken by the Service against many trust planning opportunities in the Final Regulations, it is important that planners be aware of how the Final Regulations may impact trusts and that they plan for flexibility by using trust protectors or other mechanisms to allow trusts that are implemented to be adapted as needed.

For example:

> A high earner, married couple may own 100% of an S corporation that may have $100,000 per year of income and does not pay wages or have Qualified Property.

Since none of the income from this entity will qualify for the Section 199A deduction for this high earner couple, if they were to transfer the ownership of this S corporation to a separately taxed trust, the trust may qualify for the Section 199A deduction and would be taxed at the highest rate allowed of 29.6% in lieu of being taxed at a 37% rate.

The trust would also not be subject to the Medicare tax on the first $12,500 of undistributed income and could distribute income to beneficiaries who may be in lower tax brackets or to charities that would pay no tax at all.

Additionally, under Section 642, complex trusts are not required to distribute their income and are allowed a $100 personal exemption.[353] Simple trusts are required to distribute all of their income to the beneficiaries of the trust each year and are allowed a $300 personal exemption.[354] Distributions of income made by simple trusts to charity cannot qualify for the income tax charitable deduction under Section 642(c)(1).[355]

Users of trusts should be aware that while the exemption for the alternative minimum tax was raised for individuals, as discussed in Chapter 9, the exemption amount for trusts and estates stayed the same, at $22,500. Similarly, the phase-out of the alternative minimum tax exemption was increased for married joint filers and surviving spouses to $1,000,000 and $500,000 for single filers, while the phase-out for trusts and estates remains at $75,000. Those who have high-earning trusts should be aware of this potentially large tax liability.

When this book refers to "separately taxed trusts," the authors mean trusts that are separately taxed on undistributed income, which are also known as "Complex Trusts," as further described below. The tax law refers to a trust that is disregarded as "defective" because the income of the trust is considered to be income of the Grantor of the trust, as opposed to being taxed to the trust or the beneficiaries who receive distributions from the trust.

Technically, a trust that is taxed at its own brackets is known as a "complex trust," but the authors find the term "separately taxed trust" to be easier for laymen and many advisors to work with.

Besides disregarded trusts and separately taxed trusts, there are also Section 678 trusts, Charitable Remainder Trusts, ESBTs ("Electing Small Business Trusts") which can own S corporation stock, and QSSTs (Qualified Subchapter S Trusts") which can also own subchapter S stock, as indicated below.[356]

A.   SUMMARY OF PRIMARY TERMS AND CONCEPTS

The following terms are used above and below and are repeated here for convenience and future reference:

Separately taxed trust or complex trust. A complex trust is considered a separate taxable entity and pays income tax on undistributed income. Further, Medicare tax will be payable on

---

[353] IRC § 642(b)(2)(A). A trust which may retain its income is also known as a complex trust.

[354] IRC § 642(b)(2)(B). A trust which is required to distribute its income currently is also known as a simple trust. Estates are allowed a $600 personal exemption per § 642.

[355] IRC § 651(a)(2). These trusts "do not provide that any amounts are to be paid, permanently set aside, or used for the purposes specified in section 642(c) (relating to deduction for charitable, etc., purposes)."

[356] The income from trusts that are disregarded for income tax purposes is normally taxed to the grantor of the trust, except that under Section 678 a trust can be considered as owned by a beneficiary who has had certain withdrawal rights, as discussed below.

accumulated income that exceeds $12,500 for 2018 and $12,750 for 2019. A complex trust can distribute income to its beneficiaries, who are then taxed on the income to the extent received.

Example:

> A separately taxed trust receives $100,000 of income and distributes $30,000 of income to each of three children. The trust pays income tax on $10,000, and the three children pay income tax on $30,000 each.

The tax brackets that apply to a complex trust in 2018 and in 2019 can be found earlier in this book in Charts 13 and 13A.

Further discussion of complex trust planning is set forth below.

A *simple trust* is required to pay all income each year to its beneficiaries under the trust document, and the beneficiaries pay income tax on the trust's income, whether it has actually been paid out or not.

Disregarded or "defective" trusts. The grantor/contributor of a disregarded trust is considered to have received all income that the trust otherwise would have reported for income tax purposes. The trust does not have to distribute income or file an income tax return but should file an informational return with the IRS annually. When these rules were enacted, individuals were in higher tax brackets than trusts, so a trust that was "defective" resulted in a higher income tax liability. This is no longer the case, so in many circumstances, planners want a trust to be "defective."

A Section 678 trust is like a disregarded trust, except the income is all taxed to one or more beneficiaries who have had the right to withdraw all corpus or income, triggering status as a Section 678 trust. It is possible for a complex trust to be converted to a Section 678 trust by providing a beneficiary with the right to withdraw. PLR 200848017 discusses the conversion of a complex trust to a grantor trust. The same logic should apply to the conversion of a complex trust to a Section 678 trust by providing the beneficiary with the right to withdraw all trust assets for a specified period. An extensive discussion of Section 678 trusts can be found below.

An Electing Small Business Trust ("ESBT") makes a special election to enable it to own S corporation stock and may be treated as a complex trust, a disregarded trust or a Section 678 trust, depending upon design and implementation. When an ESBT is a complex trust, all income from S corporation ownership is taxed at the highest bracket (presently 37%), and, originally, it seemed that due to a technical glitch in the Section 199A language, flow-through income or trade or business income of an ESBT would not qualify for the Section 199A deduction. The Final Regulations provide that ESBTs may take the Section 199A deduction on flow-through income from an S corporation.

As noted above, an ESBT that is disregarded as a "defective" trust during the Grantor's lifetime will not be subject to the "two separate trusts rule" described above until the Grantor has died or the trust is no longer considered to be owned by the Grantor for income tax purposes. Grantor Trust status will therefore "trump" the Section 199A ESBT rules described herein.

Once an ESBT election is made, Treasury Regulation Section 1.641(c)-1 requires that an ESBT will be treated as being two separate trusts, one consisting of the portion of the trust which holds the S corporation stock, and the other consisting of assets that are not S corporation stock. The S corporation K-1 income is taxed at the highest tax bracket, even if it is distributed out to beneficiaries who are in lower tax brackets. The non-S portion is taxed under the traditional rules that apply to the taxation of complex trusts.

A chart illustrating the above is as follows:

Chart 21 - Electing Small Business Trust (ESBT) Chart

NOTE: As written by the statute, any ESBT will not qualify for the Section 199A deduction, and, although the Proposed Regulations say that it will, can regulations override an incorrect statute?

If the Grantor is Living:	After the Grantor's Death:
If disregarded (Grantor Trust) – Income is taxed at Grantor's individual income tax bracket	S corporation income taxed at a highest income tax bracket
If Complex: 1. S corporation income is taxed at highest income tax bracket 2. Other income taxed at beneficiary's bracket if distributed; if not, income is taxed at compressed trust brackets	Other income taxed at beneficiary's bracket if distributed; if not, income is taxed at compressed trust brackets.

The Final Regulation makes it clear that an ESBT receives only one $157,500 threshold for SSTB income or trade or business income where wages or qualified property are not sufficient to allow the deduction. The $157,500 threshold is apportioned between the S corporation portion and non-S corporation portion pro rata to the income that is received and not distributed to the beneficiaries of the ESBT.

As noted above, the Grantor Trust rules will trump the ESBT rules during the grantor's or beneficiary's lifetime if the trust has certain provisions that would cause the trust to be considered as owned by the grantor or a beneficiary for income tax purposes.

Qualified Subchapter S Trusts ("QSSTs") fall under a fourth category of trust taxation called "simple trusts," where the income of the trust is all taxed to one or more beneficiaries who have the absolute right to receive the trust income each year. The Final Regulations treat QSSTs as grantor trusts, thus enabling planning, whereby the income of a QSST will be considered the income of the individual or entity having the right to receive the QSST income.

QSSTs are further discussed after Section 678 trusts below, and can be a very good candidate for Section 199A planning, including when an income will be coming from an activity or a partnership entity that could partly be owned by an S corporation that is in turn owned in whole or in part by a QSST.

Charitable Remainder Trusts ("CRTs") are the fifth category of trusts, which require no tax on normal income. Individuals with appreciated assets sometimes contribute these assets to Charitable Remainder Trusts and receive a charitable contribution while deferring the payment of income tax until the appreciated assets contributed to the trust are sold. The beneficiaries of a Charitable Remainder Trust pay tax only when they receive distributions, which carries the income out on a "worst first basis." For example, if a Charitable Remainder Trust has received $20,000 of ordinary income and $60,000 of capital gain income in the past and makes its first distribution of $30,000 to beneficiaries, then the beneficiaries are considered to have received $20,000 of ordinary income and $10,000 of capital gains income.

Income tax that has come from a trade or business owned by a Charitable Remainder Trust or via partnership ownership should qualify for the Section 199A deduction, assuming all other requirements have been met. The Treasury released Proposed Regulations on how to calculate the Section 199A deduction on distributions from a charitable trust that has Qualified Business Income and provided further guidance on how W-2 wages and UBIA of qualified property will be allocated to the non-charitable beneficiary of a Charitable Remainder Trust.

The Proposed Regulations discussing the possible treatment of Charitable Remainder Trusts have not yet become final, but taxpayers may rely upon them until Final Regulations are issued.

Under the Proposed Regulations, a Charitable Remainder Trust will not be considered a separate taxpayer and will not receive its own threshold limitation. The Proposed Regulations provide that a non-charitable beneficiary of a Charitable Remainder Trust will only be treated as having received QBI eligible for the Section 199A deduction after all other ordinary income items have been distributed from the CRT, effectively treating QBI as a new category of income in the "worst first" distribution categories.[357]

To give more detail, there have been four tiers of income that come from a Charitable Remainder Trust when the income has been retained in one year and paid out in another year. Normally Charitable Remainder Trusts do not pay income tax themselves, but the non-charitable beneficiaries pay taxes as and when monies or other assets are distributed to them, based upon a "worst first approach," where ordinary income comes out first, capital gains income comes out second, and tax-free income comes out third.[358] Technically, the first tier of income to be

---

[357] Letter from Annette Nellen to David J. Kautter, I.R.S., and William M. Paul, I.R.S., *supra*, note 39.
[358] Treas. Reg. § 1.664-1(d)(1)(ii)(a).

distributed is ordinary income, then capital gain, then other income,[359] and finally as a distribution of the trust corpus.[360]

The Proposed Regulations provide for a new second tier of distributions under Section 199A. The first tier is ordinary income that cannot qualify for the Section 199A deduction, the second tier is ordinary income that may qualify for the Section 199A deduction, and the third tier will be capital gains income.

An example is as follows:

> A Charitable Remainder Trust that pays $20,000 a year to the individual income beneficiary of the trust receives $15,000 of QBI in year one and $10,000 of interest income. It distributes $20,000 to the beneficiary, which carries out $10,000 of interest and $10,000 of QBI income.
>
> If there is no interest income in the second year, then the $20,000 payment carries out $15,000 of QBI and $5,000 of corpus.
>
> In the first year, two-thirds of the W-2 wages paid by the trade or business owned by the Charitable Remainder Trust will be allocated to the beneficiary of the Charitable Remainder Trust, since two-thirds of the QBI was distributed from such trust. The remaining one-third of W-2 wages will be allocated to the trust, and since the trust does not pay income taxes, this allocation of wages does not help in the qualification for the Section 199A deduction.
>
> In the second year, all wages will be allocated to the beneficiary since all of the QBI was distributed from the Charitable Remainder Trust.

To the extent that the distribution is treated as carrying out QBI, W-2 wages and UBIA of qualified property will be allocated to the non-charitable beneficiary pro rata to the non-charitable beneficiary share of the trust's total QBI (whether or not distributed) and the undistributed wages and UBIA are treated as retained by the trust and does not carry over to subsequent years. The Regulations provide the following explanation:

> Accordingly, if 10 percent of the QBI of a Charitable Remainder Trust is distributed to the recipient and 90 percent of the QBI is retained by the trust, 10 percent of the W-2 wages and UBIA of qualified property is allocated and reported to the recipient and 90 percent of the W-2 wages and UBIA of qualified property is treated as retained by the trust. However, any W-2 wages retained by the trust do not carry over to subsequent taxable years for Section 199A purposes.

---

[359] Treas. Reg. § 1.664-1(d)(1)(i)(a)(3). Other income is the Charitable Remainder Trust's income that is not in the ordinary income or capital gains tiers, and includes items excluded from gross income under IRC §§ 101-140.
[360] IRC § 664(b).

Advisors should be aware that trusts and beneficiaries who receive K-1 income via a complex trust, a simple trust, an ESBT or a Charitable Remainder Trust cannot use the Section 179 accelerated depreciation deduction, but are able to take Section 168(k) bonus depreciation, which is generally the same for most situations through 2023, as discussed in greater detail beginning in Chapter 11.

Trusts which themselves are taxed on income that is not distributed will be important tools in Section 199A and associated planning. The following example and subsequent discussion should be of assistance to those who wish to learn how to plan with complex trusts:

Complex Trust Example:

> Jack is married and files jointly with his wife. He has taxable income of $430,000, which includes $310,000 of K-1 income from an LLC taxed as an S corporation CPA firm that he owns 100% of. He works part time for the firm, receiving a salary of $120,000, and currently is not eligible for the Section 199A deduction because of the income thresholds.

By allowing an existing trust that was formed or funded prior to the effective date of Section 199A to purchase 50% of the stock of the CPA firm,[361] Jack can lower his income and reduce his tax burden. The trust can be for the benefit of his wife and his children if properly drafted and administered, and Jack can still receive a salary, but his flow-through income would be significantly reduced. As much as $157,500 could be put into the trust, which does not have to distribute income to the beneficiaries. With a taxable income of $275,000 ($120,000 salary + $155,000 flow-through income), Jack can take a Section 199A deduction of $31,000.

The trust's income will be taxed at 37% on all income above $12,500 for 2018 ($12,750 applies for 2019). However, the trust will qualify for the Section 199A deduction on its $155,000 of flow-through income. The trust is therefore effectively taxed at 29.6%, which is less than Jack's otherwise applicable 35% individual tax bracket.

It is important to note that several requirements must be met to prevent the subject trust from being considered as owned by Jack for income tax purposes, including that (1) Jack's wife is not the trustee of the trust, (2) Jack's wife can only receive distributions with the approval of an "adverse party," and (3) neither Jack nor his wife can replace trust assets with assets of equal value or exercise any power to appoint where trust assets pass during Jack's lifetime. In addition, no party should have the right to add beneficiaries to the trust or to allow Jack or his wife to borrow from the trust without providing adequate collateral and security.

---

[361] It is important to check state law before attempting to transfer stock or other ownership in a professional entity to a trust. For example, Florida restricts the ownership of stock of a CPA firm. If the trust was formed or funded after the effective date of Section 199A it will be hard to avoid the anti-abuse rules, which would aggregate the trust and the grantor income for purposes of calculating or disallowing the Section 199A deduction.

Further discussion of complex trust planning is set forth below.

If the trust instead distributes some or all of its income to the beneficiaries, the income will be taxed at their brackets, and the beneficiaries may also qualify for Section 199A on the flow-through income they receive from the trust. Just like others who qualify for the deduction, if their taxable income is below the $157,500 (for single filers) or $315,000 (for married filing jointly) thresholds, they will receive the Section 199A deduction regardless of whether wages were paid or Qualified Property is owned by the flow-through entity. By having a portion of income go to charities, the trust can have the equivalent of an income tax charitable deduction under Section 642(c) that is not limited by the itemized deduction and percentage of Adjusted Gross Income limitations that can apply to individuals.

Irrevocable trusts have been popular for many decades as a way to assure that family wealth can be held safely for spouses, descendants, and others. A primary purpose for establishing irrevocable trusts in the past has been to avoid federal estate tax. Oftentimes, this has involved making the trust "defective" for income tax purposes so that the trust's income will be considered to be the income of the grantor. This enables the grantor to pay income taxes on behalf of the trust, which reduces the grantor's estate. This worked well for grantors who had concerns that they would be subject to federal estate tax at the time of death but is no longer needed for a high percentage of individuals who set these trusts up and would be just as happy now to have the assets back in their own name, or to at least have the trust pay its own taxes, in addition to accomplishing other planning objectives.

A common arrangement is an irrevocable trust that benefits a spouse and descendants. These are commonly known as "Irrevocable Life Insurance Trusts" ("ILITs") where the trustee can own life insurance on the grantor, and the Trust can benefit the Grantor's spouse and descendants, and also "Spousal Limited Access Trusts" ("SLATs") which can hold assets other than life insurance.

These trusts are normally protected from creditors of either spouse and considered as owned by the donor spouse for income tax purposes, although it is possible to have a SLAT taxed as a complex ("separately taxed") trust if the spouse/beneficiary is not a trustee and one or more other beneficiaries of the entire trust corpus are required to consent to any distribution to the spouse/beneficiary.

There will be no step-up in basis when the grantor of a complex trust dies, unless he or she holds a power to appoint (direct) trust assets to the grantor, the grantor's estate, the grantor's creditors, or creditors of the grantor's estate, and having this power can affect how the trust is taxed. Below is a chart that describes some of the most common forms of trusts and their characteristics:

Chart 22 – Categories of Trusts Chart

Complex Electing Small Business Trust "ESBT"

Beneficiary Defective Trust (aka BDIT or 678 Trust)

Complex Trust

Qualified Subchapter S Trust "QSST"

Grantor Trust

Can be owner of an S corporation.

Can allow a non-resident alien beneficiary to effectively be a member of an S corporation.

S corporation income taxed at the highest rate bracket, regardless of whether income is distributed to beneficiaries.

ESBTs may have multiple beneficiaries, and mandatory distributions of income are not required.

Distributions made to charity will be subject to the same rules that apply to individuals.

3.8% Medicare tax begins to apply at $12,500+ of AGI.

Grantor treated as the owner for federal income tax purposes

Beneficiary treated as owner for federal income tax purposes.

Can be owner of an S corporation.

Can have only one named beneficiary.

Must pay all "fiduciary accounting income" to trust beneficiary each year.

All S corporation K-1 income taxed to beneficiary of trust.

Taxed as a separate entity to the extent that income is not distributed.

"Distributable Net Income" paid out can carry the income to lower bracket taxpayers.

The trust has an effective tax rate of 24.1% on the first $12,500 of income and 37% above that.

Distributions made within 65 days of the next tax year can be considered to have been made in the previous tax year.

Distributions made to charity can carry income to the charity to in effect give a tax deduction without a 60% adjusted gross income limitation or itemized deduction considerations.

3.8% Medicare tax begins to apply at $12,500+ of AGI.

Unlike a C Corporation – No tax upon liquidation of the trust.

Can shield trustee and beneficiaries from operational liability similar to a corporation depending upon state law.

Separate and apart from Section 199A planning, advisors should determine whether trust assets will receive a new income tax basis on the death of the grantor or any other older individual to reduce income taxes that would otherwise be due when trust assets are sold. Some trusts are designed to include a "power of appointment" that can be held by a senior family member in order to facilitate this. Other trusts can have such "powers of appointment" installed by trust amendment, agreement between the beneficiaries and trustees, trust protectors, court reformation, or "decanting" the trust assets into a new trust having such features.

It is noteworthy that under Internal Revenue Code Section 1014(b)(9), the basis of a taxpayer's property acquired from a decedent by reason of death, form of ownership, or through the exercise or non-exercise of a Power of Appointment is reduced by the amount of depreciation taken by the taxpayer on such property, if the taxpayer is considered to own or have an interest in such property prior to the death of the decedent.

Section 1014(b)(9) does not apply to reduce basis by depreciation taken by the decedent, and only applies if depreciation is taken by a taxpayer that has an ownership or interest in the property prior to the death of the decedent.

For example, A transfers property worth $100,000 to B, and A retains a general Power of Appointment over the property. Four years later, A predeceases B when the property is worth $200,000, and B has taken $10,000 of depreciation deductions. Section 1014 will apply to step-up the basis of the property to the current fair market value of $200,000; however, Section 1014(b)(9) will also apply to reduce the basis by the amount of depreciation taken by B. B will therefore receive a stepped up basis in the property equal to $190,000 ($200,000 less $10,000 of depreciation taken by B).

Section 1014(b)(9) also applies when property is treated as owned as tenants by the entireties or joint tenants with rights of survivorship, but only to the extent that the depreciation deductions or income from the property is allocated to the joint owner under applicable local law.

For example, Husband and Wife own property worth $30,000 as tenants by the entireties. Under local law, each spouse is entitled to one-half of the income produced by the property. Husband dies when the property is worth $50,000, and the entire value of the property is included in Husband's estate by reason of Husband retaining a general Power of Appointment over the property. Husband and Wife have taken $10,000 of depreciation deductions on their jointly filed income tax return. As a result, Wife will receive a stepped up basis in the property equal to $45,000 ($50,000 less $5,000 of depreciation that was allocated to Wife).

B. COMPLEX TRUSTS

Complex Trusts are trusts which pay income tax on "distributable net income" that is not distributed to beneficiaries. The Proposed Regulations had provided that the $157,500 threshold that applied to complex trusts would not be reduced by distributions made to beneficiaries that carry-out "distributable net income" for income tax purposes. The Final Regulations eliminated this provision, and there is some confusion as to what can and cannot be done with a Complex Trust, as discussed in the section below entitled "Complex Trust Anti-Abuse Rule" in this Chapter.

Example:

> A complex trust with $300,000 of distributable net income that distributed $150,000 to a beneficiary having no other taxable income would not have been able to take a Section 199A deduction on its remaining $150,000 of income from a Specified Service Trade or Business or an entity that pays no wages and has no qualified property under the Proposed Regulations, and the beneficiary of the trust would also not be able to take a Section 199A deduction on the income that was distributed from the trust to the beneficiary.

Distributions May Carry Out Taxable Income to Use a Beneficiary's Threshold. This provision of the Proposed Regulations was appropriately criticized, and the Final Regulations did not discuss or give examples that would give indication as to whether distributions that carry out distributable income to beneficiaries may be aggregated with the income of the trust and a high-income grantor if formed for a primary purpose of avoiding tax under Section 199A.

Depreciation Flow-Through Confusion Was Resolved. The Proposed Regulations relating to the allocation of depreciation deductions under a trust as between the trust itself and beneficiaries were criticized as being incorrect. The Final Regulations include a revised example to clarify the allocation of Qualified Business Income and depreciation as between a trust and its beneficiaries and continue to require that a trust or estate allocate Qualified Business Income, including any negative losses, among the trust and its beneficiaries based on the relative portions of DNI distributed or retained.

Times Have Changed for a Great Many. *An $11,400,000 per person (and growing with the chained Consumer Price Index) estate tax exemption now applies, and even though this amount is scheduled to be reduced by half in 2026, a great many families have very little, if any, risk of ever paying federal estate tax.*

At the same time, the federal income tax law now often favors complex, separately taxed trusts, which are taxed at their own bracket on retained income and can distribute income to low tax bracket beneficiaries to reduce the overall federal income taxes paid by a family. These are called "Complex Trusts," although they are usually not very complicated. If, for example, a "complex" trust receives $112,500 worth of income during a calendar year, it might distribute $20,000 of income to each of five young adult beneficiaries whose income would be taxed in the 22% tax bracket (assuming that the Kiddie Tax discussed earlier in this book in Chapter 9, Part Two does not apply), and it could retain $12,500 of income and pay $3,011.50 of tax on such income, as compared to having a high bracket grantor of the trust pay a 37% income tax plus a 3.8% Medicare tax. This results in a total income tax savings of $25,011.50 for the family.[362]

---

[362] 40.8% times $12,500 is $5,100, thus saving $2,088.50 in income taxes on income retained by the trust. 40.8% times $112,500 is $45,900. 22% of $100,000 equals $22,000 of incomes taxes paid by the beneficiaries, plus $3,011.50 of income taxes paid by the trust, equals $25,011.50 in total taxes paid by the trust and the beneficiaries. $45,900 minus $25,011.50 equals $20,888.50 of income tax savings for the family.

Chart 23 – Example of Use of Trusts in Section 199A Planning Chart

This chart demonstrates how trusts can be used in the context of Section 199A.

In the example below, a flow-through business distributes money to an owner, as well as to a trust established for the benefit of the owner's three children. The three children receive distributions from the trust and that income is taxed at their rates.

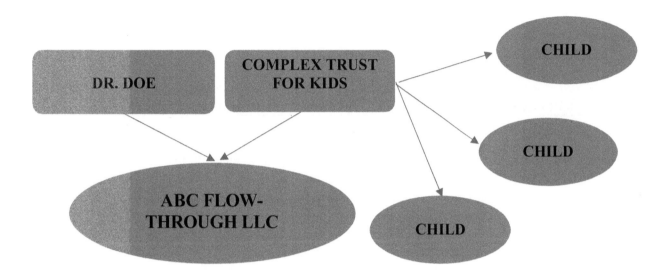

If each child in the chart has $50,000 a year in taxable income, they could each receive over $100,000 of flow-through income and take the Section 199A deduction on it, even if they were single and regardless of whether it was from a Specified Service Trade or Business or not. If each of them receives $100,000 of flow-through income, each can receive a $20,000 Section 199A deduction, amounting to total tax savings of $4,800 (assuming the children were in the 24% bracket).

Additionally, the trust can be set up to retain any income up to when the trust earnings, in addition to its distributions, are equal to the lower income threshold of $157,500 and take a separate 20% deduction. If the trust retained $12,500 (the maximum amount before the 3.8% Medicare tax would apply), this alone would save $1,614 in income taxes and $475 in employment taxes.

The situation with trusts can be even better where the trust allows for other tax savings as described below.

C.   **CHARITABLE DISTRIBUTIONS**

If the trust agreement authorizes distributions to charity, then such distributions can carry otherwise taxable income out to the charity that is not taxed. The family therefore gets the equivalent of a charitable deduction that might not otherwise be available because of the high itemized deduction threshold that now applies to individuals ($12,000 for single individuals and $24,000 for married couples filing jointly). For example, a $20,000 charitable contribution made by a 37% tax bracket individual will commonly not result in any tax deduction whatsoever because of the $24,000 standard deduction that now applies. Using a complex trust that specifically allows for charitable payments could save 37% of $20,000 ($7,400) in taxes for a high income bracket family that can place income producing property or S corporation or partnership interests under a complex trust.

Charitable contributions can be made by the end of a calendar year and still count to reduce the income of the trust for the previous year, assuming an election to do so is filed on the trust's amended tax return for the previous year.[363] For example, if a trust makes a charitable contribution in Year 2, it can elect to have the contribution treated as if it was made in Year 1 as long as the election is made on an amended tax return for Year 1, which can be filed as late as the deadline for Year 2's tax return on April 15 of Year 3, or October 15 if extended. The distribution can reduce the trust's taxable income for Year 1 or Year 2, as decided by the trustee.

D. STATE AND LOCAL TAX (SALT) DEDUCTION AND STATE INCOME TAX SAVINGS

Complex trusts can deduct up to $10,000 of state and local taxes each year, including real estate taxes, so that they can own personal use real estate and receive a tax deduction that the grantor and other family members may not be eligible for because of the $10,000 per year, per taxpayer limit on the deductibility of state and local taxes.

For example, a vacation home that is subject to $30,000 a year in property taxes could be owned one-third each by three separate trusts for the primary benefit of each separate child of a married couple to enable all of the property taxes to be deductible, assuming that each of the trusts has $10,000 or more of otherwise taxable income.

In addition, for taxpayers who live in states that impose a high state income tax, a complex trust may be established in a state that does not have a state income tax, thus avoiding state income taxes that would have otherwise been owed. These types of trusts are commonly referred to as NING (Nevada Incomplete Non-Grantor) Trusts or DING (Delaware Incomplete Non-Grantor) Trusts. Complex rules must be followed to ensure that the trust is taxed in the low-income tax state, and not that of the high income tax state where the grantors or beneficiaries live.[364]

1. ADVANTAGES.

(a) **Spraying and Allocation Flexibility**

The trustee can decide which beneficiaries receive how much each year. The trust may exert polite pressure on the beneficiaries or even pay beneficial expenses on their behalf instead of outright to them to influence behavior in a way that can be far superior to letting them have direct ownership in a management or intellectual property company. This provides significant flexibility that is not

---

[363] IRC § 642(c)(1). *See also* Treas. Regs. § 1.642(c)-1(b).
[364] For more information on NINGS and DINGS see Ed Morrow's white paper on the subject entitled "*Incomplete Gift, Non Grantor Trusts (aka DINGS, NINGS): Not Just for State Income Tax Avoidance.*"

available for S corporations and partnerships because of the second class of stock and substantial economic effect rules.[365]

(b) **65 Day Look Back**

In addition, distributions made during the first 65 days of the calendar year can be considered to have been made in the previous calendar year for income distribution purposes. This allows the trustee and family members to confer with their tax advisors after December 31st to determine where income can best be allocated for the previous year.

(c) **Reduced Chance of Audit**

Having income payable to a trust and distributed to low bracket taxpayers can reduce the chances of audit. Complex trusts file a Form 1041, and 1041 audits are very rare, if existent at all. Audits of low bracket taxpayers occur at a much lower frequency than the audits of high bracket taxpayers. This is certainly not a good sole reason to use irrevocable trusts, but it is an advantage.

Trusts have other income tax advantages, which include the following:

(d) **Tax-Free Distributions of Appreciated Assets**

Appreciated assets can be transferred out of a trust to beneficiaries without triggering income tax that would apply if a trust were taxed as a corporation, or as a partnership if certain "mixing bowl" and related rules apply.

(e) **New Fair Market Value Income Fair Market Value Tax Basis on Death of Power Holders**

Assets held in a trust can receive a new income tax basis to avoid payment of capital gains tax on appreciation that occurs up through the date of the grantor's death, if the grantor has what is known as general Power of Appointment over trust assets. Court Orders or non-judicial reformation agreements may provide an individual with a short life expectancy with the right to direct how trust assets might pass within reasonable parameters, which can result in a new fair market value date of death income tax basis as if the Power Holder was the owner of the assets. This would include a power to appoint assets to creditors of the estate of the Power Holder, even if such Power is only exercisable with the consent of an independent party. This would be consistent with the intention of a grantor who set up a trust for estate tax purposes and now wants to assert a reasonable degree of control because estate tax is no longer an issue, and the situation among family members may have changed.

---

[365] S corporation distributions must be pro rata to ownership under IRC § Section 1368, and for entities taxed as partnerships, the substantial economic effect rules under § 704(b)(2) prevent special allocations of income without satisfaction of the complicated substantial economic effect regulations that are found at Treasury Regulations §§ 1.704-1(b)(2)(i) – (iii)(c).

(f)   **Ability to Deduct Expenses Incurred in Connection with the Administration of the Trust**

The 2017 Tax Cuts and Jobs Acts eliminated the ability for individuals to deduct miscellaneous itemized deductions; however, this does not apply to trust expenses for costs which are paid or incurred in connection with the administration of the trust that would not have been incurred if the property were not held in such trust.

2.   **DISADVANTAGES.**

(a)   **Formation and Annual Carrying Costs**

Costs and possible repercussions of forming or changing irrevocable trusts should of course be considered. This includes consideration of the cost of forming a trust or changing a disregarded trust to a complex trust, filing of income tax returns, and associated formalities.

(b)   **Loss of 179 Deductions**

As mentioned in the introduction to this chapter, Section 179 deductions that allow for the immediate expensing of certain property are not available for trusts, or for beneficiaries who receive trust distributions in the year that Section 179 property is acquired. Trusts may have to write off furniture, equipment, and other acquired business property over the life of the asset under the normal depreciation rules that apply under Code Section 168.

Fortunately, the Section 168(k) bonus depreciation can be taken by a trust, which, in many cases, will often be as good as the Section 179 deduction. The Tax Cut and Jobs Act expanded Section 168(k) to enable taxpayers to immediately expense 100% of qualified business property placed in service between September 27, 2017 and January 1, 2023.[366] Although, the percentage of qualified business property that may be immediately expensed begins to decrease after 2023, and is eliminated after 2027, Section 168(k) bonus depreciation provides temporary relief from the inability of trusts to take a Section 179 deduction.

For example, if a construction business purchases trucks for its workers to use, the company can choose to depreciate the property all at once under Section 168(k) (because it has a life of less than 20 years). A trust could have part ownership in the company and be able to claim the deduction on its tax return, assuming the company is a flow-through entity. In addition to the instant deduction the company will get in the first year, the owners, including the trust, can continue to use the trucks as Qualified Property under Section 199A for at least 10 years.

---

[366] IRC § 168(k)(1)(A) allows a depreciation deduction equal to the "applicable percentage" of the adjusted basis in qualified property under the statute. IRC § 168(k) (6)(A) defines applicable percentage as 100% for September 27, 2017- December 31, 2022, and then decreases 20% each year afterward. IRC § 168(k)(2)(A) defines qualified property as one of the following: (1) property to which § 168 applies with a depreciable life of less than 20 years, (2) computer software, (3) water utility property, (4) a qualified film or television production, and (5) a qualified theatrical production. Additionally, the property does not have to be new, only that the property has not been used by the taxpayer previously.

(c)   **Partnership Taxation May Apply**

Trusts that engage in business may be taxed as partnerships instead of complex trusts if the case law that existed before the "check the box" regulations were issued in 1997 would have caused the trust to be considered to be an "association" under the Supreme Court decision of *Morrissey v. Commissioner*, and the subsequent Section 7701 Regulations. There are no known cases where this has occurred, and the result would be that the beneficiaries of the trust will be considered to be partners and thus taxable on the retained income of the trust that would have otherwise been taxed at the trust level.

(d)   **Disclosure and Fiduciary Duty Differences**

The trustee of a trust normally has a duty to account annually, disclose trust actions, and to act for the best interest of the beneficiaries. These fiduciary duties will commonly exceed the duties that a general partner has under a partnership, or that a manager has under an LLC, but may be altered by agreement with adult beneficiaries, and selecting an appropriate situs ("state or country of formation") for a given trust normally is a duty.

Clients with irrevocable trusts currently in place that are treated as disregarded for income tax purposes should review the situation and discuss with their advisors whether these structures should be altered in order to take advantage of the income tax planning opportunities that may exist for irrevocable trusts and the structures associated therewith. [367]

E.   **COMPLEX TRUST ANTI-ABUSE RULE**

The Proposed Regulations had unusual language which provided that certain trusts would be "disrespected" for Section 199A purposes if they were established for the purpose of avoiding tax under Section 199A. The Final Regulations clarify that the anti-abuse rule is designed to "thwart the creation of even one single trust with a principal purpose of avoiding, or using more than one, threshold amount."

The Final Regulations indicate that if the trust is created or funded for "a principal purpose" of avoiding tax under Section 199A, then the trust will be aggregated with the grantor or other trusts from which it was funded for purposes of determining the threshold amount for calculating the Section 199A deduction.

Specifically, the Regulation reads as follows:

> ***Anti-abuse rule for creation of a trust to avoid exceeding the threshold amount.***
> *A trust formed or funded with a principal purpose of avoiding, or of using more than one, threshold amount for purposes of calculating the deduction under Section 199A will not be respected as a separate trust entity for purposes of determining the threshold amount for purposes of Section 199A.*

---

[367] *Stephenson Trust v. Commissioner*, 81 T.C. 283 (1983); *Estelle Morris Trusts v. Commissioner*, 51 T.C. 20 (1968), *aff'd per curiam*, 427 F.2d 1361 (9th Cir. 1970).

The term "a primary purpose" is an interesting choice of words, since the word "a" denotes that there can be multiple "primary purposes," while the word "primary" indicates that this would have to be the main purpose, or that there might be equally ranked "primary purposes."

These words have been used in other Internal Revenue Code Sections and Federal Statutes and have been the subject of decisions by the U.S. Supreme Court, the Tax Court, and two Circuit Courts of Appeals.

The majority of case law and regulations seem to define this term as being singular, meaning that there can be only one principal purpose. Therefore, "if the purpose to evade or avoid federal income tax exceeds in importance any other purpose, it is the principal purpose."[368] In determining the purpose, "entire circumstances in which the transaction or course of conduct occurred, in connection with the tax result," must be considered. In cases where multiple purposes are apparent, it might be "appropriate to aggregate all tax avoidance purposes and compare them with the aggregate business purpose for the acquisition."[369]

An excellent article which reviews these decisions can be read to conclude that the IRS would have to prove that no other purpose was more important than the objective of avoiding tax under Section 199A in order for the "a primary purpose" test to be met.[370]

Once the IRS makes the determination that an acquisition was made with the principal purpose to evade tax, the determination is presumed correct, and the burden then shifts to the taxpayer to show otherwise.[371]

For example, the vast majority of estate and trust planning performed by the authors will involve trusts that will benefit descendants and never be paid outright to them. Many of these trusts are formed after the death of a parent for the primary purpose of providing lifetime creditor, estate tax, divorce and unwise decision protection for a child and the descendants of a child, which has nothing to do with Section 199A income tax savings.

Quite often, clients form such trusts during their lifetimes to facilitate avoidance of federal estate tax, and to protect assets going to descendants from potential future creditors of the parent.

These trusts have been formed routinely by the authors for decades, and the authors will not stop forming these trusts, even if establishing them would cause loss of income tax savings under Section 199A.

But, if and when such a trust is formed, if an "incidental benefit" is to save income taxes under Section 199A, would that be "a primary purpose"?

---

[368] 26 C.F.R. § 1.269-3.
[369] *Love v. C.I.R.*, 103 T.C.M. (CCH) 1887 (Tax 2012).
[370] *A Principal Purpose; There Can Only Be One* by Benjamin M. Willis (2013).
[371] TAX CT Rule 142 Burden of Proof.

The answer to this question will be based upon the facts and circumstances of each situation, but the fact that a trust is formed and may save tax money under Section 199A will not make it automatically considered to have been established for "a primary purpose" of avoiding such tax.

The Final Regulations provide no examples to give any further guidance with respect to this.

> *In an April 4, 2019 ABA webinar with two Treasury officials[372], an example was discussed where a mother had gifted part ownership in a business earning $400,000 of income to her son so that the mother was then considered to have $200,000 of income and the son was considered to have $200,000 of income. The example explained that the gift was directly to the son, solely for the purposes of qualifying income for the Section 199A deduction, and that there is no anti-abuse rule to prevent this type of planning. The example then explained that if the gift of the 50% interest in the business was to a Complex Trust for the benefit of the son and the trust was established for the purpose of avoiding tax under Section 199A, then the trust would be disregarded for purposes of determining the threshold and the $200,000 of income allocated to the trust would be aggregated with the Grantor of the trust (the mother), so that the mother would be considered to have $400,000 of Section 199A income. As a result of this, none of the mother's income would be eligible for the Section 199A deduction. The trust would still be taxed on the $200,000 of income, and the Treasury officials declined to comment on whether the son or the trust would be able to take the Section 199A deduction.*

The following takes into account that income distributed from a complex trust to a low income beneficiary may nevertheless be aggregated with the grantor of the trust and the trust itself for the $157,500 / $315,000 threshold calculation purposes.

---

[372] ABA Section of Real Property Trust & Estate Law Webinar on April 4, 2019 entitled *Recent 199A Guidance: Hear from Practicing Experts and Government Officials*, presented by Audrey Ellis, Office of Tax Policy, Department of the Treasury (Washington, DC) and Wendy Kribell, Office of Chief Counsel, IRS (Washington, DC).

The following charts illustrate the above examples:

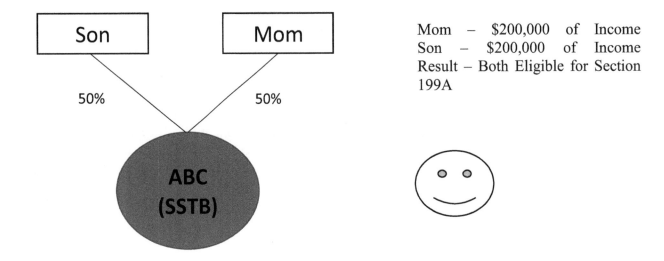

Mom – $200,000 of Income
Son – $200,000 of Income
Result – Both Eligible for Section 199A

Earns $400,000 of Income

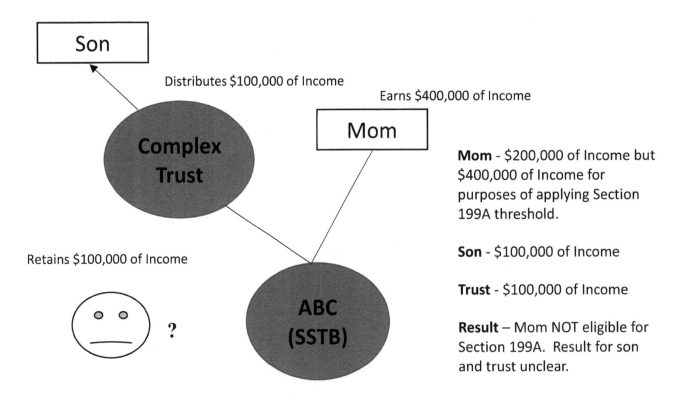

Mom - $200,000 of Income but $400,000 of Income for purposes of applying Section 199A threshold.

Son - $100,000 of Income

Trust - $100,000 of Income

Result – Mom NOT eligible for Section 199A. Result for son and trust unclear.

The only language in the Preamble to the Final Regulations which discusses this rule reads as follows (we have bolded the most important language):

One commenter requested clarification on whether a trust with a reasonable estate or business planning purpose would be respected. Another commenter argued that the rule is overbroad and lacks clarity as to what would be abusive and what the consequences would be of not respecting the trust for Section 199A purposes. The commenter also stated that the rule is not needed because of §1.643(f)-1 and if both rules are retained, they should use the same test (principal versus significant purpose).

Finally, the commenter asked for clarification on whether the rule applies to a single trust and suggested it should apply on an annual basis. This last suggestion has not been adopted because the test goes to the creation of the trust, factors which would not change in later years. **The Final Regulations clarify that the anti-abuse rule is designed to thwart the creation of even one single trust with a principal purpose of avoiding, or using more than one, threshold amount. If such trust creation violates the rule, the trust will be aggregated with the grantor or other trusts from which it was funded for purposes of determining the threshold amount for calculating the deduction under Section 199A. [Emphasis added].**

The above language does not explicitly state that income distributed from a Complex Trust to a low-income beneficiary would be aggregated with the income of the Grantor of the trust for purposes of measuring the $157,500 / $315,000 limitation, notwithstanding that this was the apparent intention of the drafters.

Read literally, a separately taxed trust which has been formed and funded before enactment of Section 199A cannot have been "formed or funded with a principal purpose of avoiding, or of using more than one, threshold amount . . . under Section 199A," and should therefore not be subject to the anti-abuse rules.

This means that trusts that were in existence and funded before the law was passed in February of 2017 could use their existing assets, or perhaps debt taken on at arm's-length by borrowing or using purchase money financing, to purchase ownership interests in SSTBs or entities that do not have sufficient wages or qualified property to allow the income to qualify for the Section 199A deduction. This can be accomplished by having the trustee of the trust use trust assets to make capital contributions to the entity or purchase interests owned by high income taxpayers who would not be eligible for the deduction.

In addition, trusts that are established under estate plans that were in place before Section 199A was enacted, and which will be funded under such plans without substantial change, should also be immune by the same rationale.

In many situations, trusts exist under state law that are disregarded for income tax purposes, with their assets considered to be owned by their grantors for income tax purposes. These trusts become complex trusts when the grantor dies or releases certain powers that exist over the trust. Time will tell whether such converted trusts may be considered to have been "formed or funded with a principal purpose of avoiding, or of using more than one, threshold amount for purposes of calculating the deduction under Section 199A" when they existed as grantor trusts before Section 199A was passed, but are voluntarily, or involuntarily, converted to complex trusts thereafter.

Further, many taxpayers have, and will, fund separately taxed trusts without having any knowledge, or any family situation, that would give rise to the avoidance of income tax under Section 199A at the time of formation and funding.

When subsequent Section 199A opportunities arise or become apparent, and the trust can purchase interests in a business or entity by making a capital contribution or buying an interest therein, the anti-abuse rule would not seem to apply.

It is noteworthy that the income tax benefits of being able to deduct up to $10,000 of trust income to pay for residential trust property taxes, and to make distributions to charity, if permitted in the trust agreement, being taxed at lower brackets of income tax and avoiding the 3.8% Medicare tax on up to $12,750 of income for 2019, and practical planning advantages make many separately taxed trusts worthwhile, regardless of whether a Section 199A deduction advantage applies.

F.   TREATMENT OF MULTIPLE COMPLEX TRUSTS

This Section discusses the Section 643(f) multiple trust rules and includes the original Section 643(f) statute that was enacted in 1984, the Committee Report examples that were issued shortly thereafter, private letter rulings that were issued in 2015 and 2017, the Proposed Regulations, and the Final Regulations, all of which should be understood by those who wish to work with multiple trusts in planning.

Internal Revenue Code Section 643(f) was enacted in 1984 for the purpose of preventing multiple trusts funded by one grantor, or a married couple, from benefitting the same beneficiaries while having separate and multiple lower tax brackets.

The IRS's intentions with respect to requiring multiple trusts to be aggregated for both tax bracket and Section 199A $157,500 threshold purposes is clear, as further discussed below.

The actual language of Section 643(f) is as follows:

(f) Treatment of Multiple Trusts - For purposes of this subchapter, under regulations prescribed by the Secretary, 2 or more trusts shall be treated as 1 trust if–

(1) such trusts have substantially the same grantor or grantors and substantially the same primary beneficiary or beneficiaries, and

(2) a principal purpose of such trusts is the avoidance of the tax imposed by this chapter. For purposes of the preceding sentence, a husband and wife shall be treated as 1 person.

The IRS's position has been that the statute is "self-implementing," as further discussed below, even though a plain reading of the statute suggests that it would not apply until Regulations were issued. Commentators have not agreed as to whether this is the case for multiple trusts that have been established before the effective date of the Regulations. The IRS did issue private letter rulings on the statute in 2015 and thereafter, which would certainly be indicative of the statute being effective upon enactment.

The Final Regulations issued under Section 643(f) are basically a restatement of the Statute and read as follows:

§1.43(f)-1 Treatment of multiple trusts.

    (a) General rule. For purposes of subchapter J of chapter 1 of subtitle A of Title 26 of the United States Code, two or more trusts will be aggregated and treated as a single trust if such trusts have substantially the same grantor or grantors and substantially the same primary beneficiary or beneficiaries, and if a principal purpose for establishing one or more of such trusts or for contributing additional cash or other property to such trusts is the avoidance of Federal income tax. For purposes of applying this rule, spouses will be treated as one person.

    (b) Applicability date. The provisions of this section apply to taxable years ending after August 16, 2018.

The Proposed Regulations contained extensive provisions that were not included in the Final Regulations which detailed when multiple trusts would be considered to be subject to the Section 643(f) rules and included examples that demonstrated that multiple trusts that each benefitted only one of multiple siblings during their lifetimes would be considered as separate and not aggregated, even if they might be held for common multiple descendants after the death of the then living sibling and descendants thereof.

In one fact pattern, two separate trusts were established by parents, one for the benefit of their son, and the other for the benefit of their daughter. The trust for the son would pay income to him for his life, and after his death the remainder would be held for the daughter. The trust established for the grantors' daughter would pay her all income and principal in the discretion of the trustee for her education, support and maintenance, and further provided that distributions could be made during the daughter's life to provide medical expenses for the son, who would also receive the remainder of the trust upon the daughter's death. The Proposed Regulations concluded that the terms of these trusts contained significant non-tax differences and would not be presumed to be established for the principal purpose of avoiding income taxes, and thus would be permitted to be considered to have separate exemptions. This is consistent with Example 2 of the 1984 Committee Reports, which is reproduced below.

The Preamble to the Final Regulations indicates that the IRS is still considering whether and how the questions posed should be addressed in future guidance, including whether the terms "principal purpose" and "identical grantors and beneficiaries" should be defined, and what examples might appropriately be provided.

The Preamble to the Final Regulations indicates that the following comments were received:

1.   Requests for clarification of what it means to form or fund a trust with a significant purpose of receiving a Section 199A deduction, while stating that trusts should not be combined simply because the deduction is increased if there is a legitimate non-tax reason that led to the creation of the trusts.

2.	Objections were received to the presumption of a tax avoidance purpose that would apply if there was a reduction of income tax under Section 199A and arguing that the focus should be on whether there is a non-tax purpose for creating multiple trusts.

3.	One commenter noted that the use of "substantial purpose" rather than "principal purpose" was inconsistent with the statutory language.

It is important to keep in mind that any single complex trust formed or funded for a primary purpose of avoiding income tax under Section 199A may be aggregated with its grantor or grantor under the anti-abuse rule described above, so that the Section 643(f) multiple trust rule may not be needed by the Service to disallow the Section 199A deduction in such circumstances.

> *The above multiple trust anti-abuse rule will apply only to tax years ending after December 22, 2017.*

The IRS has applied and interpreted Section 643(f) in several Private Letter Rulings. In PLR 201709020, the IRS issued a ruling that when a trust divided into separate trusts for each of the grantor's children upon the grantor's death, that such trust would not be treated as one trust under Section 643(f) because each trust has a different primary beneficiary. Under the facts of the Ruling, it does not appear that the trust for one child could be invaded for another child of the grantor.

The PLR specifically stated that "the trust will each have different primary beneficiaries. We conclude that as long as the trust created by the pro rata transfer of assets from trust are separately managed and administered; they will be treated as separate trusts for federal income tax purposes."

Based on the above, it appears to the authors that the IRS did not consider the grantor's motive in establishing the trusts and held that they would not be treated as one trust solely because of the fact that each trust has different primary beneficiaries.

Other Private Letter Rulings that came to the same conclusion include PLR 201722007, PLR 201532011, and a series of other Rulings related to the 201709020 request.

Additionally, the 1984 Committee Reports issued with the statute provide the following examples:

Example 1:

> Grantor (G) has two brothers and two sisters. G creates four trusts, each providing the trustee with discretion to distribute current or accumulated income to any one or more of the trust beneficiaries. Each trust has three beneficiaries - three of G's four siblings. Each sibling is a beneficiary of three of the four trusts. If G established the four trusts for the principal purpose of avoiding the federal income tax, the four trusts will be treated as one for federal income tax purposes.

Example 2:

Grantor (G) has two children, a son (S) and a daughter (D). G creates one trust, with all income payable currently to S and with the remainder payable to D upon S's death. G creates a second trust, with discretionary income and principal for S's medical expenses and discretionary income for D's education, support and maintenance, and with the remainder payable to D upon S's death. These trusts should be treated as separate trusts for federal income tax purposes and not aggregated into one even though the trusts have the same remainder beneficiary.

Notice that Example 2 did not consider the grantor's purpose in establishing the trust and simply concluded that the subsection would not apply to aggregate trusts which have different primary beneficiaries.

As mentioned above, the Treasury issued Proposed Regulations under Section 643(f) on August 8th that provided two heavily criticized examples that were deleted from the Final Regulations. These prior and now eliminated examples read as follows:

Example 1 from Proposed Regulations – Not Adopted by Final Regulations:

A owns and operates a pizzeria and several gas stations. A's annual income from these businesses and other sources exceeds the threshold amount in Section 199A(e)(2), and the W 2 wages properly allocable to these businesses are not sufficient for A to maximize the deduction allowable under Section 199A. A reads an article in a magazine that suggests that taxpayers can avoid the W 2 wage limitation of Section 199A by contributing portions of their family businesses to multiple identical trusts established for family members. Based on this advice, in 2018, A establishes three irrevocable, non-grantor trusts: Trust 1 for the benefit of A's sister, B, and A's brothers, C and D; Trust 2 for the benefit of A's second sister, E, and for C and D; and Trust 3 for the benefit of E. Under each trust instrument, the trustee is given discretion to pay any current or accumulated income to any one or more of the beneficiaries. The trust agreements otherwise have nearly identical terms. But for the enactment of Section 199A and A's desire to avoid the W 2 wage limitation of that provision, A would not have created or funded such trusts. A names A's oldest son, F, as the trustee for each trust. A forms a family limited partnership and contributes the ownership interests in the pizzeria and gas stations to the partnership in exchange for a 50% general partner interest and a 50% limited partner interest. A later contributes to each trust a 15% limited partner interest. Under the partnership agreement, the trustee does not have any power or discretion to manage the partnership or any of its businesses on behalf of the trusts, or to dispose of the limited partnership interests without the approval of the general partner. Each of the trusts claims the Section 199A deduction on its Form 1041 in full based on the amount of QBI allocable to that trust from the limited partnership, as if such trust was not subject to the wage limitation in Section 199A(b)(2)(B).

Under these facts, for federal income tax purposes under this Section, Trust 1, Trust 2, and Trust 3 would be aggregated and treated as a single trust.

The second deleted example seemed to suggest that having different siblings as beneficiaries suffices to break the substantially same primary beneficiary test, but then appeared to say that the two trusts could be aggregated back to the grantor if the trusts were funded with a tax avoidance motive even if there are separate grantors or separate primary beneficiaries in place.

Here is the second example:

Example 2 from Proposed Regulations – Not Adopted by Final Regulations:

> X establishes two irrevocable trusts: one for the benefit of X's son, G, and the other for X's daughter, H. G is the income beneficiary of the first trust and the trustee is required to apply all income currently to G for G's life. H is the remainder beneficiary of the first trust. H is an income beneficiary of the second trust and the trust instrument permits the trustee to accumulate or to pay income, in its discretion, to H for H's education, support, and maintenance. The trustee also may pay income or corpus for G's medical expenses. H is the remainder beneficiary of the second trust and will receive the trust corpus upon G's death.

Under these facts, there are significant non-tax differences between the substantive terms of the two trusts, so tax avoidance will not be presumed to be a principal purpose for the establishment or funding of the separate trusts. Accordingly, in the absence of other facts or circumstances that would indicate that a principal purpose for creating the two separate trusts was income tax avoidance, the two trusts will not be aggregated and treated as a single trust for federal income tax purposes under this Section.

The Final Regulations do not give any examples.

It is also noteworthy that prior to the enactment of Section 643(f), the IRS tried on at least two occasions to aggregate multiple trusts as one trust. The Tax Court held in both situations that the Code did not support a subjective test of tax avoidance motive as a basis for determining the existence of multiple trusts and that the motive for establishing and maintaining multiple trusts was irrelevant for tax purposes.

1. **GRANTOR TRUSTS.**

The Final Regulations fortunately were unchanged from the Proposed Regulations in indicating the trusts that are considered as owned by the grantor or a beneficiary of the trust will be treated as such. As indicated in other LISI Newsletters and Alan Gassman's Forbes Blog entitled 678 Ways To Qualify for the 199A 20% Deduction, 678 Trusts can be used very effectively under the Section 199A rules to allow income to be considered as having been paid to low income bracket trust beneficiaries without having to give the income or other amounts to such beneficiaries. Any planner who is not yet using Section 678 Trusts owes it to him or herself and his or her clients to begin to do so, especially in Section 678 planning.

2. UNRELATED BUSINESS INCOME.

Section 501(a) "Tax Exempt Entities," including charitable trusts and 501(c)(3) charitable corporations, are subject to income tax on income that is not related to their charitable or tax-exempt functions. This is known as "Unrelated Business Taxable Income." The Preamble to the Final Regulations indicates that eligibility to receive a Section 199A deduction by tax exempt companies and trusts are beyond the scope of the Final Regulations, and that the IRS will study the issue and request comments on the interaction of Sections 199A and 512.

G.   USE OF SECTION 678 TRUSTS

Certain trusts cannot be used to deflect income that would not be deductible by professionals or high-income taxpayers.

Trusts which are separately taxed and held for the benefit of family members can be structured to receive income that is either accumulated or distributed, whereby the trust will pay tax on income accumulated, and the beneficiary or beneficiaries will pay tax to the extent of income distributed. When Section 199A was first passed, the estate planning community was ready to mobilize a great number of these trusts that would own interests in SSTBs, management companies and non-SSTB companies owned by high earner taxpayers, so that each separate trust could accumulate up to $157,500 of income and also spray out an amount sufficient so that each child and grandchild would have income of up to $157,500 (or $315,000 if married filing jointly), and articles describing this technique were published and mentioned in the Preamble to the Proposed Regulations.

The Final Regulations carry forth the intention of the Proposed Regulations by providing that a separately taxed trust that is "formed or funded with a principal purpose of avoiding, or of using more than one, threshold amount for purposes of calculating the deduction under Section 199A" will be considered as aggregated with its contributor for Section 199A purposes.

The language of the Final Regulations was also changed from referencing "Trusts formed or funded..." under the Proposed Regulations to "A trust formed or funded..." under the Final Regulations, meaning that this not only applies to the creation of multiple trusts, but can also apply to the creation of a single trust as specifically stated in the Preamble to the Final Regulations.

For example, if a high earner married couple owning 50% of a manufacturing company that does not pay sufficient wages or have sufficient qualified property to allow them to receive a Section 199A deduction transfers part ownership of the S corporation to a trust for their daughter for no other purpose than to allow for the Section 199A deduction, then the income accumulated within the trust will not qualify for the Section 199A deduction as long as the father and the mother who fund the trust continue to be high income taxpayers, based upon their personal income and the income of the trust being aggregated.

The Proposed Regulations went even farther and provided that income distributed from the trust to a beneficiary of the trust would be considered to have stayed in the trust for the purposes of "disrespecting" the arrangement.

While the Final Regulations now allow for the taxable income of the "tax avoidance trust" to be determined after considering the DNI deduction for income distributed to a beneficiary, it is unclear if the net income that is transferred from a separately taxed trust to a beneficiary will be treated as having been received by the beneficiary and not subject to aggregation under the Anti-Abuse provisions of the Final Regulations, although the two Treasury lawyers who participated in the April 4, 2019 ABA webinar described in Chapter 9 and Chapter 13 indicated that even if the income was distributed by trust out to a beneficiary, it will be aggregated with any remaining trust income and the Grantor's income for purposes of determining whether the Grantor's income of the trust exceeds the threshold levels, assuming that the trust was established for the principal purpose of avoiding, or using more than one, threshold amount.

The Final Regulations did not impose any limitation on the use of Section 678 Trusts, which are irrevocable trusts which are considered as owned by the beneficiary or beneficiaries thereof.

In fact, Final Regulations specifically state that trusts that are considered as owned by a specific individual or individuals under the "Grantor Trust Rules" will be "treated as owned by the grantor or other person," and therefore appear to not be subject to these rules.

Therefore, in the example above, the mother and father could place part ownership of their S corporation stock into a trust that is considered as owned by their daughter for income tax purposes.

This is accomplished by special provisions in the trust that may give the daughter the right to withdraw the stock contributed to the trust within thirty days of when it is contributed thereto. After the thirty days lapses, the daughter will have no further withdrawal or control rights, and an Independent Trustee who is replaceable by the parents (which may be the daughter) can determine if and when the trust will make distributions to the daughter.

The K-1 income from the S corporation with respect to such stock will be reported on the daughter's personal income tax return, to qualify for the Section 199A deduction assuming that the daughter's income is below the threshold levels.

This will work just as well with a Specified Service Trade or Business, if state law allows this, or an MSO established to provide services to a Specified Service Trade or Business, if state law does not allow for ownership to be transferred.

Chart 24 – Comparison of 678 Trusts to Complex Trusts Chart

Comparison of 678 Trusts to Complex Trusts

Complex Trusts	678 Trusts
1. Attempt to spray taxable income among multiple beneficiaries.	1. All taxable income considered as taxed to one beneficiary who may receive limited or no distributions.
2. Will need a separate tax return and must pay income before 65 days after the end of each calendar year to carry out DNI.	2. No separate tax return has to be prepared for the trust.
3. Ability to retain up to $12,750 of income to be taxed at lower brackets to save up to $2,127 if Medicare tax applies.	3. If beneficiary has less than $157,500 of taxable income, including 678 income, 199A deduction may be taken on SSTB or income otherwise limited by wage/replacement property requirements.
4. Up to $157,500 of retained income may qualify for the Section 199A deduction for SSTB or low wage/qualified property income if trust not formed or funded to avoid tax under 199A.	4. Section 121 deduction may apply to primary residence of withdrawal power beneficiary.
5. May pay income to charity to avoid tax if allowed under Trust Agreement.	5. The trust may benefit a spouse, descendants and other individuals – spouse may only receive benefits with consent of adverse party while grantor is living.
6. May pay up to $10,000 per year in property taxes to receive deduction.	6. Deemed owner/beneficiary may deduct up to $10,000 per year in property taxes cumulatively.
7. Medicare tax savings may also apply.	7. Spouse or another individual may have a testamentary power of appointment while grantor is living to divest the withdrawal power beneficiary and/or others.

Qualified Subchapter S Trusts (QSSTs)

The QSST is defined in Internal Revenue Code Section 1361 as trust which holds S corporation stock and is required to pay all income to a named individual who is also entitled to receive all principal from the trust during his or her lifetime. The fact that a QSST cannot have a beneficiary other than the one individual who is considered to be the S corporation shareholder for income tax purposes limited the utility thereof.

It is possible to have a trust which holds S corporation ownership as a "subtrust" to satisfy the statute, while having other parts of the trust own other assets that may be held for the benefit of other beneficiaries.

Since the income beneficiary of the QSST is considered to be the owner of the trust for income tax purposes, the trust is considered to be a "grantor trust" under Internal Revenue Code Section 678, and is therefore not subject to the Section 199A Regulation anti-abuse rule, even if a primary purpose of the formation or funding of the trust is to qualify for an income tax deduction under Section 199A. If a trust holds a QSST subtrust and non-QSST subtrusts, then only the QSST subtrust will be considered to be a Section 678 "Grantor Trust."

Like a Section 678 Trust, all income of a QSST is reported on the income tax return of the beneficiary who is the deemed owner of the trust, but unlike many Section 678 Trusts, all income of the QSST must be paid by the trustee to the income beneficiary by the end of the trust's tax year, or within 65 days of the next calendar year if an election is made under Section 663(b) to treat the distribution as having been made in the previous tax year. Any principal payments must also be made only to the income beneficiary. On the income beneficiary's death, the trust may continue for a successor income beneficiary, in which case it would continue to qualify as a QSST and eligible S corporation shareholder.

Under a conventional non-QSST Section 678 Trust, there is no obligation to pay trust income or principal to the beneficiary who is deemed to be the owner of the trust, and income can be distributed to any one or more beneficiaries other than the deemed owner.

While at first glance the strict income payout requirement of a QSST would cause it to be undesirable, there are planning mechanisms that can be used to make a QSST arrangement more desirable:

1.   The Definition of Income. The amount of income that is required to be paid out to the QSST income beneficiary is determined by reference to state income and principal law, and will therefore only include dividends that are actually received from the S corporation by the Trustee of the QSST, and other forms of income that the QSST receives.

        If the QSST owns a limited liability company that is disregarded for income tax purposes, and the limited liability company owns the S corporation stock, then the payment of distributions from the S corporation to the disregarded LLC may not be considered as the payment of income to the trustee of the QSST, depending upon state law.

        Most states have adopted the Uniform Principal and Income Act, which generally defines income to be the amount of cash and property distributed from a disregarded LLC to its owner.

        Eventually, however, when distributions are made from the LLC to the trustee of the QSST, some or all thereof will be considered as income, while some may be considered to be a distribution of principal.

2.   A distribution to an LLC solely owned by the income beneficiary may be considered to be a distribution to the beneficiary, even if the LLC is irrevocably managed by a manager, who will have a fiduciary duty to manage the LLC reasonably, but no specific duty to make distributions to the beneficiary.

        Nevertheless, an income beneficiary may have to have the right to require that future distributions be made from the QSST to that beneficiary in order for the trust to qualify.

Advisors now have stable Final Regulations and multiple avenues to allow for the responsible structuring of business and professional arrangements to maximize tax deductions that may be received under Section 199A.

Clients who would like to reduce family income tax burdens and enhance multiple generation and trust and estate planning stand ready to be helped and advisors should act with reasonable speed to make these structures available.

The authors believe that the decision of whether or not to aggregate and how to keep SSTBs and Non-SSTBs separate when a taxpayer is involved in multiple trades or businesses is another important area in the Final Regulations. Stay tuned for a future newsletter discussing this planning opportunity.

While the 247 pages of the Final Regulations and their interaction with the inner workings of the Internal Revenue Code must be carefully studied and understood, seeing opportunities where they exist is an important function of tax advisors in the form of this special gift from the Treasury Department delivered just after the holiday season.

CHAPTER 14.
FINAL REGULATIONS AND HOW THEY ARE
DIFFERENT FROM THE PROPOSED REGULATIONS

As early as February of 2018, the IRS noted that it had plans to release guidance on Section 199A for definitional, computational, and other purposes by mid-to late-June. This deadline passed, and Proposed Regulations issued on August 8, 2018 were found by many to be "anti-taxpayer" in a number of ways. The key points and highlights of the Proposed Regulations, many of which remained unchanged in the Final Regulations can be found in the authors' article *Proposed Regulations for 199A - The Good, The Bad, the Taxpayer-Unfriendly* LISI Income Tax Planning Newsletter #152 (August 13, 2018) at http://www.leimbergservices.com.

Knowledge of the Proposed Regulations is important for purposes of filing 2018 tax returns, because each taxpayer must decide whether to follow the Proposed Regulations as to each and every issue associated with that taxpayer, or the Final Regulations. The following chart gives a summary of primary differences between the Final and Proposed Regulations that advisors can consider. These items are further discussed below.

Proposed vs. Final Regulations Under Section 199A

Reasons to Rely Upon Proposed Regulations for 2019	Reasons to Rely Upon Final Regulations for 2019
A flow-through entity renting property to a commonly controlled C corporation will be considered an active trade or business whereas the Final Regulations require that the property be rented to another flow-through entity or an individual.	Taxpayers may take into account Section 743 basis adjustments, including Section 754 elections for partnerships.
The field of health was limited to those who provide medical services directly to patients which could be beneficial for those in the health field that do not have direct contact with patients.	Taxpayers may aggregate at the entity level.
If an entity provides services to a commonly controlled SSTB then such entity will be treated as part of the SSTB that it is providing services to. This could be beneficial to taxpayers within the phase-out range in which the entity providing services does not have sufficient wages or qualified property to qualify for the Section 199A deduction and would be impacted by the double phase-out. The Final Regulations require the entity providing services to be treated as a separate SSTB which would require separate testing under the Wage and Qualified Property Test.	UBIA will be carried over for contributions of property to a partnership or an S corporation.

Reasons to Rely Upon Proposed Regulations for 2019	Reasons to Rely Upon Final Regulations for 2019
ESBTs - Electing Small Business Trusts may be able to use two threshold limitations, one for the S portion of the trust and another for the non-S portion of the trust under the Proposed Regulations.	The incidental rule that would require an SSTB offering products or services as part of the SSTB to be more than 5% of gross receipts in order to be considered separate and apart from the SSTB.
Examples under the multiple trust rules were deleted from the Final Regulations which provide additional guidance on when a trust is considered to have substantially different beneficiaries.	Presumption that an employee is an independent contractor will only last for three years and additional guidance is provided through examples in the Final Regulations on how the presumption can be rebutted.
Examples under the multiple trust rules were deleted from the Final Regulations which provide additional guidance on when a trust is considered to have substantially different beneficiaries.	Trusts have the ability to take into account the distributable net income "DNI" deduction for distributions made from a trust.
	Under the anti-abuse rules the Proposed Regulations provided that if the trust was funded for the "significant purpose of receiving a deduction under Section 199A" it would not be respected, whereas the Final Regulations changed this to "a principal purpose of using more than one threshold," which seems to be a lesser standard.
	The Final Regulations do not include a presumption that the trust was formed or funded for a principal purpose if a significant income tax benefit would result.

Even before then advisors were given hints as to how the IRS intended to regulate some important issues. At the American Bar Association's San Diego meeting in February, attorney- advisor at the Treasury's Office of Tax Policy Audrey Ellis had given indications that the scope of the term "reasonable compensation" under Section 199A(c)(4)(A) would not be expanded.[373] This was explicitly confirmed in the Preamble to the Final Regulations. A great many advisors had also wondered if, and feared that, the term would be applied to all entities beyond its traditional application to S corporations.

---

[373] *Stephenson Trust v. Commissioner*, 81 T.C. 283 (1983); *Estelle Morris Trusts v. Commissioner*, 51 T.C. 20 (1968), *aff'd per curiam*, 427 F.2d 1361 (9th Cir. 1970).

The text of the Final Regulations can be found in **Error! Reference source not found.**. This Chapter will be dedicated to analyzing the substance and implication of this guidance, which is presented in condensed, bullet-point format for convenience of the reader.[374]

The Final Regulations do not eliminate all potential Section 199A planning opportunities. Despite the proposed limitations on having related entities provide management, billing, marketing, and other services and products to a Specified Service Trade or Business, "Crack and Pack" entities can still provide significant tax savings when held at arm's-length and owned by taxpayers who have income under the $157,500 (or $315,000 if married, filing jointly) threshold.

For example, a partnership owned 51% by a dentist and 49% by the children of the dentist that receives rent or other arm's-length payments can have profits that are considered to pass 49% to the children, who may qualify for the Section 199A deduction, based upon their lower tax brackets.

Also, the proposed "disrespecting" of separately taxed Complex Trusts established to avoid tax under Section 199A will not apply to pre-existing trusts that were funded before Section 199A was enacted, or Section 678 trusts, which are funded by a grantor and considered as owned by a beneficiary or beneficiaries who had or have the opportunity to withdraw the assets placed into trust or the income therefrom. The lower tax brackets of children and other family members can therefore be safely used for Section 199A planning without any risk of aggregation of separate Section 678 trusts. These trusts are discussed in more detail in Chapter 13.

In addition, the new Regulations under Section 643(f) with respect to multiple trusts will not apply if there are completely separate lifetime beneficiaries as demonstrated in Section 1.643(f)-1(c), Example 2, which is discussed in Chapter 13, so long as the principal reason in establishing the trusts is not tax avoidance.

Abbreviations from Final Regulations and Their Meanings

Final Regulations Abbreviations	New Meaning
PTP	Publicly Traded Partnership
QBI	Qualified Business Income
REIT	Real Estate Investment Trust
RPE	Relevant Pass-Through Entity
SSTB	Specified Service Trade or Business
UBIA	Unadjusted Basis Immediately After Acquisition (of Qualified Property)

---

[374] Eric Yauch, *ABA Section of Taxation Meeting: Existing Tax Code Helpful for Addressing Section 199A Issues,* Tax Notes Today (May 28, 2018).

Final Regulations Abbreviations	New Meaning
DNI	Distributable Net Income (referring to trusts and estates)

The Final Regulations are comprised of seven Sections, with six dedicated to Section 199A, and one dedicated to Section 643. They are as follows:

- *Section 1.199A-1* covers calculation rules of Section 199A, as well as definitional guidance on the standard of being engaged in a trade or business, and loss carry-over rules.

- *Section 1.199A-2* covers the rules regarding the determination of W-2 wages and UBIA of Qualified Property.

- *Section 1.199A-3* provides guidance surrounding the terms and calculations regarding QBI, Real Estate Investment Trust dividends, and qualified Publicly Traded Partnership income.

- *Section 1.199A-4* covers the rules relating to aggregation non-Specified Service Trades or Businesses and Specified Service Trades or Businesses.

- *Section 1.199A-5* covers definitional guidance of Specified Service Trades or Businesses.

- *Section 1.199A-6* covers computational guidance for individuals who own or are beneficiaries of Relevant Pass-Through Entities, Publicly Traded Partnerships, trusts and estates.

- *Section 1.643(f)-1 covers the treatment of multiple trusts, and possible* aggregation thereof, when the trusts have significantly the same beneficiaries and the same grantors, namely that the IRS has the power to aggregate them into singular trusts.

Section 199A Subsections – Grants of Authority

For reference, the authors have included the subsections and text of the grants of authority below for readers:

Topic	Code Section	Specific Language
Short Taxable Years	§ 199A(b)(5)	"The Secretary shall provide for the application of this subsection in cases of a short taxable year or where the taxpayer acquires, or disposes of, the major portion of a trade or business or the major portion of a separate unit of a trade or business during the taxable year."

Topic	Code Section	Specific Language
Allocation of Items/Wages	§ 199A(f)(4)(A)	"The Secretary shall prescribe such regulations … for requiring or restricting the allocation of items and wages under this Section and such reporting requirements as the Secretary determines appropriate."
Tiered Entity Situations	§199A(f)(4)(B)	"The Secretary shall prescribe such regulations … for the application of this Section in the case of tiered entities."
Depreciable Periods/ 1031 Exchanges	§ 199A(h)	"The Secretary shall (1) apply rules similar to the rules under Section 179(d)(2) in order to prevent the manipulation of the depreciable period of qualified property using transactions between related parties, and (2) prescribe rules for determining the UBIA of qualified property acquired in like-kind exchanges or involuntary conversions."
Agricultural and Horticultural Cooperatives	§ 199A(g)(3)(C) & § 199A(g)(6)	"Secretary shall prescribe rules for the proper allocation of items described in subparagraph (A) for purposes of determining qualified production activities income. Such rules shall provide for the proper allocation of items whether or not such items are directly allocable to domestic production gross receipts"

and

"The Secretary shall prescribe such regulations as are necessary to carry out the purposes of this subsection, including regulations which prevent more than 1 taxpayer from being allowed a deduction under this subsection with respect to any activity described in paragraph (3)(D)(i). Such regulations shall be based on the Regulations applicable to cooperatives and their patrons under Section 199 (as in effect before its repeal)." |

Time will tell whether many of these provisions will be within the authority of the Treasury Department to issue these Regulations.

On the whole, the Final Regulations do not substantially differ from Proposed Regulations, much to the dismay of many practitioners. However, the Final Regulations stop short of certain limitations espoused by the Proposed Regulations, and also leave open many planning opportunities, some of which are not so obvious. We discuss these opportunities in Chapter 11 and throughout this book.

The following is a list of material changes under the Final Regulations relative to the Proposed Regulations:

1.   The new definition for performances of services in the field of health is no longer limited to those who provide medical services directly to a patient, and certain functions associated with providing services or products for those who provide services directly to patients.

This has the effect of including additional healthcare professionals as SSTBs. For example, the Final Regulations contain an example where a board certified pharmacist who performs part-time services to a small medical facility in a rural area where he receives and reviews orders from physicians who are providing medical care at the facility, makes recommendations on dosing and alternative medications, performs inoculations, checks for drug interactions, and fills pharmaceutical orders for patients receiving care at the facility would be considered as being engaged in the field of health for the purposes of this Section 199A deduction.

Another example under the Final Regulations provides that a company that operates day surgery centers but does not employ physicians, nurses or medical assistants, does not perform services in the field of health for the purposes of the Section 199A deduction. However, it seems that if the surgery center directly employs any physicians, nurses or medical assistants, then it would be considered as performing services in the field of health (and therefore would be an SSTB) for purposes of Section 199A deduction.

Interestingly, both state and federal law require that ambulatory surgery centers directly hire medical support staff, so it seems that any ambulatory surgery center would be considered an SSTB.

The Final Regulations also classify veterinarians and physical therapists as being included in the definition of performing services in the field of health, which therefore causes such trades or businesses to be SSTBs. Further, remote radiologists and non-patient contact medical professionals are treated as SSTBs because the Final Regulations have removed the requirement that medical services be provided directly to a patient in order to be classified as performing services in the field of health for the purposes of the Section 199A deduction.

For a more detailed discussion on the "field of health" see Chapter 9.

2.   Architects and engineers were specifically excluded from the definition of performance of services in the field of consulting. Many commentators were concerned that architects and engineers could be considered an SSTB if they provided consulting services. The Final Regulations again saved the day for this industry by specifically stating that "Services within the fields of architecture and engineering are not treated as consulting services."

3.   Consulting also does not include providing training and other educational courses or the performance of consulting services that are embedded in, or ancillary to, the sale of goods or performance of services on behalf of a trade or business that is otherwise not an SSTB (such as typical services provided by a building contractor) if there is no separate payment for the consulting services.

It is noteworthy that lobbyists and other similar professionals will be treated as consultants and thus an SSTB. Further, based upon an example contained in the Final Regulations, staffing services will not be considered as consulting if the staffing company is paid on a commission or per procured employee basis.

4.   The definition of performances of services in the field of law was specified to include "the performance of **legal** [emphasis added] services by individuals such as lawyers, paralegals, legal arbitrators, mediators, and similar professionals performing services in their capacity as such. The performance of services in the field of law does not include the provision of services that do not require skills unique to the field of law; for example, the provision of services in the field of law does not include the provision of services by printers, delivery services, or stenography services."

The addition of the word legal seems to mean that services offered by law firms which are not limited to the "legal" profession will not be considered to be SSTBs.

5.   Life insurance and real estate sales agents and activities are excluded from being SSTBs.

The now Final Section 199A Regulations provide that "the performance of services in the field of brokerage services includes services in which a person arranges transactions between a buyer and a seller with respect to securities (as defined in Section 475(c)(2)) for a commission or fee. This includes services provided by stockbrokers and other similar professionals but *does not include services provided* by real estate agents and brokers, or *insurance agents and brokers.*"

The Preamble to the Final Regulations provided further guidance on this exclusion by explaining that ancillary services related to the commission-based sale of an insurance policy will generally not be considered to be the provision of financial services for purposes of Section 199A. Further, the Preamble states that the commission-based sales of insurance policies generally will not be considered the performance of services in the field of investing and investing management for purposes of Section 199A.

This means that entities which sell life insurance will not be considered to be SSTBs, and groups that sell life insurance in addition to providing investment advice and annuity sales might want to separate the life insurance functions into a separate company, or at minimum maintain separate books and records, in order to have any revenues therefrom be exempt from SSTB classification.

Statutory employee treatment of life insurance agents is described in Chapter 11.

6.   The Final Regulations clarify that the performance of services in the field of financial services does not include taking deposits or making loans but does include arranging lending

transactions between a lender and borrower.

As a result, banks and other financial institutions will not be treated as SSTBs, however this change in the definition would include mortgage brokers as SSTBs.

7.   The Preamble to the Final Regulations provides that real estate settlement agents may be considered to be performing services in the field of accounting, specifically stating that "Whether a real estate settlement agent is engaged in the performance of services in the field of accounting depends on the facts and circumstances including the specific services offered and performed by the trade or business."

8.   The Final Regulations eliminated the incidental SSTB limitation that was included under the Proposed Regulations whereby SSTBs that provide products and/or services incidental to the operation of the SSTB activity trade or business would need to exceed 5% of the total combined gross receipts of the trade or business in order to be considered a separate trade or business and not aggregated as part of the SSTB.

This means that an entity that generates SSTB income and also actively provides non-SSTB products and/or services that are incidental to the SSTB trade or business can be considered as a separate trade or business that is not aggregated to be a part of the SSTB. For example, if a landscaping company providing lawn care and landscaping equipment (not an SSTB) also provides consulting services with respect to landscape design for large office parks and residential buildings (an SSTB), then the lawn care and landscaping equipment arm of the business would not be considered to be an SSTB if a separate set of books and records are maintained with respect thereto.

9.   The Preamble to the Final Regulations refers to Regulations under Section 446 and indicates that at a minimum books and records must be separable in order to separate SSTB from non-SSTB income, but the examples seem to indicate that separate books and records must be maintained, and that separation would best include having separate employees for each function and other indicia of separateness.

Specifically, the Preamble to the Final Regulations provides as follows:

The Treasury Department and the IRS acknowledge that an entity can conduct more than one Section 162 trade or business. This position is inherent in the reporting requirements detailed in §1.199A-6, which require an entity to separately report QBI, W-2 wages, UBIA of qualified property, and SSTB information for each trade or business engaged in by the entity. Whether a single entity has multiple trades or businesses is a factual determination. However, court decisions that help define the meaning of "trade or business" provide taxpayers guidance in determining whether more than one trade or business exists. As discussed in Part II.A.3.a. of this Summary of Comments and Explanation of Revisions, generally under Section 162, to be engaged in a trade or business under Section 162, the taxpayer must be involved in the activity with continuity and regularity, and the taxpayer's primary purpose for engaging in the activity must be for income or profit [Emphasis added]. [Groetzinger, at 35.]

The Treasury Department and the IRS also believe that multiple trades or businesses will generally not exist within an entity unless different methods of accounting could be used for each trade or business under §1.446-1(d). Section 1.446- 1(d) explains that no trade or business is considered separate and distinct unless a complete and separable set of books and records is kept for that trade or business. Further, trades or businesses will not be considered separate and distinct if, by reason of maintaining different methods of accounting, there is a creation or shifting of profits and losses between the businesses so that income of the taxpayer is not clearly reflected [Emphasis added].

The example referenced above reads as follows, with important items and characteristics underlined:

> Animal Care LLC provides veterinarian services performed by licensed staff and also develops and sells its own line of organic dog food at its veterinarian clinic and online. The veterinarian services are considered to be the performance of services in the field of health under paragraphs (b)(1)(i) and (b)(2)(ii) of this section. Animal Care LLC separately invoices for its veterinarian services and the sale of its organic dog food. Animal Care LLC maintains separate books and records for its veterinarian clinic and its development and sale of its dog food. Animal Care LLC also has separate employees who are unaffiliated with the veterinary clinic and who only work on the formulation, marketing, sales, and distribution of the organic dog food products. Animal Care LLC treats its veterinary practice and the dog food development and sales as separate trades or businesses for purposes of Section 162 and 199A. Animal Care LLC has gross receipts of $3,000,000. $1,000,000 of the gross receipts is attributable to the veterinary services, an SSTB. Although the gross receipts from the services in the field of health exceed 10 percent of Animal Care LLC's total gross receipts, the dog food development and sales business is not considered an SSTB due to the fact that the veterinary practice and the dog food development and sales are separate trades or businesses under Section 162. [Emphasis added]

For more detail see Chapter 9.

10.   The Final Regulations make it clear that an entity having more than 10% in SSTB gross revenues will be considered to have 100% SSTB income, unless there is an adequate "books and records and associated separation."[375]   A 5% threshold will apply if the entity has revenues exceeding $25 million.

---

[375] Treas. Reg. § 1.199A-5(c)(1)(i).

Chart 25 – When Separate Books and Records Must Be Maintained

A chart outlining when separate books and records need to be maintained is as follows:

When Separable Books and Records Should Be Maintained When SSTB and Non-SSTB Activities are Under One Entity

Type of Business	Percentage of SSTB Gross Receipts When Divided by Total Gross Receipts	Are Separate Books and Records Maintained?	Tax Treatment
Mainly Non-SSTB *De minimis* Rule	Under 10% of gross receipts, provided that if total gross receipts exceed $25 million, then under 5%.	Does not affect treatment.	All income is treated as non-SSTB income.
Over 10% Non-SSTB (or 5% if total gross receipts exceed $25 million)	Over 10% with gross receipts under $25 million or over 5% with gross receipts over $25 million.	If separable books and records are not maintained.	All income is treated as SSTB income.
Mainly Non-SSTB	Over 10% with gross receipts under $25 million or over 5% with gross receipts over $25 million.	If separable books and records are not maintained.	The taxpayer may treat non-SSTB income as non-SSTB if books and records are "separable."
Mainly SSTB	Does not affect treatment.	If maintain, separable books and records.	All non-SSTB income is treated as non-SSTB income.
Mainly SSTB	Does not affect treatment.	If separable books and records are not maintained.	All income is treated as SSTB income.

11.   The Final Regulations confirm that Electing Small Business Trusts ("ESBTs"), which are certain trusts that are eligible to hold S corporation stock, can qualify for the Section 199A deduction on S corporation income, even though the ESBT statute was not properly conformed by the 2017 Tax Act to allow this. This result is what Congress intended, so this was an anticipated correction that is hopefully within the power of the Treasury Department, if not confirmed by a statutory change to Section 1361. It is noteworthy that in the *Bobrow* case,[376] a taxpayer followed the IRS Publication on IRA rollover rules and was penalized when the Tax Court determined that the publication was erroneous. This should not be the case for taxpayers who rely upon the Regulations, which specifically state that they can be relied upon by taxpayers.

The Final Regulations clarify that the S portion and non-S portion of an ESBT will be treated as a single trust for the purpose of determining the applicable threshold amount. This eliminates what some commentators believed to be a loophole in the Proposed Regulations.

---

[376] *Bobrow v. Commissioner of the Internal Revenue*, U.S. Tax Ct., Jan. 28, 2014 pg. 24.

12.   Consider using a Qualified Subchapter S Trust, which is considered to be owned by the beneficiary who has the right to receive all income of the trust. Income is defined under state law, so the S corporation may have significant income that is not actually distributed to the trust. Other planning aspects of QSSTs are described in Chapter 13.

13.   The Final Regulations confirm that the SSTB limitation also applies to publicly traded partnerships, while the Wage and Qualified Property limitations do not.
Accordingly, high income owners of publicly traded partnerships do not need to be concerned with the amount of Wages paid or Qualified Property owned by the partnership, but the Section 199A deduction may be limited if the publicly traded partnership engages in one or more SSTB activities.

14.   If property is inherited and immediately placed in service by an heir, the UAB in the property will generally be its fair market value at the time of the decedent's death, and the Regulations confirm that Section 1014 applies for the purposes of Section 199A, even if there is personal or other use of the property, not directly related to the applicable trade or business.

The Final Regulations allow a partnership to take into account basis adjustments using a modified version of Section 743(b) when a Section 754 election is in place, but any prior depreciation taken is not restored for UBIA purposes. The increase is allowed to the extent that it is attributable to an increase in the fair market value of the property from the original UBIA of the property, but not to the extent of depreciation that would be recaptured.

Example:

> A, B and C are equal partners in ABC partnership. A, B and C purchase a building for $900,000, and each partner's share of the UBIA is $300,000.
>
> A sells his interest to D for $500,000 when the building is worth $1,500,000 and the tax basis of the building is $600,000 (assuming $300,000 of depreciation has been taken). Under a typical 743 basis adjustment, D would receive a basis increase of $300,000. However, for purposes of Section 199A, this adjustment is limited to $200,000, which is the difference between the purchase price ($500,000) and A's original UBIA in the property ($300,000). The depreciated portion is not restored for UBIA purposes.

The $200,000 "excess 743(b) basis adjustment" is treated as a new item of qualified property that is placed into service on the day the partnership interest was transferred.

Although further analysis is necessary, this may not result in a full step up in basis for a partnership owning appreciated property on a partner's death or when there is a sale of a partnership interest.

The Final Regulations contain two examples that illustrate the above and read as follows:

Example 1:

(i) Facts. A, B, and C are equal partners in partnership, PRS. PRS has a single trade or business that generates QBI. PRS has no liabilities and only one asset, a single item of qualified property with a UBIA equal to $900,000. Each partner's share of the UBIA is $300,000.

(ii) A sells its one-third interest in PRS to T for $350,000 when a section 754 election is in effect. At the time of the sale, the tax basis of the qualified property held by PRS is $750,000. The amount of gain that would be allocated to T from a hypothetical transaction under §1.743-1(d)(2) is $100,000. Thus, T's interest in PRS's previously taxed capital is equal to $250,000 ($350,000, the amount of cash T would receive if PRS liquidated immediately after the hypothetical transaction, decreased by $100,000, T's share of gain from the hypothetical transaction). The amount of T's section 743(b) basis adjustment to PRS's qualified property is $100,000 (the excess of $350,000, T's cost basis for its interest, over $250,000, T's share of the adjusted basis to PRS of the partnership's property).

(iii) Analysis. In order for T to determine its UBIA, T must calculate its excess section 743(b) basis adjustment. T's excess section 743(b) basis adjustment is equal to an amount that would represent T's section 743(b) basis adjustment with respect to the same item of qualified property, as determined under §1.743-1(b) and §1.755-1, but calculated as if the adjusted basis of all of PRS's property was equal to the UBIA of such property. T's section 743(b) basis adjustment calculated as if adjusted basis of the qualified property were equal to its UBIA is $50,000 (the excess of $350,000, T's cost basis for its interest, over $300,000, T's share of the adjusted basis to PRS of the partnership's property). Thus, T's excess section 743(b) basis adjustment is equal to $50,000.

(iv) Therefore, for purposes of applying the UBIA limitation to T's share of QBI from PRS's trade or business, T's UBIA is equal to $350,000 ($300,000, T's one-third share of the qualified property's UBIA, plus $50,000, T's excess section 743(b) basis adjustment).[377]

Example 2:

(i) Facts. Assume the same facts as in Example 1, except that A sells its one-third interest in PRS to T for $200,000 when a section 754 election is in effect. At the time of the sale, the tax basis of the qualified property held by PRS is $750,000, and the amount of loss that would be allocated to T from a hypothetical transaction under §1.743-1(d)(2) is $50,000. Thus, T's interest in

---

[377] Treas. Reg. § 1.199A-2(a)(3)(iv)(D), Example 1.

PRS's previously taxed capital is equal to $250,000 ($200,000, the amount of cash T would receive if PRS liquidated immediately after the hypothetical transaction, increased by $50,000, T's share of loss from the hypothetical transaction). The amount of T's section 743(b) basis adjustment to PRS's qualified property is negative $50,000 (the excess of $250,000, T's share of the adjusted basis to PRS of the partnership's property, over $200,000, T's cost basis for its interest).

(ii) Analysis. In order for T to determine its UBIA, T must calculate its excess section 743(b) basis adjustment. T's excess section 743(b) basis adjustment is equal to an amount that would represent T's section 743(b) basis adjustment with respect to the same item of qualified property, as determined under §1.743-1(b) and §1.755-1, but calculated as if the adjusted basis of all of PRS's property was equal to the UBIA of such property. T's section 743(b) basis adjustment calculated as if adjusted basis of the qualified property were equal to its UBIA is negative $100,000 (the excess of $300,000, T's share of the adjusted basis to PRS of the partnership's property, over $200,000, T's cost basis for its interest). T's excess section 743(b) basis adjustment to the qualified property is limited to the amount of T's section 743(b) basis adjustment of negative $50,000.

(iii) Therefore, for purposes of applying the UBIA limitation to T's share of QBI from PRS's trade or business, T's UBIA is equal to $250,000 ($300,000, T's one-third share of the qualified property's UBIA, reduced by T's negative $50,000 excess section 743(b) basis adjustment).[378]

Because many taxpayers will not benefit from discounts these entities afford for estate tax purposes while exemptions are high, it may be advantageous to liquidate entities before a partner's death or before the sale of a partnership interest in some instances.

This could allow for various planning techniques where the partnership distributes the property to its partners before the death of a partner or a combined sale of the partnership interest and the appreciated property. Some practitioners have indicated that the partnership should hold the property until after the death of a partner or sale of the partnership interest and distribute the property immediately thereafter. This apparently would allow the appreciated property to receive a basis increase due to Section 1014 and the Section 754 election, and the heir can place the property back into the partnership with an increased basis for the purposes of Section 199A.

15.   The Final Regulations corrected the taxpayer unfriendly position under the Proposed Regulations that the UBIA of property contributed immediately after acquisition to an S corporation or partnership would be based upon the basis of the property on the date of contribution, which could result in a step-down in basis if the property was depreciable.

---

[378] Treas. Reg. § 1.199A-2(a)(3)(iv)(D), Example 2.

The Final Regulations provide that the UBIA of contributed property will retain a carryover basis for the property when it was first placed into service by the contributing partner or shareholder.

16. The Final Regulations confirm that qualified property that is eligible to receive a new fair market value income tax basis under IRC Section 1014 will be considered to have been placed in service on the date of death, with a new depreciation period having started, which will allow for the new fair market value basis of the asset to be the UBIA for a minimum of ten years.

17. The Final Regulations provide that a separately taxed trust that is "formed or funded with a principal purpose of avoiding, or of using more than one, threshold amount for purposes of calculating the deduction under Section 199A" will be considered as combined with its contributor for Section 199A purposes.

The Proposed Regulations had referenced "trusts formed or funded..." meaning that it was conceivable that the Proposed Regulations were to only apply to multiple trusts. The Final Regulations make it clear that they are to apply to both individual and multiple trusts.

The Final Regulations confirm that a trust that is considered to be a grantor trust as to any taxpayer under current Revenue Code Sections 671 and 679 (which includes the Section 678 trust that is treated as being owned by someone other than the grantor for federal income tax purposes) will be respected. This keeps open the possibility of using Section 768 trusts, such as BDIT's and BDOT's, might be beneficial in qualifying for the Section 199A deduction.

18. The Proposed Regulations had provided special rules that apply when a trade or business had 50% or more common ownership with an SSTB and provides property or services to the SSTB by providing that that a trade or business that provides more than 80% of its property or services to an SSTB and has at least 50% common related party ownership will be treated as an SSTB. When there was at least 50% common ownership and less than 80% of the property or services were provided to the related party SSTB, then the Proposed Regulations provided that the related entity was considered to be an SSTB in proportion to the products and services provided to the SSTB.

> The Final Regulations eliminate the 80% rule, and simply provide that if there is more than 50% or more common ownership, the portion of the trade or business that provided property or services to the 50% or more commonly owned SSTB, will be treated as a separate SSTB, with the income attributable to the services provided to non-SSTBs being considered to be non-SSTB income.

19. The Final Regulations create the presumption that a person who was an employee of a business continues to be an employee for a period of three years following termination of his or her employment. The Final Regulations provide that an individual may rebut this presumption by providing records that are sufficient to collaborate the individual's status as a non-employee for federal employment tax purposes. Such records can include contracts and partnership or shareholder agreements.

20.   The Preamble to the Final Regulations recognized that any expense that is deductible for federal income tax purposes will be considered as an expense in the determination of Qualified Business Income under Section 199A, including the deductible portion (50%) of employment taxes on self-employment income under Section 164(f), the self-employed health insurance deduction under Section 162(l) and the deduction for contributions to qualified retirement plans under Section 404.

The Treasury Department and the IRS declined to address whether deductions for unreimbursed partnership expenses, the interest expensed to acquire partnership and S corporation interest, and state and local taxes are attributable to a trade or business, stating that "such guidance is beyond the scope of such regulations." The punting by the Treasury and the IRS on this issue does not instill confidence in taxpayers as to the interpretation of these rules and their position on any such deductions when employed in practice.

21.   The Final Regulations confirm that real estate leasing activities can qualify for the 20% deduction without regard to whether the landlord is an active trade or business if the tenant is an active trade or business owned by an individual taxpayer, partnership, or S corporation, and the landlord and the tenant are "commonly controlled entities," which are defined as common ownership of 50% or more in each entity, including direct or indirect ownership by related parties under Sections 267(b) and 707(b).[379]

---

[379] Related parties under 267(b) and 707(b) include:
(1) Members of the family, defined as brothers and sisters (whether by whole or half-blood), spouse, ancestors and lineal descendants;
(2) An individual and a corporation more than 50 percent in value of the outstanding stock of which is owned, directly, or indirectly, by or for such individual:
(3) Two corporations which are members of the same controlled group (as defined in subsection (f));
(4) A grantor and a fiduciary of any trust;
(5) A fiduciary of a trust and a fiduciary of another trust, if the same person is a grantor of both trusts;
(6) A fiduciary of a trust and a beneficiary of such trust;
(7) A fiduciary of a trust and a beneficiary of another trust, if the same person is a grantor of both trusts;
(8) A fiduciary of a trust and a corporation more than 50 percent in value of the outstanding stock of which is owned, directly or indirectly, by or for the trust or by or for a person who is a grantor of the trust;
(9) A person and an organization to which Section 501 (relating to certain educational and charitable organizations which are exempt from tax) applies and which is controlled directly or indirectly by such person or (if such person is an individual) by members of the family of such individual;
(10) A corporation and a partnership if the same persons own (A) more than 50 percent in value of the outstanding stock of the corporation, and (B) more than 50 percent of the capital interest, or the profits interest in the partnership;
(11) An S corporation and another S corporation if the same persons own more than 50 percent in value of the outstanding stock of each corporation;
(12) An S corporation and a C corporation, if the same persons own more than 50 percent in value of the outstanding stock of each corporation;
(13) Except in the case of a sale or exchange in satisfaction of a pecuniary bequest, an executor of an estate and a beneficiary of such estate;
(14) A partnership and a person owning, directly or indirectly, more than 50 percent of the capital interest, or the profits interest, in such partnership; or
(15) Two partnerships in which the same persons own, directly or indirectly, more than 50 percent of the capital interests or profits interests.

The Final Regulations added the following underlined language to the exception to the active trade or business requirement of the Section 162 trade or business requirement:

In addition, rental or licensing of tangible or intangible property (rental activity) that does not rise to the level of a Section 162 trade or business is nevertheless treated as a trade or business for purposes of Section 199A, if the property is rented or licensed to a trade or business conducted <u>by the individual or an RPE</u> [Relevant Pass-through Entity] which is commonly controlled under §1.199A-4(b)(1)(i) (regardless of whether the rental activity and the trade or business are otherwise eligible to be aggregated under §1.199A-4(b)(1)).

Under the Proposed Regulations, if the rental or licensing of property was to a commonly controlled C corporation, the entity receiving the rent payments would be considered to be a trade or business eligible for the Section 199A deduction. By adding that the trade or business must be conducted by the individual or Relevant Pass-Through Entity, the rental or licensing of property to a commonly controlled C corporation will need to separately rise to the level of an active trade or business in order to be eligible for the Section 199A deduction. If the rental is to a commonly controlled trade or business that is taxed as a sole proprietorship, partnership, or S corporation (a "Relevant Pass-Through Entity"), then the rental activity will qualify for the Section 199A deduction regardless of whether the activity is considered to be an active trade or business.

The Final Regulations apply the Section 162 definition of a trade or business for non-commonly controlled rental activities, which can be problematic for passive landlords, lessors of non-real estate personal items, and licensors of intellectual property rights that are not active enough to qualify as a Section 162 trade or business. These taxpayers will instead have to rely upon case law or the safe harbor under IRS Notice 2019-7 discussed below to qualify as an active trade or business to be eligible for the Section 199A deduction.

22.   IRS Notice 2019-7 sets forth a safe harbor for taxpayers in real estate rental activities, and real estate activities, and requires that 250 hours or more of rental services be performed by owners, employees, and other agents in order to qualify for the safe harbor, which is discussed in more detail in Chapter 12, Part Two.

Under the Final Regulations, "active" leasing activities will be considered to be a Trade or Business for the purposes of the Section 199A deduction. Additionally, a passive lease for the active Trade or Business with common ownership will be considered active if the tenant is not an SSTB. An active lease between an SSTB and an affiliated entity will be considered to be a separate SSTB.

Under the Final Regulations, a triple net lease will normally not qualify as a Trade or Business for the purpose of determining eligibility for the Section 199A deduction under any circumstance.

The following items remain largely unchanged by the Final Regulations:

For further clarification on the complex ripple effects of the new Final Corrected Regulations, the esteemed co-author to this book, Martin Shenkman, has provided the following breakdown:[380]

RIPPLE EFFECTS OF THE NEW FINAL CORRECTED REGULATIONS

The Regulations include a myriad of provisions that might affect how a trade or business is defined and whether or not that trade or business will qualify for the QBI deduction. Many of these nuanced rules have direct application to determining whether income from real estate activities will or will not qualify. Marty Shenkman has provided the following discussion with respect to this:

A. MULTIPLE TRADES OR BUSINESSES

"Whether a single entity has multiple trades or businesses is a factual determination. However, court decisions that help define the meaning of "trade or business" provide taxpayers guidance in determining whether more than one trades or businesses exist." The aggregation, or decision not to aggregate, or the inability to aggregate (e.g. real estate properties that are not trades or businesses cannot be aggregated), may all affect the outcome of the analysis.

B. ACTIVITY TO CONSTITUTE A TRADE OR BUSINESS

The Regulations refer to case law to interpret what it means "…to be engaged in a trade or business, the taxpayer must be involved in the activity with continuity and regularity and the taxpayer's primary purpose for engaging in the activity must be for income or profit. *Groetzinger*, at 35."

C. BOOKS AND RECORDS

'Section 1.446-1(d) explains that no trade or business is considered separate and distinct unless a complete and separable set of books and records is kept for that trade or business. Further, trades or businesses will not be considered separate and distinct if, by reason of maintaining different methods of accounting, there is a creation or shifting of profits and losses between the businesses of the taxpayer so that income of the taxpayer is not clearly reflected." This appears to mean that if several businesses do not have "complete and separable sets of books and records" they cannot be separate businesses. If there is a shifting of profits that is not "clearly reflected" then to businesses cannot be separated. This might all affect the calculus of QBI for the overall enterprise. This adds requirements that practitioners will have to address in delineating businesses for purposes of the QBI deduction.

D. COMBINATION OF MULTIPLE ENTITIES

The determination of a trade or business is made more complex by the possibility of combining multiple entities so that the combined business enterprise rises to the level of a trade or business. "As described in part II of this Summary of Comments and Explanation of Revisions, the Proposed Regulations incorporate the principles of Section 162 for determining whether a trade or business exists for purposes of Section 199A. A taxpayer can have more than one Section 162 trade or

---

[380] All quotations in the following section have been pulled directly from the New Final Corrected Regulations for Section 199A.

business.[381] Multiple trades or businesses can also be conducted within one entity. A trade or business, however, cannot generally be conducted across multiple entities for tax purposes. The preamble to the Proposed Regulations acknowledges that it is not uncommon for what may be thought of as single trades or businesses to be operated across multiple entities, for various legal, economic, or other non-tax reasons. It is because trades or businesses may be structured this way that the Final Regulations permit combining the entities for purposes of determining whether a trade or business exists. So merely determining whether the developer's activities constitute a trade or business is only part of the analysis. The Regs. further provide: "The aggregation rules are intended to allow aggregation of what is commonly thought of as a single trade or business where the business is spread across multiple entities. Common ownership is an essential element of a single trade or business."

E.   CONSISTENCY

The Regulations also impose a consistently requirement on the delineation of a trade or business: "In cases in which other Code provisions use a trade or business standard that is the same or substantially similar to the Section 162 standard adopted in these Final Regulations, taxpayers should report such items consistently. For example, if taxpayers who own tenancy in common interests in rental property treat such joint interests as a trade or business for purposes of Section 199A but do not treat the joint interests as a separate entity for purposes of §301.7701-1(a)(2), the IRS will consider the facts and circumstances surrounding the differing treatment." This may be a factor in determining whether future restructuring can be done to enhance QBI deductions from real estate and related endeavors since a restructuring that changes prior reporting may violate the consistency requirement.

F.   ALLOCATIONS

The consistency requirements are broad and appear in several contexts in the Proposed Regulations. So, in addition to the above provision, consistency in allocations is also required. "The Proposed Regulations provide that if an individual or a Relevant Pass-Through Entity directly conducts multiple trades or businesses and has items of QBI which are properly attributable to more than one trade or business, the individual or Relevant Pass-Through Entity must allocate those items among the several trades or businesses to which they are attributable using a reasonable method based on all the facts and circumstances. The chosen reasonable method for each item must be consistently applied from one taxable year to another and must clearly reflect the income and expenses of each trade or business."

G.   1099 FILINGS

The Regulations also impose an additional requirement that if an operation does not comply with Form 1099 reporting requirements, it may not meet the requirements of constituting a trade or business. The Regulations provide: "Similarly, taxpayers should consider the appropriateness of treating a rental activity as a trade or business for purposes of Section 199A where the taxpayer does not comply with the information return filing requirements under Section 6041." Section 6041 provides in part: "All persons engaged in a trade or business and making payment in

---

[381] See §1.446-1(d)(1).

the course of such trade or business to another person, of rent, salaries, wages, premiums, annuities, compensations, remunerations,… of $600 or more in any taxable year…required to make returns in regard thereto by the regulations hereinafter provided for, shall render a true and accurate return to the Secretary, under such regulations" So a failure of a rental activity to file 1099s will preclude it from being characterized as a trade or business for 199A even if it passes the gauntlet of the 162 analysis discussed below.

H. DISREGARDED ENTITIES

"…trades or businesses conducted by a disregarded entity will be treated as conducted directly by the owner of the entity for purposes of Section 199A." This could be useful for real estate developers. For example, most developers structure operations so that every property is in a separate LLC. So, if a developer has brother-sister disregarded entities the trade or business test should be determined at the aggregate/developer level. If a developer has a family limited partnership ("FLP") that owns brother-sister "subsidiary" single member LLCs holding each property, then the trade or business test should be handled at the FLP level. However, if as many developers do the structure is a non-disregarded management company that owns 1% of each property LLC and the developer or a grantor trust owns the other 99% then it would appear that the trade or business testing and QBI calculations would have to be done at the level of each property LLC.

I. ENTITY LEVEL CALCULATIONS

Apropos to the above comments concerning disregarded entities is further comments in the Regs. about testing at the entity level: "For purposes of Section 199A, the determination of whether an activity is a trade or business is made at the entity level. If a Relevant Pass-Through Entity is engaged in a trade or business, items of income, gain, loss, or deduction from such trade or business retain their character as they pass from the entity to the taxpayer – even if the taxpayer is not personally engaged in the trade or business of the entity. Conversely, if a Relevant Pass-Through Entity is not engaged in a trade or business, income, gain, loss, or deduction allocated to a taxpayer from such entity will not qualify for the Section 199A deduction even if the taxpayer or an intervening entity is otherwise engaged in a trade or business. As described in part II.A.3 of this Summary of Comments and Explanation of Revisions, a trade or business for purposes of Section 199A is generally defined by reference to the standards for a Section 162 trade or business. A rental real estate enterprise that meets the safe harbor described in Notice 2017-07, released concurrently with these Final Regulations, may also treated as trades or businesses for purposes of Section 199A. Additionally, the rental or licensing of property if the property is rented or licensed to a trade or business conducted by the individual or a Relevant Pass-Through Entity which is commonly controlled under §1.199A- 4(b)(1)(i) is also treated as a trade or business for purposes of Section 199A. In addition to these requirements, the items must be effectively connected to a trade or business within the United States as described in Section 864(c)." For developers who have, as illustrated above, an entity that is not disregarded, if that entity's activities do not rise to the level of a trade or business then its revenue will not qualify as QBI. This appears to be so even if the aggregate of the taxpayer's activities with respect to all entities arises to the level of a trade or business, as these cannot be aggregated if the individual entities themselves do not meet the trade or business requirement.

J.   PENALTIES

The Regs. provide for the following: "Section 6662(a) provides a penalty for an underpayment of tax required to be shown on a return. Under Section 6662(b), the penalty applies to the portion of any underpayment that is attributable to a substantial underpayment of income tax. Section 6662(d)(1) defines substantial understatement of tax, which is generally an understatement that exceeds the greater of 10 percent of the tax required to be shown on the return or $5,000. Section 6662(d)(1)(C) provides a special rule in the case of any taxpayer who claims the Section 199A deduction for the taxable year, which requires that Section 6662(d)(1)(A) is applied by substituting "5 percent" for "10 percent." Section 1.199A-1(e)(6) cross-references this rule. One commenter asked for guidance on how the Section 6662 accuracy penalty would be applied if an activity was determined by the IRS not to be a trade or business for purposes of Section 199A. The Treasury Department and the IRS decline to adopt this suggestion as guidance regarding the application of Section 6662 is beyond the scope of these regulations." Thus, when the continued lack of clarity on what real estate rentals activities might constitute a trade or business is discussed later in this article, practitioners should bear in mind that the penalty for incorrectly making that determination is based on the lower 5% threshold and the Treasury refused to provide further guidance in this regard. Perhaps practitioners making "close calls" for real estate clients might mention the harsher penalty rules.

K.   PREVIOUSLY SUSPENDED 469 LOSSES

The Regs. provide that previously suspended losses under Section 469 are to be treated as losses from a separate trade or business for purposes of Section 199A.

L.   GUARANTEED PAYMENTS FOR USE OF CAPITAL

"…for purposes of Section 199A, guaranteed payments for the use of capital should be treated in a manner similar to interest income. Interest income other than interest income which is properly allocated to trade or business is specifically excluded from qualified items of income, gain, deduction or loss under Section 199A(c)(3)(B)(iii)."

M.   U.S. QBI

"Section 199A(c)(3)(A)(i) provides that for purposes of determining Qualified Business Income, the term "qualified items of income, gain, deduction, and loss means items of income, gain, deduction and loss to the extent such items are effectively connected with the conduct of a trade or business within the United States…" Therefore, businesses with international activities will need to carefully allocate income and expenses to determine what the Qualified Business Income amount is for Section 199A purposes.

Common Law Employees and Officers. The Final Regulations did not change the guidance provided under the Proposed Regulations for common paymaster and employee leasing scenarios and state that wages paid to "common law employees and officers" of a trade or business will be treated as having come from the actual employer, notwithstanding whether the payment is made by an employee leasing or other organization, including certified professional employer organizations described in Section 7705, statutory employers described in Section 1401(d)(1), and agents described in Section 3504.

- 299 -

When Wages May Be Considered Paid. The Final Regulations specify that wages can be considered as paid as long as they are timely recorded in an appropriate manner within sixty days after the end of the applicable calendar year in which they are paid, with a possible extension of an additional sixty days when needed to correct wage reporting returns.

Wage Allocation. The Final Regulations make clear that wages are to be allocated to the trade or business that actually employed the individual, as opposed to being considered as paid by an affiliated company that might be acting as a common paymaster but did not actually use the employee in that business.

Wages When Ownership Changes. The Final Regulations further provide that wages will be tracked separately for any short years that result from the change of ownership of a trade or business by tracking the actual wages paid in each portion of the year, as opposed to prorating them. The vast majority of advisors are not aware that Section 199A allows certain pension plan contributions, health insurance costs, and other items of compensation to be included in the calculation of wages.

Qualified Property Under the 2.5% Test. The Final Regulations also disallow including Qualified Property under the 2.5% test if it is purchased within 60 days of the end of the taxable year and disposed of within 120 days after the end of the taxable year, if the trade or business does not use the property for at least 45 days prior to disposition, unless the principal purpose of the acquisition and disposition was for other than increasing the Section 199A deduction.

Improvements to Qualified Property. Improvements to Qualified Property are treated as a separate Qualified Property, with its own basis and holding period. Therefore, if a taxpayer buys a new air-conditioning system for a building in year one, it would constitute Qualified Property through year 10, and then if the taxpayer adds additional components to the system in year three, the cost of the additional components can be considered as Qualified Property until year 13.

The recordkeeping requirements of the new Final Regulations and other rules under the statute will be quite difficult and costly for many taxpayers.

Section 162 Allocation of Wages and Qualified Property Among Multiple Entities. When an entity conducts multiple trades or businesses, as determined under Section 162, wages and Qualified Property must be allocated among them using reasonable allocation methods, which include gross income or direct tracing methods. While there appears to be some flexibility in these rules, there is no offset for the harsh treatment accorded to Specified Service Trades or Businesses. The Final Regulations provide that taxpayers may make an election to aggregate businesses, which is discussed in more detail below, and provide details on the netting of losses and profits on various businesses.

Section 199A Application of Wage and Qualified Property Limitations and Deductions. The Final Regulations do not use the Section 469 passive loss rules for grouping trades or businesses; instead, the Preamble to the Proposed Regulations explains that Section 469 dealt with the level of taxpayer involvement in a particular endeavor and that this is not the paradigm under Section 199A. The Final Regulations create a new method of aggregation of trades or businesses so that taxpayers can combine multiple trades or businesses for the purposes of applying the Wage and Qualified Property limitations and maximizing the deduction. In order to be aggregated, the businesses must meet the following requirements:

A.   The same person or group of people directly or indirectly own 50% or more of each trade or business;

B.   For purposes of determining ownership under this subsection, ownership by spouses, as well as children, grandchildren, siblings and parents, can be attributed to each other;

C.   The ownership existed for a majority of the tax year;

D.   The items must be reported on returns within the same taxable year;

E.   None of the businesses must be a Specified Service Trade or Business; and

F.   The aggregated trades or businesses must also satisfy at least two of the following requirements:

> (1)   The trades or businesses provide products or services that are the same or customarily offered together;
>
> (2)   The trades or businesses share facilities or significant centralized business elements such as personnel, accounting, legal, manufacturing, purchasing, human resources, or information technology resources; and
>
> (3)   The trades or businesses are operated in coordination with, or reliance upon, one or more of the businesses in the aggregated group (for example, supply chains interdependencies).

Aggregation of Minority Interests. A series of fourteen well-written examples beginning at Section 1.199A-4(d), which are reproduced in Chapter 9, demonstrate that a taxpayer owning less than 50% of multiple entities, when another taxpayer or related taxpayer owns more than 50% of each entity, can elect to aggregate the minority interests therein, if the other rules are satisfied.

Aggregating Losses Among Multiple Entity Owners. Aggregation will allow wages and Qualified Property to be considered as paid for by all of the entities, so that the deduction can be taken for an entity that has little or no wages or Qualified Property if another entity has sufficient wages and Qualified Property for both its own income and the income of affiliates. The examples point out that losses from an entity that could be aggregated must be netted against the aggregate profits of other applicable entities, if any aggregation occurs. Aggregation is discussed in more detail in Chapter 9, Part Two.

Example:

> One example in the Final Regulations indicates that ownership of a sailboat racing team and a marina by separate companies would not be aggregated, but that ownership of a trucking company that delivers lumber and other supplies in one company, operation of a lumber yard

in another company, and operation of a construction business that presumably uses lumber and other supplies, can be aggregated.

Ramifications of Aggregating to Two or More Trades. Once a taxpayer chooses to aggregate two or more trades or businesses, they must be consistently reported and aggregated for all subsequent taxable years, unless there is a change in facts and circumstance so that the separate trades and businesses no longer qualify for aggregation. The implications of all of this to professional advisers can be daunting. In some instances, modeling the various options may be the only way to determine what the actual impact of various decisions might be. Practitioners should be cautious about providing conclusions to clients with specificity without the opportunity to perform the appropriate analysis. The costs of the level of detailed analysis that might be necessary in many instances will be a concern for many clients. It will be easy to make mistakes in advising on this law, which raises the stakes by lowering the substantial understatement threshold to 5% of the tax required to be reported for the year (essentially what the IRS says should have been paid), in lieu of the normal 10% threshold that applies. There is no explanation as to why taking a Section 199A deduction would cause this unfair tripwire standard that will apply to many innocent taxpayers who may not even know that they are eligible for the deduction and may not even claim the deduction or reduce tax liability as the result of it.

Tax Penalties for Underpayment. Many people incorrectly believe that tax penalties are only imposed on those who are negligent or have bad intent, but this is not the case. There are eight enumerated ways for the IRS to impose accuracy-related penalties, and while negligence is one of these reasons, the IRS only needs to demonstrate that the taxpayer substantially underpaid their taxes in order to impose a sanction on the taxpayer under Section 6662, which provides an additional tax of 20% of the underpayment. There is a reasonable cause exception where no penalty will apply if the taxpayer can show there was reasonable cause for the underpayment and that the taxpayer acted in good faith.

Specified Service Trades or Businesses Phase-Out Range. The Final Regulations enumerate the categories of Specified Service Trades or Businesses, which are treated differently because income derived therefrom by high earner taxpayers (over $157,500 for single filers, and $315,000 for married filing jointly filers) will be limited during the $100,000 phase-out range (a $50,000 phase-out range applies for single filers) and not qualify for the deduction above that phase-out range. The Final Regulations give some useful examples of which functions are considered to be under these definitions and which functions are not, and the following chart illustrates all of the points made in the Final Regulations in this regard. While there are a few points of leniency, overall the tone of the Final Regulations is to broadly ensnare as much as possible under the Specified Service Trades or Businesses taint.

Exclusions From Specified Service Trades or Businesses. It is notable that the Final Regulations specifically state that banking, real estate brokerage services and insurance agencies (including life insurance agents) are not Specified Service Trades or Businesses. However, investment banking, hedge funds management, lobbying and veterinary medicine are Specified Service Trades or Businesses.

Chart 26 – Activity Chart

The below chart is similar to the separate charts set forth in Chapter 9 under each category of Specified Trade or Business:

Activity Chart		
Activity	**Includes**	**Does Not Include**
Health	The provision of medical services by physicians, pharmacists, nurses, dentists, veterinarians, physical therapists, psychologists, and other similar healthcare professionals who provide medical services directly to the patient.	The provision of services not directly related to a medical field, even though the services may purportedly relate to the health of the service recipient. For example, the performance of services in the field of health does not include the operation of health clubs or health spas that provide physical exercise or conditioning to their customers, payment processing, or research, testing and manufacture and/or sales of pharmaceuticals or medical devices. Payment processing is quite limited and would not appear to facilitate medical practices dividing off significant practice administrative activities as producing non-Specified Service Trade or Business revenue. Practitioners also need to read these very limited exclusions with consideration to the broad aggregation rules which further limit planning.
Law	The provision of services by lawyers, paralegals, legal arbitrators, mediators, and similar professionals in their capacity as such. Please note that in most states mediators do not need to be licensed lawyers.	The provision of services that do not require skills unique to the field of law, for example, the provision of services in the field of law does not include the provision of services by printers, delivery services, or stenography services. Excluding delivery services is of no help and demonstrates the broad all-encompassing view the Final Regulations have taken of Specified Service Trades or Businesses. There is no discussion as to whether trustee, executor and executrix, title insurance, and other services that do not require a

Activity Chart		
Activity	**Includes**	**Does Not Include**
		law license, are considered to be legal services.
Accounting	The provision of services by accountants, enrolled agents, return preparers, financial auditors, and similar professionals in their capacity as such, limited to services requiring state licensure as a certified public accountant (CPA)...which includes tax return and bookkeeping services, even though the provision of such services may not require the same education, training, or mastery of accounting principles as a CPA.	Payment processing and billing analysis. The inclusion of bookkeeping services, an activity that does not require the professional training or licensing of a CPA, further illustrates the broad Specified Service Trade or Business view of the Final Regulations.
Actuarial Science	Is based on the ordinary meaning "actuarial science" and provides that the term "performance of services in the field of actuarial science" means payment processing and billing analysis.	The provision of services by analysts, economists, mathematicians, and statisticians not engaged in analyzing or assessing the financial costs of risk or uncertainty of events.
Performing Arts	The performance of services by individuals who participate in the creation of performing arts, such as actors, singers, musicians, entertainers, directors, and similar professionals performing services in their capacity as such.	The provision of services by persons who broadcast or otherwise disseminate video or audio of performing arts to the public. Does not include the performance of services that do not require skills unique to the creation of performing arts, such as maintenance and operation of equipment or facilities used in the performing arts.
Consulting	The provision of professional advice and counsel to clients to assist the client in achieving goals and solving problems...includes providing advice and counsel regarding advocacy with the intention of influencing decisions	The performance of services other than advice and counsel. This determination is made based on all the facts and circumstances of a person's business.

Activity Chart		
Activity	**Includes**	**Does Not Include**
	made by a government or governmental agency and all attempts to influence legislators and other government officials on behalf of a client by lobbyists and other similar professionals performing services in their capacity as such.	Does not include the performance of services in the field of consulting services embedded in, or ancillary to, the sale of goods or performance of services on behalf of a trade or business that is not otherwise a Specified Service Trade or Business (e.g., services provided by a building contractor) if there is no separate payment for the consulting services. This may require some businesses to modify their billing practices and incorporate fees for what would otherwise have been separately stated services into the product price.
Athletics	Is most similar to the field of performing arts. Provides that the term "performance of services in the field of athletics" means the performances of services by individuals who participate in athletic competition, such as athletes, coaches, and team managers in sports, such as baseball, basketball, football, soccer, hockey, martial arts, boxing, bowling, tennis, golf, skiing, snowboarding, track and field, billiards, and racing.	The provision of services that do not require skills unique to athletic competition, such as the maintenance and operation of equipment or facilities for use in athletic events; the provision of services by persons who broadcast or otherwise disseminate video or audio of athletic events to the public.
Financial Services	Limits the definition of financial services to services typically performed by financial advisors and investment bankers and provides that the field of financial services includes the provision of financial services to clients, including managing wealth, advising clients with respect to finances, developing retirement plans, developing wealth transition plans, the provision of advisory and	Taking deposits or making loans. Please note that interest earned on notes owed by customers or on notes receivable resulting from the financed sale of products to customers will be included in Section 199A income, but that normal interest income earned on accounts owned by a trade or business will not.

Activity Chart		
Activity	**Includes**	**Does Not Include**
	other similar services regarding valuations, mergers, acquisitions, dispositions, restructurings (including in Title 11 or similar cases), and raising financial capital by underwriting, or acting as the client's agent in the issuance of securities, and similar services. Services provided by financial advisors, investment bankers, wealth planners, and retirement advisors and other similar professionals.	
Brokerage Services	The performance of services in the field of brokerage services includes services in which a person arranges transactions between a buyer and a seller with respect to securities for a commission or fee. This includes services provided by stockbrokers and other similar professionals.	Does not include services provided by real estate agents and brokers, or insurance agents and brokers.
Investment Management	The performance of services that consist of investing and investment management refers to a trade or business involving the receipt of fees for providing investing, asset management, or investment management services, including providing advice with respect to buying and selling investments.	The performance of services of investing and investment management does not include directly managing real property.
Trading Services	The performance of services that consist of trading means a trade or business of trading in securities, commodities, or partnership interests. Whether a person is a trader in securities, commodities, or partnership interests is determined by considering all relevant facts and circumstances, including the source and type of	A taxpayer who engages in hedging transactions as part of their business is not considered to be engaged in the trade or business of trading commodities.

Activity Chart		
Activity	**Includes**	**Does Not Include**
	profit that is associated with engaging in the activity, regardless of whether that person trades for the person's own account, for the account of others, or any combination thereof.	
Dealing in Securities	The performance of services that consist of dealing in securities means regularly purchasing securities from and selling securities to customers in the ordinary course of a trade or business or regularly offering to enter into, assume, offset, assign, or otherwise terminate positions in securities with customers in the ordinary course of a trade or business.	A taxpayer that regularly originates loans in the ordinary course of a trade or business of making loans but engages in no more than negligible sales of the loans is not dealing in securities.
Dealing in Commodities	The performance of services that consist of dealing in commodities means regularly purchasing commodities from and selling commodities to customers in the ordinary course of a trade or business, or regularly offering to enter into, assume, offset, assign, or otherwise terminate positions in commodities with customers in the ordinary course of a trade or business.	A taxpayer who engages in hedging transactions as part of their business is not considered to be engaged in the trade or business of dealing in commodities.
Where the Principal Asset of The Trade or Business is the Reputation or Skill of One or More Employees or Owners	**SEE DISCUSSION BELOW**	

Principal Asset – Reputation or Skill. The final category of a Specified Service Trade or Business involves a situation where the principal asset of the trade or business is the reputation or skill of one or more employees or owners. Many advisors were concerned with the potential breadth of this "catch all" provision. Fortunately, the Treasury chose to narrowly construe this category in both the Proposed and Final Regulations, so that the definition will not apply unless one of the following exists:

- Fees or other compensation is received for endorsement of products or services;

- License or fees are received for the use of an individual's image, likeness, name, signature, voice, trademark, or any other symbols associated therewith; or

- Compensation is received for appearing at an event or on radio, television, or other media.

For the purposes of the above, compensation includes ownership in a business entity that is received in lieu of cash.

An example in the Final Regulations is as follows:

> A famous chef may own a restaurant, and the income from the restaurant would qualify for the Section 199A deduction, but any income earned as a license fee for the use of his or her name to brand the restaurant or sell cookware would be considered as income from a Specified Service Trade or Business. What if instead of a pure license fee for the use of the chef's name on the island-themed margarita cookware, the chef instead received a share in the profits from the sales of cookware? Would that alternatively be characterized as non-Specified Service Trade or Business income? Consideration should be given to how to structure license arrangements in light of this. It therefore appears that not all of Jimmy Buffett's Section 199A deduction will get wasted away in Margaritaville. [382]

Property Acquired in a Like-Kind Tax-Free Exchange. The Final Regulations provide that property that has been received in a like-kind tax-free exchange will be considered as acquired when the property that it is replacing was acquired and will be considered to have the basis of the property that it is replacing. Advisors familiar with the Section 1031 like-kind exchange rules know that it was cut back to apply only to real estate and buildings and other fixed improvements

---

[382] Some of them are running to lovers
Leaving no forward address
Some of them are running tons of ganja
Some are running from the IRS
Late at night you will find them
In the cheap hotels and bars
Hustling the senoritas
While they dance beneath the stars
Spending those renegade pesos
On a bottle of rum and a lime
Singin' give me some words I can dance to
Or a melody that rhymes

from BANANA REPUBLICS BY JIMMY BUFFETT.

thereto, and that the older property traded away is called the "relinquished property," and that the new property acquired is called the "replacement property." The holding period and basis of the relinquished property is what applies under Section 199A when applying this to the 2.5% Qualified Property hurdle. If the replacement property has excess basis (that is basis in excess of the cost of the relinquished property), then such excess is treated as a separate item of Qualified Property placed in service when the replacement property is acquired. In addition, if boot is received by the taxpayer in the transaction then the boot received will reduce the basis in the replacement property for purposes of Section 199A.

Taxpayers that have previously made elections under Section 168(f)(1) to exclude property from standard depreciation methods (depreciation based upon MACRS tables) and use an alternative method, such as depreciation based upon units of production, can make a new election under Treasury Regulation Section 1.168(i)- 6(i)(1) to bring the replacement property back under standard deprecation methods (MACRS) in a like-kind exchange, in which event the basis in the replacement property would be treated as placed in service in the year the replacement property is acquired.

The Final Regulations contain the following examples to illustrate the UBIA calculations for property acquired in a like-kind exchange:

Example 1:

> (A) On January 5, 2012, A purchases Real Property X for $1 million and places it in service in A's trade or business. A's trade or business is not an SSTB. A's basis in Real Property X under section 1012 is $1 million. Real Property X is qualified property within the meaning of section 199A(b)(6). As of December 31, 2018, A's basis in Real Property X, as adjusted under section 1016(a)(2) for depreciation deductions under section 168(a), is $821,550.
>
> (B) For purposes of section 199A(b)(2)(B)(ii) and this section, A's UBIA of Real Property X is its $1 million cost basis under section 1012, regardless of any later depreciation deductions under section 168(a) and resulting basis adjustments under section 1016(a)(2).[383]

Example 2:

> (A) The facts are the same as in Example 1, except that on January 15, 2019, A enters into a like-kind exchange under section 1031 in which A exchanges Real Property X for Real Property Y. Real Property Y has a value of $1 million. No cash or other property is involved in the exchange. As of January 15, 2019, A's basis in Real Property X, as

---

[383] Treas. Reg. 1.199A-2(c)(4), Example 1.

adjusted under section 1016(a)(2) for depreciation deductions under section 168(a), is $820,482.

(B) A's UBIA in Real Property Y is $1 million as determined under paragraph (c)(3)(ii) of this section. Pursuant to paragraph (c)(2)(iii)(A) of this section, Real Property Y is first placed in service by A on January 5, 2012, which is the date on which Real Property X was first placed in service by A.[384]

Example 3:

(A) The facts are the same as in Example 1, except that on January 15, 2019, A enters into a like-kind exchange under section 1031, in which A exchanges Real Property X for Real Property Y. Real Property X has appreciated in value to $1.3 million, and Real Property Y also has a value of $1.3 million. No cash or other property is involved in the exchange. As of January 15, 2019, A's basis in Real Property X, as adjusted under section 1016(a)(2), is $820,482.

(B) A's UBIA in Real Property Y is $1 million as determined under paragraph (c)(3)(ii) of this section. Pursuant to paragraph (c)(2)(iii)(A) of this section, Real Property Y is first placed in service by A on January 5, 2012, which is the date on which Real Property X was first placed in service by A.[385]

Example 4:

(A) The facts are the same as in Example 1, except that on January 15, 2019, A enters into a like-kind exchange under section 1031, in which A exchanges Real Property X for Real Property Y. Real Property X has appreciated in value to $1.3 million, but Real Property Y has a value of $1.5 million. A therefore adds $200,000 in cash to the exchange of Real Property X for Real Property Y. On January 15, 2019, A places Real Property Y in service. As of January 15, 2019, A's basis in Real Property X, as adjusted under section 1016(a)(2), is $820,482.

(B) A's UBIA in Real Property Y is $1.2 million as determined under paragraph (c)(3)(ii) of this section ($1 million in UBIA from Real Property X plus $200,000 cash paid by A to acquire Real Property Y).

---

[384] Treas. Reg. 1.199A-2(c)(4), Example 2.
[385] Treas. Reg. 1.199A-2(c)(4), Example 3.

Because the UBIA of Real Property Y exceeds the UBIA of Real Property X, Real Property Y is treated as being two separate qualified properties for purposes of applying paragraph (c)(2)(iii)(A) of this section. One property has a UBIA of $1 million (the portion of A's UBIA of $1.2 million in Real Property Y that does not exceed A's UBIA of $1 million in Real Property X) and it is first placed in service by A on January 5, 2012, which is the date on which Real Property X was first placed in service by A. The other property has a UBIA of $200,000 (the portion of A's UBIA of $1.2 million in Real Property Y that exceeds A's UBIA of $1 million in Real Property X) and it is first placed in service by A on January 15, 2019, which is the date on which Real Property Y was first placed in service by A.[386]

Example 5:

(A) The facts are the same as in Example 1, except that on January 15, 2019, A enters into a like-kind exchange under section 1031, in which A exchanges Real Property X for Real Property Y. Real Property X has appreciated in value to $1.3 million. Real Property Y has a fair market value of $1 million. As of January 15, 2019, A's basis in Real Property X, as adjusted under section 1016(a)(2), is $820,482. Pursuant to the exchange, A receives Real Property Y and $300,000 in cash.

(B) A's UBIA in Real Property Y is $1 million as determined under paragraph (c)(3)(ii) of this section ($1 million in UBIA from Real Property X, less $0 excess boot ($300,000 cash received in the exchange over-reduced by $300,000 in appreciation in Property X, which is equal to the excess of the $1.3 million fair market value of Property X on the date of the exchange over $1 million fair market value of Property X on the date of acquisition by the taxpayer)). Pursuant to paragraph (c)(2)(iii)(A) of this section, Real Property Y is first placed in service by A on January 5, 2012, which is the date on which Real Property X was first placed in service by A.[387]

Example 6:

(A) The facts are the same as in Example 1, except that on January 15, 2019, A enters into a like-kind exchange under section 1031, in which A exchanges Real Property X for Real Property Y. Real Property X has appreciated in value to $1.3 million. Real Property Y has a fair market

---

[386] Treas. Reg. 1.199A-2(c)(4), Example 4.
[387] Treas. Reg. 1.199A-2(c)(4), Example 5.

value of $900,000. Pursuant to the exchange, A receives Real Property Y and $400,000 in cash. As of January 15, 2019, A's basis in Real Property X, as adjusted under section 1016(a)(2), is $820,482.

(B) A's UBIA in Real Property Y is $900,000 as determined under paragraph (c)(3)(ii) of this section ($1 million in UBIA from Real Property X less $100,000 excess boot ($400,000 in cash received in the exchange over-reduced by $300,000 in appreciation in Property X, which is equal to the excess of the $1.3 million fair market value of Property X on the date of the exchange over the $1 million fair market value of Property X on the date of acquisition by the taxpayer)). Pursuant to paragraph (c)(2)(iii)(A) of this section, Real Property Y is first placed in service by A on January 5, 2012, which is the date on which Real Property X was first placed in service by A.[388]

Example 7:

(A) The facts are the same as in Example 1, except that on January 15, 2019, A enters into a like-kind exchange under section 1031, in which A exchanges Real Property X for Real Property Y. Real Property X has declined in value to $900,000, and Real Property Y also has a value of $900,000. No cash or other property is involved in the exchange. As of January 15, 2019, A's basis in Real Property X, as adjusted under section 1016(a)(2), is $820,482.

(B) Even though Real Property Y is worth only $900,000, A's UBIA in Real Property Y is $1 million as determined under paragraph (c)(3)(ii) of this section because no cash or other property was involved in the exchange. Pursuant to paragraph (c)(2)(iii)(A) of this section, Real Property Y is first placed in service by A on January 5, 2012, which is the date on which Real Property X was first placed in service by A.[389]

Example 8:

(A) C operates a trade or business that is not an SSTB as a sole proprietorship. On January 5, 2011, C purchases Machinery Y for $10,000 and places it in service in C's trade or business. C's basis in Machinery Y under section 1012 is $10,000. Machinery Y is qualified property within the meaning of section 199A(b)(6). Assume that

---

[388] Treas. Reg. 1.199A-2(c)(4), Example 6.
[389] Treas. Reg. 1.199A-2(c)(4), Example 7.

Machinery Y's recovery period under section 168(c) is 10 years, and C depreciates Machinery Y under the general depreciation system by using the straight-line depreciation method, a 10-year recovery period, and the half-year convention. As of December 31, 2018, C's basis in Machinery Y, as adjusted under section 1016(a)(2) for depreciation deductions under section 168(a), is $2,500. On January 1, 2019, C incorporates the sole proprietorship and elects to treat the newly formed entity as an S corporation for Federal income tax purposes. C contributes Machinery Y and all other assets of the trade or business to the S corporation in a non-recognition transaction under section 351. The S corporation immediately places all the assets in service.

(B) For purposes of section 199A(b)(2)(B)(ii) and this section, C's UBIA of Machinery Y from 2011 through 2018 is its $10,000 cost basis under section 1012, regardless of any later depreciation deductions under section 168(a) and resulting basis adjustments under section 1016(a)(2). The S corporation's basis of Machinery Y is $2,500, the basis of the property under section 362 at the time the S corporation places the property in service. Pursuant to paragraph (c)(3)(iv) of this section, S corporation's UBIA of Machinery Y is $10,000, which is C's UBIA of Machinery Y. Pursuant to paragraph (c)(2)(iv)(A) of this section, for purposes of determining the depreciable period of Machinery Y, the S corporation's placed in service date of Machinery Y will be January 5, 2011, which is the date C originally placed the property in service in 2011. Therefore, Machinery Y may be qualified property of the S corporation (assuming it continues to be used in the business) for 2019 and 2020 and will not be qualified property of the S corporation after 2020, because its depreciable period will have expired.[390]

Example 9:

(A) LLC, a partnership, operates a trade or business that is not an SSTB. On January 5, 2011, LLC purchases Machinery Z for $30,000 and places it in service in LLC's trade or business. LLC's basis in Machinery Z under section 1012 is $30,000. Machinery Z is qualified property within the meaning of section 199A(b)(6). Assume that Machinery Z's recovery period under section 168(c) is 10 years, and LLC depreciates Machinery Z under the general depreciation system by using the straight-line depreciation method, a 10-year recovery period, and the half-year convention. As of December 31, 2018, LLC's basis in Machinery Z, as adjusted under section 1016(a)(2) for depreciation deductions under section 168(a), is $7,500. On January 1, 2019, LLC distributes

---

[390] Treas. Reg. 1.199A-2(c)(4), Example 8.

Machinery Z to Partner A in full liquidation of Partner A's interest in LLC. Partner A's outside basis in LLC is $35,000.

(B) For purposes of section 199A(b)(2)(B)(ii) and this section, LLC's UBIA of Machinery Z from 2011 through 2018 is its $30,000 cost basis under section 1012, regardless of any later depreciation deductions under section 168(a) and resulting basis adjustments under section 1016(a)(2). Prior to the distribution to Partner A, LLC's basis of Machinery Z is $7,500. Under section 732(b), Partner A's basis in Machinery Z is $35,000. Pursuant to paragraph (c)(3)(iv) of this section, upon distribution of Machinery Z, Partner A's UBIA of Machinery Z is $30,000, which was LLC's UBIA of Machinery Z.[391]

Non-Like-Kind Property Exchanges. It is noteworthy that non-recognition provisions under Section 1031 are mandatory, and taxpayers do not have the option to elect out of Section 1031 to treat the transaction as a sale and purchase of replacement property in order to obtain a new stepped-up basis in the replacement property. However, nothing prevents a taxpayer from structuring a transaction so that the exchange will not qualify as a Section 1031 exchange by exchanging non-like-kind property or not meeting the applicable timing requirements. Although the failure to meet the like-kind requirements will cause any gain on the transaction to be recognized, the replacement property will have a basis equal to the purchase price and a new holding period will apply for purposes of the Section 199A Qualified Property calculation. This may also be beneficial in situations where the taxpayer has an expiring loss carryforward that could be used to offset the gain on the exchange and result in a new basis for the replacement property.

Trust Planning. Many taxpayers will establish trusts for children or others that are separately taxed and can own interests in S corporations and partnerships and qualify for the deduction under situations where the parents would not qualify because of their income levels or other factors. The Final Regulations specifically state that "a Trust formed or funded with a principal purpose of receiving a deduction under Section 199A will not be respected for purposes of Section 199A" under the title "Anti-Abuse Rule for Creation of Multiple Trusts to Avoid Exceeding the Threshold Amount."

One question is whether the IRS has the ability to require that income that has passed into or through a complex trust must be aggregated with the income of its grantor for threshold purposes. The apparent authority for this Regulation is the following language under Section 199A(f)(4), ("Anti-Abuse Rules"), which is the only Subsection of Section 199A to grant the Secretary authority to issue Anti-Abuse Rules and does not, in the opinion of some authors, authorize such a discriminatory provision:[392]

---

[391] Treas. Reg. 1.199A-2(c)(4), Example 9.

[392] If Aretha Franklin knew about these Regulations, she might have said "R-E-S-P-E-C-T, what the hell are you going to do to my trust and me?" Aretha Franklin's hit song "Respect" was recorded on February 14, 1967 in New York's Atlantic Studios, and the song won Franklin two Grammy awards.

The Secretary shall prescribe such Regulations as are necessary to carry out the purposes of this Section, including Regulations—

- for requiring or restricting the allocation of items and wages under this Section and such reporting requirements as the Secretary determines appropriate, and

- for the application of this Section in the case of tiered entities.

Nowhere under Section 199A is the Secretary given the express authority to issue regulations regarding the treatment of trusts, nor is the Secretary given the ability to treat discriminatorily or to "disrespect" (for lack of a better term) a specific class of taxpayers eligible under the statute.

The authority for the multiple trust rule in the Final Regulations comes from IRC Section 643(f), which provides for the aggregation of multiple trusts if there are not significant non-tax differences between the trusts.

Judge Learned Hand's famous quotation from the early 1900s comes to mind:

> *Anyone may so arrange his affairs that his taxes shall be as low as possible; he is not bound to choose that pattern which best pays the Treasury; there is not even a patriotic duty to increase one's taxes. Everyone does it, rich and poor alike, and I'll do it right, for nobody owes any public duty to pay more than the law demands.*[393]

Section 643(f) was enacted in 1989 to provide that Regulations could be issued to allow the IRS to treat two or more trusts as a single trust if they (1) were formed by substantially the same grantor, (2) had substantially the same primary beneficiaries,[394] and (3) were formed for the principal purpose of avoiding income taxes. Regulations were never issued, and some commentators (writing in LISI and elsewhere) pointed out that the IRS could not assert the multiple trust provision of the Code without having Regulations issued. We now have Final Regulations under Section 643(f) so the above is mostly an academic question.

The Final Regulations under Section 199A were connected to the new Section 643 Regulations, which state that a principal purpose to avoid taxes will be presumed if it results in a significant income tax benefit, unless there are significant non-tax purposes that could not have been achieved without the creation of the separate trust.

The Proposed Regulations contained two heavily criticized examples that were subsequently deleted from the Final Regulations. For a more detailed discussion of Section 643 and the anti-abuse rules related to trust planning under Section 199A see Chapter 13.

---

[393] *Gregory v. Helvering*, 293 U.S. 465(1935), was a landmark decision by the United States Supreme Court concerned with U.S. income tax law.

[394] Section 643(f) explicitly aggregates multiple trusts where the trusts have substantially the same grantors and primary beneficiaries, and a principal purpose of such trusts is the avoidance of income tax. It seems that separate trusts can be established which have different primary beneficiaries and remainder beneficiaries, and significant non-tax differences, and that such trusts would not be subject to aggregation.

Pre-2018 Losses Will Not Reduce QBI Income When Released. The Final Regulations provide that losses that were built up through December 31, 2017 will not reduce Qualified Business Income, and provides for how losses will be applied.

Where Code provisions block and delay the recognition of losses, such as under the passive loss rules under Section 469, and the S corporation rules that limit losses to the basis of stock, the losses that are released after 2017 will only reduce Qualified Business Income to the extent accumulated after 2017.

Fiscal Year Entity Coordination. Almost uniformly, the Final Regulations provide that S corporations, trusts, estates and partnerships that are not on a calendar year basis for 2017 and 2018 will be considered to have all items of income and deduction occur for Section 199A calculation purposes for the period ending in 2018. The Final Regulations appear to contemplate that the income and deductions that such entities will have for the fiscal year beginning in 2018 will be counted in 2019 when the subsequent fiscal year ends, but this is not specifically mentioned so it is not clear what becomes of income and deductions for fiscal years that begin in 2018 and will end in 2019.

The Final Regulations provide taxpayers with substantial guidance on many key issues under Section 199A, but leave many items unexplained, and, as would be expected, create many new issues that will need to be clarified, or will remain unclear.

The Treasury and Internal Revenue Service did an admirable job to issue voluminous regulations that were vitally needed to facilitate tax compliance, but much more work is needed, and will hopefully be forthcoming without significant delay or hardship.

INDEX